Microsoft®

Microsoft®
SQL Server™ 2000
Administrator's
Pocket
Consultant

D1138025

William R. Stanek

PUBLISHED BY
Microsoft Press
A Division of Microsoft Corporation
One Microsoft Way
Redmond, Washington 98052-6399

Copyright © 2000 by William R. Stanek

Library of Congress Cataloging-in-Publication Data
Stanek, William R.
    Microsoft SQL Server 2000 Administrator's Pocket Consultant / William R. Stanek.
      p. cm.
    Includes index.
    ISBN 0-7356-1129-7
    1. Client/server computing.   2. SQL server.   3. Relational databases.   I. Title.
QA76.9.C55 S795 2000
005.75'85--dc21   00-056226

Printed and bound in the United States of America.

2 3 4 5 6 7 8 9   MLML   5 4 3 2 1 0

Distributed in Canada by Penguin Books Canada Limited.

A CIP catalogue record for this book is available from the British Library.

Microsoft Press books are available through booksellers and distributors worldwide. For further information about international editions, contact your local Microsoft Corporation office or contact Microsoft Press International directly at fax (425) 936-7329. Visit our Web site at mspress.microsoft.com. Send comments to *mspinput@microsoft.com*.

Acquisitions Editor: Juliana Aldous
Project Editors: Maureen Williams Zimmerman and Julie Miller
Technical Editor: John Panzarella

Contents at a Glance

Table of Contents

Part II
Microsoft SQL Server 2000 Administration

Part III
Microsoft SQL Server 2000 Data Administration

Part IV
Performance, Optimization, and Maintenance

Tables

Samples

Acknowledgments

Writing this book was a great experience that *really* put my years of Microsoft SQL Server administration and consulting knowledge to the test. It is gratifying to see techniques that I've used time and again to solve problems put into a printed book so that others may benefit from them. But no man is an island, and this book couldn't have been written without help from some very special people.

As I've stated in previous Administrator's Pocket Consultants, the team at Microsoft Press is top-notch. I owe huge "thank yous" to Anne Hamilton as senior acquisitions manager and Stuart Stuple as managing editor, both for recognizing the potential of my practical and useful approach to the Administrator's Pocket Consultant series and for their willingness to run with the approach. Juliana Aldous handled acquisitions and helped out whenever possible to keep the project rolling.

Julie Miller and Maureen Zimmerman watched over the editorial process from the Microsoft Press side. Lisa Wehrle managed the editorial process for nSight, Inc. Their thoroughness and attention to every detail is greatly appreciated!

Joseph Gustaitis was the copy editor for the book, and John Panzarella was the technical editor. Together, they did a great job of ensuring the copy and content was accurate. Thank you, thank you, thank you!

Thanks also to Studio B literary agency and my agents, David Rogelberg and Neil Salkind. Hopefully, I haven't forgotten anyone, but if I have, it was an oversight. *Honest.* ;-)

Introduction

Microsoft SQL Server 2000 Administrator's Pocket Consultant is designed to be a concise and compulsively usable resource for SQL Server 2000 administrators. It covers everything you need to perform the core administrative tasks for SQL Server and is the readable resource guide that you'll want on your desk at all times. Because the focus is on giving you maximum value in a pocket-sized guide, you don't have to wade through hundreds of pages of extraneous information to find what you're looking for. Instead, you'll find exactly what you need to get the job done.

This book is designed to be the one resource you turn to whenever you have questions about SQL Server administration. To this end, the book zeroes in on daily administration procedures, frequently used tasks, documented examples, and options that are representative while not necessarily inclusive. One of the key goals is to keep content concise enough so the book is compact and easy to navigate while also ensuring that the book contains as much information as possible. Instead of a 1000-page tome or a 100-page quick reference, you get a valuable resource guide that can help you quickly and easily perform common tasks, solve problems, and implement advanced SQL Server technologies like Data Transformation Services (DTS), replication, distributed queries, and multiserver administration.

Who Is This Book For?

Microsoft SQL Server 2000 Administrator's Pocket Consultant covers the Small Business Server (SBS), Standard, and Enterprise editions of SQL Server. The book is designed for:

- Current SQL Server 2000 database administrators
- Accomplished users who have some administrator responsibilities
- Administrators migrating to SQL Server 2000 from previous versions
- Administrators transitioning from other database architectures

To include as much information as possible, I had to assume that you have basic networking skills and a basic understanding of SQL Server, and that SQL Server is already successfully installed on your systems. With this in mind, I don't devote entire chapters to understanding SQL Server architecture, installing SQL Server, or running simple SQL queries. But I do cover SQL Server configuration, enterprise-wide server management, performance tuning, optimization, maintenance, and much more.

I also assume that you're fairly familiar with SQL commands and stored procedures as well as the standard Microsoft Windows user interface. If you need help learning SQL basics, you should read other resources (many of which are available from Microsoft Press).

How Is This Book Organized?

Microsoft SQL Server 2000 Administrator's Pocket Consultant is designed to be used in the daily administration of SQL Server and as such, the book is organized according to job-related tasks rather than SQL Server features. Before you use this book, you should be aware of the difference between Administrator's Pocket Consultants and Administrator's Companions. Although both books are designed to be a part of an overall administrator's library, Administrator's Pocket Consultants are the down-and-dirty, in-the-trenches books and Administrator's Companions are the comprehensive tutorials and references that cover every aspect of deploying a product or technology in the enterprise.

Speed and ease of reference are essential parts of this hands-on guide. The book has an expanded table of contents and an extensive index for finding answers to problems quickly. Many other quick reference features have been added to the book as well. These features include quick step-by-steps, lists, tables with fast facts, and cross-references. The book is broken down into both parts and chapters. The parts contain a part-opener paragraph or two about the chapters grouped in that part.

Part I, "Microsoft SQL Server 2000 Administration Fundamentals," covers the fundamental tasks you need for SQL Server administration. Chapter 1 provides an overview of SQL Server administration tools, techniques, and concepts. Chapter 2 explores configuring and tuning SQL Server. You'll learn about optimizing memory usage, parallel processing, authentication, auditing, and more.

In Part II, "Microsoft SQL Server 2000 Administration," you'll find the essential tasks for administering SQL Server. Chapter 3 details management techniques for server groups and servers. You'll also learn how to control services and server processes. The core administration tasks for creating and managing databases are covered in Chapter 4 with a logical follow-up Chapter 5 on SQL Server security. To manage server security, you'll create user logins, configure login permissions, and assign roles. The permissions and roles you assign determine the actions users can perform as well as what types of data they can access.

SQL Server data administration is the subject of Part III. Chapter 6 covers techniques for creating, managing, and optimizing tables, indexes, and views. In Chapter 7, you'll find tasks for importing and exporting data using DTS as well as the old standby bulk copy program (BCP). Chapter 8 focuses on integrating SQL Server databases with other SQL Server databases and with other data sources. You'll find detailed discussions on distributed queries, distributed transactions, Microsoft Distributed Transaction Coordinator (MS DTC), and linked servers.

Chapter 9 explores data replication. You'll learn all about the latest replication techniques, including merge replication and immediate-updating subscribers.

Part IV, "Performance, Optimization, and Maintenance," covers administration tasks you'll use to enhance and maintain SQL Server. Chapter 10 provides the essentials for working with server logs, monitoring SQL Server performance, and solving performance problems. Chapter 11 starts by explaining how to create a backup and recovery plan. Afterward, the chapter dives into common tasks for creating and restoring backups. Chapter 12 explores database automation and maintenance, showing how to create alerts, schedule jobs, handle operator notifications, and more. You'll also learn how to create maintenance plans and resolve database consistency problems.

Conventions Used in This Book

I've used a variety of elements to help keep the text clear and easy to follow. You'll find code terms and listings in monospace type, except when I tell you to actually type a command. In that case, the command appears in **bold** type. When I introduce and define a new term, I put it in *italics*.

Other conventions include:

Note   To provide additional details on a particular point that needs emphasis.

Tip   To offer helpful hints or additional information.

Caution   To warn you when there are potential problems you should look out for.

More Info   To point to more information on the subject.

Real World   To provide real-world advice when discussing advanced topics.

Best Practice   To explain the best technique to use when working with advanced configuration and administration concepts.

I truly hope you find that *Microsoft SQL Server 2000 Administrator's Pocket Consultant* provides everything you need to perform essential administrative tasks on SQL Server as quickly and efficiently as possible. Your thoughts are welcome at sql-consulting@tvpress.com. Thank you.

Support

Every effort has been made to ensure the accuracy of this book. Microsoft Press provides corrections for books through the World Wide Web at *http://mspress.microsoft.com/support/*.

If you have comments, questions, or ideas regarding this book, please send them to Microsoft Press using either of the following methods:

Postal Mail:

> Microsoft Press
> Attn: *Microsoft SQL Server 2000*
> *Administrator's Pocket Consultant* Editor
> One Microsoft Way
> Redmond, WA 98052-6399

E-mail:

> MSPINPUT@MICROSOFT.COM

Please note that product support is not offered through the above mail addresses. For support information visit Microsoft's Web site at *http://support.microsoft.com/directory/*.

Part I
Microsoft SQL Server 2000 Administration Fundamentals

Part I of this book examines the fundamental tasks you need for Microsoft SQL Server 2000 administration. Chapter 1 provides an overview of SQL Server administration tools, techniques, and concepts. Chapter 2 explores configuring and tuning SQL Server. You'll learn about optimizing memory usage, parallel processing, authentication, auditing, and more.

Chapter 1

Microsoft SQL Server 2000
Administration Overview

As you get started with Microsoft SQL Server 2000, you should concentrate on these areas:

- How SQL Server 2000 works with your hardware
- What versions and editions of SQL Server 2000 are available
- How SQL Server 2000 works with Microsoft Windows-based operating systems
- What administration tools are available

SQL Server 2000 and Your Hardware

Successful database server administration depends on three things:

- Good database administrators
- Strong database architecture
- Appropriate hardware

The first two ingredients are covered: you're the administrator, you're smart enough to buy this book to help you through the rough spots, and you've enlisted SQL Server 2000 to provide your high-performance relational database management system (RDBMS) needs. This brings us to the issue of hardware. SQL Server 2000 should run on a system with adequate memory, processing speed, and disk space. You also need an appropriate data and system protection plan at the hardware level.

Key guidelines for choosing hardware for SQL Server are as follows:

- **Memory** A minimum of 256 MB of RAM for Standard Edition and 512 MB of RAM for Enterprise Edition. This is several times the minimum memory requirement of 32 MB and 64 MB respectively; the primary reason for this extra memory is performance. SQL Server 2000 and standard Windows 2000 services together use between 80 and 100 MB of memory as a baseline. User connections consume about 24 KB each. Data requests and other SQL Server processes use memory as well, and this memory usage is in addition to all other processes and applications running on the server.

- **CPU** SQL Server 2000 runs only on Intel *x*86 or compatible hardware. It won't run on Motorola MIPS R4000, PowerPC or DEC Alpha processors. SQL Server achieves solid benchmark performance with Intel Pentium III Xeon 733 MHz and AMD Athlon 1000 MHz. Both CPUs provide good starting points for the average SQL Server system. You can achieve significant performance improvements with a high level of on processor cache. Most Xeon processors ship with 512 KB, 1 MB or 2 MB of on processor cache—and 2 MB of cache yields much better performance overall.

- **SMP** SQL Server 2000 supports symmetric multiprocessors and can process complex parallel queries. Parallel queries are valuable only when few users are on a system and you're processing large queries. On a dedicated system that runs only SQL Server and supports fewer than 100 simultaneous users, a single CPU should suffice. If the server supports more than 100 users or doesn't run on a dedicated system, you may want to consider adding processors (or using a system that can support additional processors as your needs grow).

- **Disk drives** The amount of data storage capacity you need depends entirely on the number and size of the databases the server supports. You need enough disk space to store all your data plus work space, system files, virtual memory, transaction logs, and, in the case of a cluster, the quorum disk. I/O throughput is just as important as drive capacity. In most cases SCSI (Small Computer System Interface) drives are faster than IDE/EIDE (Integrated Device Electronics/Enhanced Integrated Device Electronics), and therefore I recommend them. For the best I/O performance, FC (Fiber Channel) is the recommended choice for high-end storage solutions. Instead of using a single large drive, you should use several smaller drives, which allows you to configure fault tolerance with RAID (redundant array of independent disks). I recommend separating data and logs and placing them on separate drives. This includes the quorum disk for clustering.

- **Data protection** You should add protection against unexpected drive failures by using RAID. For data, use RAID 0 or RAID 5. For logs, use RAID 1. RAID 0 (disk striping without parity) offers good read/write performance, but any failed drive means that SQL Server can't continue operation on an affected database until the drive is replaced. RAID 1 (disk mirroring) creates duplicate copies of data on separate drives, but recovery from drive failure usually interrupts operations while you restore the failed drive from transaction logs or database backups. RAID 5 (disk striping with parity) offers good protection against single drive failure but has poor write performance. For best performance and fault tolerance, RAID 0 + 1 is recommended, which consists of disk mirroring and disk striping without parity.

- **UPS** SQL Server is designed to maintain database integrity at all times and can recover information using transaction logs. This doesn't protect the server hardware, however, from sudden power loss or power spikes. Both of these can seriously damage hardware. To prevent this, get an uninterruptible power supply. A UPS system gives you time to shut down the system properly in the event of a power outage, and it's also important in maintaining database integrity when the server uses write-back caching controllers.

If you follow these hardware guidelines, you'll be well on your way to success with SQL Server 2000.

SQL Server 2000 and SQL Server Desktop

SQL Server 2000 is distributed in three main editions: Standard, Enterprise, and Developer. In all of these editions, you'll find a server installation and a desktop installation. The server installation includes the full version of SQL Server. The desktop installation includes a scaled-down version of SQL Server with some limitations.

The most widely deployed edition is the Standard Edition, which is designed for the average-sized organization. The Standard Edition

- Runs on multiple versions of the Microsoft Windows operating system, including Windows NT 4.0 Server, Windows NT 4.0 Server Enterprise, and all Windows 2000 Server variants.

Note   For all editions of SQL Server 2000 running on Microsoft Windows NT Server 4.0, Service Pack 5 (SP 5) or later must be installed. For additional requirements pertaining to the operation of SQL Server 2000 on Windows NT Server 4.0, refer to the SQL Server 2000 Books Online.

- Supports an unlimited database size, up to 2 GB of RAM, four CPUs for symmetric multiprocessing, full-text search, and Microsoft SQL Server Analysis Services. Supports up to eight CPUs on Windows NT 4.0 Server Enterprise only.

While the Standard Edition is a strong database server solution, large organizations will want to consider the Enterprise Edition. The Enterprise Edition adds

- Support for up to 64 GB of RAM and 32 CPUs on Windows 2000 Datacenter Server, 8 GB of RAM and 8 CPUs on Windows 2000 Advanced Server, which provides for exceptional performance and the ability to scale SQL Server to support large database installations.

Note   Refer to SQL Server 2000 Books Online for maximum amount of physical RAM and number of CPUs supported on all versions of the Windows operating systems. Search for "Maximum Capacity Specifications."

- Log shipping, which allows SQL Server to send transaction logs from one server to another. Use this feature to create a standby server.
- Federated databases, which allows you to create distributed partition views by horizontally partitioning tables across multiple servers. Use this feature

when you want a group of servers to work together to support a large Web site or enterprise data processing.

- Failover clustering, which allows you to create four-node clusters on Windows 2000 Datacenter Server and two-node clusters on Windows 2000 Advanced Server. Use this feature to provide failover and failback support.

- Indexed views, parallel DBCC, parallel CREATE INDEX, and enhanced read-ahead. Use these features to enhance the performance of SQL Server.

As you might expect, the SQL Server 2000 Enterprise Edition runs on Windows NT 4.0 Server Enterprise, Windows 2000 Advanced Server, and Windows 2000 DataCenter. The Developer Edition supports all the features of the Enterprise Edition but is licensed for development use only.

Other editions of SQL Server 2000 are available. These editions are the Windows CE Edition, the Personal Edition, and the Desktop Engine. The Windows CE Edition allows you to use SQL Server as the data store on Windows CE devices. The Personal Edition is the version you run when you want to work with the SQL Server desktop. The Desktop Engine is a version of the SQL Server 2000 database engine that can be distributed with third-party applications.

All editions of SQL Server 2000 automatically and dynamically configure user connections. This is different from previous versions, where specific limitations were placed on the number of simultaneous user connections. So you don't have to worry about managing user connections as much as you used to. Just keep in mind that as the number of user connections increases so does the amount of resource usage on the server. The server has to balance the workload among the many user connections, which can result in decreased throughput for user connections and the server as a whole.

Whether you use the Standard or Enterprise Edition, you have four options for working with SQL Server. You can

- **Work with the full server and tool installation**   Perform a complete installation of SQL Server, choosing the Server And Client Tools option. The installation can be performed locally or remotely.

- **Work with only the management or development tools, or both**   Start a normal installation but choose the Client Tools Only option on the Installation Definition page. This gives you the management tools and books online. Add development tools and code samples if you plan to do any development. Don't select the server components. (If you use per server licensing, this is the best option for management and development.)

- **Work with the SQL Server Desktop**   Install the SQL Server Desktop (Personal Edition) on any Windows workstation or server operating system, including Windows 95, Windows 98, and Windows 2000. For best performance, I recommend five or fewer connections. (If you use per seat licensing, this is the best option for management and development.)

- **Work with only the data access components and network libraries**
Start a normal installation but choose the Connectivity Only option on the Installation Definition page. This installs the Microsoft Data Access Components and network libraries a client needs to connect to SQL Server 2000.

The Personal Edition provides a full SQL Server database, but it has some limitations. Features not supported by the Personal Edition include

- Parallel queries when multiple CPUs are available
- Failover clusters and federated databases
- Extended memory addressing
- Log shipping and transactional replication
- Read-ahead scans and indexed views

Additionally, the Personal Edition has limited support for transactional replication and Analysis Services. Personal Edition databases can only be subscribers for transactional replication. Personal Edition databases don't support user-defined OLAP (online analytical processing database) partitions, linked OLAP cubes, custom rollups, and other key analytical functions.

Note As you can see, most of the differences between various editions of SQL Server are below the surface and don't affect the interface. Because of this, I refer to specific editions or differentiate between the server and the desktop installation only when necessary.

SQL Server and Windows 2000

When you install SQL Server on server operating systems, SQL Server makes several modifications to the environment. These modifications include new system services, additions to the taskbar, integrated authentication, new domain/workgroup accounts, and registry updates.

Services for SQL Server

When you install SQL Server on Windows NT or Windows 2000, several services are installed on the server. These services include

- **SQL Server** The SQL Server service is the primary database service. For the default database instance this service is named MSSQLServer. When multiple instances of SQL Server are installed, you'll also see MSSQL$*instancename* where *instancename* is the name of the SQL Server instance.

- **SQL Server Agent** The SQL Server Agent service is used with scheduling. For the default database instance this service is named SQLServerAgent. When multiple instances of SQL Server are installed, you'll also see SQLAgent$*instancename* where *instancename* is the name of the SQL Server instance.

- **Distributed Transaction Coordinator** The Distributed Transaction Coordinator service coordinates distributed transactions between two or more database servers.
- **Microsoft Search** Used with full-text searches on databases. Only available when full-text search is installed as a custom component.
- **Active Directory Helper** MSSQLServerADHelper adds and removes objects used to register SQL Server and Analysis Server instances. Also updates object permissions related to SQL Server service accounts.

 Note SQL Server Desktop doesn't use services or service accounts. You'll learn more about managing services and configuring service-related options in Chapter 3, "Managing the Enterprise."

Taskbar Extras for SQL Server

A taskbar shortcut is available for SQL Server. You can use this shortcut to manage services and display service status by completing the following steps:

1. Double-click the shortcut to start the SQL Server Service Manager.
2. Right-click the shortcut and then select the Current Service On \\COMPUTER-NAME option to configure which service's icon is displayed on the taskbar.
3. Right-click the shortcut and then select Start, Stop, or Pause to control the active service.
4. Right-click the shortcut and then select Options to configure options for SQL Server Service Manager.
5. Right-click the shortcut and then select Exit to temporarily remove the SQL Server shortcut from the taskbar.

 Note To permanently remove the SQL Server shortcut from the taskbar, you must remove SQL Service Manager as a startup option. Right-click Start on the taskbar and then select Explore All Users. You'll see Windows Explorer with the Start Menu folder selected. Double-click Programs, select Startup, right-click Service Manager, and then select Delete. When prompted to confirm the action, click Yes.

Authentication Enhancements

SQL Server security is completely integrated with Windows domain security, allowing for authentication based on user and group memberships as well as standard SQL Server user accounts. These authentication techniques make it much easier to manage logons and security. You can

- Combine Windows and SQL Server authentication so users in Windows domains can access the server using a single account and other users can be logged on using a SQL Server login ID. This is the default setting.

- Use authentication based on Windows domain accounts only, so only users with a domain account can access the server.

Service Accounts

On Windows NT and Windows 2000, the MSSQLServer and SQLServerAgent services are configured to use Windows logon accounts. You can also configure additional SQL Server services to use Windows logon accounts. Two types of accounts are supported:

- **Local system accounts**   Provide administrative privileges to SQL Server on the local system but no privileges on the network. If the server requires resources on the local server only, use the local system account. Use local system accounts when you want to isolate SQL Server and restrict it from interacting with other servers. The Microsoft Search service must always use the local system account.

- **Domain accounts**   Set the service to use a standard domain account with privileges you configure. Use domain accounts when the server requires resources across the network, when you need to forward events to the application logs of other systems, and when you want to configure e-mail or pager notification.

Caution   With Windows accounts, make sure the SQL Server service has Administrator privileges on the local system. If you don't do this, the tasks you can perform with the server are restricted. You'll learn more about accounts and security in Chapter 5, "Microsoft SQL Server 2000 Security."

SQL Server and Active Directory

A directory is an important part of any computing environment. Businesses use directories to store information about objects on the network, such as users, contacts, and computers. You access information in a directory using a directory service. The directory service in Windows 2000 is called Active Directory. Active Directory service is used to store information in the directory and to make the information available to authorized users, services, and applications.

SQL Server 2000 includes enhancements for integrating with Active Directory service. Instances of SQL Server and their attributes are registered in Active Directory service during installation. Additional entries are created each time a database, server cube, or data mining model is created. These entries allow users and applications to search the directory for a particular instance of SQL Server and to search for characteristics of the server instance.

Custom applications can use Active Directory service to manage replication objects and to analyze directory data using Microsoft SQL Server 2000 Analysis Services. Active Directory service is also used with replication services to provide the ability to browse for and subscribe to publications. For example, you can search for SQL Server publications in Active Directory Users And Computers. Right-click the domain node, select Find and then in the Find Users, Contacts, And Groups dialog box select SQL Server Publications on the Find selection list.

Custom applications use the OLE DB Provider for Microsoft Directory Services to access information in Active Directory service. This OLE DB Provider exposes an LDAP and a SQL object interface. The Lightweight Directory Access Protocol (LDAP) interface is used to search Active Directory service using LDAP paths. The SQL interface is used to search Active Directory service using SQL syntax. Using the OLE DB Provider for Microsoft Directory Services, applications can also use Active Directory service as a data source for Data Transformation Services (DTS).

The key to using the OLE DB Provider for Microsoft Directory Services is to create a linked server using *ADSDSOObject* as the provider name and *adsdatasource* as the data source argument for the *sp_addlinkedserver* stored procedure. An example follows:

```
EXEC sp_addlinkedserver 'ADSI', 'Active Directory Services 2.5',
'ADSDSOObject', 'adsdatasource
GO
```

Results from an Active Directory query are returned in a tabular format that can be queried using SQL Server distributed queries. Linked servers and the *sp_addlinkedserver* stored procedure are discussed in depth in Chapter 8.

SQL Server Administration Tools

SQL Server provides many administration tools. The tools you'll use the most are

- **Graphical administration tools**   The key tools for managing SQL Server. You can access them by selecting them individually. Select Start, choose Programs, and then use the Microsoft SQL Server menu.

- **Administration wizards and the Taskpad**   Tools designed to automate key administration tasks. You access them in SQL Server Enterprise Manager.

- **Command-line utilities**   Additional utilities designed to be run at the command line or accessed in scripts.

The following sections provide brief introductions to these administration tools. Additional details for key tools are provided throughout the book. Keep in mind that you may need administration access to SQL Server to use these utilities.

Graphical Administration Tools

SQL Server 2000 provides several types of tools for administration. The graphical administration tools are the ones you'll use the most. You can access these tools by selecting Start, choosing Programs, and then using the Microsoft SQL Server menu.

SQL Server 2000 is designed for local and remote management. You can use most of the tools to manage local resources as well as remote resources. For example, in SQL Server Enterprise Manager you can register a new server and then connect to it. Afterward, you can remotely manage the server and all its databases from your system. Table 1-1 provides a list of the key graphical administration tools and their uses.

Table 1-1. Quick Reference for Key SQL Server 2000 Administration Tools

Administration Tool	Purpose
Client Network Utility	Configures the client network libraries and DB Library. Covered in Chapter 2.
ODBC Data Source Administrator	Allows you to view and configure ODBC (open database connectivity) data sources for all ODBC drivers on the workstation or server.
Performance Monitor	A customized version of the standard performance monitor, featuring special objects and counters for SQL Server. (Not available with Windows 95 or Windows 98 desktop installations.) See Chapter 10.
SQL Profiler	Allows you to analyze user activity and generate audit trails. Covered in Chapter 10.
SQL Query Analyzer	A visual utility for making queries and SQL scripts. Used anytime you want to execute SQL statements, check queries, or perform index analysis. See Chapter 4.
SQL Server Enterprise Manager	The main administration tool for SQL Server 2000. Manages SQL servers, databases, security, and more. Key aspects are discussed in Chapter 3.
SQL Server Network Utility	Configures server network libraries.
SQL Server Service Manager	Manages and configures SQL services. Easier to use than the Services utility in the Control Panel. See Chapter 3.

Administration Wizards and the Taskpad

Administration wizards are designed to make database administration easier. Wizards guide you through common database administration tasks using a series of dialog boxes, and they free you from having to remember what to enter when. SQL Server provides more than 20 wizards.

You start most Administration wizards by selecting Taskpad entries in SQL Server Enterprise Manager (see Figure 1-1). The Taskpad is a key feature in SQL Server 2000. You use the Taskpad to navigate through SQL Server options by clicking hypertext links. While some links access other Taskpad pages, others launch

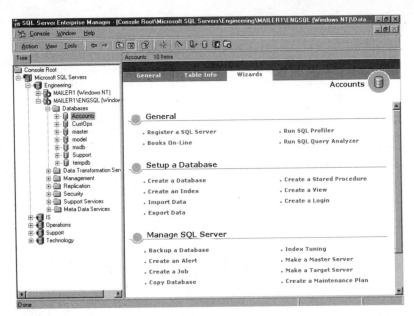

Figure 1-1. *SQL Server Enterprise Manager provides many wizards to make database administration easier.*

wizards or display database information pages. Buttons on the toolbar allow you to move backward or forward as well as refresh the display if necessary.

The Taskpad is disabled by default in full installations and disabled by default in desktop installations. To enable or disable the Taskpad, complete the following steps:

1. In SQL Server Enterprise Manager, select a database server entry. The database server entry is labeled <SERVERNAME (OS)> or <SERVERNAME\DBINSTANCE (OS), such as SQL1 (Windows NT/2000) or SQL1\Engineering1 (Windows NT/ 2000).

2. Choose Taskpad from the View menu.

You'll learn more about SQL Server Enterprise Manager in Chapter 3. SQL Server also provides an additional wizard for migrating from previous versions. This wizard is called the SQL Server Upgrade Wizard. Use this wizard to migrate databases from a SQL Server 7.0 database and import the data into an existing SQL Server 2000 installation.

You run the SQL Server Upgrade Wizard by selecting Start, choosing Programs, and then choosing the SQL Server Upgrade Wizard option from the Microsoft SQL Server-Switch submenu. During the installation you'll need to stop and restart both database servers; consequently, you'll probably want to perform this operation after regular business hours.

Command-Line Tools

The graphical administration tools provide just about everything you need to work with SQL Server. Still, there are times when you may want to work from the command line, especially if you want to automate installation, administration, or maintenance with scripts. Key command-line tools you'll use include BCP.EXE, ISQL.EXE, OSQL.EXE, TEXTCOPY.EXE, ODBCPING.EXE, and REBUILDM.EXE. These command-line executables are usually stored in the \Mssql\Binn directory.

BCP

BCP is the bulk copy program. You can use BCP to import and export data or copy data between instances of SLQ Server 2000. BCP's major advantage is speed. It's much faster than standard database import/export procedures. Unfortunately, its command-line syntax makes it much harder to use.

The syntax for BCP is shown in Sample 1-1.

Sample 1-1. BCP Syntax

```
bcp {dbtable | query} {in | out | queryout | format} datafile

  [-m maxerrors] [-f formatfile] [-e errfile]

  [-F firstrow] [-L lastrow] [-b batchsize]

  [-n native type] [-c character type] [-w Unicode characters]

  [-N keep non-text native] [-V file format version] [-q quoted
  id]

  [-C code page specifier] [-t field terminator] [-r row
  terminator]

  [-i inputfile] [-o outfile] [-a packetsize]

  [-S server name\instance name] [-U username] [-P password]

  [-T trusted connection] [-v version] [-R regional enable]

  [-k keep null values] [-E keep identity values]

  [-h "load hints"]
```

ISQL

ISQL is a SQL query tool that you can run from the command line. ISQL communicates with SQL Server through the DB Library and is used primarily because it runs within scripts. You'll find that ISQL has very little overhead, making it a good choice when system resources are a concern. Sample 1-2 shows the syntax for ISQL.

Sample 1-2. ISQL Syntax

```
isql [-U login id] [-P password]
    [-S server] [-H hostname] [-E trusted connection]
    [-d use database name] [-l login timeout] [-t query timeout]
    [-h headers] [-s colseparator] [-w columnwidth]
    [-a packetsize] [-e echo input] [-x max text size]
    [-L list servers] [-c cmdend]
    [-q "cmdline query"] [-Q "cmdline query" and exit]
    [-n remove numbering] [-m errorlevel]
    [-r msgs to stderr]
    [-i inputfile] [-o outputfile]
    [-p print statistics] [-b On error batch abort]
    [-O use Old ISQL behavior disables the following]
    <EOF> batch processing
    Auto console width scaling
    Wide messages
    default errorlevel is -1 vs 1
    [-? show syntax summary (this screen)]
```

 Note ISQL does not support connecting to named instances of SQL Server 2000. ISQL will always connect to the default instance of SQL Server.

When you start ISQL, you can issue Transact-SQL statements to run queries, execute stored procedures, and more. Because you're working at the command line, these commands aren't executed automatically and you need to use additional commands to tell ISQL when to execute statements, when to ignore statements, and so on. These additional statements must be entered on separate lines and are summarized in Table 1-2.

Table 1-2. Commands for Use with ISQL and OSQL

Command	Description
GO	Executes all statements entered up to the previous GO or RESET
RESET	Clears statements you've entered so they aren't executed
ED	Calls the editor

(continued)

Table 1-2. *(continued)*

Command	Description
!! command	Executes the specified Windows NT shell command or script
QUIT	Exits ISQL
EXIT	Exits ISQL
CTRL+C	Ends a query without exiting from ISQL

OSQL

An alternative to ISQL is OSQL. You'll use OSQL to execute queries using ODBC connections instead of DB Library. The syntax for OSQL is shown in Sample 1-3. With OSQL, you can also use the commands listed in Table 1-2.

Sample 1-3. OSQL Syntax

```
osql [-U login id] [-P password]

  [-S server name\instance name] [-H hostname] [-E trusted
  connection]

  [-d use database name] [-1 login timeout] [-t query timeout]

  [-h headers] [-s colseparator] [-w columnwidth]

  [-a packetsize] [-e echo input] [-I Enable Quoted Identifiers]

  [-L list servers] [-c cmdend] [-D ODCB DSN name]

  [-q "cmdline query"] [-Q "cmdline query" and exit]

  [-n remove numbering] [-m errorlevel]

  [-r msgs to stderr] [-V severitylevel]

  [-i inputfile] [-o outputfile]

  [-p print statistics] [-b On error batch abort]

  [-u outputfile stored in Unicode format]

  [-R ODBC use client settings when converting currency, date,and
  time] [-O use Old ISQL behavior disables the following]

  <EOF> batch processing

  Auto console width scaling

  Wide messages

  default errorlevel is -1 vs 1

  [-? show syntax summary]
```

Textcopy

Textcopy is a command-line utility for importing and exporting text or images files with SQL Server. When you import with Textcopy, data from a specified file is copied into SQL Server, replacing an existing text or image value. When you export with Textcopy, a text or image value is copied from SQL Server into a specified file. The syntax and switches for Textcopy are shown in Sample 1-4 and Table 1-3, respectively.

Sample 1-4. Textcopy Syntax

```
TEXTCOPY [/S [sqlserver]] [/U [login]] [/P [password]]

    [/D [database]] [/T table] [/C column] [/W "where clause"]

    [/F file] [{/I | /O}] [/K chunksize] [/Z] [/?]
```

Table 1-3. Textcopy Switches

Switch	Definition
/?	Displays syntax and usage help.
/C column	Specifies the table column.
/D database	Sets the database to use. If the database isn't specified, the default database for the user login is used.
/F file	Sets the input/output file name.
/I Input	Specifies that you're copying into SQL Server from a file.
/K chunksize	Sets the size of the data transfer buffer in bytes. While the minimum value is 1024 bytes, the default value is 4096 bytes.
/O Output	Specifies that you're copying from SQL Server to a file.
/P password	Sets the login password. If password isn't set, NULL is used.
/S sqlserver	Designates the SQL Server to connect to. If *sqlserver* isn't specified, the local SQL Server is used.
/T table	Specifies the database table.
/U login	Sets the login to connect with. If the login isn't set, Textcopy attempts to use a trusted connection.
/W "*where* clause"	Used to set the necessary *where* clause that must specify a single row in the designated table.
/Z	Displays debug information while running.

Odbcping

If you need to verify an ODBC connection between a client and server, you can use Odbcping. You can use Odbcping to perform two types of tests. You can test the ability of a client to connect directly to a server, and you can test the integrity of an ODBC data source.

Odbcping is a command-line utility with the following syntax:

```
odbcping [ {-Sserver_name [\instance_name] | -Ddata_source]
[-Ulogin_id] [-Ppassword]
```

Note   SQL Server 2000 doesn't install the Odbcping utility during setup. It's located in the \x86\Binn directory on the SQL Server 2000 compact disc.

Rebuildm

Rebuildm is a utility for rebuilding the master database. Rebuilding the master database removes all database objects and data. Because of this, you'll need to re-create database objects and reload data by restoring backups of system and user databases, or use *sp_attach_db* to reattach the data and log files if recent copies are available. You need to rebuild the master database only in these situations:

- To repair a corrupted master database
- To change the default collation settings for a SQL Server instance

Note   Unlike SQL Server 7, SQL Server 2000 allows you to specify collations at several levels. The default collation is the setting for all system databases, and you can't change this without rebuilding the master database. You can set a different collation when you create databases, tables, parameters, and literal strings.

To start the Rebuild Master utility, type **rebuildm** on the command line. Then follow the prompts.

Chapter 2

Configuring and Tuning Microsoft SQL Server

Microsoft SQL Server 2000 is designed to balance the workload dynamically and to self-tune configuration settings. For example, SQL Server can dynamically increase or decrease memory usage based on overall system memory requirements.

SQL Server also manages memory efficiently, especially when it comes to queries and user connections—and memory is just one of dozens of areas where the configuration is automatically adjusted.

While self-tuning works in most cases, there are times when you'll need to configure SQL Server settings manually. For example, if you're running a large database with special constraints and the database isn't performing the way you expect it to, you may need to customize the configuration. You may also need to modify configuration settings for SQL Server accounts, authentication, and auditing. Key tools you'll use to modify configuration settings are

- **SQL Server Setup**   Allows you to create new instances of SQL Server, add components, rebuild the SQL Server registry, uninstall SQL Server, and more.

- **SQL Server Enterprise Manager**   Provides an easy-to-use interface that updates the database and registry settings for you.

- **Stored Procedures**   Lets you view and manage configuration settings through stored procedures, such as *sp_configure* and *xp_regwrite*. Note that you can change some options of *sp_configure* only when Show Advanced Options is set to 1, as in the following example:

  ```
  exec sp_configure 'show advanced options', 1
  ```

- **SQLSERVR.EXE**   Starts SQL Server from the command line, and you can use it to set configuration parameters at startup.

In this chapter I use a task-oriented approach to explain how you use these tools to configure SQL Server.

Running and Modifying SQL Server Setup

SQL Server Setup is the utility you use to perform key installation tasks for SQL Server. Using SQL Server Setup, you can

- Create new instances of SQL Server
- Add or remove components
- Rebuild the SQL Server registry
- Uninstall SQL Server
- Create an unattended installation file for SQL Server installations

Creating New Instances of SQL Server

You can install multiple instances of the SQL Server 2000 database engine on a single computer. Running multiple instances of the database engine is ideal when

- You need to support multiple test and development environments on a single large server.
- You need to run multiple applications on a desktop and each application installs its own instance of the SQL Server 2000 desktop engine.
- You need to securely isolate the databases that are available on a single server.

In most other situations, however, you should not run multiple instances of the SQL Server 2000 database engine. Each instance of the SQL Server 2000 database engine has its own set of system and user databases. Each instance also has separate SQL Server and SQL Server Agent services. All other components and services are shared, and this adds to the overhead on the server.

Understanding SQL Server Instances

When you install SQL Server 2000, you have the option of installing a default instance of the SQL Server 2000 database engine or a named instance of the SQL Server 2000 database engine. In most cases, you'll want to install the default instance first and then install additional named instances of the SQL Server database engine as necessary. There is no limit to the number of named instances that you can run on a single computer.

A default instance is identified by the name of the computer on which the SQL Server 2000 database engine is running and doesn't have a separate instance name. Applications connect to the default instance by using the computer name in their requests. Only one default instance can run on any computer, and this default instance can be any version of SQL Server.

All instances of SQL Server other than the default instance are identified by the instance name that you set during installation. Applications connect to a named instance by specifying the computer name and the instance name in the format *computer_name\instance_name*. Only the SQL Server 2000 database engine can run as a named instance. Previous versions of SQL Server do not support named instances.

Note When you run SQL Server 2000 Enterprise Edition, you can cre- ate server clusters that link up to four servers together in a node. Applications connect to the default instance on a SQL Server cluster by specifying the virtual server name. Applications connect to a named instance on a SQL Server cluster by specifying the virtual server name and the named instance in the format *virtual_server_name\instance_name*.

Installing a SQL Server Instance

To install an instance of the SQL Server 2000 database engine, complete the following steps:

1. Log on to the server using an account with administrator privileges. Then insert the SQL Server 2000 CD-ROM into the CD-ROM drive.

Tip Be sure to keep a detailed record of the actions you perform in steps 6-9. These actions should explicitly state the server, server instance, and installation options you're using. You'll need this record if you ever need to rebuild the SQL Server registry settings for the server instance.

2. If Autorun is enabled, the SQL Server 2000 setup program should start automatically. Otherwise, you'll need to double-click AUTORUN.EXE in the root directory of the CD-ROM.

3. Click SQL Server 2000 Components and then select Install Database Server. This starts the Microsoft SQL Server Installation Wizard. Click Next.

4. You can install SQL Server 2000 on local or remote computers. Select Local Computer or Remote Computer as appropriate. Click Next.

Note You can also install SQL Server 2000 as part of a cluster. If a cluster is detected, the Virtual Server option is selected by default.

5. Select Create A New Instance Of SQL Server and then click Next. Afterward, complete the user information and license agreement windows.

6. Select Server And Client Tools and then click Next. As shown in Figure 2-1, you must now determine the instance type to install. To install a default instance of SQL Server, select Default and then click Next. Otherwise, clear the Default check box and then type the instance name in the field provided. The instance name can be up to 16 characters in length and must follow the naming rules for nondelimited identifiers.

Note You can install only one default instance on a computer. If a de- fault instance already exists, you can't select the Default check box.

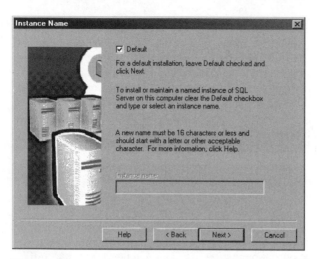

Figure 2-1. *Use the options to select the instance type as either default or named.*

7. In the Setup Type dialog box, select the installation type as Typical, Minimum, or Custom. With a custom installation, you'll be able to select subcomponents and networking libraries. You'll also be able to set the default character set and collation.

 Caution When you install SQL Server using the Typical or Minimal installation type, the default character set and collation are set. You can't change these settings on an existing SQL Server installation without rebuilding the master database. Rebuilding the master database detaches all other databases on the server, making them unusable. For more information, see the section of this chapter entitled "Changing Collation and Rebuilding the Master Database."

8. In the Services Accounts dialog box, determine how the SQL Server and SQL Server Agent services will run (see Figure 2-2). To use the same account information and autostart each service, select Use The Same Account For Each Service and then set the options using the Service Settings panel. Otherwise, choose Customize The Settings For Each Service and then set options for SQL Server and SQL Server Agent using the options of the Services and Service Settings panels.

 Tip The SQL Server and SQL Server Agent services can run under the Local System account or a Domain User account. If the server requires resources on the local server only, use the Local System account. Otherwise, use a domain account.

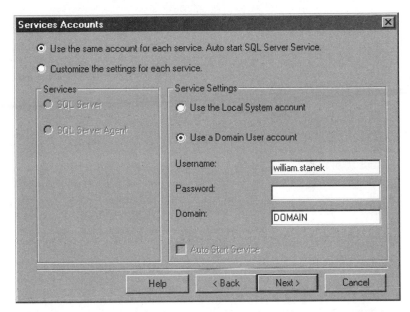

Figure 2-2. *Use the Services Accounts dialog box to determine how the SQL Server and SQL Server Agent services will run.*

9. Use the Authentication Mode dialog box to configure the authentication settings. The SQL Server instance can run under Microsoft Windows authentication or mixed mode authentication. With Windows authentication, you use only domain accounts to authenticate connections to the SQL Server instance. With mixed mode authentication, users can access the SQL Server instance using domain accounts or SQL Server IDs.

10. Click Next, choose an appropriate licensing mode, and then click Continue to begin the installation process. Anytime there are tasks using files that setup needs to install, you'll see a prompt. The prompt tells you which tasks you need to shut down to avoid having to reboot after installation. Stop tasks as necessary. If you stop services, be sure to note dependent services that are stopped as well. You'll need to restart these services later. Click Next and then click Finish to complete the process.

11. Register the instance of the SQL Server database engine as discussed in the section of Chapter 3 entitled "Managing Servers." You can then manage the server instance in Enterprise Manager.

Adding Components

SQL Server keeps track of those components you've installed and those you haven't. If you ever want to add components, you can do so by completing the following steps:

1. Log on to the server using an account with administrator privileges. Then insert the SQL Server 2000 CD-ROM into the CD-ROM drive.

2. If Autorun is enabled, the SQL Server 2000 setup program should start automatically. Otherwise, you'll need to double-click AUTORUN.EXE in the root directory of the CD-ROM.

3. Click SQL Server 2000 Components and then select Install Database Server. This starts the Microsoft SQL Server Installation Wizard. Click Next.

4. Select Local Computer, Remote Computer, or Virtual Server as appropriate. Click Next.

5. Select Upgrade, Remove, Or Add Components and then click Next.

6. Use the Instance Name dialog box to select the instance you want to work with. If necessary, clear the Default check box so that you can use the Instance Name selection list. Click Next.

7. Select Add Components To Your Existing Installation and then click Next. You can now add components to the installation.

The installation program detects currently installed components and then allows you to select additional components. Components you might want to add through the installation program include

- **Server components**   SQL Server, upgrade tools, replication support, full-text search, debug symbols, and performance counters

- **Management tools**   Enterprise Manager, Query Analyzer, Profiler, DTC Client Support, and Conflict Viewer

- **Books online**   Help documentation, installed on the system's hard disk drive or accessed from a CD-ROM, or both

- **Development tools**   Headers and libraries, Backup/Restore API, and Debugger Interface

 Note   As the installation dialog box says, selecting components already installed doesn't reinstall them and canceling components already installed doesn't remove them.

The SQL Server CD-ROM provides other tools that aren't part of the standard installation. You access these tools on the initial installation screen and they include

- **Analysis Services**   Used with online analytical processing applications and data warehousing

- **English Query**   Used with applications that allow plain-English queries of the SQL database

Restoring the SQL Server Registry

Each instance of the SQL Server 2000 database engine running on the computer has settings that are stored in the Windows registry. If these settings are corrupted or accidentally deleted, you can restore them by using the SQL Server Setup program. Setup rebuilds the registry settings based on information you provide and won't copy files. You must know how you installed the corrupted instance of SQL Server. If you don't remember how you installed the SQL Server instance, you'll need to uninstall and then reinstall SQL Server.

Note   The registry settings are only for the specific instance of the SQL Server 2000 database engine you identify. The restore process doesn't restore registry settings for other applications and services.

To rebuild the SQL Server registry settings, follow these steps:

1. Log on to the server using an account with administrator privileges. Then insert the SQL Server 2000 CD-ROM into the CD-ROM drive.

2. If Autorun is enabled, the SQL Server 2000 setup program should start automatically. Otherwise, you'll need to double-click AUTORUN.EXE in the root directory of the CD-ROM.

3. Click SQL Server 2000 Components and then select Install Database Server. This starts the Microsoft SQL Server Installation Wizard. Click Next.

4. Select Local Computer, Remote Computer, or Virtual Server as appropriate. Click Next.

5. Select Advanced Options and then click Next. Afterward, select Rebuild Registry and then click Next again.

6. Proceed through the installation process, choosing the same options you previously selected for the instance of the SQL Server database engine. When you finish, Setup will begin the restoration process. If the rebuild is successful, you'll see a prompt indicating this. If the rebuild is unsuccessful, you'll see a prompt notifying you that you need to uninstall and then reinstall SQL Server for this particular database instance.

Uninstalling SQL Server

You use the SQL Server Setup program to uninstall SQL Server 2000. You can uninstall each instance of the SQL Server database engine separately.

To uninstall an instance of SQL Server, complete these steps:

1. Log on to the server using an account with administrator privileges. Then insert the SQL Server 2000 CD-ROM into the CD-ROM drive.

2. If Autorun is enabled, the SQL Server 2000 setup program should start automatically. Otherwise, you'll need to double-click AUTORUN.EXE in the root directory of the CD-ROM.

3. Click SQL Server 2000 Components and then select Install Database Server. This starts the Microsoft SQL Server Installation Wizard. Click Next.

4. Select Local Computer, Remote Computer, or Virtual Server as appropriate. Click Next.

5. Select Upgrade, Remove, Or Add Components and then click Next.
6. Use the Instance Name dialog box to select the instance you want to remove and then click Next.
7. Select Uninstall Your Existing Installation and then click Next. The installation wizard removes the SQL Server instance.
8. Click Next and then click Finish to complete the process.

Configuring SQL Server with Enterprise Manager

Enterprise Manager provides the easiest way to configure SQL Server. In Enterprise Manager you access the Properties dialog box of a registered server and then use the tabs and options provided to configure the server. Behind the scenes, SQL Server executes commands that modify server settings. If the changes affect the master database or other databases, the stored procedure *sp_configure* is used to make changes in the *sysconfigures* system table. If the changes affect the Microsoft Windows Registry, the stored procedure *xp_regwrite* is used to update the Registry. SQL Server also uses stored procedures to read configuration settings. For example, the stored procedure *xp_regread* is used to read most registry settings.

Once you register a server in Enterprise Manager, you can connect to it and manage its configuration with the SQL Server Properties dialog box. To access this dialog box, complete the following steps:

1. Select Start, choose Programs, choose Microsoft SQL Server, and then choose Enterprise Manager.
2. Access the server group containing the server you want to work with. Right-click the server name in the Enterprise Manager tree view and choose Properties from the shortcut menu. This opens the dialog box shown in Figure 2-3.
3. You can now configure common SQL Server settings. For more advanced settings, you'll need to use a stored procedure, such as *sp_configure*.

The SQL Server Properties dialog box has many tabs. The sections that follow discuss each of them. To obtain a summary of current settings in SQL Server Query Analyzer, run the following command:

```
exec sp_configure
```

Figure 2-3. *The SQL Server Properties dialog box allows you to configure SQL Server without having to use stored procedures like* sp_configure. *Pointing and clicking is easy, so it's definitely recommended.*

Determining System and Server Information

General system and server information is available on the General tab of the SQL Server Properties dialog box (see Figure 2-3). The information provided by the General tab helps you determine the following:

- SQL Server edition: Standard, Enterprise, or Personal
- Operating system version
- SQL Server version
- Default language
- Platform and chip architecture
- Amount of RAM installed on the system
- Number of CPUs
- SQL Server root directory location
- Default server collation

Using the extended stored procedure *xp_msver*, you can obtain similar information. Execute the following command:

```
exec xp_msver 'ProductName', 'ProductVersion', 'Language',
'Platform', 'WindowsVersion', 'PhysicalMemory', 'ProcessorCount'
```

 Tip You can use the SQL Query Analyzer to execute the command shown. Basic techniques for using this utility are covered in the section of this chapter entitled "Configuring SQL Server with Stored Procedures."

Configuring Startup

SQL Server provides many ways to configure server startup. One of them is through the General tab of the SQL Server Properties dialog box. Use the check boxes in the Autostart Policies When The Operating System Starts area. These check boxes determine whether the related services start automatically when the operating system starts. You can use these check boxes as follows:

- **Configuring SQL Server startup** To automatically start SQL Server (MSSQLServer service) when the system boots, select the Autostart SQL Server check box. Otherwise, clear the check box.

- **Configuring SQL Server Agent startup** To automatically start SQL Server Agent (SQLServerAgent service) when the system boots, select the Autostart SQL Server Agent check box. Otherwise, clear the check box.

 Note The MSSQLServer and SQLServerAgent services are used with the default server instance only. When you're working with a named instance of SQL Server, these services are named MSSQL$*instancename* and SQLAgent$*instancename*.

- **Configuring MSDTC startup** To automatically start MSDTC (MSDTC service) when the system boots, select the Autostart MSDTC check box. Otherwise, clear the check box.

Enterprise Manager uses the stored procedure *xp_regwrite* to modify the service startup settings. These settings affect the startup values registry keys.

 Caution Don't write directly to the Registry unless it's absolutely necessary. Use the Properties dialog box instead—that's what it's for.

Setting Startup Parameters

Startup parameters control how SQL Server starts and what options are set when it does. The easiest way to configure startup options is through the General tab of the SQL Server Properties dialog box. Click Startup Parameters to display the dialog box shown in Figure 2-4. You can now add and remove startup parameters.

Tip Startup parameters can be passed to the command-line utility SQLSERVR.EXE as well. Passing this utility the –c option starts SQL Server without using a service. You must run SQLSERVR.EXE from the Binn directory that corresponds to the instance of the SQL Server database engine that you want to start. For the default instance, the utility is located in mssql\Binn. For named instances, the utility is located in mssql$*instancename*\Binn.

Adding Startup Parameters

You can add startup options by completing the following steps:

1. Type a parameter in the Parameter field.

2. Choose Add.

3. Click OK to apply the changes.

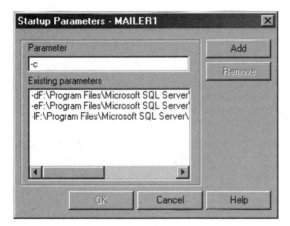

Figure 2-4. *Configure startup parameters for SQL Server by adding or removing options. Don't delete the default options (-d, -e, and -l) or you may have problems.*

Removing Startup Parameters

You can remove startup parameters by completing the following steps:

1. Select the parameter, and then choose Remove.

2. Click OK to apply the changes.

Common Startup Parameters

Table 2-1 shows startup parameters and how they're used. The first three parameters (-d, -e, and -l) are the defaults for SQL Server. The remaining parameters allow you to configure additional settings.

Table 2-1. Startup Parameters for SQL Server

Parameter	Description	Example
-d\<path\>	Sets the full path for the master database.	-dC:\MSSQL\data\master.mdf
-e\<path\>	Sets the full path for the error log.	-eD:\LOGS\ERRORLOG
-l\<path\>	Sets the full path for the master database transaction log.	-lD:\LOGS\mastlog.ldf
-B	Sets a breakpoint on error; used with the -y option when debugging	
-c	Prevents SQL Server from running as a service. This makes startup faster when you're running SQL Server from the command line.	
-f	Starts SQL Server with minimal configuration. Enables the *sp_ configure* Allow Updates option, which is disabled by default.	
-g number	Specifies the amount of memory in MB to reserve for SQL Server.	-g 192
-m	Starts SQL Server in single-user mode. Only a single user can connect and the checkpoint process isn't started.	
-n	Tells SQL Server not to log errors in the application event log.	
-p\<level\>	Sets the precision level for numeric and decimal data types. Default is 38 digits but the range is 1–38. Maximum precision (38) is assumed if you use the switch without setting a level.	-p38
-s\<altreg\>	Sets an alternative Registry key for SQL Server. This is used during startup instead of the default key.	-sHKEY_LOCAL_MACHINE\ SYSTEM\CurrentControlSet\ Services\MSSQLServerMod
-T\<tnum\>	Sets a trace flag. Trace flags set nonstandard behavior and are often used in debugging or diagnosing performance issues.	-T237

(continued)

Table 2-1. *(continued)*

Parameter	Description	Example
-t<tnum>	Sets an internal trace flag for SQL Server. Used only by SQL Server support engineers.	-t8837
-x	Disables statistics tracking for CPU time and cache-hit ratio. Allows maximum performance.	
-y number	Sets an error number that causes SQL Server to dump the stack.	-y 1803

Setting the Startup Service Account

SQL Server inherits rights and permissions from the startup service account. These permissions are used whenever SQL Server performs tasks on the local system or across the network. As discussed in the section of Chapter 1 entitled "Service Accounts," you can use two types of accounts: local system accounts and domain accounts. If SQL Server performs only local operations, use the local system account. Otherwise, use a properly configured domain account.

Note   If you plan on using SQL mail or SQLAgent mail, it's a good idea to make sure that the domain user account you set to run the SQL Server and SQL Agent services is a member of the local administrators group and that you assign both services to the same account. If you change the account after you've installed SQL Server, you'll have to make several changes to security settings to restart the services.

Using the Local System Account

Specify the local system account for SQL Server startup by completing the following steps:

1. Access the Security tab of the SQL Server Properties dialog box.

2. Use the local system account by choosing the System Account option button in the Startup Service Account area.

3. Click OK. Now the server can only access local resources.

Using a Domain Account

Specify a domain account for SQL Server startup by completing the following steps:

1. Set appropriate privileges for the SQL Server account and make sure the user account has the "log on as a service" local security policy setting enabled.

2. From the SQL Server Properties dialog box, go to the Security tab.

3. Choose the This Account option button. Then type the designated account name and password. If necessary, specify the domain as part of the account

name, such as cordata\wrstane, where cordata is the domain name and wrstane is the account name.

4. Click OK.

Authentication and Auditing

You configure authentication and auditing options with the Security tab of the SQL Server Properties dialog box. This tab is shown in Figure 2-5.

Setting Authentication Mode

As discussed in the section of Chapter 1 entitled "Authentication Enhancements," SQL Server can use combined domain and SQL Server authentication or domain authentication only. To use combined authentication, select the SQL Server And Windows option button. Now users in Windows domains can access the server using a domain account and other users can be logged on using a SQL Server logon ID.

To use domain authentication only, select the Windows Only option button. Now only users with a domain account can access the server.

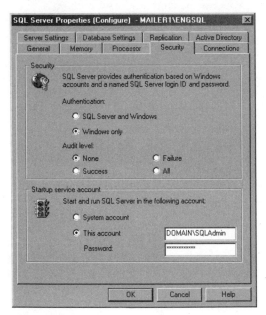

Figure 2-5. *Configure authentication and auditing with the Security tab's options.*

Tip With combined authentication, SQL Server first checks to see if a new logon is a SQL Server logon. If the logon exists, SQL Server then uses the password provided to authenticate the user. If the logon doesn't exist, it uses domain authentication. Note also that domain authentication isn't available on SQL Server Desktop running on Windows 95 or Windows 98.

Setting Auditing Level

Auditing allows you to track user access to SQL Server. You can use auditing with both authentication modes as well as with trusted and untrusted connections.

When auditing is enabled, user logons are recorded in the Windows application log, the SQL Server error log, or both, depending on how you configure logging for SQL Server. The available auditing options are

- **None** Disables auditing (the default setting)
- **Success** Audits successful logon attempts
- **Failure** Audits failed logon attempts
- **All** Audits both successful and failed logon attempts

Tuning Memory Usage

SQL Server is designed to manage memory needs dynamically, and it does an excellent job in most cases. Using dynamic memory allocation, SQL Server can add memory to handle incoming queries, free up memory for another application you're starting, or reserve memory for possible needs. The default memory settings are the following:

- Dynamically configure SQL Server memory
- Minimum memory allocation of 0 MB
- Maximum memory allocation is set to the total amount of RAM on the system
- No memory is reserved specifically for SQL Server
- Minimum memory for query execution of 1024 KB

You can change these settings if you like, but you need to be very careful about allocating too little or too much memory to SQL Server. Too little memory and SQL Server has to throttle back and may not handle tasks in a timely manner. Too much memory and SQL Server may take essential resources away from other applications like the operating system, which may result in excessive paging and a drain on overall system performance.

Tip Statistics that can help you better allocate memory are the number of page faults per second and the cache-hit ratio. Page faults per second helps track paging to and from virtual memory. Cache-hit ratio helps track whether data being retrieved is in memory. You'll learn more about this in Chapter 10, "Profiling and Monitoring Microsoft SQL Server."

The following sections examine key areas of memory management. The primary way to configure memory usage is to use the Memory tab of the SQL Server Properties dialog box, shown in Figure 2-6. I'll also show you a better way to configure Windows memory usage for SQL Server.

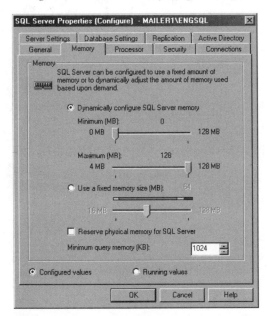

Figure 2-6. *You can use the Memory tab to dynamically or manually configure memory usage, but keep in mind that you shouldn't change these settings unless you're experiencing performance problems.*

Working with Dynamically Configured Memory

With dynamically configured memory, SQL Server configures memory usage automatically, based on workload and available resources. Total memory usage varies between the minimum and maximum values you set. To use dynamically configured memory, complete the following steps:

1. Select the Dynamically Configure SQL Server Memory option button in the Memory tab.

2. If desired, set minimum and maximum memory usage values with the Minimum and Maximum sliders, respectively. It's recommended that you set the Maximum value at or near total RAM for stand-alone servers.

3. Click OK.

You can use the stored procedure *sp_configure* to change the minimum and maximum settings. Use the following Transact-SQL commands:

```
exec sp_configure 'min server memory', <number of megabytes>
exec sp_configure 'max server memory', <number of megabytes>
```

Best Practice   With dynamically configured memory, you usually don't need to set minimum and maximum memory usage values. On a dedicated system running only SQL Server, however, you may achieve smoother operation by setting minimum memory to 4 MB + (24 KB * NumUsers), where NumUsers is the average number of users simultaneously connected to the server. You may also want to reserve physical memory for SQL Server. SQL Server uses about 3.5 MB for its code and internal structures. Additional memory is used as follows: 96 bytes for locks, 2880 bytes for open databases, and 276 bytes for open objects, which include all tables, views, stored procedures, extended stored procedures, triggers, rules, constraints, and defaults. To simplify tracking additional memory, I just add 500 KB. This gives a total of 4 MB.

Using Fixed Memory

If you want to override the dynamic memory management features, you can do this by setting a fixed memory size for SQL Server. Complete the following steps:

1. From the SQL Server Properties dialog box, go to the Memory tab, and select Use A Fixed Memory Size.

2. Adjust memory setting to the desired value using the slide control.

3. Click OK.

Caution   Setting fixed memory incorrectly can cause serious perfor- mance problems on SQL Server. Use fixed memory only in circumstances when you need to ensure that an exact amount of memory is available for SQL Server.

Reserving Physical Memory

You can also reserve memory specifically for SQL Server. When you reserve physical memory for SQL Server, the operating system doesn't swap out SQL Server memory pages even if that memory could be allocated to other processes when SQL Server is idle. On a dedicated system, reserving memory can improve SQL Server performance by cutting down on paging and cache hits.

To reserve physical memory for SQL Server, complete the following steps:

1. From the SQL Server Properties dialog box, go to the Memory tab and select Reserve Physical Memory For SQL Server.

2. Click OK.

You can also use the stored procedure *sp_configure* to reserve physical memory. The Transact-SQL command you would use is

```
exec sp_configure 'set working set size', 1
```

Allocating Memory for Queries

By default, SQL Server allocates a minimum of 1024 KB of memory for query execution. This memory allocation is guaranteed per user, and you can set it anywhere from 512 KB to 2 GB. If you increase the minimum query size, you can improve the performance of queries that perform processor-intensive operations, such as sorting or hashing. If you set the value too high, however, you can degrade the overall system performance. Because of this, adjust the minimum query size only when you're having trouble executing queries quickly.

 Best Practice The default setting of 1024 KB of RAM works in most cases. However, you may want to consider changing this value if the server operates in an extremely busy environment, with lots of simultaneous queries running in separate user connections, or in a relatively slow environment, with few (but large or complex) queries. In this case, four factors should determine your decision to adjust the minimum query size: the total amount of free memory (when the system is idle and SQL Server is running), the average number of simultaneous queries running in separate user connections, the average query size, and the query response time you hope to achieve. There's often a trade-off to be made with these values. You can't always get an instant response, but you can optimize performance based on available resources.

Use the following equation to get a starting point for the optimization:

FreeMemory / (AvgQuerySize * AvgNumSimulQueries).

For example, if the system has 200 MB of free memory, the average query size is 2 MB, and the average number of simultaneous queries is five, the optimal value for query size is 200 MB / (2*5) or 20 MB. Generally, this value represents the maximum you should assign given the current environment, and you'll want to lower this value.

To allocate memory for queries, complete the following steps:

1. From the SQL Server Properties dialog box, go to the Memory tab and set a value for the Minimum Query Memory box. This value is set in kilobytes.

2. Click OK.

You can also use the stored procedure *sp_configure* to set the minimum query size. The related command is

```
exec sp_configure 'min memory per query', <number of kilobytes>
```

Configuring Processors and Parallel Processing

Systems that use multiprocessors can take advantage of SQL Server's enhancements for parallel and symmetric multiprocessing. You can control how and when processors are used by SQL Server as well as when queries are processed in parallel. On Windows 2000, standard editions of SQL Server support up to four processors. Enterprise Editions support up to 32 processors (8 with Advanced Server and 32 on Data Center Server).

Optimizing CPU Usage

Processor settings are automatically configured and optimized when you install SQL Server. Don't change these settings without careful forethought. That said, you can manually configure processor usage by completing the following steps:

1. Select Start, choose Programs, choose Microsoft SQL Server, and then choose Enterprise Manager.

2. Right-click the server name in the Enterprise Manager tree view and choose Properties from the shortcut menu.

3. From the SQL Server Properties dialog box, go to the Processor tab, as shown in Figure 2-7.

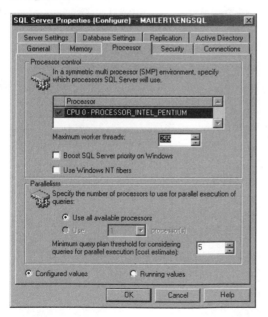

Figure 2-7. *Use the Processor tab to control which processors are used by SQL Server and when parallel processing is used. Read the notes before making changes.*

4. Use the Processor list to determine which processors SQL Server uses. Select the check box for processors you want to use and clear the check box for processors you don't want to use. The first CPU on the system is identified as CPU 0, the second as CPU 1, and so on.

 Best Practice If the system has more processors than SQL Server supports, SQL Server doesn't use all of them. For example, on an eight-way symmetric multiprocessing (SMP) system, SQL Server Standard can use only four processors. This leaves four processors for other applications and system-level tasks.

While you may be tempted to assign SQL Server to the higher numbered processors (5, 6, 7, and 8), this isn't a good idea. Windows assigns deferred process calls associated with network interface cards (NICs) to the highest numbered processors. Here, if the system had two NICs, these calls would be directed to CPU 8 and CPU 7. Definitely consult with the equipment manufacturer before changing these values.

5. Click OK.

6. These settings take effect when the server is stopped and restarted.

You can also use the stored procedure *sp_configure* to set the affinity mask. The related command is

```
exec sp_configure 'affinity mask', <integer value>
```

SQL Server interprets the integer value as a bit mask representing the processors you want to use. In this bit mask, CPU 0 is represented by bit 0, CPU 1 with bit 1, and so on. A bit value of 1 tells SQL Server to use the CPU. A bit value of 0 tells SQL Server not to use the CPU. For example, if you wanted to turn on support for processors 1, 2, and 5, you would have a binary value of

000100110

The corresponding integer value is 76:

64 + 8 + 4 = 76

Setting Parallel Processing

A lot of calculations go into determining when parallel processing is and isn't used. Generally, SQL Server processes queries in parallel

- When the number of CPUs is greater than the number of active connections.
- When the estimated cost for the serial execution of a query is higher than the query plan threshold. (The estimated cost refers to the elapsed time in seconds required to execute the query serially.)

That said, certain types of statements can't be processed in parallel unless they contain clauses. For example, UPDATE, INSERT, and DELETE aren't normally processed in parallel even if the related query meets the criteria. However, if the UPDATE or DELETE statements contain a *where* clause or an INSERT statement contains a *select* clause, the *where* and *select* can be executed in parallel. Changes are then serially applied to the database.

You can configure parallel processing by completing the following steps:

1. From the SQL Server Properties dialog box, go to the Processor tab.

2. To use all available processors for parallel processing (the maximum supported by SQL Server), select the Use All Available Processors option button.

3. To use a set amount of processors for parallel processing (up to the maximum supported by SQL Server), select the Use N Processor(s) option button and then select the number of processors to use. A value of 1 tells SQL Server not to use parallel processing.

4. Set a cost estimate in the Minimum Query Plan Threshold field. You can use any value from 0 to 32,767. On a single CPU the cost threshold is ignored.

5. Click OK. These changes take effect immediately. You don't need to restart the server.

You can use the stored procedure *sp_configure* to configure parallel processing. The Transact-SQL commands are

```
exec sp_configure 'max degree of parallelism', <integer value>
exec sp_configure 'cost threshold for parallelism',
   <integer value>
```

Note Transact-SQL is an enhanced version of the standard structured query language (SQL) that is used by SQL Server. You may also see Transact-SQL referenced as T-SQL.

Configuring Threading, Priority, and Fibers

Threads are a very important part of a multitasking operating system and enable SQL Server to do many things at once. Threads aren't processes, however. They're concurrent execution paths that allow applications to use the CPU more effectively.

SQL Server tries to match threads to user connections. When the number of threads that are available is greater than the number of user connections, there is at least a one-to-one ratio of threads to user connections, which allows each user connection to be handled uniquely. When the number of threads available is less than the number of user connections, SQL Server must pool threads; as a result, the same thread may serve multiple user connections, which can reduce performance and response time if additional resources are available and aren't being used.

Normally, the operating system handles threads in kernel mode but handles applications and user-related tasks in user mode. Switching between modes, such as when the kernel needs to handle a new thread, requires CPU cycles and resources. To allow the application to handle threading directly, you can use fibers. Switching fibers doesn't require changing modes and therefore can sometimes improve performance. Another way to improve performance is to increase the priority of SQL Server threads. Normally, threads have a priority of 1 to 31, and higher priority threads get more CPU time than lower priority threads. Higher priority threads can also preempt lower priority threads, forcing threads to wait until higher priority threads finish executing. By increasing thread priority, you can give the threads a higher preference for CPU time and ensure that other threads don't preempt them.

 Note The complete range for thread priority is from 0 to 31. Thread priority 0 is reserved for operating system use.

You configure worker threads, fibers, and thread priority using the SQL Server Properties dialog box. Go to the Processor tab and use these options:

- **Maximum Worker Threads** Sets the maximum number of threads. By default, the field is set to 255. However, you can use any value from 10 to 32,767 (except on the desktop version). On a busy server with lots of user connections, you may want to increase this value. On a slow server with few connections, you may want to decrease this value. Computers with multiple processors can concurrently execute one thread per CPU.

- **Boost SQL Server Priority On Windows** Increases the priority of SQL Server threads. Without boosting, SQL Server threads have a priority of 7 (normal priority). With boosting, SQL Server threads have a priority of 13 (high priority). On a dedicated system running only SQL Server, this option can improve performance. However, if the server runs other applications, the performance of those applications may be degraded.

- **Use Windows NT Fibers** Configures SQL Server to use fibers, which it can handle directly. SQL Server still needs threads to carry out tasks. SQL Server allocates one thread per CPU and then allocates one fiber per concurrent user connection up to the Maximum Worker Threads value. You must restart the server for this option to take effect.

 Tip Fibers work best when the server has multiple CPUs and a relatively low user to CPU ratio. For example, on an Enterprise installation with 32 CPUs and 250 users, you may see a noticeable performance boost with fibers. But when you have eight CPUs and 5000 users, you may see performance *decrease* with fibers.

You can use *sp_configure* to set fibers, maximum worker threads, and priority boost. The commands are

```
exec sp_configure 'lightweight pooling', <0 or 1>
exec sp_configure 'max worker threads', <integer value>
exec sp_configure 'priority boost', <0 or 1>
```

Configuring User and Remote Connections

Requests for data are handled through user connections to client systems. The client opens a connection to SQL Server, makes a request, and waits for a response from SQL Server. When the client is finished with its request, it closes the connection. Other servers and applications can also connect to SQL Server remotely. To configure client connections and remote server connections, you can use the Connections tab in the SQL Server Properties dialog box.

As you see in Figure 2-8, there are many settings associated with client and server connections. The sections that follow examine these settings.

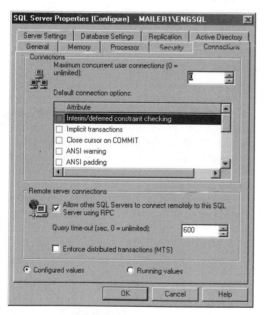

Figure 2-8. *The default connection settings seen in the Connections tab are usually sufficient. Note the original settings before you make any changes.*

Setting Maximum User Connections

In the Connections tab, the Maximum Concurrent User Connections field allows you to configure the maximum number of user connections that SQL Server allows at any one time. SQL Server allows you to set this value to anywhere from 0 to 32,767. By default, the value is set to zero, which means an unlimited number of connections is allowed. However, the actual number of user connections allowed really depends on hardware, application, and other server limitations. You can determine the number of user connections allowed on your system by executing the following command in SQL Server Query Analyzer:

```
select @@max_connections
```

To set the maximum number of user connections, complete the following steps:

1. From the SQL Server Properties dialog box, go to the Connections tab.

2. Type a new value in the Maximum Concurrent User Connections field and then click OK.

3. Stop and restart the server for the changes to take effect.

You can also set the maximum user connections by using the following command:

```
exec sp_configure 'user connections', <integer value>
```

 Best Practice You shouldn't need to change the maximum connections value. If you do, be careful. When the maximum number of connections is reached, users receive an error message and aren't able to connect until a connection becomes available. The only time you'll need to set this option is in an environment where you have a large number of users and need to limit the number of active connections to ensure that requests for connected users are handled in a timely manner. A better alternative is to add sufficient memory to the system or configure a cluster to balance the workload, or both. For large numbers of users, you should also ensure that SQL applications connect and then disconnect promptly when finished to free resources.

Default Connection Options

On the Connections tab you'll find a list box labeled Default Connection Options. You'll use the list box options to set default query-processing options for user connections. Select an option by selecting its related check box. Cancel an option by clearing its related check box. Any changes you make affect new logons only. Current logons aren't affected. Furthermore, users can override the defaults by using *set* statements, if necessary.

Table 2-2 provides a summary of the connection options as well as the default state for ODBC (open database connectivity) and OLE DB (object linking and embedding database, which may be different from the SQL Server default). You'll also find a list of commands you can use with *sp_configure*, the corresponding value for the configuration bit mask, and the SET commands used to override the default settings in a user session.

Table 2-2. Configuring Connection Options

Connection Option	Description	Default State	Bit Mask Value	SET Command
Interim/deferred constraint checking	When on, disables deferred checking of foreign key constraints. This applies stricter referential integrity checking.	Off	1	DISABLE_DEF_ CNST_CHK
Implicit transactions	When on, uses transactions implicitly whenever statements are executed.	Off	2	IMPLICIT_ TRANSACTIONS
Close cursor on COMMIT	When on, automatically closes a cursor at the end of a transaction.	Off	4	CURSOR_ CLOSE_ ON_COMMIT
ANSI warning	When on, SQL Server displays null, overflow, and divide-by-zero warnings. Otherwise no error or null may be returned.	On	8	ANSI_ WARNINGS
ANSI padding	When on, data in fixed-length fields are padded with trailing spaces to fill out the width of the column.	On	16	ANSI_PADDING
ANSI nulls	Controls how NULL is used with equality operators. When on, comparing anything with NULL gives an unknown result.	On	32	ANSI_NULLS
Arithmetic abort	When on, causes a query to terminate when an overflow or divide-by-zero error occurs.	On	64	ARITHABORT
Arithmetic ignore	Returns NULL when an overflow or divide-by-zero error occurs during a query.	On	128	ARITHIGNORE

(continued)

Table 2-2. *(continued)*

Connection Option	Description	Default State	Bit Mask Value	SET Command
Quoted identifier	When on, SQL Server interprets double quotation marks as indicating an identifier rather than as delimiting a string.	On	256	QUOTED_IDENTIFIER
No count	When on, turns off the display of the number of rows returned in a query.	Off	512	NOCOUNT
ANSI null defined ON	When on, new columns are defined to allow nulls (if you don't explicitly allow or disallow nulls).	Off	1024	ANSI_NULL_DFLT_ON
ANSI null defined OFF	When on, new columns are defined not to allow nulls (if you don't explicitly allow or disallow nulls).	Off	2048	ANSI_NULL_DFLT_OFF

For *sp_configure*, the default options are set with the *user options* parameter

```
exec sp_configure 'user options', <integer bit mask value>
```

Here, the bit mask value is the sum of the numeric values for all the options you want to use. Each option has a corresponding SET command as well. When you make a connection, you can use the SET command to override the default setting for the session. For example, if you wanted to turn on ANSI padding, ANSI nulls, and ANSI warning, you'd use the bit mask value 56, such as

```
exec sp_configure 'user options', 56
```

In a user session, you could later turn these options on or off using

```
set ansi_padding on
set ansi_nulls off
```

Configuring Remote Server Connections

Connections from other servers are handled differently than user connections. You can determine whether servers can connect using remote procedure call (RPC), how long it takes for remote queries to time out, and whether distributed transactions are used. To configure remote connections, complete these steps:

1. From the Server Properties dialog box, go to the Connections tab.

2. To allow servers to connect by means of RPC, select Allow Other SQL Servers To Connect Remotely To This SQL Server Using RPC. Remote servers can then log on to the server to execute stored procedures remotely. You must stop and restart the server if you change this option.

Caution   RPC connections are allowed by default. If you change this behavior, remote servers can't log on to SQL Server. This secures SQL Server from remote server access.

3. By default, queries executed by remote servers don't time out. To change this behavior, type a time-out value in the Query Time-Out field. Time-out values are set in seconds, and the acceptable range of values is from 0 to 2,147,483,647. A value of 0 means that there is no query time-out for remote server connections.

4. Stored procedures and queries executed on the server can be handled as distributed transactions by using MS DTC. If you want to execute procedures in this way, select the Enforce Distributed Transactions (MTS) check box. If you change this option, you must stop and restart the server.

5. Click OK.

These options can also be set with *sp_configure* and the related Transact-SQL statements are

```
exec sp_configure 'remote access', <0 or 1>
exec sp_configure 'remote query timeout', <number of seconds>
exec sp_configure 'remote proc trans', <0 or 1>
```

Note   A value of 0 is off and a value of 1 is on.

Server Settings

You use the Server Settings tab of the SQL Server Properties dialog box to configure general server settings. As shown in Figure 2-9, you can set the default language, general server behavior, and more.

Setting Default Language for SQL Server
The default language determines default display formats for dates as well as the names of months and days. All output is in U.S. English unless you're running a localized version of SQL Server. Localized versions of SQL Server are available for French, German, Japanese, and Spanish. On a localized server, there are two sets of system messages, one in U.S. English and one in the local language. If the default language is set to the local language, SQL Server messages are displayed in the local language. Otherwise, they're displayed in U.S. English.

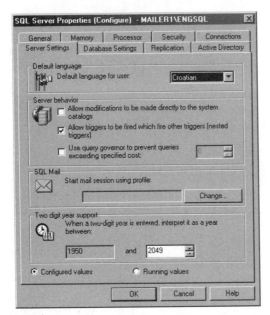

Figure 2-9. *You set general configuration options for the server in the Server Settings tab.*

In the Server Settings tab of the SQL Server Properties dialog box, you use the Default Language For User drop-down list box to set the default language and then click OK. Afterward, you must stop and restart the server for the changes to take effect. With *sp_configure*, the related Transact-SQL statement is

```
exec sp_configure 'default language', <language id number>
```

The language ID number for U.S. English is always 0.

Allowing and Disallowing System Updates

By default, users can only update the systems table with system-stored procedures, even if they have proper permissions. This is a valuable feature because it prevents users from executing statements that may corrupt the database or prevent SQL Server from starting. Still, you may want to change this behavior and allow direct updates to system tables. Once you allow modifications, anyone with proper permissions can update systems tables by executing statements or stored procedures.

This is very risky. Rather than take chances, you may want to follow this procedure:

1. From the SQL Server Properties dialog box, go to the Server Settings tab.

2. Enable system table modifications by selecting Allow Modifications To Be Made Directly To The System Catalogs.

3. Click OK, and then stop SQL Server.

4. Start SQL Server in single-user mode at the command line by typing **sqlservr -m**.

Note If multiple instances are installed, you'll need to use the –s instancename option here to start the instance.

5. Make the necessary changes to the system tables.

6. From the SQL Server Properties dialog box, go to the Server Settings tab.

7. Disable system table modifications by clearing Allow Modifications To Be Made Directly To The System Catalogs.

8. At the window running SQL Server from the command line, press Ctrl+C. Then, when prompted, type **Y** for Yes. This stops SQL Server. Restart the SQL Server service.

With *sp_configure*, the related Transact-SQL statement is

```
exec sp_configure 'allow updates', <0 or 1>
```

Note If you use *sp_configure* to allow updates, you must use the *reconfigure with override* statement as well. Then stop and restart the server.

Allowing and Disallowing Nested Triggers

By default, SQL Server allows you to nest up to 32 levels of triggers. Nested triggers are useful for executing a series of tasks within a single transaction. For example, an action can initiate a trigger that starts another trigger, which in turn can start another trigger, and so on. Because the trigger is handled within a transaction, a failure at any level causes the entire transaction to roll back, which reverses all changes to the database. As a fail-safe measure, triggers are terminated when the maximum nesting level is exceeded. This protects against an infinite loop.

To allow or disallow nested triggers, complete the following steps:

1. From the SQL Server Properties dialog box, go to the Server Settings tab.

2. Set or clear Allow Triggers To Be Fired Which Fire Other Triggers (Nested Triggers).

3. Click OK.

With *sp_configure*, the related Transact-SQL statement is

```
exec sp_configure 'nested triggers', <0 or 1>
```

Controlling Query Execution

The Query Governor disallows execution of any query that has a running time that exceeds a specified query cost. The query cost is the estimated time, in seconds, required to execute a query, and it's estimated prior to execution based on the query engine's analysis of execution time. By default, the Query Governor is turned off, meaning there is no maximum cost. To set the Query Governor, complete the following steps:

1. From the SQL Server Properties dialog box, go to the Server Settings tab.
2. Select Use Query Governor To Prevent Queries Exceeding Specified Cost.
3. In the Query Governor field, type a maximum query cost limit. The valid range is from 0 to 2,147,483,647. A value of 0 disables the Query Governor. Any other value sets a maximum query cost limit.
4. Click OK.

With *sp_configure*, the related Transact-SQL statement is

```
exec sp_configure 'query governor cost limit', <limit>
```

You can also set a per connection query cost limit in Transact-SQL using

```
set query_governor_cost_limit <limit>
```

 Tip Before you set the Query Governor, you should use Query Analyzer to estimate the cost of current queries you're running on the server. This will give you a good idea of a value to use for the maximum query cost. You can also use Query Analyzer to optimize queries.

Setting the Default SQL Mail Profile

You can use e-mail facilities with SQL Server in two ways. You can

- Configure stored procedures that are triggered by e-mail through SQL Mail.
- Send notifications to designated operators through SQLAgentMail.

These SQL Server features can use separate mail profiles, or they can use the same mail profile. You must configure the profile(s) on the server and on associated valid e-mail account(s). Afterward, you need to complete the following steps:

1. Tell SQL Server about the SQL Mail profile by accessing the SQL Mail Configuration dialog box and then typing the profile name in the Profile Name field. Once you configure mail properly, you can access the SQL Server Properties dialog box and type a mail logon name for SQL Mail in the Mail Login Name field of the Server Settings dialog box.
2. Tell SQL Server Agent about the SQLAgentMail profile by accessing the SQL Server Agent Properties dialog box and then typing the profile name in the Mail Profile field in the General tab.

 Note You'll find detailed information on SQL Mail and SQL Server Agent in Chapter 3 and Chapter 12, respectively.

Configuring Year 2000 Support

SQL Server allows you to insert or modify dates without specifying the century part of the date. However, to be Year 2000 compliant, SQL Server interprets two-digit dates as being within a certain time span. By default, this time span is from 1950 to 2049. With this setting, all two-digit dates from 50 to 99 are treated as having 19 in front of them and all two-digit dates from 00 to 49 are treated as having 20 in front of them. Thus, SQL Server would interpret a two-digit year of 99 as 1999 and a two-digit year of 02 as 2002.

To maintain backward compatibility, Microsoft recommends that you leave the setting at the default value. You can, however, change this value by completing the following steps:

1. From the SQL Server Properties dialog box, go to the Server Settings tab.

2. In the When A Two-Digit Year Is Entered, Interpret It As A Year Between list box, select a value that is the ending year of the time span you want to work with. The valid range for the ending year is 1753 to 9999.

3. Click OK.

Note   The time span affects all databases on the current server. Also, some older OLE clients support only a date range of 1931 to 2030. To be compatible with these clients, you may want to type 2030 as the ending year for the time span.

With *sp_configure*, the related Transact-SQL statement is

```
exec sp_configure 'two digit year cutoff', <ending year>
```

Database Settings

You use the Database Settings tab of the SQL Server Properties dialog box to configure server-wide database settings. As shown in Figure 2-10, you can use the tab to set index fill, backup and restore options, and checkpoint execution.

Setting the Index Fill

The default index fill determines how much space SQL Server should reserve when it creates a new index using existing data. A tradeoff is involved when setting the fill factor. Setting the fill factor too high slows down SQL Server when you add data to a table. However, setting a fill factor too low can affect read performance by an amount inversely proportional to the fill factor. For example, a fill factor of 25 percent can degrade read performance by a factor of 4 (or 4 times normal) but makes large updates faster initially. Ideally, you'll balance the need to quickly make updates against the need for good read performance and select a fill factor that makes sense for your situation.

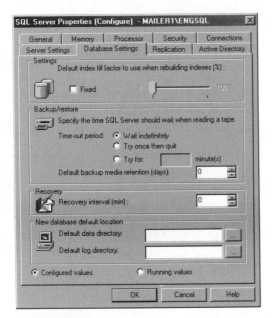

Figure 2-10. *You set general configuration options for the databases in the Database Settings tab.*

 Best Practice The fill factor is used only when an index is created and isn't maintained afterward. This allows you to add, delete, or update data in a table without worrying about maintaining a specific fill factor.

Because of this, the empty space in the data pages can fill up if you make extensive additions or modifications to the data. To redistribute the data, re-create the index and specify a fill factor when you do so. Indexes are discussed more in Chapter 6.

By default, the index fill is set to 0 but the valid range is from 0 to 100. The setting of 0 is an optimized setting for SQL Server. Any other value is an actual fill percentage.

SQL Server handles the optimized setting in much the same way as a fill percentage of 100. Here, SQL Server creates clustered indexes with full data pages and nonclustered indexes with full leaf pages. But unlike an index fill of 100, the optimized setting of 0 leaves room for growth in the upper level of the index tree. On the other hand, with an index fill of 100, there's no room for growth, which is why you should use this value only with read-only tables where you'll never add data.

If you need to, you can override the default when you create indexes. But you have to remember to do this. You can also set a fixed index fill as the default by completing the following steps:

1. From the SQL Server Properties dialog box, go to the Database Settings tab.
2. Select the Fixed check box.
3. Use the Fixed slider to set a fill percentage. A low fill factor allows more room for insertions without requiring page splits, but the index takes up more space. A high fill factor allows less room for insertions that don't require page splits, but the index uses less space.
4. Click OK.

With *sp_configure*, the related Transact-SQL statement is

```
exec sp_configure 'fill factor', <integer percentage>
```

Backup and Restore Time-Out

You often make SQL Server backups on tape devices. When you work with tape devices and the DB-Library, you may want to control whether or not you want to enforce a read/write time-out. The default is to have DB-Library "wait indefinitely" for a response from SQL Server, which is sometimes less than ideal. With an indefinite time-out, you won't necessarily get errors that let you know that you're having backup problems. To change this behavior, you may want to set a specific time-out, such as "try once and then quit" or "try for a certain number of minutes and then quit."

You set the time-out period by completing the following steps:

1. From the SQL Server Properties dialog box, go to the Database Settings tab.
2. To set an indefinite time-out, select the Wait Indefinitely option button.
3. To try once and then quit, select the Try Once Then Quit option button.
4. To try for a specified amount of time, select the Try For N Minute(s) option button and then enter the time-out period in the field provided.
5. Click OK.

Backup and Restore Retention

As you'll learn in Chapter 11, SQL Server has many features to help you back up and restore data. When you write data to tapes using DB-Library, you can specify the number of days to maintain old files. This value is called the *retention period*, and you set it by completing the following steps:

1. From the SQL Server Properties dialog box, go to the Database Settings tab.
2. Enter the number of days you'd like to maintain old files in the Default Backup Media Retention (Days) field. The minimum value is 0, which specifies that old files are always overwritten. The valid range is from 0 to 365.
3. Click OK.

With *sp_configure*, the related Transact-SQL statement is

```
exec sp_configure 'media retention', <number of days>
```

Flushing Cache with Checkpoints

Database checkpoints flush all cached data pages to the disk and are done on a per database basis. In SQL Server you control how often checkpoints occur using the recovery interval. By default, the recovery interval is set to 0, which allows SQL Server to dynamically control when checkpoints occur. This usually means that checkpoints occur about once a minute on active databases. Unless you're experiencing performance problems that are related to checkpoints, you shouldn't change this option.

You set the checkpoint interval manually by completing the following steps:

1. From the SQL Server Properties dialog box, go to the Database Settings tab.

2. Enter the checkpoint time in minutes in the Recovery Interval (Min) field. The valid range is from 0 to 32,767. This is a server-wide setting.

3. Click OK.

With *sp_configure*, the related Transact-SQL statement is

```
exec sp_configure 'recovery interval', <number of minutes>
```

Replication

You use the Replication tab of the SQL Server Properties dialog box to manage and configure publishing and distribution services for SQL Server. This section discusses the available options on the Replication tab and how to start the Configure Publishing And Distribution Wizard.

Distribution and Publishing

Initially the Replication tab will display COMPUTERNAME\SQLINSTANCE Is Not Configured As A Publisher Or Distributor in the Publishing and Distribution section. To configure Publishing and Distribution services, you must run the Configure Publishing And Distribution Wizard first by selecting the Configure button. This will start the wizard and allow you to perform the following actions:

- Specify the local SQL Server Instance or another server as a Distributor.
- Configure the properties of the local SQL Server Instance as a Distributor.
- Configure the properties of the local SQL Server Instance as a Publisher.

If you configure the local SQL Server Instance as a Publisher and Distributor, the Publishing and Distributor section will display View Or Change The Configuration Of COMPUTERNAME\SQLINSTANCE As A Publisher And Distributor. Selecting the Configure button using this configuration will access the Publisher and Distributor Properties page for the local SQL Server. The Publisher and Distributor Properties page will allow you to access and modify the properties for Distributors, Publishers, Publication Databases, and Subscribers.

If you configure the local SQL Server Instance as a Publisher, the Publishing and Distributor section will display View Or Change The Configuration Of COMPUTERNAME\SQLINSTANCE As A Publisher. Selecting the Configure button using this configuration will access the Publisher and Distributor Properties page, but you will only have access to the properties for Distributors, Publication Databases, and Subscribers.

Selecting the Disable button will start the Welcome To The Disable Publishing And Distribution Wizard, which will allow you to disable publishing, distribution, or both on the local SQL Server.

Replication Monitor Group

You will also see a new section on the Replication tab entitled Replication Monitor Group. Selecting the Add COMPUTERNAME\SQLINSTANCE As A Distributor In The Replication Monitor Group option will add the local SQL Server to the Replication Monitor group as a Distributor. This will allow you to monitor the replication activity of Distributors from the local computer.

Specific details covering Replication modes and setting up and configuring Publishing and Distribution servers for Subscribers will be covered in Chapter 9, "Configuring Snapshot, Merge, and Transactional Replication."

Adding and Removing Active Directory Information

You use the Active Directory tab of the SQL Server Properties dialog box to manage SQL Server information published in Active Directory services. The tab has three buttons:

- **Add**   Publishes information about a SQL Server instance in Active Directory.
- **Refresh**   Updates information related to a SQL Server instance in Active Directory. Useful when you create databases, server cubes, or data mining models and want the updates reflected throughout the directory before normal replication.
- **Remove**   Removes information about a SQL Server instance from Active Directory.

Configuring SQL Server with Stored Procedures

You can configure many areas of SQL Server through the SQL Server Properties dialog box. As you've learned in this chapter, you can also configure SQL Server with stored procedures, such as *sp_configure*. You execute stored procedures and other queries in Query Analyzer. Query Analyzer is a client tool that sends commands to the SQL Server query engine, which in turn parses, compiles, and executes the commands.

The following sections explain how you can configure SQL Server using Query Analyzer and stored procedures. You'll find more detailed coverage of Query Analyzer in other chapters.

Starting Query Analyzer

You can start Query Analyzer using any of these techniques:

- Select Start, choose Programs, choose Microsoft SQL Server, and then choose Query Analyzer.
- Run ISQLW.EXE at the command line.
- From the Enterprise Manager, select the Tools menu, and then select the SQL Server Query Analyzer option.

When you start Query Analyzer from the menu or the command line, you have to specify connection information using the dialog box shown in Figure 2-11. You use the fields of this dialog box as follows:

- **SQL Server** Use this option to select the database server instance to which you want to connect. If the server instance isn't available in the drop-down list box, you can type in a server name or click the ellipsis button to display the SQL Active Directory Search dialog box, which you can use to search for all SQL servers within an entire Active Directory Forest.
- **Start SQL Server If It Is Stopped** Starts the MSSQLServer service and the database if it's stopped.
- **Windows Authentication** Uses your current domain account and password to establish the database connection. This works only if Windows authentication is enabled and you have appropriate privileges.
- **SQL Server Authentication** Allows you to specify a SQL Server logon ID and password.

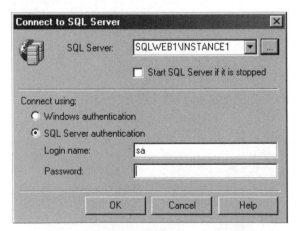

Figure 2-11. *Use the Connect To SQL Server dialog box to select the server you want to use and then specify connection information. If you start Query Analyzer in Enterprise Manager you can often bypass this dialog box.*

If you're working with an active database in Enterprise Manager and have already authenticated the connection, Query Analyzer automatically connects to the currently selected database server instance and uses this authentication information to log on. If there is no active database connection or if the logon fails, you'll see the dialog box shown in Figure 2-11.

Tip Query Analyzer normally connects you to the master database on the active server. You can use the DB drop-down list box on the Query Analyzer toolbar to change to any of the available databases on the server.

Changing Settings with *sp_configure*

The Query Analyzer window is normally divided into three panes (see Figure 2-12). The left pane allows you to browse objects that are available on the currently selected database server instance. The top right pane is for entering queries. The bottom right pane is for displaying results.

If you don't see the bottom right pane, don't worry. It's automatically displayed when you type a query. You can also set the pane to display by default. Select the Show Results Pane option on the Window menu.

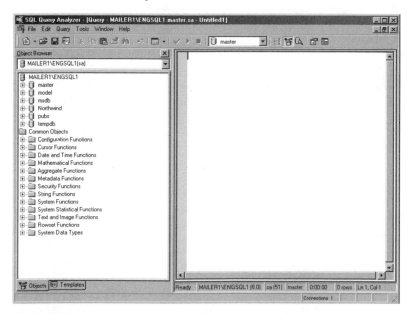

Figure 2-12. *Query Analyzer's newest feature is the object browser pane. You can use this pane to browse databases, tables, functions, and more.*

As you know, you can use *sp_configure* to view and change SQL Server configuration settings. Two types of configuration settings are available: those that are dynamic and those that aren't. In this instance, a dynamic setting is one that you can change without having to stop and restart SQL Server. To execute *sp_configure* or other types of queries, type a command in the top pane and then click the toolbar's Execute Query button (it's the green arrow). You can also execute commands using these key sequences:

- F5
- Ctrl+E
- Alt+X

Whenever you use *sp_configure* to modify settings, the changes don't actually take place until you also execute the RECONFIGURE command. You can change some highly risky settings only with the RECONFIGURE WITH OVERRIDE command. Additionally, *sp_configure* settings are divided into two categories: standard and advanced. You can execute standard commands at any time, but you can execute advanced commands only when Show Advanced Options is set to 1. With this setting in effect, you can modify both standard and advanced settings by following this procedure:

1. In Query Analyzer, type

```
exec sp_configure 'show advanced options', 1
go
reconfigure
go
```

 Note You could later disable advanced options by setting this value to 0.

2. Execute the commands by pressing Ctrl+E.
3. Clear the query windows by clicking the toolbar's Clear Query Window button.
4. Now type one *sp_configure* command for each option you want to change.
5. Type **reconfigure** (or **reconfigure with override**).
6. Execute the commands by pressing Ctrl+E.
7. If you changed any nondynamic settings, stop and start the server. (See Table 2-3 and Table 2-4 for details.)

Configuration Parameters

Table 2-3 provides a summary of the standard configuration parameters. You'll find parameters listed in alphabetical order with the minimum, maximum, and default values shown. The dynamic parameter column tells you whether the setting is dynamic. If you see a "No" in this column, you'll need to stop and restart the server to enforce changes.

Table 2-3. Quick Reference Summary for Standard Configuration Parameters

Parameter Name	Description	Minimum Value	Maximum Value	Default Value	Dynamic Yes/No
allow updates	Allow updates to systems tables.	0	1	0	Yes
default language	Sets language formatting for dates. With localized versions, can change to local language or U.S. English.	0	9999	Varies, 0 is U.S. English	Yes
max text repl size	Sets maximum number of bytes to be written to a replicated column.	0	2147483647	65536	Yes
nested triggers	Determines whether nested triggers are allowed.	0	1	1	Yes
remote access	Controls access from remote servers. 0 denies access.	0	1	1	No
remote login timeout	Sets remote logon time-out in seconds. 0 sets no time-out.	0	2147483647	5	Yes
remote proc trans	Use DTC for distributed transactions.	0	1	0	Yes
remote query timeout	Sets time-out in seconds for queries from remote servers. 0 sets no time-out.	0	2147483647	0	Yes
show advanced options	Set to 1 to turn on advanced options.	0	1	1	Yes
user options	Sets global defaults for user connections using a bit mask.	0	16383	0	Yes

Table 2-4 provides a summary of the advanced configuration parameters. To view or change these parameters, you have to set the parameter Show Advanced Options to 1. Note also that you can't change some advanced options (you can only view them).

Table 2-4. Quick Reference Summary for Advanced Configuration Parameters

Parameter Name	Description	Minimum Value	Maximum Value	Default Value	Dynamic Yes/No
affinity mask	Associates threads with processors.	0	2147483647	0	No
AWE enabled	Enables support for very large address spaces.	0	1	0	Yes
cost threshold for parallelism	Helps determine when queries are processed in parallel.	0	32767	5	Yes
cursor threshold	-1 to generate synchronous key sets for cursors. 0 sets asynchronous. Other values perform row comparison.	-1	2147483647	-1	Yes
default full-text language	Sets the default language for full-text searches in the database.	0	2147483647	0	Yes
default language	Sets the default language in the database	0	9999	0	Yes
fill factor	Sets index fill factor percentage. 0 lets SQL Server configure.	0	100	0	No
index create memory	Sets KB of memory used when creating index to sort data.	704	2147483647	0	Yes
lightweight pooling	1 switches to fibers.	0	1	0	Yes
locks	Sets the number of available locks.	5000	2147483647	0	No
max degree of parallelism	With SMP, sets number of threads to execute a parallel plan.	0	32	0	Yes
max server memory	Sets maximum memory (MB) used by SQL Server.	4	2147483647	Varies	Yes
max worker threads	Sets the maximum number of threads.	10	32767	255	Yes

(continued)

Table 2-4. *(continued)*

Parameter Name	Description	Minimum Value	Maximum Value	Default Value	Dynamic Yes/No
media retention	Sets number of days to retain backup media.	0	365	0	No
min memory per query	Sets minimum memory in KB to reserve for queries.	512	2147483647	1024	Yes
min server memory	Sets minimum memory (MB) used by SQL Server.	0	2147483647	0	Yes
network packet size	Sets the byte size of network packets.	512	65535	4096	Yes
open objects	Sets maximum number of open objects. 0 for SQL control.	0	2147483647	0	No
priority boost	Set to 1 to boost thread priority.	0	1	0	No
query governor cost limit	Sets cost limit for queries. 0 turns off limit.	0	2147483647	0	No
query wait	Sets time-out value for queries.	-1	2147483647	-1	Yes
recovery interval	Sets time interval in minutes for checkpoints. 0 for SQL control.	0	32767	0	Yes
scan for startup procs	Set to 1 to scan for stored procedure to execute on startup.	0	1	0	No
set working set size	1 sets no swapping for memory.	0	1	0	No
two digit year cutoff	Sets date range for two-digit dates.	1753	9999	2049	Yes
user connections	Controls maximum number of user connections for the database server instance. Set to 0 for unlimited.	0	32767	0	No

Troubleshooting Configuration Problems

The sections that follow examine two specific techniques that you can use to resolve SQL Server configuration problems. You'll learn how to recover from a bad configuration and how to rebuild the master database.

Recovering from a Bad Configuration

Although SQL Server 2000 has many safeguards that help you avoid configuration settings that keep SQL Server from starting, you may occasionally find that a configuration change prevents SQL Server from starting. In this case you can recover the server instance by completing the following steps:

1. Log on to the affected server locally or remotely through Telnet or Terminal Server. You must log on as using a local administrator account or the account used by the database server instance.

2. Make sure that the MSSQLServer or MSSQL$*instancename* service is stopped. If it isn't, stop the service using one of the following methods:

   - SQL Server Service Manager
   - Windows NT Service Manager
   - Windows 2000 Services

3. If the instance of SQL Server was installed as a default installation, you can stop the service by using the following command:

   `net stop MSSQLSERVER`

4. From the command prompt, switch to the directory of the associated SQL Server instance (either mssql\binn or mssql$*instancename*\Binn). You must be in this directory to use the sqlservr utility.

5. Start SQL Server from the command line with the following option:

   `sqlservr -s(instancename) -f`

6. You must use the -s option to specify the instance of SQL Server if multiple instances of SQL Server are installed. The -f option starts SQL Server in single-user mode with a minimum configuration. This ensures that the bad configuration isn't loaded.

7. Wait for the server to start up. SQL Server should write a few pages of output to the screen. Leave the server running.

8. In another command prompt window or Telnet session, start ISQL with the username of a SQL account with administrator privileges and password:

   `isql -U username -P password`

 Note You must specify the instance you are connecting to (isql –U username –P password –S*computername**instancename*) if multiple instances of SQL Server 2000 are installed.

9. If you've accessed ISQL properly, you should see the prompt change to >.

10. Reverse the changes made to the configuration by entering commands much like you would in Query Analyzer. The key difference is that you execute the commands with *go*, as in the following example:

```
exec sp_configure 'max server memory', 128
go
reconfigure
go
```

11. When you're finished, exit ISQL by typing **exit**.

12. At the window running SQL Server from the command line, press Ctrl+C. Then, when prompted, type **Y** for Yes. This stops SQL Server.

13. Restart SQL Server as you normally would. If you've made the appropriate changes, the server should start normally. Otherwise, repeat this procedure.

Changing Collation and Rebuilding the Master Database

The key reasons for rebuilding the master database are

- When you need to set a new default collation for a database server instance.

- When you need to repair a corrupted master database.

After you rebuild the master database, all user databases are detached and unreadable. To recover them, you must re-create all your user databases. You can't restore the user databases from backup—the restore maintains the information that was set when you created the backup and you may instead want to move the databases to another server by means of Data Transformation Services (DTS), which are covered in Chapter 7.

Note   Before you rebuild the master database, you should know that collation plays a different role on SQL Server 2000 than it did on SQL Server 7. Previous versions of SQL Server used the same collation for all databases and database objects within each instance. SQL Server 2000 can specify different collations for separate databases and columns within a database. When you install SQL Server, the default collation is set. You can't change the default setting on an existing SQL Server installation without rebuilding the master database. You can, however, set separate collation options for each database that you install on the server. You can also set separate collation options for tables, parameters, and literal strings.

You can rebuild the master database by completing the following steps:

1. Stop the SQL Server service for the database server instance that you want to work with. For the default instance, the service is named MSSQLServer. For named instances, the service is named MSSQL$*instancename*.

Tip To learn how to stop the SQL Server service, see the section of Chapter 3 entitled "Starting, Stopping, and Pausing SQL Server."

2. Run Rebuild Master from the command line using the following command:

   `rebuildm`

3. You should see the Rebuild Master dialog box. Use the Server selection list to choose the database server instance that you want to work with.

4. Source Directory Containing Data Files shows the original install location for the database server instance. Normally, the source directory refers to a location on the SQL Server CD-ROM. As necessary, type a new directory path or click Browse to find a directory path.

5. Click Settings, and then use the options of the Collation Settings dialog box to configure the new server settings. Click OK when you're finished.

6. In Rebuild Master, click Rebuild. When prompted to confirm the action, click Yes. Rebuild Master copies the master database source files to the server and then begins remapping and reconfiguring the server.

Part II

Microsoft SQL Server 2000 Administration

In this part you'll learn about the essential tasks for administering Microsoft SQL Server 2000. Chapter 3 explains management techniques for server groups and servers. You'll also learn how to control services and server processes. Chapter 4 covers the core administration tasks for creating and managing databases, with a logical follow-up on SQL Server security in Chapter 5. To manage server security, you'll create user logons, configure logon permissions, and assign roles.

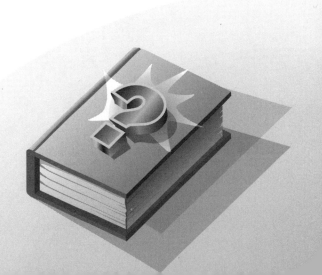

Chapter 3

Managing the Enterprise

Enterprise Manager is the primary tool you'll use to manage database servers. Other tools you may want to use to manage local and remote servers are SQL Server Service Manager, Performance Monitor, and Event Viewer. You'll use Service Manager to manage SQL-related services, such as MSSQLServer and SQLServerAgent. You'll use Performance Monitor to track SQL Server activity and performance. You'll use Event Viewer to examine events generated by SQL Server, which can provide helpful details on problems. This chapter covers Enterprise Manager and Service Manager. For details on Performance Monitor and Event Viewer, see Chapter 10.

Note SQL Server 2000 restricts permissions for the Mssql directory (either Mssql or mssql$*instancename*). Only the local Administrators group and the user account specified to start the SQL Server service instance have access to the Mssql folder and its subdirectories.

Starting, Stopping, and Pausing SQL Server

SQL Server has two modes of operation. It can run as a command-line application (SQLSERVR.EXE) or as a service. You'll use the command-line application when you need to troubleshoot problems or modify configuration settings in single-user mode. Other than that, the normal technique is to run SQL Server as a service.

Managing SQL Server Service with Service Manager

SQL Server Service Manager is the primary tool you'll use to manage SQL Server services. Most database administrators prefer SQL Server Service Manager to the alternatives because you can manage both local and remote servers. You can also configure these services to start automatically. Start SQL Server Service Manager by double-clicking the SQL Server shortcut on the taskbar or by clicking Start, then Programs, then Microsoft SQL Server, and finally Service Manager. This opens the dialog box shown in Figure 3-1.

Figure 3-1. *SQL Server Service Manager makes it easy to manage services on local and remote systems.*

You can manage the SQL Server service with Service Manager by completing the following steps:

1. Use the Server drop-down list box to select an available server. Or type the server name. For database server instances, type the server name and the instance name separated by a backslash, such as Server1\Engineering1.

2. On the Services drop-down list box, select SQL Server. Service Manager automatically selects the correct instance of the SQL Server service, which is MSSQLServer or MSSQL$*instancename*.

3. The status of the currently selected service is shown on the status bar. In Figure 3-1, for example, SQL Server is running on the selected server instance.

4. Use the available options to work with the service as follows:

    • Select Refresh Services to update the service state information.

    • Select Start/Continue to start the service.

    • Select Pause to temporarily stop the service.

    • Select Stop to stop the service.

    • Select Auto-Start Service When OS Starts in order to have SQL Server automatically start when the system boots.

 Note On Microsoft Windows 95 and Windows 98, Service Manager can only be used to manage local resources. The reason for this is that these "services" are actually running as executables on Windows 95 and Windows 98.

Managing SQL Server Service from the Command Line

You can start, stop, and pause SQL Server as you would any other service. On a local system, you type the necessary command at a standard command prompt. On a remote system, you could connect to the system using Telnet and then issue the necessary command. With Windows 2000 Server, you could also establish a remote Terminal Server session to the server and access the command console remotely. To manage the Default database server instance, the commands you use are

- **NET START MSSQLSERVER** Starts SQL Server as a service
- **NET STOP MSSQLSERVER** Stops SQL Server when running as a service
- **NET PAUSE MSSQLSERVER** Pauses SQL Server when running as a service
- **NET CONTINUE MSSQLSERVER** Resumes SQL Server when running as a service

To manage named instances of SQL Server, you use the following commands:

- **NET START MSSQL$*instancename*** Starts SQL Server as a service where *instancename* is the actual name of the database server instance
- **NET STOP MSSQL$*instancename*** Stops SQL Server when running as a service where *instancename* is the actual name of the database server instance
- **NET PAUSE MSSQL$*instancename*** Pauses SQL Server when running as a service where *instancename* is the actual name of the database server instance
- **NET CONTINUE MSSQL$*instancename*** Resumes SQL Server when running as a service where *instancename* is the actual name of the database server instance

Note If you choose not to install the default instance of SQL Server during the initial setup and instead create a new named instance as the initial SQL Server instance, you will not be able to use the NET command to manage services from the command line.

Managing the SQL Server Command-Line Executable

The SQL Server command-line executable (SQLSERVR.EXE) provides an alternative to the SQL Server service. You must run SQLSERVR.EXE from the Binn directory that corresponds to the instance of the SQL Server database engine that you want to start. For the default instance, the utility is located in \mssql\Binn. For named instances, the utility is located in \mssql$*instancename*\Binn.

When SQL Server is installed on a local system, you start SQL Server by changing to the directory for the instance of SQL Server you want to start and then typing

sqlservr at the command line. On a remote system, you connect to the system by using Telnet, changing to the appropriate directory, and then issuing the startup command. In Windows 2000 Server Editions, you can also establish a remote Terminal Server session and access the command line remotely. Either way, SQL Server reads the default startup parameters from the registry and starts execution.

You can also enter startup parameters and switches that override the default settings. The available parameters were summarized in Table 2-1 in Chapter 2. You can still connect Enterprise Manager to the server (though when you do, it may incorrectly report that it's starting the SQL Server service).

To stop an instance of SQL Server started from the command line, complete the following steps:

1. Press Ctrl+C to break into the execution stream.

2. When prompted, press N to stop SQL Server.

Using SQL Server Enterprise Manager

With its graphical point-and-click interface, Enterprise Manager makes server, database, and resource management a snap. Using Enterprise Manager, you can manage both local and remote server instances by establishing a connection to SQL Server and then administering its resources. If you've disabled remote server connections to a particular server, however, you can only work with the server locally (by logging in to the system at the keyboard or by establishing a remote Terminal Server session in Windows 2000 and then running the local management tools) or through a Telnet session.

Getting Started with Enterprise Manager

To run Enterprise Manager, choose Start, then Programs, then Microsoft SQL Server, and finally Enterprise Manager. As shown in Figure 3-2, Enterprise Manager presents information in a directory tree structure. The left pane is called the Console Root, and it can be used to work your way down through successive levels of server hierarchy, including

- **Microsoft SQL Servers**   The top level of the SQL Server hierarchy
- **SQL Server Groups**   Groupings of related SQL Server instances as defined by you
- **SQL Servers**   Entries for individual SQL Server instances and their related resource folders

The right pane shows resources you can work with, such as databases or logons. If you have the Taskpad enabled, the right pane also shows tasks you can perform. (To enable or disable the Taskpad, select a SQL Server in the Console Root and then from the View menu, choose the Taskpad option.)

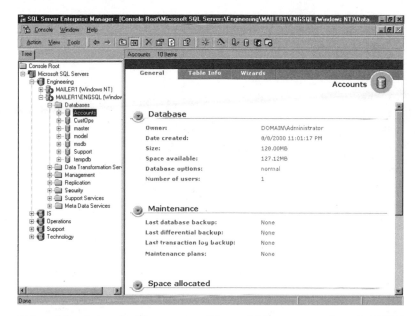

Figure 3-2. *Enterprise Manager is a Microsoft Management Console (MMC) snap-in. In many cases, you can add Enterprise Manager to an MMC you already use by choosing Add/Remove Snap-In from the Console menu and then following the prompts.*

Managing SQL Server Groups

You use SQL Server groups to organize sets of SQL servers. You define these server groups, and you can organize them by function, department, or any other criteria. Creating a server group is easy. You can even create subgroups within a group if you want to. If you make a mistake, you can delete groups as well.

Creating a Server Group

You can create a server group or a subgroup by completing the following steps:

1. In Enterprise Manager's Console Root (the left pane), right-click Microsoft SQL Servers or any group-level entry.

2. From the shortcut menu, choose New SQL Server Group. This displays the dialog box shown in Figure 3-3.

3. In the Server Groups dialog box, type a name for the new group in the Name field.

4. Top-level groups follow the Microsoft SQL Servers entry in the console hierarchy. Create a top-level group by selecting the Top Level Group option button.

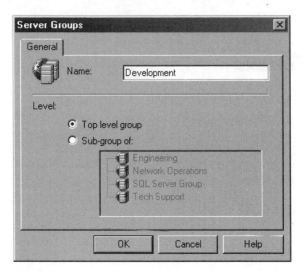

Figure 3-3. *Use the Server Groups dialog box to create new server groups or subgroups.*

5. Subgroups are organized under their primary group, such as Engineering SQL Servers. Create a subgroup by clicking the Sub-Group Of option button and then choosing the primary group from the list provided.

6. Click OK.

Deleting a Server Group

You can delete a group or subgroup by completing the following steps:

1. In Enterprise Manager's Console Root, click the plus sign (+) next to the group or subgroup you want to delete. If the group has servers registered in it, move them to a different group, as described in the section of this chapter entitled "Moving a Server to a New Group."

2. Select the group or subgroup entry.

3. Press Delete.

Adding SQL Servers to a Group

When you register a SQL Server for use with Enterprise Manager, you can choose which group you want the server to be in. You can even create a new group specifically for this server. The next section covers server registration.

Managing Servers

Servers and databases are the primary resources you manage in Enterprise Manager. Click a server group in the Console Root and the right pane shows you which servers are available for this group. If the server you want to work with isn't shown, you'll need to register it. After that, you can connect to the server to work with it and disconnect when you're finished. You can start the registration process using any of the following techniques:

- From the Action menu, choose New SQL Server Registration while Microsoft SQL Servers or any group-level entry is selected in the Console Root.
- Right-click any server or group-level entry in Enterprise Manager's Console Root and then choose New SQL Server Registration.
- Choose the Wizards option from the Tools menu and then double-click the Registry Server Wizard entry.

If you've opted not to use the Registry Server Wizard, you'll go straight to the manual registration process. Otherwise you'll use a wizard to register the server.

Registering a Server with a Wizard

The Register SQL Server Wizard makes server registration a point-and-click process. You can register multiple servers at the same time, create new groups for these servers, and more. Just complete the following steps:

1. After you start the registration process, you'll see the Register SQL Server Wizard dialog box shown in Figure 3-4. As shown, the first dialog box window provides an introduction, so click Next to continue.

2. Use the Available Servers list to select the SQL servers you want to register and then click Add to add the server to the Added Servers list. These servers should all have the same authentication account or logon account, or both. Click Next to continue.

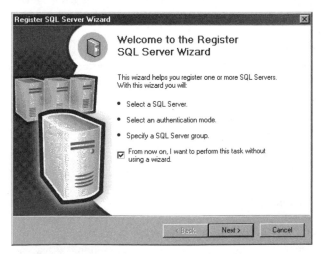

Figure 3-4. *The Register SQL Server Wizard makes it easy to register multiple servers. But if you don't like using wizards, select From Now On, I Want To Perform This Task Without Using A Wizard.*

Tip Sometimes it takes a while for servers to broadcast their names over the network. If the server you want to use isn't listed, just type the name directly in the Available Servers field and then click Add. For Default database server instances, type the server name. For named instances, type the server name and the instance name separated by a backslash, such as Server1\SQLEngineering.

3. Select the authentication mode you want to use, either Windows authentication or SQL Server authentication. With Windows authentication, you use the current domain logon for authentication. With SQL Server authentication, you use a separate SQL Server logon ID and password. Click Next to continue.

4. If you're using SQL Server authentication, the next screen asks you to specify how to log on to SQL Server. For automatic login, choose Login Automatically Using My SQL Server Account Information and then type a SQL Server logon ID and password. For manual login with each connection, choose Prompt. For The SQL Server Account Information When Connecting. Click Next to continue.

5. Select an existing server group or create a new server group for the server or servers you're registering. Click Next to continue.

6. The wizard lists the server or servers you're registering. Click Finish to complete the process and begin registration.

7. The Register SQL Server Message dialog box appears and tells you the status of each server. If a server failed to register, click Properties and edit the registration properties for the server. To stop the registration of a server that isn't responsive, click Stop. To complete the process, click Close.

Registering a Server Manually

If you don't want to use the wizard, you can manually register each server that you want to work with individually. To do this, complete the following steps:

1. In Enterprise Manager's Console Root, right-click any server or group-level entry and then choose New SQL Server Registration. If the Wizard dialog box comes up, click From Now On, I Want To Perform This Task Without Using A Wizard. Click Next. This displays the Registered SQL Server Properties dialog box shown in Figure 3-5.

2. In the Server field, type the name of the server instance you want to register. If you're unsure of the server name, use the build button (...) to display the Select Server dialog box. This dialog box shows SQL Server instances that are active on the network.

3. Select the authentication mode you want to use, either Windows authentication or SQL Server authentication. With Windows authentication, you use

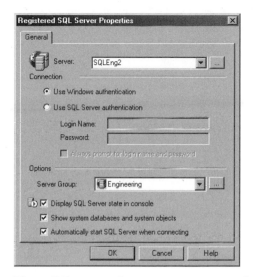

Figure 3-5. *Manual registration puts everything you need in one convenient location, but you can't simultaneously register multiple servers.*

the current domain logon for authentication. With SQL Server authentication, you use a separate SQL Server logon ID and password.

4. If you're using SQL Server authentication, type a SQL Server logon ID and password. Or select Always Prompt For Login Name And Password.

5. Using the Server Group drop-down list box, select an existing server group for the server or click the build button (...) to create a new group.

6. To display the server state in the console, select Display SQL Server State In Console. Otherwise, clear this check box and you won't see the start, stop, or pause symbols in the server icon.

Tip The server state is continually refreshed using remote procedure calls (RPCs). To cut down on network traffic, you may want to disable this feature. In addition, the server state may not be displayed when you're running Enterprise Manager on Windows 95 and Windows 98. Windows 95 and Windows 98 don't have the necessary Windows NT networking facilities.

7. To display system databases and system objects, select Show System Databases And System Objects. If you clear this option, system databases and objects are hidden, and you can display them only by editing the registration properties. The system databases are master, msdb, model, and tempdb.

Tip In Enterprise Manager you can edit the registration properties by right-clicking the server name and selecting Edit SQL Server Registration Properties.

8. To automatically start the SQL Server service when connecting, select Automatically Start SQL Server When Connecting.

 Tip Clearing this option may prevent the accidental starting of SQL Server by other administrators when you're working on the server system. This is recommended. After all, you don't want someone to accidentally start the server when you're shutting it down or performing some other type of maintenance.

9. Click OK to start the registration process. If Enterprise Manager is unable to connect to the server, you'll see an error dialog box. Choose Yes to register the server regardless of the error. Choose No to modify the registration properties and try again.

Editing Registration Properties

You can change the registration properties at any time by right-clicking the SQL Server entry in Enterprise Manager's Console Root and then selecting Edit SQL Server Registration Properties. Afterward, use the Registered SQL Server Properties dialog box as described in the "Registering a Server Manually" section of this chapter. The only property you can't change is the server name.

Moving a Server to a New Group

To move the server to a new group, complete the following steps:

1. Right-click the SQL Server entry in Enterprise Manager's Console Root and then from the shortcut menu, choose Edit SQL Server Registration Properties.
2. In the Registered SQL Server Properties dialog box, use the Server Group drop-down list box to select a new group.
3. Click OK.

Deleting a Server Registration

If you change a server name or remove a server, you may want to delete the server registration in Enterprise Manager so that Enterprise Manager no longer tries to connect to a server that can't be accessed. Right-click the server entry in the Console Root and then select Delete SQL Server Registration. When prompted to confirm the action, click Yes.

Connecting to a Server

Once you've registered a server, connecting to it is easy. Right-click the server entry in Enterprise Manager's Console Root and then from the shortcut menu, choose Connect. Or double-click the server entry to establish a connection and display the server's properties dialog box.

Note Enterprise Manager connects to other SQL servers through RPC. If you've disabled remote access to a server, however, you won't be able to connect to that server in Enterprise Manager.

Disconnecting from a Server

When you're finished working with a server, you may want to disconnect from it. This cuts down on the back-and-forth RPCs to the server. To disconnect, right-click the server's entry in Enterprise Manager and then from the shortcut menu, choose Disconnect.

Starting, Stopping, and Configuring SQL Server Agent

SQL Server Agent runs as a service and is used to schedule jobs, alerts, and other automated tasks. Once you schedule automated tasks, you'll usually want SQL Server Agent to start automatically when the system starts. This ensures that these tasks are performed as expected. Using SQL Server Service Manager, you can control the related service (SQLServerAgent or SQLAgent$*instancename*) just as you do the SQL Server service. For details, see the section of this chapter entitled "Managing SQL Server Service with Service Manager."

To configure SQL Server Agent, you'll use Enterprise Manager. Although Chapter 12 covers the agent configuration in detail, the basic steps are as follows:

1. Start Enterprise Manager and then in the left pane (Console Root) click the plus sign (+) next to the server on which you want to manage SQL Server Agent.

2. Click the Management folder.

3. Right-click the SQL Server Agent icon and then from the shortcut menu, choose Properties. You can now configure SQL Server Agent.

4. The SQL Server Agent shortcut menu also lets you start and stop the SQL Server Agent service. Click Start to start the service or click Stop to stop the service.

Starting, Stopping, and Configuring the Microsoft Distributed Transaction Coordinator

Microsoft Distributed Transaction Coordinator (MS DTC) is a transaction manager that allows client applications to work with multiple sources of data in one transaction.

When a distributed transaction spans two or more servers, the servers coordinate the management of the transaction using MS DTC. When a distributed transaction spans multiple databases on a single server, SQL Server manages the transaction internally.

SQL Server applications can call MS DTC directly to start an explicit distributed transaction. Distributed transactions can also be started implicitly by

- Calling stored procedures on remote servers running SQL Server
- Updating data on multiple OLE DB data sources
- Enlisting remote servers in a transaction

If you work with transactions under any of the previously listed scenarios, you'll want DTC to be running on the server and you'll probably also want DTC to start automatically when the server starts. As with SQL Server itself, DTC runs as a service. This service is named Distributed Transaction Coordinator. Unlike the SQL Server service, only one instance of the MS DTC service runs on a computer regardless of how many database server instances are available. This means all instances of SQL Server running on a computer use the same transaction coordinator.

As you learned in the section of this chapter entitled "Managing SQL Server Service with Service Manager," you can control the DTC service with Service Manager. You can also start and stop DTC in Enterprise Manager by completing the following steps:

1. Start Enterprise Manager and then in the left pane (Console Root) click the plus sign (+) next to the server on which you want to manage DTC.
2. Click the Support Services folder.
3. Right-click Distributed Transaction Coordinator and then click Start to start the service or click Stop to stop the service.

Installing and Configuring Full-Text Search

Full-text search allows extensive word searches of textual data and is an additional component you can add to the SQL Server installation. (For details, see the section of Chapter 2 entitled "Adding Components.") Once you install the full-text search component, you can manage full-text searches as described in the following sections.

Using Full-Text Searches

As far as administration goes, full-text searches depend on three factors:

- That you install the necessary components
- That you start the related service, which is called the Microsoft Search service
- That you create a full-text catalog for the database

When you create a full-text catalog, the search service creates full-text indexes of textual data contained in the database. Afterward, the service manages the indexes and provides the primary mechanism for examining the data they contain. As with MS DTC, only one instance of the search service runs on a computer regardless of how many database server instances are available. This means that all instances of SQL Server running on a computer use the same Microsoft Search service.

Note   In Enterprise Manager's Support Services folder, the Microsoft Search service is referred to as Full-Text Search. Don't let the terminology confuse you. These services are one and the same, and the correct name is Microsoft Search service.

The concept of a full-text index may be a bit different than you're used to. In SQL Server, a full-text index stores information about keywords and their location within a specific column. These text indexes are created for each table in the database, and groups of indexes are contained in catalogs, which are stored separately from the databases to which they belong.

Furthermore, full-text indexes are defined on base tables and not on views, system tables, or temporary tables. Indexes are populated with key values that have information about the significant words in a table, such as the column they're in and their location in the column. In Transact-SQL you can test rows against a full-text search condition using *contains* and *freetext*. You can also return the set of rows that match a full-text search condition using the functions *containstable* and *freetexttable*.

Starting, Stopping, and Configuring the Microsoft Search Service

Microsoft Search is a service that performs the necessary management and search tasks for full-text indexes and their related catalogs. Again, these indexes and catalogs are created automatically when you start and stop the search service. Using SQL Server Service Manager, you can control the search service just as you do the SQL Server service. For details, see the section of this chapter entitled "Managing SQL Server Service with Service Manager." If SQL Server uses full-text searches, you'll want to make sure that Microsoft Search starts automatically when the system boots.

Locating Files Used for Full-Text Searches

Catalogs are stored separately from the databases themselves, and although you don't have control over the where's and how's, you still should know where the related information is stored. To examine current catalog information, complete the following steps:

1. Start Enterprise Manager and then in the left pane (Console Root) click the plus sign (+) next to the server using full-text search.
2. Click the Support Services folder.
3. Right-click the Full-Text Search icon and then from the shortcut menu, choose Properties. This opens the Full-Text Search Service Properties dialog box shown in Figure 3-6.

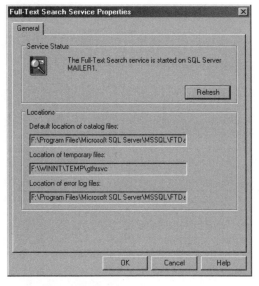

Figure 3-6. *The Full-Text Search Service Properties dialog box shows where important catalog files and logs are located.*

4. The General tab provides the following information:
   - The default location of catalog files
   - The location of temporary files used with full-text searching
   - The location of error logs

Managing Catalogs

Each database that you want to search must have its own full-text catalog. When you create a catalog, you set a schedule for populating the catalog on a regular basis or you elect to manually populate the catalog as necessary. Populating the catalog updates the full-text indexes for the catalog and ensures that the search results are accurate. SQL Server supports two methods for populating catalogs:

- **Full population** The search service builds index entries for all rows in all the tables covered by the full-text catalog. In most cases you perform a full population only when you create a catalog or need to refresh the entire contents of a catalog.

- **Incremental population** The search service only changes index entries for rows that have been added, deleted, or modified after the last population. Note that you can perform incremental population only on tables that have a timestamp column. If the table doesn't have a timestamp column, full populations are always performed.

Creating a catalog is only one part of the indexing process. After you create the catalog, you must select individual tables for indexing and associate these with the catalog. You also need to specify the individual table columns that should be indexed. Periodically, you may also need to clean up old catalogs.

Creating Catalogs

You need catalogs to perform full-text searches of databases. A single database can have multiple catalogs associated with it, and you can use these catalogs to perform different types of searches. For example, in a customer database, you could create one catalog for searching company contact information and another for searching account history.

You create a catalog for a database by completing the following steps:

1. Start Enterprise Manager and then in the left pane (Console Root) click the plus sign (+) next to the server you want to examine.

2. Right-click the database you want to catalog, point to New, and then select New Full-Text Catalog. This displays the New Full-Text Catalog Properties dialog box.

3. Type a descriptive name for the catalog in the Name field.

4. The Location field shows the default location of the catalog. You can change this location by typing a new folder path or clicking the location button (. . .) to chose a folder path.

5. If you want to automatically update the indexes in the catalog, click New Catalog Schedule on the Schedules tab and then follow the remaining steps. Otherwise, click OK and skip the remaining steps.

6. As shown in Figure 3-7, type a name for the job used to schedule the indexing.

Tip In most cases, you'll want to create two jobs. Create a one-time job to perform a full population of the catalog and then create a recurring job to perform an incremental population. SQL Server Agent runs scheduled tasks. The agent identifies scheduled tasks by the unique job name you specify. You'll learn more about SQL Server Agent in Chapter 12.

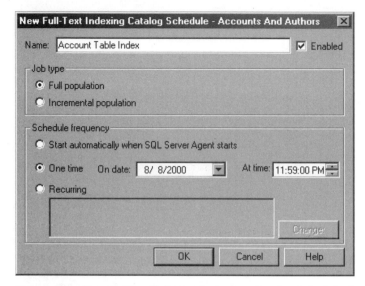

Figure 3-7. *Use the New Full-Text Indexing Catalog Schedule dialog box to create one-time or recurring jobs that populate the catalog.*

7. On the Job Type panel, select Full Population or Incremental Population as appropriate for the type of job you want to create.

8. Use the options of the Schedule Frequency panel to determine when the job runs. One-time jobs run at a specific date and time. Recurring jobs run daily, weekly, or monthly at a specific date and time.

9. Click OK twice.

Enabling Indexing of Tables and Columns

You can enable indexing of a table by completing the following steps:

1. Start Enterprise Manager and then in the left pane (Console Root) click the plus sign (+) next to the server you want to examine.

2. Click the plus sign (+) next to the database you want to work with and then click Tables.

3. In the details pane, right-click the table you want to index, point to Full-Text Index Table, and then select Define Full-Text Indexing On A Table. This starts the Full-Text Indexing Wizard.

4. Click Next and then select a unique index for the table. The index is used as a unique constraint on a single column in the table and can be used in table joins. If the table doesn't have a unique index you'll need to exit the wizard, create an index, and then restart this process.

5. As shown in Figure 3-8, select the character or image-based columns that you want to index. Each column can be set with a language constraint that identifies the natural language of the column. With text and binary data, you can also specify a document type. Click Next.

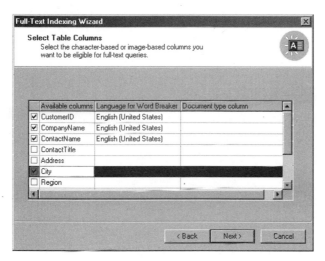

Figure 3-8. *Use the Full-Text Indexing Wizard to define how a table should be indexed. You'll need to select a unique index key and columns for indexing.*

6. Use the Select Full-Text Catalog selection menu to choose an existing catalog. Or select Create A New Catalog and then specify a name and location for the catalog.

7. Click Next. You can now select or create population schedules for the catalog. You can also select or create a population schedule for the currently selected table.

Real World In most cases, you'll want to create schedules for populating an entire catalog rather than an individual table. Still, there are times when populating individual tables makes sense, especially if the contents of a particular table change frequently and contents of other tables change rarely.

8. Click Next and then click Finish. Enterprise Manager defines the full-text index for the table but doesn't populate the index. You must populate the index manually or create a schedule for performing this task.

Editing Indexing of Tables and Columns

To change the indexing settings of a table, complete the following steps:

1. Start Enterprise Manager and then in the left pane (Console Root) click the plus sign (+) next to the server you want to examine.

2. Click the plus sign (+) next to the database you want to work with and then click Tables.

3. In the details pane, right-click the table you want to work with, point to Full-Text Index Table, and then select Edit Full-Text Indexing. This starts the Full-Text Indexing Wizard, which you can use to change the previous indexing definition.

Removing Full-Text Indexing from Tables

If you decide that you don't want to index a table any more, you can remove full-text indexing by completing the following steps:

1. Start Enterprise Manager and then in the left pane (Console Root) click the plus sign (+) next to the server you want to examine.

2. Click the plus sign (+) next to the database you want to work with and then click Tables.

3. In the details pane, right-click the table you want to work with, point to Full-Text Index Table, and then select Remove Full-Text Indexing. When prompted to confirm the action, click Yes.

Populating Catalogs

Once you select the tables and columns you want to index, you can populate the catalog manually or set a schedule that instructs SQL Server Agent to run a one-time or recurring job that populates the catalog. You can populate catalogs at the database level or at the table level. In most cases, you'll want to create schedules for populating an entire catalog rather than an individual table. Still, there are times when populating individual tables makes sense, especially if the contents of a particular table change frequently and the contents of other tables change rarely.

To manually populate a catalog with text for all tables selected for indexing, complete the following steps:

1. Start Enterprise Manager and then in the left pane (Console Root) click the plus sign (+) next to the server you want to examine.

2. Click the plus sign (+) next to the database you want to work with and then click Full-Text Catalog.

3. In the details pane, right-click the catalog you want to work with and then select Start Full Population or Start Incremental Population as appropriate. If you later need to stop the population, right-click the catalog and then select Stop Population.

To set a schedule for populating a catalog with text for all tables selected for indexing, complete the following steps:

1. Start Enterprise Manager and then in the left pane (Console Root) click the plus sign (+) next to the server you want to examine.

2. Click the plus sign (+) next to the database you want to work with and then click Full-Text Catalog.

3. In the details pane, right-click the catalog you want to work with and then select Schedules.

4. Use the Full-Text Indexing Schedules dialog box to set a schedule for populating the catalog.

5. Click OK.

To manually populate a catalog with text for a single table, complete the following steps:

1. Start Enterprise Manager and then in the left pane (Console Root) click the plus sign (+) next to the server you want to examine.

2. Click the plus sign (+) next to the database you want to work with and then click Tables.

3. In the details pane, right-click the table you want to work with, point to Full-Text Index Table and then select Start Full Population or Start Incremental Population as appropriate. If you later need to stop the population, right-click the table, point to Full-Text Index Table, and then select Stop Population.

To set a schedule for populating a catalog with text for a single table, complete the following steps:

1. Start Enterprise Manager and then in the left pane (Console Root) click the plus sign (+) next to the server you want to examine.

2. Click the plus sign (+) next to the database you want to work with and then click Tables.

3. In the details pane, right-click the table you want to work with, point to Full-Text Index Table, and then select Schedules.

4. Use the Full-Text Indexing Schedules dialog box to set a schedule for populating the table.

5. Click OK.

Rebuilding Current Catalogs

When you make frequent changes to a database, catalogs can sometimes get out of sync with the contents of a database. Over an extended period of time, catalogs can also grow quite large. To resync the catalog with the contents of the database or to squeeze out extra space in the catalog, you'll need to rebuild the catalog.

You can rebuild catalogs individually or you can rebuild all the catalogs used by a database. To rebuild a single catalog, complete the following steps:

1. Start Enterprise Manager and then in the left pane (Console Root) click the plus sign (+) next to the server you want to examine.

2. Click the plus sign (+) next to the database you want to work with and then click Full-Text Catalog.

3. In the details pane, right-click the catalog you want to work with and then select Rebuild Catalog.

To rebuild all catalogs associated with a database, complete the following steps:

1. Start Enterprise Manager and then in the left pane (Console Root) click the plus sign (+) next to the server you want to examine.

2. Click the plus sign (+) next to the database you want to work with. Right-click Full-Text Catalog and then select Rebuild All Catalogs. When prompted to confirm the action, click Yes.

 Caution Rebuilding catalogs can be time and resource intensive. In a production environment you should rebuild catalogs only during off-peak hours.

Cleaning Up Old Catalogs

Although the full-text search components do a good job of maintaining indexes and cleaning up after themselves, you'll want to keep an eye on the number and size of catalog files. You'll also want to regularly clean up old catalogs. You do this by completing the following steps:

1. Start Enterprise Manager and then in the left pane (Console Root) click the plus sign (+) next to the server using full-text search.

2. Click the Support Services folder.

3. Right-click the Full-Text Search icon and then from the shortcut menu, choose Cleanup Catalogs.

4. When prompted, choose Yes to start the cleanup. The cleanup may take a few minutes, depending on the size of the catalogs.

Removing Catalogs

To remove a single catalog, complete the following steps:

1. Start Enterprise Manager and then in the left pane (Console Root) click the plus sign (+) next to the server you want to examine.

2. Click the plus sign (+) next to the database you want to work with and then click Full-Text Catalog.

3. In the details pane, right-click the catalog you want to delete and then select Delete. When prompted to confirm the action, click Yes.

To remove all catalogs associated with a database, complete the following steps:

1. Start Enterprise Manager and then in the left pane (Console Root) click the plus sign (+) next to the server you want to examine.

2. Click the plus sign (+) next to the database you want to work with. Right-click Full-Text Catalog and then select Remove All Catalogs. When prompted to confirm the action, click Yes.

Managing SQL Mail and SQL Server Agent Mail

SQL Mail and SQL Server Agent Mail are core facilities of SQL Server. You use SQL Mail to trigger stored procedures and return result sets by e-mail. You use SQL Server Agent Mail to send e-mail and pager notifications. Both facilities rely on a Messaging Application Programming Interface (MAPI)-compliant e-mail service. SQL Mail runs through the SQL Server service. SQL Server Agent Mail, on the other hand, runs through the SQL Server Agent service. The sections that follow explain how you configure and test the mail client needed by SQL Mail and SQL Server Agent Mail and show you how to configure SQL Mail and SQL Server Agent Mail.

Setting Up SQL Server as a Mail Client

SQL Mail and SQL Server Agent Mail can use your existing e-mail infrastructure to send and receive messages as long as your e-mail server is MAPI compliant and you configure SQL Server as a valid mail client. The easiest mail service to configure a client for is Microsoft Exchange. If you're running Exchange, you must

1. Set up an Exchange mailbox for SQL Mail and SQL Server Agent Mail. Or, if you prefer, set up separate mailboxes for these facilities.

Tip By default, the SQL Mail service runs in the same security context as SQL Server service. Because of this, you must configure the Exchange mailbox for a domain account that can run the SQL Server service. SQL Server Agent Mail runs through the SQL Server Agent service and, likewise, you must configure the Exchange mailbox for a domain account that can run the SQL Server Agent service.

2. Install compatible mail client software on the server, such as Microsoft Outlook. The key components of the client used by SQL Mail and SQL Server Agent Mail are the MAPI extensions. Watch out, because you can modify these extensions accidentally when you install service packs, e-mail applications, or other applications that use e-mail.

3. Set up a mail profile for each account using the Mail utility on the Control Panel. You should configure the profiles to point to the Mail Exchange Server and the Exchange mailbox.

Tip Be sure to use a profile name that's easy to identify as the SQL Mail or SQL Server Agent Mail profile, or both. This will make it easier for others to work with the profiles and will help prevent accidental deletion.

Testing the Mail Installation

Once you configure SQL Mail as a mail client(s), you should test the installation by completing the following steps:

1. Log on to the system running SQL Server using a domain account set up for SQL Server. Remember that each database server instance has a different SQL Server service.

2. Start the mail client using the new mail profile.

3. Test the configuration by sending a message addressed to the mailbox for SQL Mail.

4. If the message doesn't show up in the mail client's inbox, you may have improperly configured SQL Mail. Take a close look at each step of the configuration and then repeat this test.

5. Repeat this process to test SQL Server Agent Mail. Remember that each database server instance has a different SQL Server Agent service.

Configuring SQL Mail

After you determine that SQL Server can send and receive mail with the mail client, you're ready to complete the configuration. You need to tell SQL Server about the profile. You do this by completing the following steps:

1. Start Enterprise Manager and then in the left pane (Console Root) click the plus sign (+) next to the server using SQL Mail.

2. Click the Support Services folder.

3. Right-click the SQL Mail icon and then from the shortcut menu, choose Properties. This opens the dialog box shown in Figure 3-9.

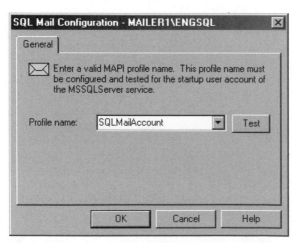

Figure 3-9. *In the SQL Mail Configuration dialog box, type the profile name in the field provided and then click Test.*

4. Type the profile name in the field provided or use the drop-down list box to select any of the available profiles on the server. If you want to test the configuration, click Test.

5. Click OK.

Configuring SQL Server Agent Mail

Next, you need to tell SQL Server about the profile for SQL Server Agent Mail. You do this by completing the following steps:

1. In Enterprise Manager, access the Management folder on the server using SQL Server Agent.

2. Right-click the SQL Server Agent icon in the left pane and then from the shortcut menu, choose Properties.

3. Type the profile name in the Mail Profile field or use the drop-down list box to select any of the available profiles on the server. If you want to test the configuration, click Test.

4. Click OK.

Managing Server Activity

As a database administrator, it's your job to make sure that SQL Server runs smoothly. One of the ways you do this is by actively monitoring the server. By monitoring server activity, you can

- Keep track of user connections and locks

- View processes and commands that active users are running

- Check the status of locks on processes and objects

- See blocked or blocking transactions

- Ensure that processes complete successfully and detect errors if they don't

When problems arise, you can send a message to a user who is running a process or even terminate a process, if necessary.

Note For more coverage of monitoring SQL Server, see Chapter 10. There you'll learn how to use Performance Monitor and SQL Server Profiler to keep track of SQL Server activity, performance, and errors.

Examining Process Information

Process information provides detailed information about the status of processes, current user connections, and other server activity. You can view process information by completing the following steps:

1. Start Enterprise Manager and then in the left pane (Console Root) click the plus sign (+) next to the server you want to examine.

2. Click the Management folder and then select Current Activity. The Current Activity entry shows a date and time when the activity snapshot was taken.

3. Choose the Process Info entry in the Console Root or double-click Process Info in the right pane. You should see a summary of process activity similar to that shown in Figure 3-10.

4. Process information isn't updated automatically. To refresh it, right-click Current Activity and from the shortcut menu, choose Refresh.

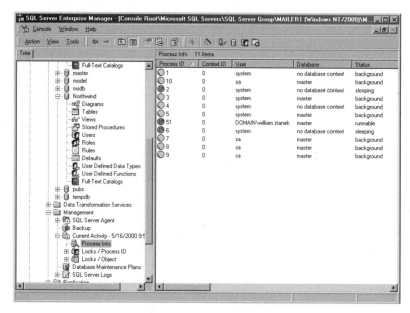

Figure 3-10. *Process Info provides a detailed look at processes and the user connections running them.*

Initially, processes are sorted by process ID, but you can order them by any of the available information categories summarized in Table 3-1. Click a category header to sort processes based on that category. Click a category header a second time to do a reverse sort on the category.

Table 3-1. Process Information Used in Database Administration

Category	Description
Process ID	Server process ID of the current user process.
Context_ID	Identifies the database context in which the process was started.

(continued)

Table 3-1. *(continued)*

Category	Description
User	User running the process by SQL Server ID or domain account, depending on the authentication technique used.
Database	The database being used. Some server processes are started before the master database is brought online, and these have no database context.
Status	The status of the process, which is usually runnable, sleeping, or background. A runnable process is active. A sleeping process is waiting for input or a lock. A background process is running in the background and periodically performing tasks.
Open Transactions	The number of open transactions.
Command	The command being executed or the last command executed.
Application	The application connecting to the server and running the process, such as SQL Server Query Analyzer.
Wait Time	The elapsed wait time in milliseconds.
Wait Type	Specifies whether the process is waiting or not waiting.
Wait Resource	The resource the process is waiting for (if any).
CPU	The amount of processor time being used by the process.
Physical I/O	The physical input/output used by the process.
Memory Usage	The amount of memory the process is using in KB.
Login Time	When the connection was established.
Last Batch Time	When the last command was executed using the connection.
Host	The host from which the connection originated.
Network Library	The network library used to establish the connection.
Network Address	The network address for the connection.
Blocked By	The number of connections blocking this process.
Blocking	The number of connections waiting for this process to finish.

Tracking Locks by Process ID and Object

Locks can be tracked by process ID and object. Either technique provides the same information, it's just presented in a different way. You can view locks by process ID or object by completing the following steps:

1. Start Enterprise Manager and then in the left pane (Console Root) click the plus sign (+) next to the server you want to examine.

2. Click the Management folder and then select Current Activity. The Current Activity entry shows a date and time when the activity snapshot was taken.

3. With processes, you can view a summary of all objects the process is locking. Click Locks/Process ID and then select the process you want to examine, such as SPID.

4. With objects, you can see a list of all processes with locks on the object. Click Locks/Object and then select the database object you want to examine, such as master.

5. Lock statistics aren't updated automatically, and you'll occasionally have to refresh the view. To do this, right-click Current Activity and from the shortcut menu, choose Refresh.

Although locks by process ID and locks by object are presented in a slightly different manner, the information contained in the listings is almost identical. With process ID, you see a list of objects the process has a lock on. With objects, you see a list of processes that have locks on the object. Beyond this, you'll also see information on the type, status, and mode of the lock as well as the lock owner, the resource being locked, and the index being locked (if applicable)—all of which are summarized in Table 3-2.

Table 3-2. Lock-Related Information Used in Database Administration

Category	Type	Description
Lock Type	RID	Row identifier. Used to lock a single row within a table.
	KEY	A row lock within an index. Used to protect key ranges.
	PAG	A lock on a data or index page.
	EXT	A lock on a contiguous group of eight data or index pages.
	TAB	A lock on an entire table, including all data and indexes.
	DB	A lock on a database.
Lock Mode	S	Shared; used for read-only operations, such as a *select* statement.
	U	Update; used when reading/locking an updateable resource. Prevents some deadlock situations.
	X	Exclusive; allows only one session to update the data. Used with the modification operations, such as INSERT, DELETE, and UPDATE.
	Intent	Used to establish a lock hierarchy.

(continued)

Table 3-2. *(continued)*

Category	Type	Description
	SchS	Schema stability; used when checking a table's schema.
	Sch-M	Schema modification; used when modifying a table's schema.
	BU	Bulk update; used when bulk-copying data.
Status	GRANT	The lock was obtained.
	WAIT	The lock is blocked by another process.
	CNVT	The lock is being converted—that is, it's held in one mode but waiting to acquire a stronger lock mode.
Owner	curs	The lock owner is a cursor.
	sess	The lock owner is a user session.
	xact	The lock owner is a transaction.
Index	Index Name	The index associated with the designated resource. With clustered indexes, you'll see a table name instead.
Resource	RID	A row identifier for a locked row within a table; listed by <file id>:<page>:<row id>/, where row id is a row within the specified page.
	KEY	A key shown as a hexadecimal number and used internally by SQL Server.
	PAG	A page number; listed by <file id>:<page>, where file id is the file id in the sysfiles table and page is the logical page number within that file.
	EXT	The first page number in the extent being locked; listed by <file id>:<page>.
	TAB	Table identifier.
	DB	Database identifier.

Troubleshooting Deadlocks and Blocking Connections

Two common problems you may see are deadlocks and blocking connections. Deadlocks and blocking connections can occur in just about any database environment, especially when lots of users are making connections to databases.

- Deadlocks occur when two users have locks on separate objects and each wants a lock on the other's object. Each user waits for the other to release the lock and this doesn't happen.

- Blocking connections occur when one connection holds a lock and a second connection wants a conflicting lock type. This forces the second connection either to wait or to block the first.

Both deadlocks and blocking connections can degrade server performance.

Although SQL Server can detect and correct deadlock and blocking situations, you can help speed up this process by identifying potential problems and taking action, if necessary. Process information can tell you when deadlocks or blocking occur. You'll want to examine these columns: Wait Time, Wait Type, Wait Resource, Blocking, and Blocked By. When you have a deadlock or blocking situation, you'll want to take a closer look at the locks on the objects that are causing problems, and you can do this in the manner described earlier in the "Tracking Locks by Process ID and Object" section of this chapter. You may also want to stop the offending processes, and you do this by following the steps described in the section of this chapter entitled "Killing Server Processes."

Tracking Command Execution in SQL Server

Sometimes you'll want to track the commands that users are executing, and you can do this by using the Current Activity resource viewer. The steps you take are the following:

1. Start Enterprise Manager and then in the left pane (Console Root) click the plus sign (+) next to the server you want to examine.

2. Click the Management folder and then select Current Activity. The Current Activity entry shows a date and time when the activity snapshot was taken.

 Tip If the snapshot is old, you can refresh the snapshot by right-clicking Current Activity and choosing Refresh from the shortcut menu.

3. Select Process Info. The entries in the User column can help you track user sessions and the processes they are using.

4. Double-click a process to display the dialog box shown in Figure 3-11. This dialog box shows the last command executed by the user.

5. To track commands being executed by the user, click Refresh.

6. To kill the process, click Kill Process. Then, when prompted, choose Yes.

7. To send a message to the user running the process, click Send Message.

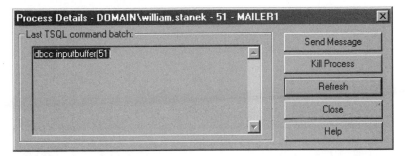

Figure 3-11. *The Process Details dialog box shows the last command or batch executed, as well as the user logon ID, process ID, and originating host.*

Sending Messages to Users Based on Connections

While you're examining processes and server activity, you may want to send messages to users based on connections. To do this, complete the following steps:

1. Start Enterprise Manager and then in the left pane (Console Root) click the plus sign (+) next to the server you want to examine.

2. Click the Management folder and then select Current Activity. The Current Activity entry shows a date and time when the activity snapshot was taken.

3. Select Process Info and then right-click a process being used by a user to whom you want to send a message.

4. From the shortcut menu, choose Send Message (see Figure 3-12).

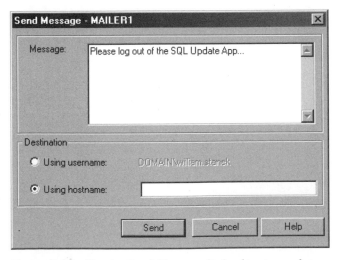

Figure 3-12. *Use the Send Message dialog box to send a message using the Messenger service. If you want to send a message to a different host, choose the Using Hostname option button and then type the new host name.*

5. In the Message area, type the text of the message.

6. Select a destination using the option buttons provided. You can send a message to the user or to the user's computer.

7. Click Send to send the message.

 Note When you send messages to users, you use the Windows Alerter and Messenger services and not SQL Mail. These services must be running on SQL Server and on the user's system. A good resource on Windows services and service management is *Microsoft Windows 2000 Server Administrator's Pocket Consultant* (Microsoft Press, 2000).

Killing Server Processes

You may need to stop processes that are blocking connections or are using up CPU time. To do this, complete the following steps:

1. Start Enterprise Manager and then in the left pane (Console Root) click the plus sign (+) next to the server you want to examine.

2. Click the Management folder and then select Current Activity. The Current Activity entry shows a date and time when the activity snapshot was taken.

3. Select Process Info and then right-click the process you want to stop.

 Note When you start SQL Server, the system starts the process IDs 1 to 6. Don't kill these processes. If you're concerned about them, stop and restart the MSSQLServer service instead of trying to kill these processes.

4. From the shortcut menu, choose Kill Process. Then, when prompted, click Yes.

Chapter 4

Core Database
Administration

Core database administration tasks involve creating, manipulating, and supporting databases. In Microsoft SQL Server 2000, a database is a collection of data and the objects that represent and interact with that data. Tables, views, stored procedures, triggers, and constraints are typical database objects.

A single database server instance can have up to 32,767 databases, and each database can have over 2 billion objects. These are theoretical limits, of course, but they demonstrate that SQL Server can handle just about any chore. To perform most administration tasks, you'll need to log in to the database using an account that has the Sysadmin role, such as the local sysadmin account (sa). Detailed information on roles and SQL Server security is found in Chapter 5.

Database Files and Logs

Each SQL Server database has a transaction log associated with it. A transaction log is a history of modifications to the database, and SQL Server uses it to ensure database integrity. All changes to the database are first written to the transaction log and then applied to the database. If the database update is successful, the transaction is completed and recorded as successful. If the database update fails, SQL Server uses the transaction log to restore the database to its original state (which is called *rolling back* the transaction). This two-phase commit process makes it possible for SQL Server to automatically restore a database in case of power failure, server outage, or other problems that occur when you enter a transaction.

SQL Server databases and transaction logs are contained in separate database files. This means that each database always has at least two files associated with it— a data file and a log file. Databases also can have secondary data files. SQL Server uses three types of database files:

- **Primary data files**   Every database has one primary data file. These files store data and maintain records of other files used in a database. By default, these files end with the .mdf extension.

- **Secondary data files**   These files store additional data for a database. By default, these files end with the .ndf extension.

- **Transaction log files**   Every database has at least one transaction log file. This file contains information necessary to restore the database. By default, log files end with the .ldf extension.

 Note   SQL Server also uses backup devices. Backup devices can be physical devices, such as tape drives, or files that are stored on a local drive or a network share. SQL Server data and log files can be stored on either FAT or NTFS partitions but can't be stored on any compressed file system.

Database files are set when you create or modify the database. By allowing for multiple database files, SQL Server can create databases that span multiple disk drives and that can grow in size as needed. Although the size of a SQL Server database is often measured in GBs, with all editions of SQL Server except the Personal Edition, databases can range in size from 1 MB to a theoretical limit of 1,048,516 TBs. With the Personal Edition, databases have a maximum size limit of 2 GB.

As you set out to work with databases, keep in mind that SQL Server is designed to expand databases automatically as necessary. This means that master, tempdb, msdb, and other critical databases won't run out of space under normal conditions—provided, of course, that there's file space on the configured drives and that you don't set a maximum database size manually. System databases are the most important ones on the server. You should never directly update tables in system databases. Instead, you should use the appropriate management tools or stored procedures to modify the databases if you need to. The only exception is the model database, which you can update with settings for new databases.

Database Administration Basics

You do most of your database administration work through Enterprise Manager. You'll use Enterprise Manager to perform many common database administration tasks, including

- Viewing database information
- Checking user and system databases
- Examining database objects

The sections that follow examine each of these tasks.

Viewing Database Information in Enterprise Manager

SQL Server organizes information using a top-down hierarchy that goes from server groups to servers to databases to objects. Accordingly, you must work your way down to the database level in order to view the databases installed on a particular server instance. If you have registered a server instance and have connected to it previously, you can view its databases by completing the following steps:

1. Start Enterprise Manager and then in the left pane (Console Root) click the plus sign (+) next to the server group you want to work with. If the SQL Server service is stopped, you'll need to restart it before accessing the server.

2. Click the plus sign (+) next to the server you want to work with and then select the Databases folder.

Note If you haven't authenticated the server connection, you may need to provide a SQL logon account and password. You may also need to reestablish a connection with the server. In either case, enter any necessary information and then click OK/Yes to continue.

3. You should see a list of the databases available on the server. Now select the database you want to work with in the left pane.

4. With the Taskpad enabled (by choosing Taskpad from the View menu, if necessary), the right pane should provide access to three different views:

   - **General** Displays database, maintenance, total size, and other important database information; also provides quick access links to start key administration tasks, such as backup database and restore database. Move the mouse pointer over a yellow category button to display a shortcut menu.

   - **Table Info** Displays the available user tables and indexes in the databases. The user tables are listed alphabetically along with their associated indexes and clustered indexes. You'll find the total table size and the number of rows in a particular table as well.

   - **Wizards** Provides quick access to the most commonly used database administration wizards. The wizards are organized into task-related categories, such as those used to manage SQL Server and those used to set up replication. Click a wizard title to start the wizard.

5. To view database information, click any of the view links in the right pane, either General, Table Info, or Wizards. Figure 4-1 shows the General view.

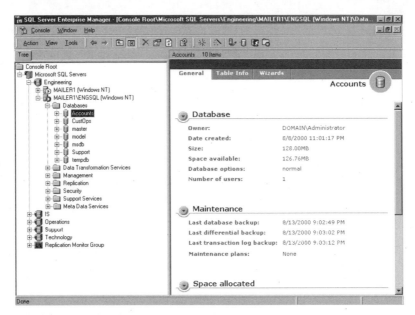

Figure 4-1. *The General view provides a summary of the selected database and also gives quick access to start key administration tasks. Move the mouse pointer over a category button to display a shortcut menu.*

Viewing Database Information Using SQL

You can also use Transact-SQL to examine database information. Transact-SQL is an enhanced version of the standard structured query language that SQL Server uses. Start Query Analyzer and then use the following command:

```
sp_helpdb <dbname>
```

where dbname is the name of the database you want to examine.

When you view database information in this way, you get an overview of the database as well as a listing of current data and log files. Table 4-1 gives a summary of this information.

Table 4-1. Database Properties Viewable Using T-SQL

Column Name	Description
compatibility_level	The current compatibility level of the database. 80 indicates SQL Server 2000 compatibility.
created	The date the database was created.
db_size	The total size of the database including all data and log files.

(continued)

Table 4-1. *(continued)*

Column Name	Description
dbid	The unique identifier for the database on the current server.
filegroup	The filegroup associated with the database file. Filegroups allow you to group sets of database files together.
fileid	The unique identifier for the file in the current database.
filename	The full filename and path.
growth	The number of megabytes or percent the file grows by.
maxsize	The maximum file size. Unlimited means there is no limit.
name	The name of the database or file (without a file extension).
owner	The database owner.
size	The current size of a file.
status	The database status.
usage	The way the file is used, such as data only or log only.

Checking System and Sample Databases

A new SQL Server installation includes the system and sample databases listed in Table 4-2. System databases are critical to the proper operation of SQL Server, and backing up and maintaining these databases is a key part of administration. Sample databases, on the other hand, are meant only to provide examples and don't need regular maintenance. The sample databases take up only 6 MB of disk space, and rather than deleting them, you may want to keep them around for testing and for use in demonstrations.

Table 4-2. Summary of System and Sample Databases

Database Name	Database Type	Description
master	System	Maintains information on all databases installed on the server. This database is modified anytime you create databases, manage accounts, or change configuration settings. Back up the master regularly.

(continued)

Table 4-2. *(continued)*

Database Name	Database Type	Description
model	System	Provides a template for all new databases. If you want new databases to have certain properties or permissions, put these changes in the model database and then all new databases will inherit the changes.
tempdb	System	Provides a temporary workspace for processing queries and handling other tasks. This database is recreated each time SQL Server is started and is based on the model database.
pubs	Sample	Provides a sample database and is often used to demonstrate SQL/Transact-SQL commands.
Northwind	Sample	Provides a sample database with application programming interface (API) examples.
msdb	System	Used by the SQL Server Agent service when performing handling alerts, notifications, and scheduled tasks. You can access all the information in this database using Enterprise Manager options.

Examining Database Objects

The key elements of a SQL Server database are referred to as *objects*. The objects you can associate with a database are:

- Constraints
- Defaults
- Indexes
- Keys
- Stored procedures
- Extended stored procedures
- Tables
- Triggers
- User-defined data types
- User-defined functions
- Views

You can also associate users, roles, rules, and full-text catalogs with databases.

To examine objects within a database, complete the following steps:

1. Start Enterprise Manager and then in the left pane (Console Root) click the plus sign (+) next to the server group you want to work with.

2. Click the plus sign (+) next to the server you want to work with again and then, if necessary, authenticate yourself or establish a connection, or both.

3. Work your way down to the database level. Expand the Databases folder and then expand the entry for the database you want to work with.

4. You should see a list of available database objects. In the left pane, click the element you want to view.

More Info   Each of these objects is covered in detail in the appropriate chapter. For example, you'll find more information on tables in Chapter 6.

Creating Databases

SQL Server uses the model database as the basis of new databases. If you want new databases to have the same setup, you should modify the model database and then create the necessary new databases. Otherwise, you'll need to manually modify the settings of each new database. The easiest way to create a new database is to use Enterprise Manager. You can also create databases using Transact-SQL.

Creating Databases in Enterprise Manager

In Enterprise Manager you set database properties with buttons and input fields and let SQL Server do all the behind-the-scenes SQL work. You create a database using the default options by completing these steps:

1. Start Enterprise Manager and then in the left pane (Console Root) click the plus sign (+) next to the server group you want to work with.

2. Click the plus sign (+) next to the server you want to work with again and then, if necessary, authenticate yourself or establish a connection, or both.

3. Right-click the Databases folder and then from the shortcut menu, choose New Database. This opens the Database Properties dialog box shown in Figure 4-2.

4. Click the General tab and type a name for the database. Although database names can have up to 128 characters, you'll be better able to track the database if it has a short but descriptive name.

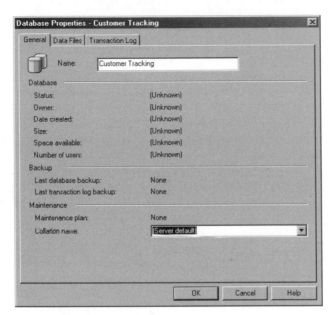

Figure 4-2. *Use the Database Properties dialog box to create new databases and to update the settings of existing databases. If you want to create databases with a wizard instead, choose the Wizards option on the Tools menu. In the Wizards dialog box expand Database and then double-click Create Database Wizard.*

Note The names of database objects are referred to as *identifiers*. Identifiers can contain from 1 to 128 characters (except for local temporary tables, which can have from 1 to 116 characters) and must follow the specific naming conventions for the identifier class to which they belong. Generally, if the identifier name uses spaces or begins with a number, you must use brackets ([]) or double quotes (" ") to delimit the name when referencing it in Transact-SQL commands.

5. Click OK. SQL Server creates the database.

To customize the creation process, follow steps 1 through 4 (but not 5) in the previous example and then continue with these steps:

1. On the General tab, use the Collation Name selection menu to choose a collation for the database. Microsoft Windows collation names have two components: a collation designator and a comparison style. The collation designator specifies the alphabet or language whose sorting rules are applied

with dictionary sorting and the code page to use when storing non-Unicode character data. The comparison style specifies additional collation style as identified by the following abbreviations:

- **CI**   Case insensitive
- **CS**   Case sensitive
- **AI**   Accent insensitive
- **AS**   Accent sensitive
- **KS**   Kanatype sensitive
- **WS**   Width sensitive
- **BIN**   Binary sort order

2. On the Data Files tab, type a name in the File Name field for the primary data file associated with this database. By default, SQL Server bases the data filename on the database name. For example, if you type Sample as the database name, the data file is named Sample_Data.

3. In the Location field, type the full path to the data file. The primary data file should end with the .mdf file extension. By default, SQL Server uses the default data location you selected when you installed the server. Click Location to find a new path or enter a new path directly.

4. In the Initial Size field, type an initial size for the database in megabytes. Use a size that makes sense for the amount of data that the database will store. By default, new databases have the same size as the model database. The size range for databases is from 1 MB to many TB.

Tip Setting the initial database size to a reasonable value cuts down on the overhead that may be associated with growing the database. Whether you grow the database manually or SQL Server grows it automatically, the database is locked until the growth is complete. This can cause delays in processing queries and handling transactions.

Note Keep in mind that you can't shrink a database to be smaller than it was when you created it. However, you can shrink individual data and log files to be smaller than their original size by using the DBCC SHRINKFILE statement. With DBCC SHRINKFILE, you must shrink each file individually, rather than trying to shrink the entire database.

5. The File Group field shows which filegroup the data file belongs to. By default, all files are placed in the primary group. While the primary data file must be in the primary group, other data files can be placed in different filegroups. Filegroups provide additional options for determining where data is stored and how it's used, as well as how data is backed up and restored.

Tip Filegroups are designed primarily for large databases and advanced administration. If your database might grow to 1 GB or larger, consider using filegroups. Otherwise, you really don't need to use filegroups. That said, the primary reason to use filegroups is to improve database response time. You do this by allowing database files to be created across multiple disks or to be accessed by multiple disk controllers, or both.

6. Secondary data files provide an additional location for data. If you want to configure secondary data files, start on a new line and then repeat steps 1 through 4. Secondary data files should end with the .ndf file extension.

7. After you configure data files, you need to configure file properties for the database. By default, data files are set to grow automatically by 10 percent each time the data files need to be expanded, and there's no limit on the maximum file size.

8. Click the Transaction Log tab shown in Figure 4-3. You can now configure one or more transaction log files in much the same way that you configured the data files. Type the file name, location, initial size, and filegroup information. Be sure to name the log files with the .ldf file extension.

Figure 4-3. *Use the Transaction Log tab to configure the size, location, and features of the transaction log.*

Real World The Autogrow feature is a good one, and I heartily recommend using it so databases don't run out of space. That said, however, the default option for file growth can lead to problems. With a 10 percent growth rate, a 500 MB database grows by a whopping 50 MB each time a data file needs to be expanded, and a server with multiple databases may run out of space as a result of the growth factor. I prefer to set the growth in megabytes, with 1 MB as a minimum growth size. When you grow in megabytes, you know exactly how much the database will grow each time. You may also want to configure an alert to notify you when the database grows to a certain size. Configuring alerts is covered in Chapter 12.

Note Sizing the transaction log can be tricky. You don't want to rob the system of needed space for data, but at the same time you want to make sure that the transaction logs aren't continually getting resized (as I noted previously, the file gets locked when it's being expanded). I recommend 2–3 MB as a minimum for most databases and 25 percent of total data file size on a moderately active database. Note also that placing transaction logs on separate drives from data files can usually improve database performance.

9. Set file properties for the transaction logs. Here, the default options usually work fine and you don't need to change anything.

10. Click OK to complete the creation process. Afterward, you should set options and permissions for the database. Setting options is covered in the section of this chapter entitled "Setting Database Options." Setting permissions is covered in Chapter 5, "Microsoft SQL Server 2000 Security."

Creating Databases Using T-SQL

Another way to create a database is to use the CREATE DATABASE command. This command has options that are similar to those in the Database Properties tab, and the best way to learn how the command works is to first create databases in Enterprise Manager and then try CREATE DATABASE.

The syntax and usage for CREATE DATABASE is shown in Sample 4-1.

Sample 4-1. CREATE DATABASE Syntax and Usage

Syntax

```
CREATE DATABASE database_name
  [ ON [PRIMARY]
  [ <filespec> [...n] ]
  [, <filegroup> [...n] ]
```

(continued)

Sample 4-1. *(continued)*
Syntax

```
]
[ LOG ON { <filespec> [,..n]} ]
[ COLLATE collation_name ]
[ FOR LOAD | FOR ATTACH ]
<filespec> ::=
( [ NAME = logical_file_name, ]
FILENAME = 'os_file_name'
[, SIZE = size]
[, MAXSIZE = { max_size | UNLIMITED } ]
[, FILEGROWTH = growth_increment] ) [,..n]
<filegroup> ::=
FILEGROUP filegroup_name <filespec> [,..n]
```

Usage

```
USE MASTER
GO
CREATE DATABASE Sample
ON
PRIMARY ( NAME = Sample1,
FILENAME = 'c:\Microsoft SQL
  Server\mssql$engone\data\sampledat1.mdf',
SIZE = 100MB,
MAXSIZE = UNLIMITED,
FILEGROWTH = 10%),
( NAME = Sample2,
FILENAME = 'c:\Microsoft SQL
  Server\mssql$engone\data\sampledat2.ndf',
SIZE = 100MB,
```

(continued)

Sample 4-1. *(continued)*
Usage

```
MAXSIZE = UNLIMITED,

FILEGROWTH = 10%)

LOG ON

( NAME = SampleLog1,

FILENAME = 'c:\Microsoft SQL
  Server\mssql$engone\data\samplelog1.ldf',

SIZE = 3MB,

MAXSIZE = UNLIMITED,

FILEGROWTH = 5MB)

GO
```

Setting Database Options

New databases inherit options from the model database. After you create a database, you can modify these settings at any time by using Enterprise Manager or Transact-SQL.

Setting Database Options in Enterprise Manager

To set database options in Enterprise Manager, complete the following steps:

1. Start Enterprise Manager and then in the left pane (Console Root) click the plus sign (+) next to the server group you want to work with.

2. Click the plus sign (+) next to the server you want to work with again and then click the plus sign (+) next to the Databases folder.

3. Right-click the database you want to work with and then from the shortcut menu, choose Properties. This opens the Properties dialog box shown in Figure 4-4. For details see the following section, "Database Options for Enterprise Manager and Transact-SQL."

4. In the Properties dialog box, click the Options tab. You can now configure options for the database by selecting or clearing the appropriate check boxes.

5. Click OK when you're finished. Your changes take effect immediately, and you don't need to restart the server.

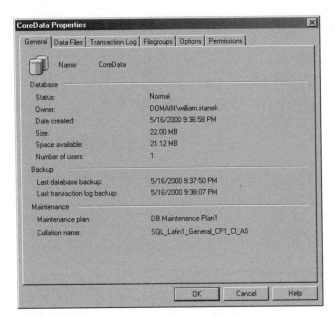

Figure 4-4. *After you create a database, you should set its options in the Properties dialog box.*

Database Options for Enterprise Manager and Transact-SQL

You use database options to configure individual databases. In most SQL Server editions, all database options are set to FALSE by default, except for Auto Create Statistics, Auto Update Statistics, and Torn Page Detection, which are set to TRUE by default in the model database. If you change these options in the model database, your default options will be different. In the following list, database Properties dialog box options are listed with initial caps, or by the related SQL command in lowercase, or both.

- **ANSI NULL Default (ANSI null default)** When TRUE, changes the database default to NULL when no value is specified. You can override this setting by explicitly stating NULL or NOT NULL when you create user-defined data types or column definitions.

- **ANSI nulls** When TRUE, any comparison to a null value evaluates to NULL. Otherwise, comparisons of non-Unicode values evaluate to TRUE only when both values are NULL.

- **ANSI warnings** When TRUE, SQL Server displays warnings when it otherwise may not. For example, if TRUE, divide-by-zero errors are displayed. Otherwise they aren't.

- **arithabort** When TRUE, terminates a query when an overflow or divide-by-zero error occurs. If the error occurs in a transaction, the transaction is rolled back. When FALSE, a warning message can be displayed, but queries and transactions continue as if no error occurred.

- **Auto Close (autoclose)** When TRUE, the database is closed and resources are freed up when the last user connection ends and all database processes are completed. The database reopens automatically when a user tries to use the database again. In the SQL Server Desktop Edition, this option is set to TRUE by default. All other editions set this option to FALSE by default. When FALSE, the database remains open even if no users are currently using it.

- **numeric roundabort** When TRUE, an error is generated when a loss of precision occurs in an expression. When FALSE, losses of precision do not generate error messages, and the result is rounded to the precision of the column or variable storing the result.

Tip With the Desktop Edition, Autoclose is a useful feature that allows databases to be treated like any other file. When the database is closed, you're free to move, copy, or change it.

- **Auto Create Statistics (auto create statistics)** When TRUE, statistics are automatically created by SQL Server for columns used in a *where* clause. These statistics are used to better determine how to evaluate a query, which in turn can improve query performance.

- **Auto Shrink (autoshrink)** When TRUE, data and log files can be reduced in size and compacted automatically. The idea is that when records are deleted or purged, you can let SQL Server automatically reduce the size of data or log files, or both. However, log files are reduced in size only when you back up the transaction log or set the Truncate Log On Checkpoint option to TRUE. In the SQL Server Desktop Edition, this option is set to TRUE by default. All other editions set this option to FALSE by default. Note also that you can't set this option on a read-only database.

Note Several caveats apply to Autoshrink. The Autoshrink option is applied only when more than 25 percent of a file contains unused space. This in turn causes SQL Server to reduce the file size so that only 25 percent of file space is free or to set the file size to its original size setting, whichever is greater. The process that shrinks the database is the server process ID 6; it checks the database size at 30-minute intervals. As with Autogrow, the database is locked when SQL Server shrinks files, which can reduce query response time. Because of this, I don't recommend using this option and prefer to periodically run the DBCC SHRINKDATABASE command or to schedule this task on a recurring basis, as explained in the section of this chapter entitled "Compacting and Shrinking a Database Manually."

- **Auto Update Statistics (auto update statistics)** When TRUE, existing statistics are automatically updated if data in the related tables changes. Otherwise, existing statistics aren't automatically updated and you can only update them manually.

- **concat null yields null** When TRUE, concatenating a string containing NULL with other strings results in NULL. Otherwise, the null value is treated as an empty string.

- **cursor close on commit** When TRUE, open cursors are closed automatically when a transaction is committed. This behavior is in compliance with SQL-92 but isn't set to TRUE by default. As a result, cursors remain open across transaction boundaries and close only when the related connection is closed or when the cursor is explicitly closed.

 Note SQL-92 is the most widely used version of the SQL standard and is sometimes referred to as ANSI SQL.

- **dbo use only** When TRUE, only the database owner can access the database. Use this option when you're modifying a database and temporarily want to block access to it. To set this option using the Properties dialog box, select Restrict Access and then choose Members of db_owner, dbcreator, or sysadmin.

- **default to local cursor** When TRUE, cursors are created with local scope unless otherwise specified, and as a result, the cursor name is valid only within this scope. When FALSE, cursors not explicitly set to LOCAL are created with a global scope and can be referenced in any stored procedure, batch, or trigger that the connection executes.

- **merge publish** When TRUE, you can use the database for merge replication publications. If you use the Replication Wizard to configure replication, this setting is changed for you automatically.

- **offline** When TRUE, the database is offline and you can mount or dismount it as necessary. You'll often want to use this option with removable media, such as CDs.

- **published** When TRUE, permits the tables of a database to be published for replication. The Replication Wizard also sets this option.

- **Read-only (read only)** When TRUE, you can read data but not modify it. Use this option to prevent users from changing data and modifying database configuration settings. When this option is set, several caveats apply: automatic recovery is skipped at system startup, locking doesn't take place, and the database won't shrink.

- **Recursive Triggers (recursive triggers)** When TRUE, a trigger can execute recursively. Triggers can be executed directly or indirectly. With a direct trigger, a trigger in Table A1 modifies Table A1, which in turn causes the trigger to fire again. With an indirect trigger, a trigger in Table A1 could modify data in Table A2, which in turn has a trigger that modifies data in Table A1, and this causes the original trigger to fire again.

- **select into/bulkcopy**   When TRUE, certain SQL commands aren't logged in the transaction log. These commands include using SELECT INTO with a permanent table, running fast bulk copy, using UPDATETEXT or WRITETEXT without logging, and using a table load. If you set this option to TRUE and execute any command that bypasses the transaction log, you can't recover the database from transaction logs and BACKUP LOG commands are prohibited. Instead, use BACKUP DATABASE to back up the entire database and then later you can back up from the log (provided you don't run any more commands that bypass the transaction log).

- **Single User (single user)**   When TRUE, only one user at a time can connect to the database. Before you can set this option, all active connections to the database must be closed. If necessary, kill the user processes as explained in Chapter 3.

- **subscribed**   When TRUE, the database can be subscribed to a replicated (or published) database.

- **torn page detection**   When TRUE, SQL Server automatically detects incomplete I/O operations known as *torn pages*. If SQL Server detects a torn page during a user connection, it raises an I/O error and terminates the user connection. If it detects a torn page during recovery, it marks the database as suspect. In either case, you may want to restore the database from backup and apply any backup transaction logs.

Tip   You can use battery-backed disk caches to ensure that data is successfully written to disk or not written at all. But don't set torn page detection to TRUE.

- **trunc. log on chkpt.**   When TRUE, the transaction log can be automatically truncated. Basically, this allows the log to be cleared out once transactions have been committed. After the transaction log has been cleared out, you can perform BACKUP/RESTORE only at the database level (and not with the transaction log). In the SQL Server Desktop Edition, this option is set to TRUE by default. All other editions set this option to FALSE by default.

Tip   Checkpoints occur at various times. A checkpoint is issued for each database when the SQL Server service shuts down normally. Checkpoints don't occur when the *shutdown with nowait* statement is used. A checkpoint is executed in a single database when a database is changed with *sp_dboption*. SQL Server also automatically issues a checkpoint on a database as necessary to ensure that the designated recovery interval can be achieved and when the log becomes 70 percent full.

Note The transaction log must be large enough to store all active transactions. Otherwise, you can't roll back transactions. In a deployment environment, you should use this option only when you can rely solely on database backups and don't supplement with transaction log backups. Note also that the tempdb database is always truncated on CHECK-POINT, regardless of the setting of this option.

- **Use Quoted Identifiers (quoted identifier)**   When TRUE, identifiers must be delimited by double quotation marks ("...") and literals must be delimited by single quotation marks ('...'). All strings that are delimited by double quotation marks are interpreted as object identifiers and don't have to follow the Transact-SQL rules for identifiers.

Viewing, Changing, and Overriding Database Options

Although Enterprise Manager makes it easy to set database options, you'll often want to view or change options using SQL commands. To do this, you can use the *sp_dboption* stored procedure, individual SET commands, or the ALTER DATABASE command. Key tasks you'll want to perform with the *sp_dboption* and SET commands are

- **Displaying an options list**   To display a list of available options, type **EXEC sp_dboption**.
- **Viewing database option settings**   To view the current option settings for a database, type **EXEC sp_dboption <dbname>** where dbname is the name of the database you want to examine, such as **EXEC sp_dboption 'Subs'**.
- **Changing database options**   To set or change a database option, type **EXEC sp_dboption <dbname>, <option>, {TRUE | FALSE}** where dbname is the name of the database you want to examine and option is the name of the option to set, such as **EXEC sp_dboption 'Subs', 'trunc. log on chkpt.', TRUE**.
- **Overriding database options**   Use SET options for individual sessions or database drivers to override default settings. You can also check options using properties of the *Databaseproperty* function. See the "Default Connection Options" section of Chapter 2 for more information.

Using ALTER DATABASE is covered in the section of this chapter entitled "Altering a Database."

 Note   The *sp_dboption* stored procedure should not be used to modify the master or tempdb databases. It is only supported for backward compatibility and primarily should be used to display database options. Whenever possible, use ALTER DATABASE to modify database options instead.

Managing Database and Log Size

With SQL Server 2000, you can manage database and log size either automatically or manually. You can configure either technique in Enterprise Manager or through Transact-SQL. This section looks primarily at configuration through Enterprise Manager.

Configuring SQL Server to Automatically Manage File Size

To configure automatic management of database and log size in Enterprise Manager, complete the following steps:

1. Start Enterprise Manager and then, using the entries in the left pane, work your way down to the Databases folder.

2. Right-click the database you want to work with, and then from the shortcut menu, choose Properties.

3. Click the Data Files tab. Under File Properties, select the Automatically Grow File check box, and then set the file growth in megabytes or as a percentage of file size.

4. Click the Transaction Log tab. Under File Properties, select the Automatically Grow File check box, and then set the file growth in megabytes or as a percentage of file size.

5. Optionally, click the Options tab and select the Auto Shrink check box. Autoshrink compacts and shrinks the database periodically.

6. Click OK when you're finished. Your changes take effect immediately; you don't need to restart the server.

Note   See the section of this chapter entitled "Creating Databases in Enterprise Manager" for tips and advice on sizing databases and transaction logs.

Expanding Databases and Logs Manually

Sometimes you'll want to increase the size of a database or log file. You can do this by completing the following steps:

1. Start Enterprise Manager and then, using the entries in the left pane, work your way down to the Databases folder.

2. Right-click the database you want to work with and then from the shortcut menu, choose Properties.

3. To expand a database, click the Data Files tab and then enter a larger file size in the Space Allocated field for a primary or secondary data file.

Tip You could also create and size a new secondary file for the database. The advantage to using a new file rather than an existing file is that SQL Server doesn't need to lock what may be an active database file in order to expand the database.

4. To expand a log, click the Transaction Log tab and then enter a larger file size in the Space Allocated field. (You could also create and size a new transaction log file.)

 Tip With data and log files, the new file size must be larger than the current size. If it isn't, you'll get an error. The reason for this is that shrinking the database is handled in a different way. See the following section, "Compacting and Shrinking a Database Manually," for details.

5. Click OK to make the changes. SQL Server locks the database while expanding it, which blocks access.

 More Info You can also expand files using Transact-SQL. The command you use is ALTER DATABASE. For more information, see the section of this chapter entitled "Altering a Database."

Compacting and Shrinking a Database Manually

Compacting and shrinking a database is a bit different from expanding it, and you'll often want finer control over the process than you get with the Autoshrink option. Fortunately, you can manually manage this process, and you can also schedule this process on a recurring basis.

To manually compact or shrink database files (both data and log files) in Enterprise Manager, complete the following steps:

1. Start Enterprise Manager and then, using the entries in the left pane, work your way down to the Databases folder.

2. Right-click the database you want to work with and from the shortcut menu, choose All Tasks. From the All Tasks menu, choose the Shrink Database option.

3. You should see the Shrink Database dialog box shown in Figure 4-5. The Database Size area shows the total amount of space allocated to all database files and the amount of free space. Use this information to help you decide whether you really want to shrink the database.

4. Use Maximum Free Space In Files After Shrinking to set the percentage of free space in the database. To squeeze all extra space out of the database, use a value of 0 percent, but be aware that the next write operation may cause the database to grow automatically.

Figure 4-5. *Shrinking a database is easy with Enterprise Manager's Shrink Database dialog box. Just make your selections and click OK, or schedule the task on a recurring basis.*

5. To reorganize data pages and move them to the beginning of the data files, select Move Pages To Beginning Of File Before Shrinking. This compacts the data pages but doesn't remove empty data pages.

Note   Log files aren't reduced in size immediately. Instead, the size is reduced when the transaction log is backed up or the log is truncated, whichever occurs first. Also, you normally can't shrink a database smaller than the model database (which is the database template).

6. Click OK to begin or continue on to step 7 for scheduling. SQL Server locks the database while shrinking it, which blocks access.

7. The property settings you make in this dialog box are saved and unique to the current database. If you want to use these properties to shrink the database on a recurring basis, select Shrink The Database Based On This Schedule and then click Change. You can now schedule this task as explained in Chapter 12, "Database Automation and Maintenance."

To manually compact or shrink individual database files in Enterprise Manager, complete the following steps:

1. Start Enterprise Manager and then, using the entries in the left pane, work your way down to the Databases folder.

2. Right-click the database you want to work with and from the shortcut menu, choose All Tasks. From the All Tasks menu, choose the Shrink Database option.

3. You should see the Shrink Database dialog box shown previously in Figure 4-5. The Database Size area shows the total amount of space allocated to all database files and the amount of free space. Use this information to help you decide whether you really want to shrink the database.

4. Click Files. This displays the Shrink Database Files dialog box.

5. Use the Database File selection menu to choose the data or log file that you want to shrink.

6. Choose a shrink action:
   - Compress pages and then truncate free space from the file
   - Truncate free space from the end of the file
   - Empty the file (data will migrate to other files in the filegroup)
   - Shrink file to __ MB

7. If you want to use these properties to shrink the data or log file at a later date and time, select Shrink The File Later and then select a date and time.

8. Click OK.

Another way to shrink a database is to use Transact-SQL. Two commands are provided:

```
DBCC SHRINKDATABASE
( database_name [, target_percent]
[, {NOTRUNCATE | TRUNCATEONLY}]
)
```

```
DBCC SHRINKFILE
( {file_name | file_id }
{ [, target_size]
| [, {EMPTYFILE | NOTRUNCATE | TRUNCATEONLY}]
 }
)
```

You use DBCC SHRINKDATABASE to shrink all data files in the database and DBCC SHRINKFILE to shrink a specific data file. By default, these commands also compact the database. You can override this option with TRUNCATEONLY or specify that you only want to compact the database with NOTRUNCATE.

The following command compacts and then shrinks the Customer database to 30 percent free space:

```
DBCC SHRINKDATABASE ( Customer, 30 )
```

The following commands compact and then shrink an individual file in the Customer database to 5 MB free space:

```
USE Customer

DBCC SHRINKFILE ( Customer_Data, 5 )
```

Note The DBCC SHRINKFILE command is the only technique you can use to shrink individual data and log files to be smaller than their origi- nal size. With DBCC SHRINKFILE, you must shrink each file individually, rather than trying to shrink the entire database. Additionally, the trunca- tion options for DBCC SHRINKDATABASE and DBCC SHRINKFILE only apply to data files and are ignored for log files. You don't truncate trans- action logs with these commands.

Manipulating Databases

Other core administration tasks that you'll often need to perform include restrict- ing, renaming, dropping, detaching, copying, and moving databases. These tasks are examined in the sections that follow.

Temporarily Restricting Database Access

As a database administrator, you'll often need to temporarily restrict access to a database during maintenance. The best way to do this is to put the data- base in single-user mode or to allow only members of db_owner, dbcreator, and sysadmin to access the database. The sections that follow explain both of these options.

Setting Single-User Mode

You'll use single user mode to perform database maintenance and recovery. Before changing to single-user mode, ask all users to disconnect from the database and then ensure that any open Enterprise Manager connections to the database are closed. If necessary, kill the user processes as explained in Chapter 3. Afterward, follow these steps to use Enterprise Manager to place the database in single-user mode:

1. Start Enterprise Manager and then, using the entries in the left pane, work your way down to the Databases folder.

2. Right-click the database you want to work with and, from the shortcut menu, choose Properties. Then in the Properties dialog box, click on the Options tab.

3. Select Restrict Access and then choose Single User.

4. Click OK.

You can also use T-SQL to place a database in single-user mode. Simply follow these steps:

1. Start Query Analyzer and then connect to the database server instance that you want to work with.

2. Use *sp_dboption* to put the database in single-user mode. The following example puts a database called SupportDB in single-user mode:

```
use master

exec sp_dboption SupportDB,'single user',true
```

Setting Members Only Access

To allow only members of db_owner, dbcreator, and sysadmin to access the database, follow these steps:

1. Start Enterprise Manager and then, using the entries in the left pane, work your way down to the Databases folder.

2. Right-click the database you want to work with. From the shortcut menu, choose Properties. In the Properties dialog box, click on the Options tab.

3. Select Restrict Access and then choose Members Of Db_owner, Dbcreator, Or Sysadmin.

4. Click OK.

Renaming a Database

You can rename user databases with the *sp_renamedb* stored procedure. To do this, complete the following steps:

1. Ask all users to disconnect from the database. Ensure any open Enterprise Manager connections to the database are closed. If necessary, kill the user processes as explained in Chapter 3.

2. Start Query Analyzer and then put the database in single-user mode. The following example puts a database called Customer in single-user mode:

```
use master

exec sp_dboption Customer, 'single user', true
```

 Tip You execute commands in Query Analyzer by clicking Execute Query or by pressing F5. With ISQL or OSQL, you can execute commands by entering the *go* statement.

3. Rename the database using the *sp_renamedb* stored procedure. In the following example, the Customer database is renamed cust:

```
exec sp_renamedb 'Customer', 'cust'
```

4. After you run the SQL commands, set the renamed database back to multiuser mode. The following example sets the cust database to multiuser mode:

```
exec sp_dboption cust, 'single user', false
```

5. Be sure that all commands, applications, and processes that use the old database name are pointed to the new database name. If you don't do this, you'll have problems.

Dropping and Deleting a Database

In SQL Server 2000, dropping and deleting a database are the same thing. When you drop a database, you remove the database and its associated files from the server. Once you drop a database, it's permanently deleted and you can't restore it without using a backup. To delete references to a database without removing the database files, use *sp_detach_db*, as described in the following section of this chapter, "Attaching and Detaching Databases."

You can drop a database by completing the following steps:

1. Close all user connections to the database.
2. Start Enterprise Manager and then, using the entries in the left pane, work your way down to the Databases folder.
3. Right-click the database you want to drop and then select Delete.
4. When prompted, choose Yes to delete the database.

Note You can't drop a database that's being used by SQL Server or by other users. For example, if you're restoring the database or the database is published for replication, you can't delete it. You also can't delete the database if there are any active user sessions.

5. Optionally, back up the master database as explained in Chapter 11, "Database Backup and Recovery." Backing up the master database ensures that the most current system information is stored and that information for the old database won't be accidentally restored with the master database.

You can also delete a database with the DROP DATABASE command. The syntax and usage for this command is shown in Sample 4-2.

Sample 4-2. DROP DATABASE Syntax and Usage

Syntax

```
DROP DATABASE database_name [,...n]
```

Usage

```
DROP DATABASE 'Customer', 'Agencies', 'Resources'
```

Attaching and Detaching Databases

The *sp_detach_db* and *sp_attach_db* stored procedures are designed primarily for use in moving database files or disabling databases without deleting their files. When you detach a database, you remove references to the server in the master database but don't delete the related database files. Detached databases aren't displayed in Enterprise Manager and aren't accessible to users. If you want to use the database again, you can reattach it with the *sp_attach_db* or *sp_attach_single_file_db* stored procedure. Attaching a database creates a new database that references data stored in existing data and log files.

Detaching a Database

When you detach a database, you can specify whether you want to update the statistics before you do. Updating statistics makes the database easier to use with read-only media; otherwise, you really don't need it. To update statistics, set the skipchecks flag to TRUE. Detach a database using *sp_detach_db*, as shown in Sample 4-3.

Sample 4-3. *sp_detach_db* **Syntax and Usage**

Syntax

```
exec sp_detach_db [@dbname =] 'dbname'
[, [@skipchecks =] 'skipchecks']
```

Usage

```
exec sp_detach_db 'sample', 'true'
```

 Tip You can't detach system databases, and you can only detach user databases when they aren't in use. Furthermore, before detaching a user database, you may want to close all current connections, put the database in single-user mode, and then run the detach operation.

Attaching a Database with Multiple Files

When you reattach a database with *sp_attach_db*, you can specify up to 16 files to associate with the database. This filename list must include the primary file, which contains pointers to the original locations of all other database files, and all files that have changed location.

Attach the database using *sp_attach_db*, as shown in Sample 4-4.

Sample 4-4. *sp_attach_db* **Syntax and Usage**

Syntax

```
exec sp_attach_db [@dbname =] 'dbname',
[@filename1 =] 'filename_n' [,...16]
exe sp_attach_db 'Sample',
'c:\Microsoft SQL Server\mssql$engone\data\sample_data.mdf',
'c:\Microsoft SQL Server\mssql$engone\data\sample_log.ldf'
```

Attaching a Database with Only a Data File

You may not need old transaction logs in a new database. Because of this, you may want only to restore a data file and let SQL Server create a new log file for you. To do this, use the *sp_attach_single_file_db* stored procedure, as shown in Sample 4-5.

Sample 4-5. *sp_attach_single_file_db* **Syntax and Usage**

Syntax

```
exec sp_attach_single_file_db [@dbname =] 'dbname',
[@physname =] 'physical_name'
```

Usage

```
exec sp_attach_single_file_db 'Customer',
  'c:\Microsoft SQL Server\mssql$engone\data\customer_data.mdf'
```

Copying Databases with Attach

One of the key reasons for using *sp_attach_db* is to create a copy of an existing database. When you do this, you copy the database's existing files to a new location and then attach them with *sp_attach_db*. The steps you take are the following:

1. Start Query Analyzer, connect to the database server instance you want to work with, and then run the *sp_helpdb* stored procedure for the database you want to copy, such as

   ```
   exec sp_helpdb Customer
   ```

2. Write down the absolute file path location of all data and log files for the database.

3. Use SQL Server Service Manager to stop the SQL Server service for the database server instance you want to work with.

4. Start Windows Explorer and then access the folders containing the database's data and log files. Use Copy to copy each file in turn and then use Paste to insert the files at the desired location. Be sure to rename the files if you need to.

5. Use SQL Server Service Manager to start the SQL Server service you previously stopped.

6. In Query Analyzer, connect to the destination database server instance and then use *sp_attach_db* to create a new database using the files you just copied, such as

   ```
   exec sp_attach_db 'Customer2',
   'c:\Microsoft SQL Server\mssql$engone\data\cust2_data.mdf',
   'c:\Microsoft SQL Server\mssql$engone\data\cust2_log.ldf'
   ```

7. In Enterprise Manager, configure the new database as necessary.

Moving Databases with Detach and Attach

You can use the *sp_detach_db* and *sp_attach_db* stored procedures to move database files to new locations. For example, if you create a database and put all the files in one location, you may want to put the data files and transaction logs on separate drives later. You would do this by detaching the database, moving database files as necessary, and then reattaching the database so that it points to the new file locations.

Moving a database is much like copying a database. You move a database by completing the following steps:

1. Close all active connections to the database you want to move and then put the database in single-user mode by typing

   ```
   exec sp_dboption Customer, 'single user', true
   ```

2. Start Query Analyzer and then run the *sp_helpdb* command for the database you want to copy, such as

   ```
   exec sp_helpdb Customer
   ```

3. Write down the absolute file path location of all data and log files for the database.

4. Use *sp_detach_db* to detach the database by typing

   ```
   exec sp_detach_db 'sample', 'true'
   ```

5. Start Windows Explorer and then access the folders containing the database's data and log files. Use Cut to cut files you want to move and then use Paste to insert these files at the desired location.

6. In Query Analyzer, use *sp_attach_db* to reattach the database. Be sure to reference the new location for files, such as

   ```
   exec sp_attach_db 'Customer',
   'c:\cust\data\cust_data.mdf',
   'c:\cust\data\cust_data2.ndf',
   'd:\cust\logs\cust2_log.ldf'
   ```

Moving a Database to Another Server

You can also move databases to a new server. You detach the database, move the related data and log files to the new server, and then reattach them. You can follow the same procedure described in the previous section, "Moving Databases with Detach and Attach."

Altering a Database

Enterprise Manager gives you an easy way to modify the configuration of a database. Another way to modify a database is to use ALTER DATABASE.

You can use ALTER DATABASE to

- Set database options. You can use it instead of the *sp_dboption* stored procedure.

- Add new data and log files to a database. All the files must be placed in the same filegroup.
- Modify properties of data and log files, such as by increasing file size, changing the maximum size, or setting file growth rules.
- Add a new filegroup to a database.
- Modify the properties of an existing filegroup, such as by determining whether the filegroup is read-only or read-write and which filegroup is the default.
- Remove files and filegroups from a database. These elements can be removed only when they don't contain data.

The ALTER DATABASE command is designed to make one database change at a time and has the syntax shown in Sample 4-6. The examples in the listing show how you could use ALTER DATABASE to perform key administration tasks. You can use Query Analyzer or ISQL/OSQL. Execute commands with either the Execute Command button or the *go* statement, respectively.

Sample 4-6. ALTER DATABASE Syntax and Usage

Syntax

```
ALTER DATABASE database
{ ADD FILE <filespec> [,...n] [TO FILEGROUP filegroup_name]

  | ADD LOG FILE <filespec> [,...n]

  | REMOVE FILE logical_file_name [WITH DELETE]

  | ADD FILEGROUP filegroup_name

  | REMOVE FILEGROUP filegroup_name

  | MODIFY FILE <filespec>

  | MODIFY FILEGROUP fgrp_name fgrp_property [NAME =
  new_fgrp_name]

  | SET <optionspec> [,...n] [WITH <termination]

  | COLLATE <collation_name>
}
<filespec> ::=
(NAME = logical_file_name
  [, NEWNAME = 'new_logical_name' ]
  [, FILENAME = 'os_file_name' ]
  [, SIZE = size]
  [, MAXSIZE = { max_size | UNLIMITED } ]
```

(continued)

Sample 4-6. *(continued)*
Syntax

```
[, FILEGROWTH = growth_increment ])

<optionspec> ::=

 < state_option >

 | < cursor_option >

 | < auto_option >

 | < sql_option >

 | < recovery_option >

 < state_option > ::=

   { SINGLE_USER | RESTRICTED_USER | MULTI_USER }

   | { OFFLINE | ONLINE }

   | { READ_ONLY | READ_WRITE }

 < termination > ::=

   ROLLBACK AFTER integer [ SECONDS ]

   | ROLLBACK IMMEDIATE

   | NO WAIT

 < cursor_option > ::=

   CURSOR_CLOSE_ON_COMMIT { ON | OFF }

   | {CURSOR_DEFAULT LOCAL | GLOBAL }

 < auto_option > ::=

   { AUTO_CLOSE ON | OFF }

   | { AUTO_CREATE_STATISTICS ON | OFF }

   | { AUTO_SHRINK ON | OFF }

   | { AUTO_UPDATE_STATISTICS ON | OFF }

 < sql_option > ::=

   ANSI_NULL_DEFAULT { ON | OFF }

   | ANSI_NULLS { ON | OFF }

   | ANSI_PADDING { ON | OFF }

   | ANSI_WARNINGS { ON | OFF }
```

(continued)

Sample 4-6. *(continued)*
Syntax

```
| ARITHABORT { ON | OFF }
| CONCAT_NULL_YIELDS_NULL { ON | OFF }
| NUMERIC_ROUNDABORT { ON | OFF }
| QUOTED_IDENTIFIER { ON | OFF }
| RECURSIVE_TRIGGERS { ON | OFF }

< recovery_option > ::=
RECOVERY { FULL | BULK_LOGGED | SIMPLE }
| TORN_PAGE_DETECTION { ON | OFF }
```

Usage: Adding a File to a Database

```
ALTER DATABASE Customer
ADD FILE
( NAME = Customerdata2,
  FILENAME = 'c:\mssql\data\customerdat2.ndf',
  SIZE = 10MB,
  MAXSIZE = 500MB,
  FILEGROWTH = 5MB )
```

Usage: Adding a Filegroup

```
ALTER DATABASE Customer
ADD FILEGROUP Secondary
```

Usage: Adding Files and Placing Them in a Filegroup

```
ALTER DATABASE Customer
ADD FILE
( NAME = Customerdata3,
  FILENAME = 'c:\mssql\data\customerdat3.ndf',
  SIZE = 10MB,
  MAXSIZE = UNLIMITED,
  FILEGROWTH = 5MB),
( NAME = Customerdata4,
  FILENAME = 'c:\mssql\data\customerdat4.ndf',
```

(continued)

Sample 4-6. *(continued)*

Usage: Adding Files and Placing Them in a Filegroup

```
  SIZE = 10MB,
  MAXSIZE = UNLIMITED,
  FILEGROWTH = 5MB)
TO FILEGROUP Secondary
```

Usage: Setting the Default Filegroup

```
ALTER DATABASE Customer
MODIFY FILEGROUP Secondary DEFAULT
```

Usage: Modifying a File

```
ALTER DATABASE Customer
MODIFY FILE
(NAME = Customerdata3,
  SIZE = 20MB)
```

Usage: Removing a File from a Database

```
USE Customer
DBCC SHRINKFILE (Customerdata3, EMPTYFILE)

ALTER DATABASE Customer
REMOVE FILE Customerdata3
```

 Note The EMPTYFILE option of DBCC SHRINKFILE empties a file by moving its data to other files in the same filegroup. You can then use the REMOVE FILE option of ALTER DATABASE to delete the file.

Tips and Techniques

All great administrators have a few tricks up their sleeves to help manage databases more efficiently and to keep things running smoothly. Here are a few tricks to keep in mind.

Moving and Resizing tempdb

The tempdb database contains temporary tables created by users or by SQL Server, or both. Unlike in previous versions of SQL Server, you can't put tempdb in memory, and SQL Server 2000 doesn't store complete transactions for temporary tables either. With temporary tables, SQL Server 2000 stores only enough information to roll back a transaction and not enough to redo a transaction.

The tempdb database is created each time you start the SQL Server service, which ensures that the database starts clean. As with other databases, the default structure of tempdb is based on the model database. This means that each time you start SQL Server, a snapshot is taken of the current model database and applied to tempdb.

By default, the tempdb primary data file has a size of 8 MB and is set to automatically grow the database by 10 percent when necessary. On a busy server, this 8 MB can fill up quickly, and as a result the server may need to frequently expand tempdb. Unfortunately, when tempdb is being expanded, SQL Server locks the database. This can slow down queries and make the server seem unresponsive. To improve the performance of tempdb, you can do a couple of things:

- Permanently expand tempdb to accommodate space needs during busy periods. To do this, follow the steps described in the section of this chapter entitled "Expanding Databases and Logs Manually." Even if the model database is smaller, tempdb will retain this new size.

- By default, tempdb is stored in the same location as other data. Unfortunately, you can't move a system database, but you can create a secondary data file for tempdb and put this file on its own drive.

Creating Secondary Data and Log Files

Secondary data and log files can improve the performance of busy databases and can help make large databases easier to manage. One occasion to create secondary files is when you want to distribute the load over several drives. For example, you could place the primary file on drive D, secondary files on drive E, and transaction logs on drive F. See the section of Chapter 1 entitled "SQL Server 2000 and Your Hardware" for more tips on drives and RAID arrays.

Another reason to create secondary files is to make it easier to restore a large database. For example, if you have a 10 GB database in a single file, you can restore the database only on a 10 GB drive, which you may not have at 3 A.M. on a Tuesday if a drive fails. Instead, create several smaller files for the database, such as five 2 GB files, and then you can restore these files to several smaller drives if necessary.

You can create secondary data or log files by completing the following steps:

1. Start Enterprise Manager and then, using the entries in the left pane, work your way down to the Databases folder.

2. Right-click the database you want to work with and from the shortcut menu, choose Properties.

3. To set a secondary data file, click the Data Files tab and then, in the Database Files area, type a new filename, location, initial size, and filegroup.

4. To set a secondary log file, click the Transaction Log tab and then, in the Transaction Log Files area, type a new filename, location, and initial size.

5. Click OK to make the changes.

Preventing Transaction Log Errors

The transaction log is essential to the smooth running of SQL Server. If the log fills up or otherwise fails, SQL Server can't process most types of queries. To ensure that the transaction log runs smoothly, you may want to use these techniques:

- To reduce the load on the transaction log, use SQL commands that aren't logged. This invalidates the transaction logs, as explained in Chapter 11.
- To ensure that the log is cleaned out periodically, set the database option Truncate Log On Checkpoint. This invalidates the transaction logs, as explained in Chapter 11.
- To prevent the log from running out of space, don't set a maximum file size but do increase the frequency of the log backup and watch the amount of free drive space closely.
- To make sure you can recover transactions, increase the permanent size of the log and increase the frequency of the log backup.

Resolving a Filegroup Is Full Error

When a data file can't be written to, you'll see a Filegroup Is Full error. This error usually occurs when the data file has reached its maximum size or you've run out of file space. To reduce the chances of this error reoccurring, you can use the following techniques:

- Don't set a maximum file size.
- Watch the amount of free drive space closely.
- Schedule data files to be compacted periodically.
- Remove unused tables, indexes, or objects.

Creating a New Database Template

The model database is used as the basis of all new databases. If you modify the options and properties of the model database, any new databases created on the server will inherit these options and properties.

Chapter 5

Microsoft SQL Server 2000 Security

Both inside and outside organizations, Microsoft SQL Server 2000 is being used more and more. Whether employees, contractors, or outside users access your databases, your job as an administrator is to manage that database access efficiently. You do this by creating user logins, configuring login permissions, and assigning roles. The permissions and roles you assign determine which actions users can perform, as well as what kinds of data they can access.

Your primary goals in managing security should be to

- Balance the user's need for access to data against your need for protection from unauthorized access to data

- Restrict database permissions so that users are less likely to execute harmful commands and procedures (whether maliciously or accidentally)

- Close off other security holes, such as those that may be caused by ordinary users being members of the Windows NT Administrators group

Note If you're working with the Personal Edition of SQL Server, the Microsoft Windows 95 or Windows 98 system hosting SQL Server can only use SQL Server logins. Thus, Windows authentication, domain user's accounts, and domain group accounts aren't available.

SQL Server 2000 Security

You control access to databases with the components of the SQL Server security model. These components include

- SQL Server authentication modes
- Server logins
- Permissions
- Roles

SQL Server 2000 Authentication Modes

The SQL Server security model has two authentication modes:

- **Windows Authentication only** Works best when the database is accessed within the organization only
- **Mixed security** Works best when outside users may access the database or when you don't use Windows domains

You configure these security modes on the server level, and they apply to all databases on the server. Keep in mind that each database server instance has a separate security architecture. This means different database server instances can have different security modes.

Windows Authentication

With Windows Authentication, you can use the user and group accounts available in the Windows domain for authentication. This lets domain users access databases without your having to provide a separate SQL Server login ID and password. The benefits of this are that domain users don't have to keep track of multiple passwords, and if they update their domain password, they don't have to change SQL Server passwords as well. However, users are still subject to all the rules of the Windows security model, and you can use this model to lock accounts, audit logins, and force users to change their passwords periodically.

When you use Windows Authentication, SQL Server automatically authenticates users based on their user account names or their group membership. If you've granted the user or the user's group access to a database, the user is automatically granted access to that database. By default, two local accounts are configured to use SQL Server. These accounts are the local Administrators group account and the local Administrator user account. (I include Administrator because it's a member of the Administrators group by default in Windows NT/2000.) Local accounts are displayed as BUILTIN\<AccountName> or COMPUTERNAME\ <AccountName> in Enterprise Manager. For example, Administrators is displayed as BUILTIN\Administrators.

 Real World Domain accounts are the best way to manage users who access the database from within the organization. Also, if you assign users to domain groups and then configure access for these groups in SQL Server, you cut down on the amount of administration you have to do. For example, if you assign users in the marketing department to a marketing group and then configure this group in SQL Server, you have only one account to manage instead of 10, 20, 50, or more. When employees leave the organization or change departments, you don't have to delete user accounts. When new employees are hired, you don't have to create new accounts either—you just make sure that they're added to the correct group in Windows NT/2000.

Mixed Security and SQL Server Logins

With mixed security, you use both Windows Authentication and SQL Server logins. SQL Server logins are primarily used by users outside the company, such as those who might access the database from the Internet. You can configure applications that access SQL Server from the Internet to use specific accounts automatically or to prompt the user for a SQL Server login ID and password.

With mixed security, SQL Server first determines whether the user is connecting using a valid SQL Server login. If the user has a valid login and has the proper password, the user connection is accepted. If the user has a valid login but has an improper password, the user connection is refused. SQL Server checks the Windows NT/2000 account information only if the user doesn't have a valid login. Here, SQL Server determines whether the Windows NT/2000 account has permission to connect to the server. If the account has permission, the connection is accepted. Otherwise, the connection is refused.

All SQL Server databases have built-in SQL Server logins with special purposes. These logins are sa, guest, and dbo, and they're discussed next under "Server Logins."

Server Logins

You configure access to SQL Server using server logins or the roles to which those logins belong, or both. Just as there are two authentication modes, there are also two kinds of server logins. You create domain logins using domain accounts, which can be domain or local user accounts, local group accounts, or universal and global domain group accounts. You create SQL Server logins by specifying a unique login ID and password. Several logins are configured by default, and these include

- The local Administrators group
- The local Administrator account
- The sa login
- The guest login (a special login configured but not automatically enabled)
- The dbo user (a special database user)

The sections that follow examine these logins.

Working with Administrators

Administrators is a local group on the database server. This group's members normally include the local Administrator user account and any other users set to administer the system locally. In SQL Server this group is granted the System Administrators (sysadmin) server role by default.

Note In Enterprise Manager, server roles are identified by full names, such as System Administrators, and regular names, such as sysadmin. When you reference server roles in procedures or Transact-SQL, you'll use the regular name, such as sysadmin. Unfortunately, SQL Server 2000 doesn't have full names for database roles, which isn't consistent with the precedent set for server roles.

Working with Administrator

Administrator is a local user account on the server. This account provides administrator privileges on the local system and you use it primarily when you install a system. If the host computer is part of a Windows domain, the Administrator account usually has domain-wide privileges as well. In SQL Server this account is granted the System Administrators server role by default.

Working with the sa Login

The sa login is the system administrator's account for SQL Server. With the new integrated and expanded security model, sa is no longer needed and is primarily provided for backward compatibility with previous SQL Server versions. As with other administrator logins, sa is granted the System Administrators server role by default. When you install SQL Server, the sa login isn't assigned a password.

To prevent unauthorized access to the server, you should set a password for this account.

 Best Practice Because the sa login is widely known to malicious users, you may want to delete or disable this account whenever possible. Instead, make System Administrators members of the System Administrators server role and have them log on using their own logins. Anyone with the System Administrators server role can then log in and administer the server. If you ever get locked out of the server, you can log on to the server locally using an account with local administrator privileges and then reset passwords or assign privileges as necessary.

Working with the Guest Login

The guest login is a special login that you can add to a database to allow anyone with a valid SQL Server login to access the database. Users who access a database by way of the guest account assume the identity of the guest user and inherit all the privileges and permissions of the guest account. For example, if you configure the domain account GOTEAM to access SQL Server, GOTEAM can access any database with a guest login, and when GOTEAM does, that person is granted all the permissions of the guest account.

By default, the guest login doesn't exist in newly created databases, but you can add it or delete it from all databases except master and tempdb. Most users access master and tempdb as guests and because of this, you can't remove the guest account from these databases. Don't worry—a guest has limited permissions and privileges in master and tempdb.

Before using the guest login, you should note the following:

- The guest login is a member of the public server role and inherits the permissions of this role.
- You must assign the guest account to a database before anyone can access it as a guest.
- The guest login is used only when a user account has access to SQL Server but doesn't have access to the database through this user account.

Working with the dbo User

The database owner, or dbo, is a special type of database user and is granted special privileges. Generally speaking, the user who created a database is the database owner. The dbo is implicitly granted all permissions on the database and can grant these permissions to other users. Because members of the System Administrators server role are mapped automatically to the special user dbo, logins with the System Administrators role can perform any tasks that a dbo can.

Objects created in SQL Server databases also have owners. These owners are referred to as the *database object owners*. Objects created by a member of the System Administrators server role belong to the dbo user automatically. Objects created by users who aren't members of the System Administrators server role belong to the user creating the object and must be qualified with the name of that user when other users reference them. For example, if GOTEAM is a member of the System Administrators server role and creates a table called Sales, Sales belongs to dbo and is qualified as dbo.Sales, or simply Sales. However, if GOTEAM isn't a member of the System Administrators server role and creates a table called Sales, Sales belongs to GOTEAM and must be qualified as GOTEAM.Sales.

Note   Technically, dbo isn't a "special login," but you may see it referred to as such. You can't log in to a server or database as dbo, but you may be the person who created the database or a set of objects in it.

Permissions

Permissions determine the actions that users can perform on SQL Server or in a database. Permissions are granted according to login ID, group memberships, and role memberships. Users must have appropriate permissions before they can perform any action that changes database definitions or accesses data. Three types of permissions are used in SQL Server:

- Object permissions
- Statement permissions
- Implicit permissions

Object Permissions

Object permissions control access to tables, views, columns, and stored procedures. You control access to these objects by granting, denying, or revoking the ability to execute particular statements or stored procedures. For example, you can grant a user the right to SELECT information from a table, but deny the right to INSERT, UPDATE, or DELETE information in the table. Table 5-1 provides a summary of object permissions.

Table 5-1. Object Permissions

Object Type	Possible Actions
Column	SELECT and UPDATE
Row	N/A (assigned at the table level as they might affect multiple columns)
Stored procedure	EXECUTE
Table	SELECT, INSERT, UPDATE, DELETE, and REFERENCES
View	SELECT, INSERT, UPDATE, and DELETE

Statement Permissions

Statement permissions control administration actions, such as creating a database or adding objects to a database. Only members of the System Administrators role and database owners can assign statement permissions. By default, normal logins aren't granted statement permissions, and you must specifically grant these permissions to logins that aren't administrators. For example, if a user needs to be able to create views in a database, you would assign permission to execute CREATE VIEW. Table 5-2 provides a summary of statement permissions that you can grant, deny, or revoke.

Table 5-2. Statement Permissions

Statement Permission	Description
CREATE DATABASE	Determines whether the login can create databases. The user must be in the master database or a member of the System Administrators server role.
CREATE DEFAULT	Determines whether the user can create a default value for a table column.
CREATE FUNCTION	Determines whether the user can create a user-defined function in the database.
CREATE PROCEDURE	Determines whether the user can create a stored procedure.
CREATE RULE	Determines whether the user can create a table column rule.
CREATE TABLE	Determines whether the user can create a table.
CREATE VIEW	Determines whether the user can create a view.
BACKUP DATABASE	Determines whether the user can back up the database.
BACKUP LOG	Determines whether the user can back up the transaction log.

Implied Permissions

Only members of predefined system roles or database/database object owners can perform implied permissions. Implied permissions for a role can't be changed or applied to other accounts (unless these accounts are made members of the role). For example, members of the System Administrators server role can perform any activity in SQL Server. They can extend databases and kill processes. You can't revoke or assign these rights to other accounts individually.

Database and database object owners also have implied permissions. These permissions allow them to perform all activities with either the database or the object they own, or with both. For example, a user who owns a table can view, add, change, and delete data. That user can also alter the table's definition and control the table's permissions.

Roles

Roles are a lot like Windows groups in that they allow you to easily assign permissions to a group of users and they can have built-in permissions (implicit permissions) that can't be changed. Two types of roles are available:

- **Server roles** Applied at the server level
- **Database roles** Applied at the database level

Server Roles

You use server roles to grant server administration capabilities. If you make a login a member of a role, users who use this login can perform any tasks permitted by the role. For example, members of the System Administrators role have the highest level of permissions on SQL Server and can perform any type of task.

You set server roles at the server level and you predefine them. This means that these permissions affect the entire server and you can't change the permission set. The list items that follow provide a summary of each server role from the lowest-level role (Database Creators) to the highest-level role (System Administrators).

- **Bulk Insert Administrators (bulkadmin)** Designed for domain accounts that need to perform bulk inserts into the database. Members of this role can add members to bulkadmin and execute the BULK INSERT command.
- **Database Creators (dbcreator)** Designed for users who need to create, modify, and drop databases. Members of this role can add members to dbcreator and perform these tasks: ALTER DATABASE, CREATE DATABASE, DROP DATABASE, EXTEND DATABASE, RESTORE DATABASE, RESTORE LOG, and *sp_renamedb*.
- **Disk Administrators (diskadmin)** Designed for users who need to manage disk files. Members of this role can add members to diskadmin and perform these tasks: DISK INIT, *sp_addumpdevice*, *sp_diskdefault*, and *sp_dropdevice*.

- **Process Administrators (processadmin)** Designed for users who need to control SQL Server processes. Members of this role can add members to processadmin and kill processes.

- **Security Administrators (securityadmin)** Designed for users who need to manage logins, create database permissions, and read error logs. Members of this role can add members to securityadmin; grant, deny, and revoke CREATE DATABASE; and read the error logs. In addition, they can also perform these tasks: *sp_addlinkedsrvlogin, sp_addlogin, sp_defaultdb, sp_defaultlanguage, sp_denylogin, sp_droplinkedsrvlogin, sp_droplogin, sp_grantlogin, sp_helplogins, sp_remoteoption,* and *sp_revokelogin.*

- **Server Administrators (serveradmin)** Designed for users who need to set server-wide configuration options and shut down the server. Members of this role can add members to serveradmin and perform these other tasks: DBCC FREEPROCCACHE, RECONFIGURE, SHUTDOWN, *sp_configure, sp_fulltext_service,* and *sp_tableoption.*

- **Setup Administrators (setupadmin)** Designed for users who need to manage linked servers and control startup procedures. Members of this role can add members to setupadmin; add, drop, and configure linked servers; and control startup procedures.

- **System Administrators (sysadmin)** Designed for users who need complete control over SQL Server and installed databases. Members of this role can perform any activity in SQL Server.

Database Roles

When you want to assign permissions at the database level, you can use database roles. You set database roles on a per database basis, which means that each database has its own set of roles. SQL Server 2000 supports three types of database roles:

- User-defined standard roles
- User-defined application roles
- Predefined (or fixed) database roles

Standard roles allow you to create roles with unique permissions and privileges. You can use standard roles to logically group users together and then assign a single permission to the role rather than having to assign permissions to each user separately. For example, you could create a role called Users that allows users to SELECT, INSERT, and UPDATE specific tables in the database but doesn't allow them to perform any other tasks.

Application roles allow you to create password-protected roles for specific applications. For example, a user could connect through a Web-based application called NetReady; this application would activate the role and the user would then gain the role's permissions and privileges. User or other roles can't be assigned to an application role. Instead, the application role is activated when the application connects to the database.

SQL Server also has predefined database roles. Predefined roles are built in and have permissions that can't be changed. You use predefined roles to assign database administration privileges, and you can assign a single login to multiple roles. These privileges are summarized in the list items that follow.

- **public**   The default role for all database users. Users inherit the permissions and privileges of the public role and this role represents their minimum permissions and privileges. Any roles that you assign to a user, beyond the public role, add permissions and privileges. If you want all database users to have specific permissions, assign the permissions to the public role.

- **db_accessadmin**   Designed for users who need to add or remove logins in a database. Members of this role can perform these tasks on the selected database: *sp_addalias*, *sp_adduser*, *sp_dropalias*, *sp_dropuser*, *sp_grantdbaccess*, and *sp_revokedbaccess*.

- **db_backupoperator**   Designed for users who need to back up a database. Members of this role can perform these tasks on the selected database: BACKUP DATABASE, BACKUP LOG, CHECKPOINT, DBCC CHECKALLOC, DBCC CHECKCATALOG, DBCC CHECKDB, DBCC TEXTALL, DBCC TEXTALLOC, and DBCC UPDATEUSAGE.

- **db_datareader**   Designed for users who need to view data in a database. Members of this role can select all data from any user table in the database.

- **db_datawriter**   Designed for users who need to modify any data in any user table in the database. Members of this role can perform these tasks on any objects in the selected database: DELETE, INSERT, and UPDATE.

- **db_ddladmin**   Designed for users who need to perform tasks related to SQL Server's data definition language (DDL). Members of this role can issue any DDL statement except for GRANT, REVOKE, or DENY. Members can also perform these tasks in the selected database: REFERENCES, *sp_changeobjectowner*, *sp_procoption*, *sp_recompile*, *sp_rename*, and *sp_tableoption*.

- **db_denydatareader**   Designed to restrict access to data in a database by login. Members of this role can deny or revoke Select permissions on any object in the database.

- **db_denydatawriter**   Designed to restrict modifications permissions in a database by login. Members of this role can deny or revoke INSERT, UPDATE, and DELETE permissions on any object in the database.

- **db_securityadmin**   Designed for users who need to manage permissions, object ownership, and roles. Members of this role can perform any of the following tasks in the selected database: DENY, GRANT, REVOKE, *sp_addapprole*, *sp_addrole*, *sp_addrolemember*, *sp_approlepassword*, *sp_changeobjectowner*, *sp_dropapprole*, *sp_droprole*, and *sp_droprolemember*.

- **db_owner**   Designed for users who need complete control over all aspects of the database. Members of this role can assign permissions, modify database settings, perform database maintenance, and perform any other administration task on the database.

Managing Server Logins

SQL Server can use Windows domain logins as well as SQL Server's own logins. If you've configured the server for mixed security, you can use both login types. Otherwise, you can use only Windows domain logins.

Viewing and Editing Existing Logins

To view or edit an existing login, follow these steps:

1. Start Enterprise Manager and then access the server you want to work with.

2. In the server's Security folder, select the Logins entry in the left pane. The right pane now displays the current logins, as shown in Figure 5-1. From this information you can learn the following:

   - **Name** The login name.

   - **Type** The login type, which is Standard for SQL Server logins, Windows User for domain user accounts, and Windows Group for domain group accounts.

   - **Server Access** The type of access permission the user has to the server. Permit means the user can access the server. Deny means the user can't access the server.

   - **Default Database** The default database for the user.

   - **Default Language** The default language for the user.

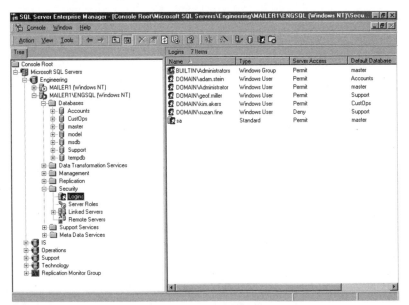

Figure 5-1. *Select the Logins entry in the Security folder to display current logins in the right pane.*

3. To view server role and database access permissions for a user, double-click the user's entry in the right pane. This opens the SQL Server Login Properties dialog box.

4. You can now edit the properties for this account using the fields of the General, Server Roles, and Database Access tabs.

To view a login with Transact-SQL, use *sp_helplogins*. The syntax and usage for this command is shown as Sample 5-1.

Sample 5-1. *sp_helplogins* **Syntax and Usage**

Syntax

```
sp_helplogins [[@LoginNamePattern =] 'login']
```

Usage

```
EXEC sp_helplogins 'goteam'
```

Creating Logins

You create new logins in Enterprise Manager by using either the Create Login Wizard or the Login Properties dialog box. Because the steps are almost identical with either method, I'll focus on the Login Properties dialog box and let you apply these techniques to the Create Login Wizard dialog boxes if you'd rather use the wizard.

To access the wizard, select the Security folder in Enterprise Manager, and then from the Tools menu, choose Wizards. This displays the Select Wizard dialog box. Click the plus sign next to Database and double-click Create Login Wizard.

Tip If you want to use Windows domain user or group accounts, you must create these accounts in the Windows domain and then create the related SQL Server logins. Ask a domain administrator to set up the necessary accounts.

To create a SQL Server login, follow these steps:

1. Start Enterprise Manager and then access the server you want to work with.

2. In the server's Security folder, right-click the Logins entry and select New Login. This opens the SQL Server Login Properties dialog box shown in Figure 5-2.

Figure 5-2. *To create new logins, you can use the SQL Server Login Proper-ties dialog box or the Create Login Wizard.*

3. In the Name field, type the name of the account you want to use, such as Sales or WRSTANEK.

4. If you're creating a login for a domain account, select the Windows Authentication option button and then use the Domain combo box to select the domain you want to use. You can also type the domain name into the combo box. The domain name should now appear in the Name field.

5. If you want to create a new SQL Server login, select the SQL Server Authentication option button and then enter the SQL Server password for the login.

6. Specify the default database and default language for the login. Assigning a default database doesn't give the login permission to access the database. Instead, it merely specifies the database that's used when no database is specified in a command.

7. Click OK to create the login. If you're creating a SQL Server login, confirm the password by reentering it when prompted.

8. You haven't assigned any roles or access permissions. Refer to the sections later in this chapter entitled "Configuring Server Roles" and "Controlling Database Access and Administration" to learn how to configure these options.

You can also create logins with Transact-SQL. To create a login for a domain account, use *sp_grantlogin,* as shown in Sample 5-2.

Sample 5-2. *sp_grantlogin* **Syntax and Usage**

Syntax

```
sp_grantlogin [@loginame =] 'login'
```

Usage

```
EXEC sp_grantlogin 'GALAXY\Sales'
```

To create a new SQL Server login, use *sp_addlogin,* as shown in Sample 5-3.

Sample 5-3. *sp_addlogin* **Syntax and Usage**

Syntax

```
sp_addlogin [@loginame =] 'login'
  [,[@passwd =] 'password']
  [,[@defdb =] 'database']
  [,[@deflanguage =] 'language']
  [,[@sid =] 'sid']
  [,[@encryptopt =] 'encryption_option']
```

Usage

```
EXEC sp_addlogin 'webtr', 'webtester', 'Customer', 'us_english'.
```

Note Although *sp_grantlogin* and *sp_addlogin* allow users to connect to SQL Server, the logins can't access databases. To configure database access, you need to run *sp_grantdbaccess* for each database the login needs access to. For details, see the section of this chapter entitled "Controlling Database Access and Administration."

Granting or Denying Server Access

When you create a new login or modify an existing login based on a Windows account, you can explicitly grant or deny access to the server for this login. Explicitly denying access to the server is useful when a particular Windows account should be temporarily restricted from accessing the server.

To grant or deny access for an existing login, complete the following steps:

1. Start Enterprise Manager and then access the server you want to work with.
2. In the server's Security folder, select the Logins entry in the left pane.
3. In the right pane, double-click the account you want to work with. This opens the SQL Server Login Properties dialog box shown previously in Figure 5-2.
4. To grant access to the server, select the Grant Access option button.
5. To deny access to the server, select the Deny Access option button.

Note Denying access to the server doesn't prevent users from logging in to SQL Server. Instead, it prevents them from using their Windows domain account to log in. Users can still log in if they have a valid SQL Server login ID and password.

6. Click OK.

You can also grant or deny logins with Transact-SQL. To grant a login for a domain account, use *sp_grantlogin*, as shown in Sample 5-4.

Sample 5-4. *sp_grantlogin* **Syntax and Usage**

Syntax

```
sp_grantlogin [@loginame =] 'login'
```

Usage

```
EXEC sp_grantlogin 'GALAXY\WRSTANEK'
```

To deny access to the server for the account, use *sp_denylogin* as shown in Sample 5-5.

Sample 5-5. *sp_denylogin* **Syntax and Usage**

Syntax

```
sp_denylogin [@loginame =] 'login'
```

Usage

```
EXEC sp_denylogin ' GALAXY\WRSTANEK '
```

Removing Logins

When a user leaves the organization or a login is otherwise not needed, you should remove the login from SQL Server. To do this, do the following:

1. Start Enterprise Manager and then access the server you want to work with.

2. In the server's Security folder, select the Logins entry in the left pane.

3. Right-click the login you want to remove and then from the shortcut menu, choose Delete.

4. When prompted, choose Yes to confirm that you want to delete the login.

The stored procedures that you use to delete SQL Server logins are *sp_revokelogin* and *sp_droplogin*. Use *sp_revokelogin* to delete Windows user and group accounts, as shown in Sample 5-6.

Sample 5-6. *sp_revokelogin* **Syntax and Usage**

Syntax

```
sp_revokelogin [@loginame =] 'login'
```

(continued)

Sample 5-6. *(continued)*

Usage

```
EXEC sp_revokelogin  ' GALAXY\WRSTANEK '
```

Use *sp_droplogin* to remove a SQL Server login as shown in Sample 5-7.

Sample 5-7. *sp_droplogin* **Syntax and Usage**

Syntax

```
sp_droplogin [@loginame =] 'login'
```

Usage

```
EXEC sp_droplogin 'TempUser'
```

Changing Passwords

You manage Windows user and group accounts in the Windows domain. Users can change their own passwords or ask the Windows administrator to reset their passwords, if necessary. For SQL Server logins, you change passwords through Enterprise Manager using the following steps:

1. Start Enterprise Manager and then access the server you want to work with.

2. In the server's Security folder, select the Logins entry in the left pane.

3. Double-click the login you want to change. This opens the SQL Server Login Properties dialog box.

4. Type the new password in the Password field and then click OK.

5. When prompted, reenter the password to confirm it and then click OK.

To change passwords with Transact-SQL, use *sp_password*, as shown in Sample 5-8.

Sample 5-8. *sp_password* **Syntax and Usage**

Syntax

```
sp_password [[@old =] 'old_password',]
{[@new =] 'new_password'}
[,[@loginame =] 'login']
```

Usage

```
EXEC sp_password 'changeme' 'h4rt5' 'GOTEAM'
```

Configuring Server Roles

Server roles set server-wide administrator privileges for SQL Server logins. You can manage server roles by role or by individual logins.

Assigning Roles by Login

To assign or change server roles for a login, follow these steps:

1. Start Enterprise Manager and then access the server you want to work with.
2. In the server's Security folder, select the Logins entry in the left pane.
3. Double-click the login you want to configure. This opens the SQL Server Login Properties dialog box.
4. Click the Server Roles tab, as shown in Figure 5-3.
5. Grant server roles by selecting the check boxes next to the roles you want to use. Server roles are discussed in the section entitled "Server Roles."
6. When you're finished configuring server roles, click OK.

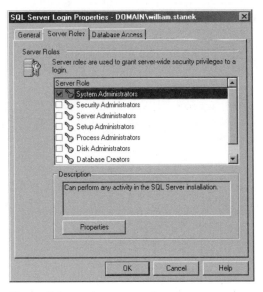

Figure 5-3. *In the Server Roles tab, you grant server roles by selecting the check boxes next to the roles you want to use.*

You can also configure server roles with Transact-SQL. The *sp_addsrvrolemember* stored procedure adds a login to a server role, and you can use it as shown in Sample 5-9.

Sample 5-9. *sp_addsrvrolemember* **Syntax and Usage**

Syntax

```
sp_addsrvrolemember [@loginame =] 'login', [@rolename =] 'role'
```

Usage

```
EXEC sp_addsrvrolemember 'GALAXY\WRSTANEK' 'sysadmin'
```

The *sp_dropsrvrolemember* stored procedure removes a login from a role and you can use it as shown in Sample 5-10.

Sample 5-10. *sp_dropsrvrolemember* **Syntax and Usage**

Syntax

```
sp_dropsrvrolemember [@loginame =] 'login', [@rolename =] 'role'
```

Usage

```
EXEC sp_dropsrvrolemember 'GALAXY\WRSTANEK' 'sysadmin'
```

Assigning Roles to Multiple Logins

The easiest way to assign roles to multiple logins is to use the Server Roles Properties dialog box. To access this dialog box and configure multiple logins, follow these steps:

1. Start Enterprise Manager and then access the server you want to work with.
2. In the server's Security folder, select the Server Role entry in the left pane.
3. In the right pane, double-click the server role you want to configure. This opens the Server Role Properties dialog box shown in Figure 5-4.
4. To add logins, click Add, and then in the Add Members dialog box, select the logins to add. Multiple logins can be selected by holding down Ctrl or Shift as you click login names.

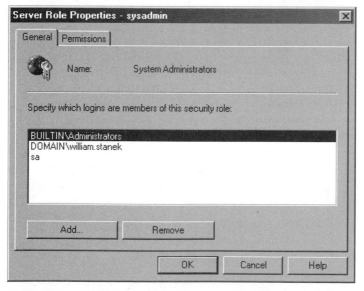

Figure 5-4. *The Server Role Properties dialog box lets you configure multiple logins to use a particular server role.*

5. To remove a login, select a login and then click Remove.

6. Click the Permissions tab to see the permissions associated with this server role.

7. When you're finished configuring server roles, click OK.

Controlling Database Access and Administration

You control database access and administration with database users and roles. Database users are the logins that have the right to access the database. Database access roles set administration privileges and other database permissions.

Assigning Access and Roles by Login

For individual logins, you can grant access to databases and assign roles as follows:

1. Start Enterprise Manager and then access the server you want to work with.

2. In the server's Security folder, select the Logins entry in the left pane.

3. Double-click the login you want to configure. This opens the SQL Server Login Properties dialog box.

4. Click the Database Access tab, as shown in Figure 5-5.

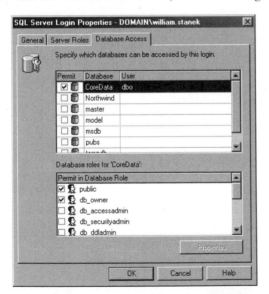

Figure 5-5. *Use the Database Access tab to grant database access, and then select roles the user should have on the currently selected database.*

5. Select the check box for a database that the login should have access to. Then, in the Permit In Database Role list box, select the check boxes next to the database roles that this login should have on the currently selected database.

6. Repeat step 5 for other databases the login should have access to.

7. When you're finished configuring database roles, click OK.

Assigning Roles for Multiple Logins

At the database level, you can assign database roles to multiple logins. To do this, complete the following steps:

1. Start Enterprise Manager and then, using the entries in the left pane, work your way down to the Databases folder.

2. In the Databases folder, click the plus sign (+) next to the database you want to work with.

3. In the left pane, select Roles to display a list of database roles in the right pane.

4. Double-click the role you want to configure. This opens the Database Role Properties dialog box shown in Figure 5-6.

5. To add role members, click Add. Then, in the Add Role Members dialog box, select the logins you want to add. You can select multiple logins by holding down Ctrl or Shift as you click login names.

6. To remove a role member, select a login and then choose Remove.

7. When you're finished configuring database roles, click OK.

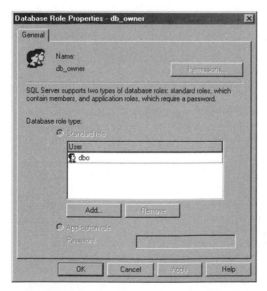

Figure 5-6. *The Database Role Properties dialog box lets you configure multiple logins to use a particular database role.*

Creating Standard Database Roles

Although predefined roles have a specific set of permissions that you can't change, you can set permissions for roles you create for a particular database. For example, suppose that a database has three different types of users: normal users who need to view data, managers who need to be able to modify data, and developers who need to be able to modify database objects. In that case you can create three roles to handle these user types. Then you need to manage only these roles and not the many different user accounts.

To create a standard database role, complete the following steps:

1. Start Enterprise Manager and then work your way down to the Databases folder using the entries in the left pane.

2. In the Databases folder, click the plus sign (+) next to the database you want to work with.

3. Right-click Roles and then from the shortcut menu, choose New Database Role. This opens the Database Role Properties dialog box shown in Figure 5-7.

4. Type a name for the role in the Name field.

 Tip Use a name that's short but descriptive, such as Normal Users, Editors, or Testers and Developers.

Figure 5-7. *When you create a database role, you can edit the Name field but you can't configure permissions until after you create the role.*

5. Select the Standard Role option button.

6. To add role members, click Add. Then, in the Add Role Members dialog box, select the logins to add. You can select multiple logins by holding down Ctrl or Shift as you click login names.

7. Click OK.

8. Enterprise Manager's right pane should display the new role. Double-click its entry to reopen the Database Role Properties dialog box.

9. Click Permissions and then use the Permissions tab to configure database access permissions for this role. For more information, see the section of this chapter entitled "Managing Database Permissions."

Creating Application Database Roles

Application roles are designed to be used by applications that access the database and don't have logins associated with them. You can configure an application role by completing the following steps:

1. Start Enterprise Manager and then, using the entries in the left pane, work your way down to the Databases folder.

2. In the Databases folder, click the plus sign (+) next to the database you want to work with.

3. Right-click Roles and then from the shortcut menu, choose New Database Role. This opens the Database Role Properties dialog box shown previously in Figure 5-7.

4. Type a name for the role in the Name field.

5. Select the Application Role option button and then type a password for this role in the Password field. You won't be asked to confirm this password.

6. Click OK.

7. Enterprise Manager's right pane should display the new role. Double-click its entry to reopen the Database Role Properties dialog box.

8. Click Permissions and then use the Permissions tab to configure database access permissions for this role. For more information, see the section of this chapter entitled "Managing Database Permissions."

Revoking Access Rights and Roles by Login

To revoke access rights or to remove a user from a role in a database, complete the following steps:

1. Start Enterprise Manager and then work your way down to the Security folder using the entries in the left pane.

2. In the Security folder, select the Logins entry in the left pane.

3. Double-click the login you want to configure. This opens the SQL Server Login Properties dialog box.

4. Click the Database Access tab.

5. Clear the check box for a database that the login should not have access to. Then, in the Permit In Database Role list box, clear the check boxes next to the database roles that this login should not have on the currently selected database.

6. Repeat step 5 for other databases the login should not have access to or rights on.

7. When you're finished, click OK.

Deleting User-Defined Roles

To delete a user-defined role, complete the following steps:

1. Start Enterprise Manager and then work your way down to the Databases folder using the entries in the left pane.

2. In the Databases folder, click the plus sign (+) next to the database you want to work with.

3. In the left pane, click Roles.

4. Select the role you want to delete and then press the Delete key.

5. When prompted, choose Yes to confirm that you want to delete the role.

 Note User-defined roles cannot be deleted if they have members. Edit the properties for the role, deleting any currently listed members, and then delete the role.

Transact-SQL Commands for Managing Access and Roles

SQL Server provides different commands for managing database access and roles. These commands are summarized in Sample 5-11.

Sample 5-11. Commands for Managing Database Access and Roles

Database Access

```
sp_grantdbaccess [@loginame =] 'login'

  [,[@name_in_db =] 'name_in_db' [OUTPUT]]

sp_revokedbaccess [@name_in_db =] 'name'
```

Predefined Roles

```
sp_dbfixedrolepermission [[@rolename =] 'role']
```

Database Standard Roles

```
sp_addrole [@rolename =] 'role' [,[@ownername =] 'owner']
```

(continued)

Sample 5-11. *(continued)*

Database Standard Roles

```
sp_droprole [@rolename =] 'role

sp_helprole [[@rolename =] 'role']
```

Database Role Members

```
sp_addrolemember [@rolename =] 'role',

 [@membername =] 'security_account'

sp_droprolemember [@rolename =] 'role',

 [@membername =] 'security_account'

sp_helprolemember [[@rolename =] 'role']
```

Application Roles

```
sp_addapprole [@rolename =] 'role', [@password =] 'password'

sp_dropapprole [@rolename =] 'role'

sp_setapprole [@rolename =] 'role' ,

 [@password =] {Encrypt N 'password'} | 'password'

 [.[@encrypt =] 'encrypt_style']
```

Managing Database Permissions

You can assign database permissions by the database owner, members of sysadmin, and members of securityadmin. The available permissions include

- **Grant**   Gives permission to perform the related task. With roles, all members of the role inherit the permission.

- **Revoke**   Removes prior grant permission but doesn't explicitly prevent a user or role from performing a task. A user or role could still inherit grant permission from another role.

- **Deny**   Explicitly denies permission to perform a task and prevents the user or role from inheriting the permission. Deny takes precedence over all other grant permissions.

Note   Deny is a Transact-SQL command and isn't part of the ANSI SQL-92 standard.

You can assign grant, deny, and revoke permissions at the database level or the object level. You can also assign permissions using database roles. For more information, see the section of this chapter entitled "Controlling Database Access and Administration."

Assigning Database Permissions for Statements

At the database level, you can grant, revoke, or deny permission to execute data definition language statements, such as CREATE TABLE or BACKUP DATABASE. These statements were previously summarized in Table 5-2.

In Enterprise Manager, you grant, revoke, or deny database permissions for statements by completing the following steps:

1. Work your way down to the Databases folder using the entries in the left pane.

2. Right-click the database you want to work with and then from the shortcut menu, choose Properties.

3. Click the Permissions tab, as shown in Figure 5-8.

4. To assign default permissions for all users, assign permissions to the public role. To assign permissions for individual users or roles, click the entries to the right of the User/Role name. A check mark grants permission. A red X denies permission. Clear a check mark to revoke permission.

5. Click OK to assign the permissions.

With Transact-SQL, you use the GRANT, REVOKE, and DENY commands to assign permissions. Sample 5-12 shows the syntax and usage of GRANT, Sample 5-13 shows the syntax and usage of REVOKE, and Sample 5-14 shows the syntax and usage of DENY.

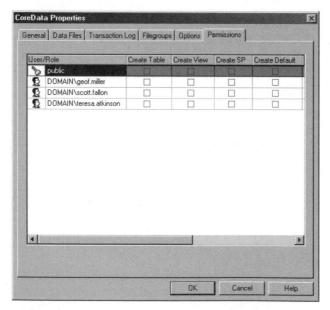

Figure 5-8. *The Permissions tab lets you assign statement permissions at the database level. The key icon indicates a role. The person icon indicates a user.*

Sample 5-12. GRANT Syntax and Usage

Syntax

```
GRANT {ALL | statement[,...n]}
TO security_account[,...n]


GRANT
  {ALL [PRIVILEGES] | permission[,...n]}
  {
    [(column[,...n])] ON {table | view}
    | ON {table | view}[(column[,...n])]
    | ON {stored_procedure | extended_procedure}
  }
TO security_account[,...n]
[WITH GRANT OPTION]
[AS {group | role}]
```

Usage

```
GRANT CREATE DATABASE, CREATE TABLE
TO Users, [GALAXY\Sales]


GRANT SELECT
ON customer..customers
TO public


GRANT INSERT, UPDATE, DELETE
ON customer..customers
TO Devs, Testers
```

Sample 5-13. REVOKE Syntax and Usage

Syntax

```
REVOKE {ALL | statement[,...n]}
FROM security_account[,...n]

REVOKE [GRANT OPTION FOR]
  {ALL [PRIVILEGES] | permission[,...n]}
  {
    [(column[,...n])] ON {table | view}
    | ON {table | view}[(column[,...n])]
    | {stored_procedure | extended_procedure}
  }
{TO | FROM}
  security_account[,...n]
[CASCADE]
[AS {group | role}]
```

Usage

```
REVOKE CREATE TABLE, CREATE DEFAULT
FROM Devs, Testers


REVOKE INSERT, UPDATE, DELETE
FROM Users, [GALAXY\Sales]
```

Sample 5-14. DENY Syntax and Usage

Syntax

```
DENY{ALL | statement[,...n]}
TO security_account[,...n]

DENY
  {ALL [PRIVILEGES] | permission[,...n]}
  {
```

(continued)

Sample 5-14. *(continued)*

Syntax

```
  [(column[,...n])] ON {table | view}
  | ON {table | view}[(column[,...n])]
  | ON {stored_procedure | extended_procedure}
}
TO security_account[,...n]
[CASCADE]
```

Usage

```
DENY CREATE TABLE
  TO Devs, Testers


DENY INSERT, UPDATE, DELETE
  ON customer..customers
  TO Users, [GALAXY\Sales]
```

Object Permissions by Login

Object permissions apply to tables, views, and stored procedures. Permissions you assign to these objects include SELECT, INSERT, UPDATE, and DELETE. A summary of permitted actions by object was listed previously in Table 5-1.

In Enterprise Manager, you grant, revoke, or deny object permissions by completing the following steps:

1. Work your way down to the Databases folder using the entries in the left pane.

2. Click the plus sign (+) next to the database you want to work with and then select Users.

3. In the right pane, you should see a list of database users. Double-click the user you want to configure. This opens the Database User Properties dialog box.

4. Click Permissions to display the Permissions tab, as shown in Figure 5-9.

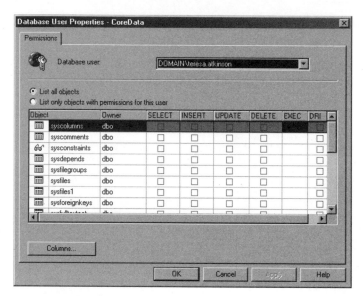

Figure 5-9. *Use the Permissions tab to assign object permissions. An eyeglasses icon indicates a view. A table icon indicates a table. An icon with the wavy blue lines indicates a stored procedure.*

5. To assign object permissions, select the List All Objects option button. You use the entries to the right of the Object and Owner names to assign permissions. A check mark grants permission. A red X denies permission. Clear a check mark to revoke permission.

6. Click Apply or OK to assign the permissions.

Object Permissions for Multiple Logins

You can also assign permission by object and in this way assign object permissions for multiple logins. To do this, complete the following steps:

1. Start Enterprise Manager and using the entries in the left pane, work your way down to the Databases folder.

2. Click the plus sign (+) next to the database you want to work with and then select the type of objects you want to work with, either Tables, Views, or Stored Procedures.

3. In the right pane, double-click the table, view, or stored procedure you want to configure. This opens a Properties dialog box.

4. In the Properties dialog box, click Permissions. This opens the Object Properties dialog box shown in Figure 5-10.

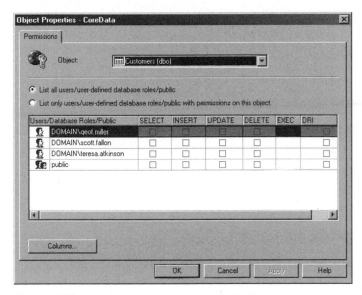

Figure 5-10. *Use the Object Properties dialog box to assign permissions by object rather than by login or role.*

5. To assign permissions for logins, select the List All Users option button. You use the entries to the right of the User/Database Roles/Public names column to assign permissions. A check mark grants permission. A red X denies permission. Clear a check mark to revoke permission.

Transact-SQL commands for assigning permissions were listed previously in the section of this chapter entitled "Assigning Database Permissions for Statements."

Part III

Microsoft SQL Server 2000 Data Administration

This part of the book covers Microsoft SQL Server 2000 data administration. Chapter 6 discusses techniques for managing tables, indexes,
and views. You'll also find tips for working with constraints and rules. In
Chapter 7 you'll learn about importing and exporting data. Chapter 8
focuses on integrating SQL Server databases with other SQL Server
databases and with other data sources. You'll find detailed discussions
on distributed queries, distributed transactions, Distributed Transaction
Coordinator, and linking remote servers. Chapter 9 explores data replication. You'll learn all about the latest replication techniques, including
merge replication and immediately updating subscribers.

Chapter 6
Manipulating Tables, Indexes, and Views

In Microsoft SQL Server 2000, the structures of tables and indexes are just as important as the database itself, especially when it comes to performance. Tables are collections of data about a specific entity, such as a customer or an order. To describe the attributes of these entities, you use named columns. For example, to describe the attributes of a customer, you could use these columns: cust_name, cust_address, and cust_phone.

Each instance of data in a table is represented as a single data entry or row. Typically, rows are unique and have unique identifiers called *primary keys* associated with them. However, a primary key isn't mandatory in ANSI SQL, and it isn't required in SQL Server. The job of the primary key is to set a unique identifier for each row in the table and to allow SQL Server to create a unique index on this key. Indexes are user-defined data structures that provide fast access to data when you search on an indexed column. Indexes are separate from tables, and you can configure them automatically with the Index Tuning Wizard.

Most tables are related to other tables. For example, a Customers table may have a cust_account column that contains a customer's account number. The cust_account column may also appear in tables named Orders and Receivables. If the cust_account column is the primary key of the Customers table, a foreign key relationship can be established between Customers and Orders as well as between Customers and Receivables. The foreign key creates a link between the tables that you can use to preserve referential integrity in the database.

Once you've established the link, you won't be able to delete a row in the Customers table if the cust_account identifier is referenced in the Orders or Receivables tables. This feature prevents you from invalidating references to information used in other tables. You would first need to delete or change the related references in the Orders or Receivables tables, or both, before deleting a primary key row in the Customers table. Foreign key relationships allow you to combine data from related tables in queries by matching the foreign key constraint of one table with the primary or unique key in another table. Combining tables in this manner is called a *table join*, and the keys allow SQL Server to optimize the query and quickly find related data.

Table Essentials

Tables are defined as objects in SQL Server databases. Tables consist of columns and rows of data, with each column having a native or user-defined data type. Tables have two units of data storage: data pages and extents. Data pages are the fundamental units of data storage. Extents are the basic units in which space is allocated to tables and indexes.

Understanding Data Pages

For all data types except *text*, *ntext*, and *image*, table data is stored in data pages that have a fixed size of 8 KB (8192 bytes). Each data page has a page header, data rows, and free space that can contain row offsets. The page header uses the first 96 bytes of each page, leaving 8096 bytes for data and row offsets. Row offsets indicate the logical order of rows on a page, which means that offset 0 refers to the first row in the index, offset 1 refers to the second row, and so on. If a table contains text and image data, the text or image may not be stored with the rest of the data for a row. Instead, SQL Server can store a 16-byte pointer to the actual data, which is stored in a collection of 8 KB pages that aren't necessarily written contiguously.

SQL Server 2000 supports six types of data pages:

- **Data**   Contain data rows with all data (except for *text*, *ntext*, and *image* data)
- **Index**   Contain index entries
- **Global Allocation Map**   Contain information about extents that have been allocated by SQL Server
- **Index Allocation Map**   Contain information about extents used by a table or index
- **Page Free Space**   Contain information about free space available in data pages
- **Text/Image**   (Binary Large Object BLOB) Contain *text*, *ntext*, and *image* data

Within data pages, SQL Server stores data in rows. Data rows don't normally span more than one page. The maximum size of a single data row is 8096 bytes (including any necessary overhead). Effectively, this means the maximum size of character columns is 8000 bytes and that columns can store up to 8000 ASCII characters or up to 4000 Unicode characters. Individual *text*, *ntext*, and *image* data values can be up to 2 GB in size, which is too large to be stored in a single data row. With *text*, *ntext*, and *image* data, data is stored in a collection of 8 KB pages, which may or may not be contiguously stored.

While collections of pages are ideal for large *text*, *ntext*, and *image* data, this storage mechanism isn't ideal when the total data size is 8096 bytes or less. Here, you'll want to store the data in a single row and to do this, you must set the *text in row* table option. The *text in row* option allows you to place small *text*, *ntext*, and *image* values directly in a data row instead of in separate pages. This can reduce the amount of space used to store small *text*, *ntext*, and *image* data and can also reduce the amount of disk input/output (I/O) needed to retrieve the values.

Note   A table that has fixed-length rows always stores the same amount of rows on each page. On the other hand, a table with variable-length rows stores as many rows as possible, based on the length of the data entered. As you might expect, there's a definite performance advantage to keeping rows compact and allowing more rows to fit on a page. With more rows per page, you'll have an improved cache-hit ratio and reduce I/O.

Understanding Extents

An extent is a set of eight contiguous data pages, which means extents are allocated in 64 KB blocks and there are 16 extents per megabyte. SQL Server 2000 has two types of extents:

- **Mixed extents**   With mixed extents, different objects can own pages in the extent. This means that up to eight objects can own a page in the extent.

- **Uniform extents**   With uniform extents, a single object owns all the pages in the extent. This means that only the owning object can use all eight pages in the extent.

When you create a new table or index, SQL Server allocates pages from a mixed extent to the new table or index. The table or index continues to use pages in the mixed extent until it grows to the point where it uses eight data pages. When this happens, SQL Server changes the table or index to uniform extents. As long as the table or index continues to use at least eight data pages, it will use uniform extents.

Working with Tables

SQL Server provides many ways to work with tables. You can create new tables using the New Table window in Enterprise Manager or the CREATE TABLE command. You can modify existing tables by using the Design Table window in Enterprise Manager or the ALTER TABLE command. You can also perform other table management functions, including copy, rename, and delete.

Creating Tables

Before you create a table, you should carefully consider the table name. Table names can be up to 128 characters long. Table names must begin with an alphabetic character but can contain underscores (_), at symbols (@), and pound signs (#). The exceptions to this rule are temporary tables. Private temporary tables begin with # and are accessible to you only during the current user session. Global temporary tables begin with ## and are accessible to anyone as long as your user session remains connected. Temporary tables are created in tempdb and are automatically deleted when your user session ends.

In Enterprise Manager you create a new table by completing the following steps:

1. Start Enterprise Manager and then work your way down to the database you want to work with. Click the plus sign (+) next to the database name to display a list of data objects and resources.

2. To create a new table, right-click the Tables node and from the shortcut menu, choose New Table. You'll then access the New Table view in Enterprise Manager, which is similar to what you see in Figure 6-1.

3. You can now create a new column by entering a column name and specifying its properties. Rows and columns displayed in the Enterprise Manager window are used as follows:

    • Rows in the New Table view correspond to columns in the table you're working with. In Figure 6-1, columns listed include CustomerID, CompanyName, ContactName, ContactTitle, Address, City, Region, PostalCode, Country, Phone, and Fax.

    • Columns in the New Table view correspond to column properties in the table you're working with. In Figure 6-1, column properties listed include Column Name, Data Type, Length, and Allow Nulls.

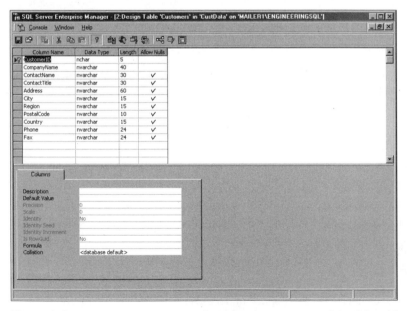

Figure 6-1. *Enterprise Manager makes it easy to create and modify tables. Work your way through the column properties from left to right.*

4. Use the Columns panel in the lower left corner to specify additional characteristics for the column you're creating. Additional characteristics are:

   * **Description** Shows a description of the column.

   * **Default Value** Shows or determines the default value for the column, which is used whenever a row with a null value for this column is inserted into the database.

   * **Precision** Shows or determines the maximum number of digits for values in the column. Only applies when the column contains numeric values.

   * **Scale** Shows or determines the maximum number of digits that can appear to the right of the decimal point for values in the column. Only applies when the column contains numeric values.

   * **Identity** Shows or determines whether the column is used as an identifier column.

   * **Identity Seed** Shows or sets the base value for generating unique identifiers. Only applies to columns whose Identity option is set to Yes or Yes (Not For Replication).

   * **Identity Increment** Shows or sets the increment for generating unique identifiers. Only applies to columns whose Identity option is set to Yes or Yes (Not For Replication).

   * **Is RowGuid** Shows or determines whether the column contains globally unique identifiers. Only applies to columns whose Identity option is set to Yes or Yes (Not For Replication).

   * **Formula** Shows or sets the formula for a computed column.

   * **Collation** Shows or sets the default collating sequence that SQL Server applies to the column whenever the column values are used to sort rows of a query result.

5. You can now create a new column by entering a column name and specifying its properties or by modifying an existing column by changing its name or its properties, or both.

6. When you're finished creating the table, click Save. Afterward type the table name when prompted and then click OK.

You can create tables with Transact-SQL using the CREATE TABLE command. The syntax and usage for this command is shown as Sample 6-1.

Sample 6-1. CREATE TABLE Syntax and Usage

Syntax

```
CREATE TABLE
  [ database_name.[ owner ] . | owner. ] table_name
  ( { < column_definition >
```

(continued)

Sample 6-1. *(continued)*
Syntax

```
    | column_name AS computed_column_expression
    | < table_constraint > } [ ,...n ]
  )


[ ON { filegroup | DEFAULT } ]
[ TEXTIMAGE_ON { filegroup | DEFAULT } ]


< column_definition > ::= { column_name data_type }
  [ [ DEFAULT constant_expression ]
    | [ IDENTITY [ ( seed , increment ) [ NOT FOR REPLICATION ] ] ]
  ]
  [ ROWGUIDCOL ]
  [ COLLATE < collation_name > ]
  [ < column_constraint > ] [ ...n ]


< column_constraint > ::= [ CONSTRAINT constraint_name ]
  { [ NULL | NOT NULL ]
    | [ { PRIMARY KEY | UNIQUE }
      [ CLUSTERED | NON-CLUSTERED ]
      [ WITH FILLFACTOR = fillfactor ]
      [ON {filegroup | DEFAULT} ] ]
    ]
    | [ [ FOREIGN KEY ]
      REFERENCES ref_table [ ( ref_column ) ]
      [ ON DELETE { CASCADE | NO ACTION } ]
      [ ON UPDATE { CASCADE | NO ACTION } ]
      [ NOT FOR REPLICATION ]
    ]
```

(continued)

Sample 6-1. *(continued)*
Syntax

```
  | CHECK [ NOT FOR REPLICATION ]
  ( logical_expression )
}


< table_constraint > ::= [ CONSTRAINT constraint_name ]
  { [ { PRIMARY KEY | UNIQUE }
  [ CLUSTERED | NON-CLUSTERED ]
  { ( column [ ASC | DESC ] [ ,...n ] ) }
  [ WITH FILLFACTOR = fillfactor ]
  [ ON { filegroup | DEFAULT } ]
  ]
  | FOREIGN KEY
  [ ( column [ ,...n ] ) ]
  REFERENCES ref_table [ ( ref_column [ ,...n ] ) ]
  [ ON DELETE { CASCADE | NO ACTION } ]
  [ ON UPDATE { CASCADE | NO ACTION } ]
  [ NOT FOR REPLICATION ]
  | CHECK [ NOT FOR REPLICATION ]
  ( search_conditions )
  }
```

Usage

```
CREATE TABLE Customers
(
  cust_lname varchar(40) NOT NULL,
  cust_fname varchar(20) NOT NULL,
  phone char(12) NOT NULL,
  uid uniqueidentifier NOT NULL
  DEFAULT newid()
)
```

Modifying Existing Tables

In Enterprise Manager you modify an existing table by completing the following steps:

1. Start Enterprise Manager and then work your way down to the database you want to work with. Click the plus sign (+) next to the database name to display a list of data objects and resources.

2. To edit an existing table, right-click the table name in the right pane and from the shortcut menu, choose Design Table. This opens the Design Table view shown previously in Figure 6-1.

3. Make any necessary changes to the table and then click Save. If the changes you make affect multiple tables, you'll see a prompt showing which tables will be updated and saved in the database. Click Yes to continue and complete the operation.

The Transact-SQL command for modifying tables is ALTER TABLE. The syntax and usage for this command is shown as Sample 6-2.

Sample 6-2. ALTER TABLE Syntax and Usage

Syntax

```
ALTER TABLE table
{ [ ALTER COLUMN column_name
  { new_data_type [ ( precision [ , scale ] ) ]
    [ COLLATE < collation_name > ]
    [ NULL | NOT NULL ]
    | {ADD | DROP } ROWGUIDCOL }
  ]
  | ADD
    { [ < column_definition > ]
    | column_name AS computed_column_expression
    } [ ,...n ]
  | [ WITH CHECK | WITH NOCHECK ] ADD
    { < table_constraint > } [ ,...n ]
  | DROP
    { [ CONSTRAINT ] constraint_name
      | COLUMN column } [ ,...n ]
```

(continued)

Sample 6-2. *(continued)*
Syntax

```
 | { CHECK | NOCHECK } CONSTRAINT
   { ALL | constraint_name [ ,...n ] }
 | { ENABLE | DISABLE } TRIGGER
   { ALL | trigger_name [ ,...n ] }
}


< column_definition > ::=
  { column_name data_type }
  [ [ DEFAULT constant_expression ]
  | [ IDENTITY [ (seed , increment ) [ NOT FOR REPLICATION ] ] ]
   ]
  [ ROWGUIDCOL ]
  [ COLLATE < collation_name > ]
  [ < column_constraint > ] [ ...n ]


< column_constraint > ::=
  [ CONSTRAINT constraint_name ]
  { [ NULL | NOT NULL ]
   | [ { PRIMARY KEY | UNIQUE }
     [ CLUSTERED | NON-CLUSTERED ]
     [ WITH FILLFACTOR = fillfactor ]
     [ ON { filegroup | DEFAULT } ]
     ]
   | [ [ FOREIGN KEY ]
     REFERENCES ref_table [ ( ref_column ) ]
     [ ON DELETE { CASCADE | NO ACTION } ]
     [ ON UPDATE { CASCADE | NO ACTION } ]
     [ NOT FOR REPLICATION ]
     ]
```

(continued)

Sample 6-2. *(continued)*
Syntax
___

```
| CHECK [ NOT FOR REPLICATION ]
   ( logical_expression )
}


< table_constraint > ::=
  [ CONSTRAINT constraint_name ]
  { [ { PRIMARY KEY | UNIQUE }
  [ CLUSTERED | NON-CLUSTERED ]
  { ( column [ ,...n ] ) } }
  [ WITH FILLFACTOR = fillfactor ]
  [ ON {filegroup | DEFAULT } ]
  ]
  | FOREIGN KEY
   [ ( column [ ,...n ] ) ]
   REFERENCES ref_table [ ( ref_column [ ,...n ] ) ]
   [ ON DELETE { CASCADE | NO ACTION } ]
   [ ON UPDATE { CASCADE | NO ACTION } ]
   [ NOT FOR REPLICATION ]
  | DEFAULT constant_expression
   [ FOR column ]
  | CHECK [ NOT FOR REPLICATION ]
   ( search_conditions )
  }
```

Usage
___

```
ALTER TABLE Customers
ADD uid uniqueidentifier NOT NULL DEFAULT newid()


ALTER TABLE Customers
ALTER COLUMN cust_fname CHAR(10) NOT NULL
```

(continued)

Sample 6-2. *(continued)*
Usage

ALTER TABLE Customers

DROP Address2

Viewing Table Row and Size Information

In Enterprise Manager you can view table row and size information by completing the following steps:

1. Start Enterprise Manager and then work your way down to the database you want to work with.

2. With the Taskpad enabled, select the database entry in the left pane and then in the right pane, click the Table Info tab, as shown in Figure 6-2. .

You can also view row, size, and space statistics for individual tables using the *sp_spaceused* stored procedure. The following accesses the Customer database and then checks the statistics for the Customers table:

USE CUSTOMER

EXEC sp_spaceused Customers

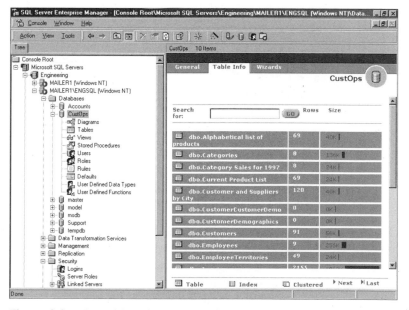

Figure 6-2. *The Table Info view provides a summary of tables and indexes used in the database, which includes the number of rows used and the table size.*

Displaying Table Properties and Permissions

In Enterprise Manager you can display table properties and permissions by completing the following steps:

1. Start Enterprise Manager and then work your way down to the database you want to work with.
2. Select the Tables node to display a table list in the right pane.
3. Double-click the table whose properties you want to examine.
4. Once the Properties dialog box is open, you can click Permissions to display and change table permissions.

Displaying Current Values in Tables

In Enterprise Manager, you modify an existing table by completing the following steps:

1. Start Enterprise Manager and then work your way down to the database you want to work with. Click the plus sign (+) next to the database name to display a list of data objects and resources.
2. To display the current values in a table, right-click the table name in the right pane and from the shortcut menu, point to Open Table and then select one of the following options:

   * **Return All Rows**   Returns all rows in the selected table.
   * **Return Top**   Returns N number of rows in the selected table. When prompted, type the maximum number of rows to fetch and then click OK.
   * **Query**   Displays a Data In Table view with a basic query that you can extend to display table data.

Copying Tables

The easiest way to create a copy of a table is to use Transact-SQL. To do that, complete the following steps:

1. Make sure that the Select Into/Bulk Copy database option is selected as specified in the section of Chapter 4 entitled "Database Options for Enterprise Manager and Transact-SQL."
2. Use SELECT INTO to extract all the rows from an existing table into the new table. The new table must not exist already. For example, if you wanted to copy the Customers table to a new table called Customers2, you could use

```
SELECT * INTO Customers2 FROM Customers
```

Renaming and Deleting Tables

In Enterprise Manager, the easiest way to rename or delete a table is to complete the following steps:

1. Start Enterprise Manager, and then work your way down to the database you want to work with.
2. Select the Tables node to display a table list in the right pane.
3. To rename a table, right-click the table and then from the shortcut menu, choose Rename. You can now type a new name for the table.
4. To delete a table, right-click the table and then from the shortcut menu, choose Delete. When prompted to confirm the action, choose Yes.

You can also rename tables using *sp_rename,* such as:

```
USE CUSTOMER

EXEC sp_rename Customers, Customers2
```

You can remove a table from the database using the DROP TABLE command, such as:

```
USE CUSTOMER

DROP TABLE Customers2
```

If you'd rather delete the rows in a table but leave its structure intact, you can use DELETE. The following DELETE command deletes all the rows in a table but doesn't remove the table structure:

```
USE CUSTOMER

DELETE Customers
```

Adding and Removing Columns in a Table

In Enterprise Manager you add or remove columns in a table as described in the section of this chapter entitled "Working with Tables." In Transact-SQL you modify table columns using the ALTER TABLE command, which was listed previously in Sample 6-2.

Adding Columns

The following example adds a unique identifier column to the Customers table:

```
USE CUSTOMER

ALTER TABLE Customers

ADD uid uniqueidentifier NOT NULL DEFAULT newid()
```

Modifying Columns

To change the characteristics of an existing column, use the ALTER COLUMN command, such as:

```
USE CUSTOMER

ALTER TABLE Customers

ALTER COLUMN cust_fname CHAR(10) NOT NULL
```

Removing Columns

The following example removes the Address2 column from the Customers table:

```
USE CUSTOMER

ALTER TABLE Customers

DROP Address2
```

Scripting Tables

You can recreate and store all the SQL commands that go into creating tables in a database in a .sql file for later use. To do this, complete the following steps:

1. Start Enterprise Manager and then work your way down to the database you want to work with.

2. Select the Tables node to display a table list in the right pane.

3. Right-click the table you want to work with and then select All Tasks. Now choose Generate SQL Script to open the dialog box shown in Figure 6-3.

4. By default, the table you clicked is listed in the Objects To Be Scripted list box. You can add other objects by clicking Show All, selecting the objects to add, and then using the Add button to add the objects to the script.

5. Use the Formatting tab fields to add formatting information that details how the objects are to be scripted.

6. Use the Options tab fields to script additional information, such as roles, logins, permissions, indexes, triggers, keys, and file options.

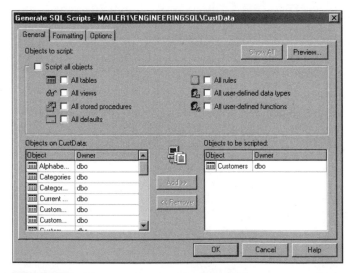

Figure 6-3. *Generate SQL commands needed to recreate tables using the Generate SQL Scripts dialog box.*

7. Click OK when you're ready to save the .sql script. When prompted, set a folder and file path for the script.

Managing Table Values

The sections that follow examine key techniques and concepts for working with table values. Whether you want to create a new table or modify an existing one, the techniques you'll use and the concepts you'll need to understand are similar.

Using Native Data Types

Native data types are those built into SQL Server and supported directly. All data types have a length value, which is either fixed or variable. Length for a numeric or binary data type is the number of bytes used to store the number. Length for a character data type is the number of characters. Most numeric data types also have precision and scale. Precision is the total number of digits in a number. Scale is the number of digits to the right of the decimal point in a number. For example, the number 8714.235 has a precision of seven and a scale of three.

Table 6-1 summarizes native data types that work with numbers and money. The first column shows the general data type or data type synonym for SQL-92 compatibility. The second column shows the SQL Server data type.

Table 6-1. Native Data Types for Numbers and Money

SQL-92 Name–Type	SQL Server Name	Range–Description
Integers		
Bit	*bit*	0 or 1
Big integer	*bigint*	-2^63 through 2^63 =1.
Integer	*int*	-2^31 (-2,147,483,648) through 2^31 =1 (2,147,483,647)
small integer	*smallint*	2^15 (-32,768) through 2^15 - 1 (32,767)
tiny integer	*tinyint*	0 through 255
Money		
Money	*money*	-922,337,203,685,477.5808 through +922,337,203,685,477.5807
small money	*smallmoney*	-214,748.3648 through +214,748.3647
Exact Numeric		
dec, decimal	*decimal*	-10^38 through 10^38 -1
numeric	*decimal*	-10^38 through 10^38 -1

(continued)

Table 6-1. *(continued)*

SQL-92 Name–Type	SQL Server Name	Range–Description
Approximate Numeric		
double precision	*float*	-1.79E + 308 through 1.79E + 308
float	*float*	-1.79E + 308 through 1.79E + 308. float[(n)] for n = 1-53
float	*real*	-3.40E + 38 through 3.40E + 38. float[(n)] for n = 1-24
Numerics		
cursor	*cursor*	A reference to a cursor.
Rowversion	*Rowversion*	A database-wide unique number that indicates the sequence in which modifications took place in the database. Formerly called a timestamp.
SQL Variant	*Sql_variant*	A special data type that allows a single column to store multiple data types (except *text*, *ntext*, *rowversion*, and *sql_variant*).
Table	*Table*	A special data type that's used to store a result set temporarily for processing. Can be used only to define local variables and as the return type for user-defined functions.
Uniqueidentifier	*uniqueidentifier*	A globally unique identifier (GUID).

Table 6-2 summarizes native data types for dates, characters, and binary data. Again, the first column shows the general data type or data type synonym for SQL-92 compatibility. The second column shows the SQL Server data type.

Table 6-2. Native Data Types for Dates, Characters, and Binary Values

SQL-92 Name–Type	SQL Server Name	Range–Description
Date		
datetime	*datetime*	January 1, 1753, to December 31, 9999; accuracy of three-hundredths of a second
small datetime	*smalldatetime*	January 1, 1900, through June 6, 2079; accuracy of one minute

(continued)

Table 6-2. *(continued)*

SQL-92 Name–Type	SQL Server Name	Range–Description
Character		
character	*char*	Fixed-length, non-Unicode character data with a maximum length of 8000 characters
character varying	*varchar*	Variable-length, non-Unicode data with a maximum of 8000 characters
text	*text*	Variable-length, non-Unicode data with a maximum length of $2^{31} - 1$ (2,147,483,647) characters
national character	*nchar*	Fixed-length, Unicode data with a maximum length of 4000 characters
national char varying	*nvarchar*	Variable-length, Unicode data with a maximum length of 4000 characters
national text	*ntext*	Variable-length, Unicode data with a maximum length of $2^{30} - 1$ (1,073,741,823) characters
Binary		
binary	*binary*	Fixed-length, binary data with a maximum length of 8000 bytes
binary varying	*varbinary*	Variable-length, binary data with a maximum length of 8000 bytes
image	*image*	Variable-length, binary data with a maximum length of $2^{31} - 1$ (2,147,483,647) bytes

When you create or modify a table in Enterprise Manager, you assign a native data type by clicking in the Data Type column and using the selection list to choose a data type. In Transact-SQL you set the data type when you create the table and populate its columns or when you alter a table and add or change columns. Sample 6-3 shows how you could create the table shown previously in Figure 6-1.

Sample 6-3. Creating a Table and Its Columns

```
USE CUSTOMER
CREATE TABLE Customers
  (CustomerID nchar(5) NOT NULL,
  CompanyName nvarchar(40) NOT NULL,
  ContactName nvarchar(30) NOT NULL,
```

(continued)

Sample 6-3. *(continued)*

```
ContactTitle nvarchar(30) NOT NULL,

Address nvarchar(60) NOT NULL,

City nvarchar(15) NULL,

Region nvarchar(15) NULL,

PostalCode nvarchar(5) NULL,

Country nvarchar(15) NULL,

Phone nvarchar(24) NULL,

Fax nvarchar(24) NULL)
```

Using Fixed-Length and Variable-Length Fields

You can create binary and character data types as fixed-length or variable-length fields. When you use fixed-length data types, the column size you specify is reserved in the database and can be written to without your having to manipulate the data around the column. This makes updates to the database quicker than with variable-length fields. When you use variable-length data types, you allow SQL Server to squeeze more rows into data pages, if possible. Generally, more rows per data page allows for more efficient reading of data, which can translate into improved performance for read operations.

To gain a better understanding of the performance implications, consider the following scenario. With fixed-length columns of 80, 120, 40, and 500 bytes each, rows would always be written using 750 bytes of storage (740 bytes for data plus 10 bytes of overhead for each row). Here, you could fit 10 rows per data page (8096/750, without the remainder). If you used variable-length columns, however, the number of bytes used per row and the amount of rows stored per page would vary. As an example, let's say that on average the variable-length rows use 400 bytes. This includes 380 bytes of data and 20 bytes of overhead (12 bytes of overhead for rows that use variable length data plus 2 bytes of overhead per variable-length column). Here, you could fit 20 rows per data page (8096/400, without the remainder), which would make data reads more efficient than the fixed-length example.

Using User-Defined Data Types

User-defined data types are special data types that are based on a native data type. You'll want to use user-defined data types when two or more tables store the same type of data in a column and these columns must have exactly the same data type, length, and nullability. Either you or SQL Server can create user-defined data types. For example, *sysname* is a user-defined data type that's used to reference database object names. The data type is defined as a variable Unicode character type of 128 characters, which is why object names are limited to 128 characters throughout SQL Server. You can apply this same concept to ensure that a particular tidbit of data is used exactly as you want it to be used.

Creating User-Defined Data Types

You create user-defined data types at the database level rather than at the table level, which is why user-defined data types are static and immutable (unchangeable). This ensures that there is no performance penalty associated with user-defined data types. User-defined data types do have some limitations, however. You can't declare a default value or CHECK constraint as part of the user-defined data type. You can't create a user-defined data type based on a user-defined data type either.

Tip When you create user-defined data types in a user-defined data- base, they apply only to that database. If you want user-defined data types to apply to multiple databases, define the data type in the model database. After that, the user-defined data type will exist in all new user-defined databases.

In Enterprise Manager you create a user-defined data type by completing the following steps:

1. Start Enterprise Manager and then work your way down to the database you want to work with.

2. Right-click the database name and select New. From the shortcut menu, select User Defined Data Type. This opens the User-Defined Data Type Properties dialog box shown in Figure 6-4.

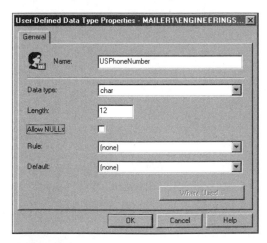

Figure 6-4. *Configure the new data type using the User-Defined Data Type Properties dialog box.*

3. Enter a name for the new data type.

4. In the Data Type list, select the data type on which you want to base the user-defined data type.

5. If the data type has a variable length, set the number of bytes or characters for the data type. For fixed-length variables, such as *int*, you won't be able to set a length.

6. To allow the data type to accept null values, select Allow Nulls.

7. Optionally, use the Rule and Default lists to select a rule or default to bind to the user-defined data type.

8. Click OK. If you open a new table or edit an existing table, you'll see the new data type as one of the last entries in the Data Type selection list.

You can also create user-defined data types with the *sp_addtype* stored procedure. Sample 6-4 shows this procedure's syntax and usage.

Sample 6-4. *sp_addtype* Syntax and Usage

Syntax

```
sp_addtype [@typename =] type,
 [@phystype =] system_data_type
 [, [@nulltype =] 'null_type']
 [, [@owner =] 'owner_name']
```

Usage

```
USE master

EXEC sp_addtype USPhoneNumber, 'char(12)', 'NOT NULL'
```

Managing User-Defined Data Types

Once you create user-defined data types, you'll often need to manage their properties. To manage user-defined data types, complete the following steps:

1. Start Enterprise Manager and then work your way down to the database you want to work with.

2. Select the User Defined Data Types node in the left pane. This displays current user-defined data types in the right pane.

3. Right-click the user-defined data type you want to manage and then select

   * Properties, to view the data type's properties and set dependencies
   * Delete, to delete the data type
   * Rename, to rename the data type

4. To see where the data type is used in the database, right-click the user-defined data type and then from the shortcut menu, choose Properties. In the User-Defined Data Type Properties dialog box, click Where Used.

Allowing and Disallowing Nulls

When you create columns in a table, you can specify whether nulls are allowed or not. A null means there is no entry in the column for that row; it isn't the same as zero or an empty string. Columns defined with a primary key constraint or identity property can't allow null values.

If you add a row but don't set a value for a column that allows null values, SQL Server inserts the value NULL—unless a default value is set for the column. When a default value is set for a column and you insert a null value, SQL Server replaces NULL with the default value. Additionally, if the column allows nulls, you can explicitly set a column to null using the NULL keyword. Don't use quotation marks when setting null explicitly.

In Enterprise Manager's New Table and Design Table views, you

- Allow nulls in a column by selecting the Allow Nulls column
- Disallow nulls in a column by clearing the Allow Nulls column

For a Transact-SQL example of allowing and disallowing nulls for a new table, see Sample 6-3.

Default Values

Null values are useful when you don't know the value or the value is missing. The use of null is controversial, though, and a better alternative is to set a default value. The default value is used when no value is set for a column you're inserting into a table. For example, you may want a character-based column to have the value N/A rather than NULL. Here, you would set the default value as N/A.

As Table 6-3 summarizes, combinations of default values and nullability are handled in different ways. The key thing to remember is that if you set a default value, the default is used whenever a value isn't specified for the column entry. This is true even if you allow nulls.

Table 6-3. Default Values and Nullability

Column Definition	No Entry, No DEFAULT Definition	No Entry, DEFAULT Definition	Enter a Null Value
Allows null values	Sets NULL	Sets default value	Sets NULL
Disallows null values	Error occurs	Sets default value	Error occurs

Using Identities and Globally Unique Identifiers

When you design tables, you'll often need to think about unique identifiers that can be used as primary keys or to ensure that merged data don't conflict with existing data. Unique identifiers for primary keys could include customer account numbers or social security numbers. However, if a unique identifier isn't available, you may want to use the identity property to generate sequential values that are unique for each row in a table. You could also use this unique identifier to automatically generate a customer account number, an order number, or whatever other unique value you need.

While the identity property provides a local solution for a specific table, it doesn't guarantee that the value will be unique throughout the database. Other tables in the database may have identity columns with the same values. In most cases, this isn't a problem because the identity values are usually used only within the context of a single table and don't relate to other tables. However, there are times when you'll need a value that's unique throughout one or more databases, and this is where globally unique identifiers come into the picture.

Globally unique identifiers are guaranteed to be unique across all networked computers in the world, which is extremely useful in merge replication. When you're merging data from multiple databases, globally unique identifiers ensure that records aren't inadvertently associated with each other. For example, the company's New York, Chicago, and San Francisco offices may have customer account numbers that are unique at local offices but not at the national level. Here, globally unique identifiers would ensure that account XYZ from New York and account XYZ from Chicago aren't merged as the same account.

Identities and globally unique identities aren't mutually exclusive. Each table can have one identifier column and one globally unique identity property. These values are often used together. For example, all clustered indexes in SQL Server should be unique, but they don't have to be unique.

In Enterprise Manager's New Table and Design Table views, you set identity values for a table by completing the following steps:

1. Create or modify other columns in the table as appropriate, and then start a new column for the identity value.

2. Give the identity column a name and then select a data type. Identifier columns must use the data type *tinyint, smallint, int, bigint, decimal,* or *numeric.* Globally unique identifier columns must have a data type of *uniqueidentifier.*

 Tip When you set the data type for an identifier column, be sure to consider how many rows are in the table as well as how many rows may be added in the future. A *tinyint* identifier would allow for only 256 unique values (0 to 255). A *smallint* identifier would allow for 32,768 values (0 to 32,767).

3. Clear the Allow Nulls check box for the identity column.

4. To assign a globally unique identifier, select the Is RowGuid check box for the identity column. A default value of *newid()* is created automatically for you.

Note The *newid()* function is used to generate new uniqueidentifier val- ues. These values are obtained by combining the identification number of a network card with a unique number from the CPU clock. If a server process generates the identifier, the network card used is the server's. If the identifier is returned by application API function calls, the network card used is the client's. Network card manufacturers guarantee that no other network card in the next 100 years will have the same number.

5. To assign a unique identifier:
   - Set Identity to Yes or Yes (Not For Replication).
   - Type a value in the Identity Seed cell. This value is assigned to the first row in the table. If you leave this cell blank, the value 1 is assigned by default.
   - Type a value in the Identity Increment cell. This value is the increment that is added to the Identity Seed for each subsequent row. If you leave this cell blank, the value 1 is assigned by default.

Note The identity seed and increment are used to determine the iden- tifier for rows. If you entered a seed value of 100 and an increment of 10, the first row would have a value of 100, the second would have a value of 110, and so on.

When you create a table in Transact-SQL, globally unique identifiers aren't generated automatically. You must reference the *newid()* function as the default value for the identifier column, such as:

```
USE CUSTOMER

CREATE TABLE Customers

  (cust_lname varchar(40) NOT NULL,

  cust_fname varchar(20) NOT NULL,

  phone char(12) NOT NULL,

  uid uniqueidentifier NOT NULL DEFAULT newid())
```

Now when you insert a new row into the table, SQL Server adds the globally unique identifier by default, such as:

```
INSERT INTO Customers

Values ('Stanek', 'William', '123-555-1212')
```

Or when you explicitly call the *newid()* function, such as:

```
INSERT INTO Customers

Values ('Stanek', 'William', '123-555-1212', newid())
```

Using Views

Views represent data in existing tables in an alternate way, and you can think of views as virtual tables. To create a view, you use a SELECT statement to select the data in one or more tables and display it as a view. For example, you could create a view that gets the customer's first name, last name, and account number from the Customers table and the order information from the Orders table, which makes the information more manageable for your company's sales representatives. As with tables, you can assign permissions to views. These permissions are specific to the view and separate from the table permissions.

Creating Views

Once you understand tables, creating views is a fairly straightforward process. You can create a view in Enterprise Manager by completing the following steps:

1. Start Enterprise Manager and then work your way down to the database you want to work with.

2. Select the Views node to display a view list in the right pane. Two types of views are available: system and user. System views provide summary information about key database information, such as table constraints and table privileges. User views are defined by you or by other database users.

3. To create a new view, right-click the Views node. From the shortcut menu, choose New View. This displays the New View window (see Figure 6-5).

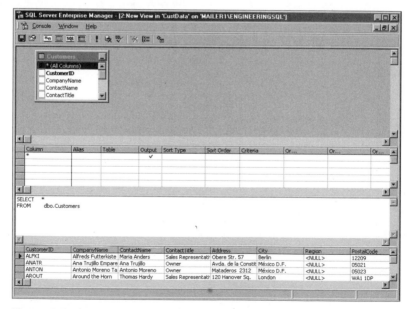

Figure 6-5. *Generate SQL commands needed to recreate tables using the New View or Design View dialog box.*

4. To modify an existing view, right-click the view name and from the shortcut menu, choose Design View. This displays the Design View window, which is similar to the window shown in Figure 6-5.

5. To add tables to the Diagram pane, right-click inside the Diagram pane window and select Add Table. In the Add Table dialog box, select the table(s) you want to add. This displays view panes for each selected table, which you can use to select table columns. Afterward, use the fields and options provided to manipulate the selection. Your actions create a *select* statement that can be used to generate the view. When you're ready, click Run on the toolbar to create the view.

Tip In the example, I entered Select * From Customer2 to create an initial view. This loaded all the column data, which I then used to set limiting criteria, as shown in Figure 6-5.

6. To set view properties, click Properties. Then use the Properties dialog box to set view properties. Key properties you'll want to set include

- **DISTINCT Values** Ensures that rows returned are unique by filtering out duplicates

- **Encrypt View** Encrypts the view so it's stored in an encoded format that can't be read using Enterprise Manager tools

7. After you run the view to update it for the latest changes, save the view. Click Save on the toolbar. If this is a new view, you'll be prompted for a view name. Enter the view name and then click OK.

You can also create views using the CREATE VIEW command. You can create a simple view by selecting all the values in a table, such as:

```
CREATE VIEW [Sales Custom View] As

SELECT *

FROM Customers2
```

You can then work directly with the view, such as:

```
SELECT * FROM [Sales Custom View]
```

To create the view shown in Figure 6-5, you would use the following command:

```
CREATE VIEW [Sales Custom View] As

SELECT cust_id AS Account, cust_lname AS [Last Name],

  cust_fname AS [First Name], state AS Region

FROM Customers2

WHERE (state = 'WA') OR

  (state = 'HI') OR

  (state = 'CA')
```

The full syntax for CREATE VIEW is shown as Sample 6-5.

Sample 6-5. CREATE VIEW Syntax

Syntax

```
CREATE [ < owner > ] VIEW view_name [ ( column [ ,...n ] ) ]
  [ WITH < view_attribute > [ ,...n ] ]
  AS
  select_statement
  [ WITH CHECK OPTION ]
  < view_attribute > ::=
    { ENCRYPTION | SCHEMABINDING | VIEW_METADATA }
```

To change an existing view without having to reset its permissions and other properties, you use ALTER VIEW. The following example changes the definition of the Sales Custom view used in previous examples:

```
ALTER VIEW [Sales Custom View] As
  SELECT cust_id AS Account, cust_lname AS [Customer Last Name],
  cust_fname AS [Customer First Name], state AS Region
  FROM Customers2
  WHERE (state = 'WA') OR
  (state = 'CA')
```

The full syntax for ALTER VIEW is shown as Sample 6-6.

Sample 6-6. ALTER VIEW Syntax

Syntax

```
ALTER VIEW view_name [ ( column [ ,...n ] ) ]
  [ WITH < view_attribute > [ ,...n ] ]
  AS
    select_statement
  [ WITH CHECK OPTION ]

  < view_attribute > ::=
    { ENCRYPTION | SCHEMABINDING | VIEW_METADATA }
```

Using Updateable Views

SQL Server supports updateable views as well. With an updateable view, you can change the information in the view using *insert, update*, and *delete* statements. You can create updateable views with one or more tables, provided the tables don't contain aggregate functions.

With updateable views, you'll usually want to set WITH CHECK OPTION. If you don't, changes to the view may result in rows no longer being displayed in the view. To see how, consider the case of the view created on the previous page. Here, you're selecting customer information for Washington, Hawaii, and California. If you change a state value to OR, the row would disappear from the view. The reason for this is that Oregon-based customers aren't displayed in the view.

Managing Views

As with tables, you can examine view properties, set view permissions, and perform other key management tasks. To get started, complete the following steps:

1. Start Enterprise Manager and then work your way down to the database you want to work with.

2. Select the Views node to display a view list in the right pane. Right-click the view you want to work with and then select

   * Rename, to rename the view

   * Delete, to delete the view

   * Properties, to examine view properties

3. To set view permissions or generate a script to recreate the view, right-click the view you want to work with and then select All Tasks. Afterward, select Manage Permissions or Generate SQL Scripts, as appropriate.

Creating and Managing Indexes

Indexes provide quick access to data without your having to search through an entire database. SQL Server 2000 allows you to create indexes on tables, views, and columns. Indexes on tables allow you to create indexes on important information in a table and quickly search through the data. Indexes on views allow you to create indexes where the result set of the view is stored and indexed in the database. Indexes on computed columns allow you to evaluate expressions and index the results (provided certain criteria are met).

Indexes are separate from tables, and you can configure them automatically using the Index Tuning Wizard. The sections that follow examine techniques you'll use to work with indexes.

Understanding Indexes

Indexes, like tables, use pages. Index pages are structured much like table data pages. They are 8 KB (8192 bytes) in size and have a 96-byte header. But unlike data pages, they don't have row offsets. Each index has a corresponding row in the *sysindexes* table with an index ID value (indid) of 1 for clustered indexes or 2–250 for nonclustered indexes. An index ID value of 255 indicates *text, ntext,* or *image* data.

SQL Server maintains indexes using a BTree structure, which is a basic tree structure consisting of a root node, intermediate level nodes, and leaf nodes. The wonderful thing about trees is that you can search them quickly and efficiently. Without the tree structure, SQL Server would need to read each table data page in the database in turn, searching for the correct record.

To put this in perspective, let's consider the limited situation where each data page contains a single row. In this case, if SQL Server searches for data in row 800 and there isn't an index, SQL Server may have to search 799 other rows before finding the right row. With a tree structure, SQL Server navigates the nodes down the index searching for the row that matches the corresponding index key. In the best-case scenario, where the index keys have been arranged in a full tree, the number of nodes that need to be searched is proportional to the height of the tree. For example, 27,000 rows may be represented with 30 levels of nodes, and if so, SQL Server would have to navigate 15 nodes on average to find the matching row.

 Note If you were paying particular attention, you know I streamlined the example to demonstrate the power of indexing. The point is that indexing can improve performance by orders of magnitude, and a database without it can seem extremely slow. By the same token, if you index the wrong information, you can make the database equally slow, which is why it's so important to select the most referenced/used column to index.

Clustered and Nonclustered Indexes

SQL Server supports two types of indexing:

- Clustered indexes
- Nonclustered indexes

You can create indexes on just about any column. The key exceptions are for columns that contain the *text, ntext, image,* and *bit* data types. You can't create indexes on these data types. You should always select the index column carefully. Selecting the correct column to index improves response time dramatically. Selecting the wrong column to index could actually degrade response time. For pointers on which column to index, use the Index Tuning Wizard.

Using Clustered Indexes

A clustered index stores the actual table data pages at the leaf level, and the table data is physically ordered around the key. A table can have only one clustered index and when this index is created, the following happens:

- Table data is rearranged.
- New index pages are created.
- All nonclustered indexes within the database are deleted.

The result is a lot of disk I/O operations and extensive use of system and memory resources. When creating a clustered index, it's a good idea to have free space that's at least 1.5 times the amount of data in the table. The extra free space ensures that you have enough space to complete the operation and do it efficiently.

Normally, you create a clustered index on a primary key. You can, however, create a clustered index on any named column, such as cust_lname or cust_id. With clustered indexes, the values you're indexing should be unique. If the values aren't unique, SQL Server creates secondary sort keys on rows that have duplicates of their primary sort keys.

Using Nonclustered Indexes

In a nonclustered index, pages on the leaf level contain a bookmark that tells SQL Server where to find the data row corresponding to the key in the index. If the table has a clustered index, the bookmark indicates the clustered index key. If the table doesn't have a clustered index, the bookmark is an actual row locator.

When you create a nonclustered index, SQL Server creates the required index pages but doesn't rearrange table data. SQL Server doesn't delete other indexes either. Each table can have up to 249 nonclustered indexes.

Which Columns Should Be Indexed?

Now that you know how indexes work, you can focus on which columns you should index. Ideally, you'll select columns for indexing based on the types of queries executed against the database. A real help in determining the types of queries being run is SQL Server Profiler. You use SQL Profiler to create a trace that contains a good snapshot of activities performed by users on the database.

You can then manually examine this trace to see what types of queries are executed, or you can use the trace file as a saved workload file in the Index Tuning Wizard. Regardless of which technique you use, keep in mind that the maximum length of all columns that comprise an index is 900 bytes. This means that the total byte size of all columns must be 900 or less.

Table 6-4. What to Index and Not to Index

Index	Don't Index
Tables with lots of rows	Tables with few rows
Columns that are often used in queries	Columns that are rarely used in queries
Columns with strong selectivity, that they have a wide range of values	Columns with poor selectivity, meaning that they have a wide range of values

(continued)

Table 6-4. *(continued)*

Index	Don't Index
Columns used in aggregate functions	Columns that have a large byte size
Columns used in group by queries	Tables with lots of modifications but few actual queries
Columns used in order by queries	
Columns used in table joins	

Table 6-5 provides suggestions for the types of columns that should use clustered or nonclustered indexes.

Table 6-5. When to Use Clustered and Nonclustered Indexes

Use Clustered Index	Use Nonclustered Index
Primary keys that are searched for extensively, such as account numbers	Primary keys that are sequential identifiers, such as identity columns
Queries that return large result sets	Queries that return small result sets
Columns used in lots of queries	Columns used in aggregate functions
Columns with strong selectivity	Foreign keys
Columns used in order by or group by queries	
Columns used in table joins	

Indexing Computed Columns and Views

With SQL Server 2000, you can index computed columns and views as well as tables. Indexes on computed columns and views involve storing results in the database for future reference. With computed columns, the column values are calculated and then used to build the keys stored in the index. With views, the result set is stored by creating a clustered index on the view. In both cases, the stored results are valid only if all connections referring to the results can generate an identical result set, which puts specific restrictions on how you can create indexes on computed columns and views.

You must establish connections referring to the results using specific SET options and these options must have the same settings. The options you must set are as follows:

- ANSI_NULLS must be set on
- ANSI_PADDING must be set on
- ANSI_WARNINGS must be set on
- ARITHABORT must be set on
- CONCAT_NULL_YIELDS_NULL must be set on

- QUOTED_IDENTIFIER must be set on
- NUMERIC_ROUNDABORT must be set off

Further, all operations referencing the view must use the exact same algorithm to build the view result set. This includes:

- The *create index* statement that builds the initial result set or is used to calculate the initial keys
- Any subsequent *insert, update,* or *delete* statements that affect the data used to build the view result set or are used to calculate keys
- All queries for which the query optimizer must determine if the indexed view is useful

Viewing Indexes

In Enterprise Manager you can view indexes by completing the following steps:

1. Start Enterprise Manager and then work your way down to the database you want to work with.
2. With the Taskpad enabled, select the database entry in the left pane and then, in the right pane, click the Table Info tab.
3. The right pane now lists the tables and indexes in the database.

You can also view indexes using the *sp_helpindex* and *sp_statistics* stored procedures, such as:

```
use customer

exec sp_help_index Customers

exec sp_statistics Customers
```

Creating Indexes

The primary ways to create indexes are to use the Create Index Wizard or the Transact-SQL CREATE INDEX command. To create indexes with the wizard, complete the following steps:

1. Start Enterprise Manager and then work your way down to the database you want to work with.
2. Click Wizards on the toolbar or from the Tools menu, choose Wizards. You'll see the Select Wizard dialog box. Expand the Database option by clicking the plus sign (+).
3. Select Create Index Wizard and click OK. Or double-click Create Index Wizard. This starts the Create Index Wizard.

4. Read the welcome message and then click Next to access the Select Database And Table dialog box shown in Figure 6-6.

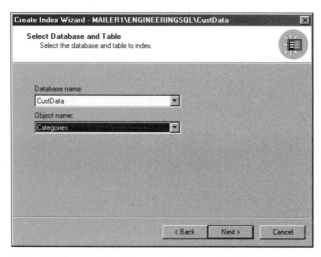

Figure 6-6. *Use the Select Database And Table dialog box to select a database and table to work with.*

5. Select the database and table on which you want to add the index. Click Next.

6. Any indexes that already exist are summarized in the Current Index Information dialog box. Click Next.

7. Select the column(s) you want to include in the index, as shown in Figure 6-7. You can only select columns that have valid data types for indexing. Any columns that aren't available for indexing are shown with a red X.

8. Each column can have a separate sort order for the index. By default, the sort order is set to ascending. You can set the sort order to descending by selecting Sort Order (DESC).

9. Next set the following indexing options:

   • **Make This A Clustered Index**   Select this option to create a clustered index on the columns selected. Otherwise, a nonclustered index is created. Keep in mind that you can have only one clustered index per table, so if the table already has a clustered index, this option is shaded and you can't select it.

   • **Make This A Unique Index**   Select this option to enforce the uniqueness of column values.

   • **Optimal Fill Factor**   Select this option to let SQL Server use an optimized fill as described in the section of Chapter 2 entitled "Setting the Index Fill."

   • **Fixed Fill Factor**   Select this option and then set a fill factor using the related field. For more information on index fill, see Chapter 2.

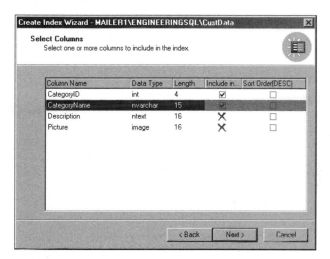

Figure 6-7. *Use the Select Columns dialog box to select columns for indexing.*

10. Click Next when you're ready to continue.

11. Type a name for the index in the Index Name field. You can use up to 128 characters for the index name. Ideally, the index name should be short and easy to associate with its purpose, such as Index For Cust ID.

12. Click Finish when you're ready to complete the process. The wizard then creates the index for you.

With the CREATE INDEX command, you create indexes using the syntax shown in Sample 6-7.

Sample 6-7. CREATE INDEX Syntax

Syntax

```
CREATE [ UNIQUE ] [ CLUSTERED | NON-CLUSTERED ] INDEX index_name
  ON { table | view } ( column [ ASC | DESC ] [ ,...n ] )
[ WITH
   [ PAD_INDEX ]
   [ [ , ] FILLFACTOR = fillfactor ]
   [ [ , ] IGNORE_DUP_KEY ]
   [ [ , ] DROP_EXISTING ]
   [ [ , ] STATISTICS_NORECOMPUTE ]
   [ [ , ] SORT_IN_TEMPDB ]
]
[ ON filegroup ]
```

Managing Indexes

After you create an index, you may need to change its properties, rename it, or delete it. You handle these tasks in Enterprise Manager by completing the following steps:

1. Start Enterprise Manager and then work your way down to the database you want to work with. Click the plus sign (+) next to the database name to display a list of data objects and resources.

2. Right-click the table name whose indexes you want to manage and then, from the shortcut menu, select Design Table. This opens the Design Table view in Enterprise Manager.

3. On the toolbar, click Table And Index Properties. This opens the Properties dialog box.

4. Click the Indexes/Keys tab, shown in Figure 6-8.

5. Use the Selected Index selection list to choose the index you want to manage. With the index selected, you can now

   - Rename the index by entering a new index name in the Index Name field

   - Delete the index by clicking Delete

   - Change the index properties by selecting new options

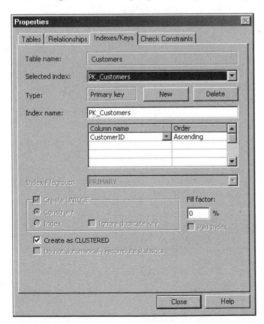

Figure 6-8. *Manage indexes using the Indexes/Keys tab in the Properties dialog box.*

You can also manage indexes with stored procedures and Transact-SQL commands, namely *sp_rename* and DROP INDEX. Unfortunately, a lot of caveats accompany these commands. For example, you can't drop an index that was created by defining a primary key or unique constraints. You must instead drop the constraint with ALTER TABLE.

Using the Index Tuning Wizard

The Index Tuning Wizard is one of the best tools a database administrator has in the indexing and optimization process. But before you start this wizard, you should create a trace containing a representative snapshot of database activity. You'll use this snapshot as the workload file in the Index Tuning Wizard. For specific pointers on creating a trace file, see the section of Chapter 10 entitled "Creating and Managing Performance Monitor Logs." To use the Index Tuning Wizard, complete the following steps:

1. Start Enterprise Manager and then work your way down to the database you want to work with.

2. Click Wizards on the toolbar or from the Tools menu, choose Wizards. You'll see the Select Wizard dialog box. Expand the Management option by clicking the plus sign (+).

3. Select Index Tuning Wizard and click OK. Or double-click Index Tuning Wizard. This starts the Index Tuning Wizard.

4. Read the welcome message and then click Next to access the Select Server And Database dialog box shown in Figure 6-9.

5. Select the server and database you wish to analyze.

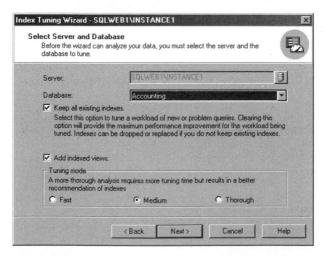

Figure 6-9. *Use the Select Server And Database dialog box to select a server, database, and indexing options.*

6. To ensure that existing indexes aren't dropped, select Keep All Existing Indexes. Otherwise, clear this option.

 Tip If you've selected a strong, representative snapshot of database activity in the trace, you'll probably want to clear the Keep All Existing Indexes option and let the Index Tuning Wizard make the appropriate suggestions for you. This ensures that existing indexes don't conflict with the recommendations the wizard may make.

7. To analyze indexed views as well as indexed tables, select Add Indexed Views.

8. Set the tuning mode as either Fast, Medium or Thorough. A more thorough analysis requires more time to perform but results in better recommendations for indexing.

9. In the Specify Workload dialog box, make sure that the My Workload file option button in the Workload section is selected. You set this option because you're using an existing trace data.

10. If you saved the trace data to a file, select My Workload File and then use the Open dialog box to find the trace file.

11. If you saved the trace data to a table, select SQL Server Table and then use the Connect to SQL Server dialog box to specify which SQL Server to connect to and the source table to use.

12. Click the Advanced Options button to set advanced options, as shown in Figure 6-10. The advanced options are

   - **Limit Number of Workload Queries To Sample** Optionally sets the maximum number of queries to sample. If you want to set this

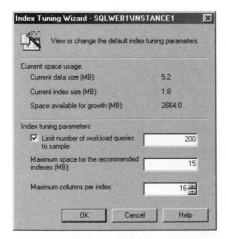

Figure 6-10. *Click the Advanced Options button and then set index tuning parameters.*

value, select the associated check box and then enter a workload query limit.

- **Maximum Space For The Recommended Indexes (MB)** Sets the maximum space that can be used by index pages. The default is 2 MB, which may not be sufficient for a large or complex database.

- **Maximum Columns Per Index** Sets the maximum number of columns that can be used in a single index. The default is 16, which is a high value for an average-sized database.

13. Next, select tables whose indexes you want to optimize, as shown in Figure 6-11. By default, all tables are deselected. You can add tables by selecting the check box for the associated table you want added or click the Select All Tables button to add all tables.

14. Click Next and the Index Tuning Wizard will begin analyzing your workload file. You can click End to stop the analysis at any time.

15. When it has finished the analysis, the wizard will make recommendations and display them in the Index Recommendations dialog box (see Figure 6-12). To see detailed analysis information, click the Analysis button.

16. Once you've completed reviewing the Index Tuning Wizard recommendations and analysis, click Next. You'll see the Completing The Index Tuning Wizard dialog box. Click Finish to apply the index tuning choices you've made. If you execute now, your changes will be updated and take effect immediately.

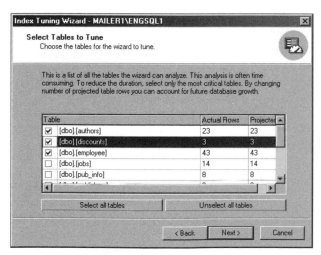

Figure 6-11. *Select tables to tune using this dialog box.*

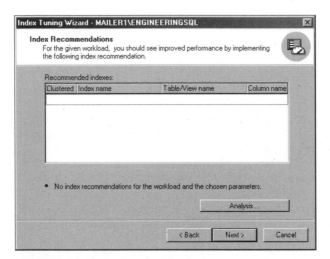

Figure 6-12. *Apply the changes, if desired. Otherwise, clear the Apply Changes option.*

Optionally, save the recommended changes as a SQL script file. You can review or edit the script using a text editor and schedule a job to implement the changes later.

Column Constraints and Rules

Column constraints and rules are important parts of database administration. You use constraints to control the way column values are used, such as whether a value must be unique or whether it must have a specific format. While you usually apply constraints directly to a specific column, you can use rules to create constraints that you can apply to multiple tables in a database.

Using Constraints

SQL Server enforces the uniqueness of column values using unique and primary key constraints. You'll often use unique constraints to create secondary keys (for nonclustered indexes) that you can use in conjunction with the primary key. Foreign key constraints identify the relationships between tables and ensure that referential integrity is maintained. Other types of constraints you may want to use are check and not null constraints. Check constraints restrict the format or range of acceptable values for columns. Not null constraints prevent null values in a column.

Constraints can apply to columns or to entire tables. A column constraint is specified as part of a column definition and applies only to that column. A table constraint is declared independently from a column definition and can apply to several columns in the table. You must use table constraints when more than one column must be included in a constraint. For example, if a table has three columns in the primary key, you must use a table constraint to include all three columns in the primary key.

Setting Uniqueness Constraints

When you set a unique constraint on a column or columns, SQL Server automatically creates a unique index and then checks for duplicate values. If duplicate key values exist, the index creation operation is cancelled and an error message is displayed. SQL Server also checks the data each time you add data to the table. If the new data contain duplicate keys, the insert or update is rolled back and an error message is generated. You can specify that duplicate keys should be ignored by using the IGNORE_DUP_KEY option.

In Enterprise Manager you set the uniqueness constraint with the Make This A Unique Index option, as described in the "Creating Indexes" section of this chapter. In Transact-SQL you can set the unique constraint when you create the index, such as:

```
USE Customer
CREATE UNIQUE INDEX [Cust ID Index]
ON Customers(cust_id)
```

A nonclustered index is created unless a clustered index is explicitly specified, such as:

```
USE Customer
CREATE UNIQUE CLUSTERED INDEX [Cust ID Index]
ON Customers(cust_id)
```

Primary Key Constraints

SQL Server also allows you to designate any column or group of columns as a primary key, but primary keys are often defined for identity columns. A table can have only one primary key, and, because unique values are required, no primary key column can accept null values. Also, when you use multiple columns, the values of all the columns are combined to determine uniqueness.

As with unique constraints, SQL Server creates a unique index for the primary key columns. With primary key constraints, however, the index is created as a clustered index—unless a clustered index already exists on the table or a nonclustered index is explicitly specified.

In Enterprise Manager you set the primary key in the New Table view or the Design Table view by completing the following steps:

1. Clear Allow Nulls for any columns that will be used in the primary key.
2. Select the column or columns that you want to use as the primary key by holding down Shift and clicking the shaded box to the left of the column name.
3. Click Set Primary Key on the toolbar.

You can also set the primary key when you create or alter tables. Examples are shown in Sample 6-8.

Sample 6-8. Creating a Table and Its Columns with a Primary Key Constraint

```
USE CUSTOMER

CREATE TABLE Customers

 (cust_id varchar(11) NOT NULL,

 cust_lname varchar(40) NOT NULL,

 cust_fname varchar(20) NOT NULL,

 phone char(12) NOT NULL,

 CONSTRAINT PK_Cust PRIMARY KEY (cust_id))


USE CUSTOMER

ALTER TABLE Customers

 (ADD CONSTRAINT PK_Cust PRIMARY KEY (cust_id))
```

Foreign Key Constraints

Foreign key constraints identify the relationships between tables and ensure that referential integrity is maintained. A foreign key in one table points to a candidate key in another table. Foreign keys prevent changes that would leave rows with foreign key values when there are no candidate keys with that value in the related table. You can't insert a row with a foreign key value if there is no candidate key with that value. The exception is when you insert a null foreign key value.

In the following example, the Order table establishes a foreign key referencing the Customer table defined earlier:

```
CREATE TABLE Order

 (order_nmbr  int,

 order_item varchar(20),

 qty_ordered  int,

 cust_id  int

  FOREIGN KEY REFERENCES Customer(cust_id)

  ON DELETE NO ACTION

)
```

The ON DELETE clause defines that actions are taken if you try to delete a row to which existing foreign keys point. The ON DELETE clause has two options:

- **NO ACTION**   Specifies that the deletion fails with an error
- **CASCADE**   Specifies that all rows with foreign keys pointing to the deleted row are to be deleted as well

You can also set an ON UPDATE clause, such as:

```
CREATE TABLE Order

(order_nmbr   int,

order_item varchar(20),

qty_ordered   int,

cust_id   int

  FOREIGN KEY REFERENCES Customer(cust_id)

  ON UPDATE CASCADE

)
```

The ON UPDATE clause defines the actions that are taken if you try to update a row to which existing foreign keys point. The clause also supports the NO ACTION and CASCADE options.

Using Check Constraints

Check constraints allow you to control the format or range of values, or both, that are associated with tables and columns. You could use this type of constraint to specify that zip codes must be entered in the format 999999999 or that phone numbers must be entered as 9999999999.

In Enterprise Manager you set check constraints in the New Table view or Design Table view by completing the following steps:

1. Click Table And Index Properties on the toolbar. Then, as shown in Figure 6-13, click the Check Constraints tab.

2. To create a new constraint, click New, enter the new constraint in the Constraint Expression text box, and then type a name in the Constraint Name field.

3. To edit an existing constraint, choose it in the Selected Constraint selection list. Then modify the existing constraint expression in the Constraint Expression text box.

4. To delete a constraint, choose it in the Selected Constraint selection list and then click Delete. When prompted to confirm the deletion, choose Yes.

You can also add and remove constraints using the CREATE TABLE or ALTER TABLE command, such as:

```
USE CUSTOMER

ALTER TABLE Customer3

ADD CONSTRAINT CheckZipFormat

CHECK (([zip] like '[09][09][09][09][09][09][09][09][09]'))
```

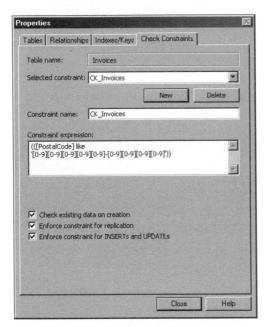

Figure 6-13. *Set constraints in the Check Contraints tab.*

Using Not Null Constraints

Not null constraints specify that the column doesn't accept null values. Normally, you set not null constraints when you create the table. You can also set not null constraints when you alter a table. In Enterprise Manager, the Allow Nulls column in the Create Table and Design Table views controls the use of this constraint. If the Allow Nulls column is cleared, the related table column doesn't accept nulls.

Using Rules

A rule is a constraint that you can apply to multiple columns or tables. However, if a rule is applied to multiple columns within a table, each rule will be independent of the others and not be aware of the other columns. Rules perform the same function as check constraints and are maintained in SQL Server 2000 for backward compatibility. Instead of using rules, Microsoft recommends that you use check constraints. Check constraints are more customizable and concise than rules. For example, while you can apply only one rule to a column, you can apply multiple check constraints to a column. Rules can be very useful in certain situations. Constraints are defined within table definitions, whereas rules are independently defined objects and therefore are not limited to being bound to a particular table. Rules are also bound to a table after the table is created and are not deleted if the table is deleted. Rules also have the advantage of being able to be bound to any user-defined data type.

With those caveats, you still can use rules if you want to. To create a rule in Enterprise Manager, complete the following steps:

1. Start Enterprise Manager and then work your way down to the database you want to work with. Click the plus sign (+) next to the database name to display a list of data objects and resources.

2. To create a new rule, right-click the Rules node and from the shortcut menu, choose New Rule. This opens the dialog box shown in Figure 6-14.

3. In the Name field type a name for the rule. Although the name can be up to 128 characters long, you should use a fairly short name so you can easily reference it.

4. In the Text field, enter the constraint to set as a database rule. Substitute the *@value* function in the place of a specific column reference.

Once you create a rule, it's displayed in the Rules view, and you can manage it much as you would any other database resource. The corresponding Transact-SQL commands for creating and managing rules are CREATE RULE and DROP RULE. You can use CREATE RULE as follows:

```
CREATE RULE CheckFormatZip
AS @value LIKE '[09][09][09][09][09][09][09][09][09]'
```

After you have created a rule, you must activate the rule in order to use it. You use a special stored procedure called *sp_bindrule* to bind the rule to a particular table column or user-defined data type. You can also use *sp_unbindrule* to remove a rule that's bound to a table column or user-defined data type. Use the following syntax when binding and unbinding rules:

```
sp_bindrule <'rule'>, <object_name'>, [<'futureonly_flag'>]
EXEC sp_unbindrule 'object name'
```

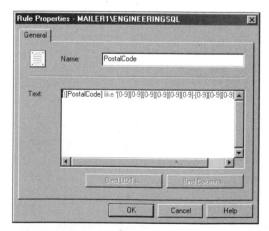

Figure 6-14. *Type a rule name and set the text of the constraint.*

Chapter 7

Importing and Exporting Data with DTS and BCP

In the old days, bulk copy program (BCP) was just about the only tool Microsoft SQL Server administrators could use to move data around. BCP is extremely fast and has a minimal overhead, but it also has a very rigid (and sometimes unforgiving) syntax. Then along came Data Transformation Services (DTS), an improved method for importing and exporting data between heterogeneous data sources. Whether you want to move data from a legacy system on a onetime basis or continually move data back and forth for data warehousing, DTS should be your first choice. With DTS you don't need to struggle with BCP anymore. DTS is extremely flexible and surprisingly fast, and you can use the technology to copy and transform data to or from any OLE DB or ODBC data source.

Understanding DTS

DTS is designed to move data accurately and efficiently as well as to convert or transform data between heterogeneous data sources. You can use DTS when you want to

- Move data between heterogeneous systems, such as from Oracle to SQL Server or vice versa

- Move data between SQL Servers, including primary and foreign keys

- Move data from Microsoft Access or Microsoft Excel to SQL Server or vice versa

- Extract data; transform the data by performing column mappings, filling in missing values, and so on; and then import the data on the destination system

- Copy views from one database to another

Tip The DTS Import/Export Wizard can run the import/export process between any of the available data sources. You don't have to set SQL Server as either the source or the destination. For example, you can use the DTS Import/Export Wizard to copy data from a text file to an Excel spreadsheet.

The key components of DTS are database drivers, packages, and other support tools.

DTS and Database Drivers

OLE DB and ODBC drivers are a key part of DTS. Without these drivers, you couldn't communicate with other systems. SQL Server provides native OLE DB and ODBC drivers for

- SQL Server
- Oracle
- Microsoft OLAP Services
- Microsoft Internet Publishing
- Access and Excel
- ASCII text files
- Other ODBC data sources

The text file driver is the catchall for import and export procedures. If you don't have a native driver for your legacy database and you can't use the generic ODBC driver, you can usually export the data to a text file and then import it into SQL Server. You can go from SQL Server to a legacy system using the same technique.

DTS Packages

At the heart of DTS you'll find the DTS Import/Export Wizard. You use the DTS Import/Export Wizard to create DTS packages, which you can later view or modify using DTS Designer. Packages are simply sets of tasks for importing, transforming, and exporting data that you can reuse or schedule to run as often as needed. Packages can be

- Stored in the repository database on a local or remote server
- Shared through SQL Server Meta Data Services
- Stored outside the database in COM-structured storage files, which is useful when you want to copy, move, and e-mail packages to another location
- Stored in Visual Basic files where you can use them in Visual Basic programs.

You execute packages directly from Enterprise Manager using the DTS Designer, DTS Import/Export Wizard, or from the Data Transformation Services section. You can also execute packages from the command prompt using the Dtswiz command-line utility, the DTS Run utility for Windows, or the Dtsrun command-line utility. Within DTS packages, you'll find

- **Connections** Store information about the source or destination of data. In a connection, you specify the data provider to use (such as the Microsoft OLE DB Data Provider for SQL Server), the server to which you want to connect, the logon to use for the connection, and the database to work with for the import/export operation. In DTS Designer, you select connections using the Data menu.

- **Tasks** Set the operations that need to be performed within the package. Tasks can consist of ActiveX scripts, SQL scripts, SQL queries, commands to transfer SQL Server objects, data-driven queries, bulk insert commands, and external processes to execute. You can even have DTS send e-mail when a package completes.

- **Workflow procedures** Set when and how a particular task should be executed, such as on completion, on failure, or on success. For example, you could schedule a task that sends e-mail on failure or on success.

- **Data transformation procedures** Set the step-by-step transformation process for the data. Also referred to as Data Pumps.

You can store a DTS package on any SQL Server and you don't need to create or store it on the source or destination server associated with the package. If you're editing, modifying, scheduling, or just viewing a DTS package, you need to use the user account of the package owner or an account that operates under the Sysadmin role on the SQL Server where the package is actually stored.

You can set general properties for all packages created on a particular SQL Server database instance using DTS application options. To set DTS application options, complete the following steps:

1. Start Enterprise Manager and then access the server instance you want to use.
2. Right-click the Database Transformation Services folder and then select Properties.
3. You can now set the following general options for packages:

   - **Cache** Enables caching of DTS application environment. Caching decreases the time needed to open packages in DTS Designer, but you must remember to refresh cache when you change the DTS environment by adding new scripting languages, custom transformations, OLE DB providers, or custom tasks. Only applies to SQL Server 2000 on Microsoft Windows 2000.

   - **Refresh Cache** Clears and refreshes the DTS Cache. When caching is enabled, you must refresh when you change the DTS application environment. You should refresh after you add a new installation of SQL Server 2000 to a server, register any new objects or tasks in DTS packages, or add a new OLE DB provider.

   - **Show Multi-Phase Pump In DTS Designer** Displays the multi-phase data pump options in any DTS package that has transformation tasks. You can access multi-phase data pump options when you're configuring transformations in either the Data Driven Query Task or Transform Data Task.

   - **Turn On Just-In-Time Debugging** Allows DTS Designer to use the Visual InterDev script debugger to debug Microsoft ActiveX scripts. Only applies if you are running Microsoft Visual InterDev or have installed the Microsoft Windows NT 4.0 Option Pack.

Other DTS Tools

Other tools available for DTS are

- **DTS Designer** A tool for developing and maintaining packages. With DTS Designer you have complete control over every step of the transformation process. After you create a package in the DTS Import/Export Wizard, you can use DTS Designer to modify the package and to set additional tasks, workflow, and other procedures.

- **DTS COM objects** Extensible components for integrating DTS functionality into external applications and scripts. A powerful scripting utility is integrated into DTS Designer.

Creating Packages with the DTS Import/Export Wizard

Creating a DTS package is one of the most complex tasks you'll perform as a database administrator. Although the DTS Import/Export Wizard, fortunately, is designed to help you build DTS packages without a lot of fuss, the process is still involved. To help reduce complexity, I'll divide the creation process into stages and then examine each stage individually. The stages you use to create DTS packages are

- Stage 1: Source and Destination Configuration
- Stage 2: Copy, Query, or Transfer
- Stage 3: Formatting and Transformation
- Stage 4: Save, Schedule, and Replicate

To get started with DTS, start the DTS Import/Export Wizard and then click Next to advance to the Source selection page. You start the DTS Import/Export Wizard in Enterprise Manager by completing the following steps:

1. Start Enterprise Manager and then access the server instance you want to work with.

2. Right-click the Database Transformation Services folder and then select All Tasks. Then select either Import Data or Export Data.

You don't need to start Enterprise Manager to run the DTS Import/Export Wizard. Instead, you can start the DTS Import/Export Wizard from the menu by completing the following steps:

1. Access the Microsoft SQL Server menu by selecting Start and then Programs.

2. Select Import And Export Data.

You can also run the DTS Import/Export Wizard from the command line by entering **dtswiz**.

If necessary, you can specify setup options through the command line as well. You can use these options to preconfigure information needed for the source or for the destination connection (but not both). The Dtswiz options are shown in Sample 7-1, and they are defined in Table 7-1. As shown in the usage example, you configure source information using the /i switch and then enter additional options. You configure the destination information using the /x switch and then enter additional options.

Sample 7-1. Dtswiz Syntax and Usage

Syntax

```
dtswiz [{/i or /x}] [/s<servername\instancename>] [/u<username>]
[/p<password>]

   [/d<database>] [/m] [/y] [/n] [/?]
```

Usage

```
dtswiz /i /szeta /usa /pgorilla /dcustomer
```

```
dtswiz /x /somega /usa /pgorilla /dcustomer2
```

Table 7-1. Dtswiz Switches Defined

Switch	Definition
/i	Sets import operation and configures source with other options.
/x	Sets export operation and configures destination with other options.
/s<servername>	Sets server name.
/u<username>	Sets user name for SQL Login id.
/p<password>	Sets password for SQL Login id.
/d<database>	Sets database.
/m	Sets the execution on main thread property for the package.
/y	Hides system databases.
/n	Sets Microsoft Windows authentication. Windows Authentication has precedence over the SQL Logon ID and password.
/?	Displays syntax and usage help.

Stage 1: Source and Destination Configuration

In Stage 1 you choose the source and destination for the import/export operation. If you started a DTS Import/Export Wizard and clicked Next, you should be on the Choose A Data Source page. At this stage you should complete the following steps:

1. Use the Source drop-down list box to select the source for the import/export operation. SQL Server provides native drivers for OLE DB and ODBC data sources. Select the data source that matches the type of file, application, or database you want to use as the source. For example, if you were copying from an Excel 2000 spreadsheet, you would choose Microsoft Excel 97-2000.

2. Fill in any additional information required to establish a connection to the source. The source you select determines what additional information you need to supply. Click Next.

3. Use the Destination drop-down list box to select the destination for the import/export operation.

4. Fill in any additional information required to establish a connection to the destination. As with the source, the destination you select determines what additional information you need to supply.

5. Click Next to go on to Stage 2: Copy, Query, or Transfer.

If choosing a source and destination were that easy, it would be a snap. But sometimes it isn't clear what additional information you need to provide. Basically, this is because there are several types of sources and destinations that you can select. These sources include

- File-based data connections
- DSN connections through ODBC drivers
- Server-based connections to databases other than SQL Server
- Server-based connections to SQL Server
- Text files

The sections that follow take a closer look at each of these connection categories.

File-Based Data Connections

You use file-based data connections with applications and databases that are file-based. You'll use this type of connection with dBase, Access, Excel, and Paradox. With file-based connections, you use a dialog box similar to the one shown in Figure 7-1. You need to enter the following information:

- **File Name**   The full file or Uniform Naming Convention (UNC) path to the source or destination file, such as //omega/data/excel/cust.xls
- **Username**   A valid username for accessing the source or destination file
- **Password**   A valid password for accessing the source or destination file

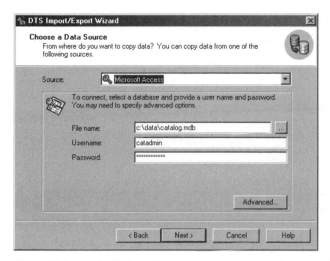

Figure 7-1. *With file-based connections, you need to specify the full path to the source/destination file and give authentication information, if necessary.*

DSN Connections Through ODBC Drivers

Data source name (DSN) connections are used with most databases that use ODBC drivers. You'll use this type of connection with dBase VFP, Microsoft Fox Pro, Microsoft Visual Fox Pro, Oracle, and other ODBC data sources. If you're setting up an ODBC connection to an Oracle database, you'll need the client connectivity tools or a third-party ODBC driver installed on the server you're establishing a connection from. Further, it's usually much easier to use the Oracle ODBC client driver with an associated system DSN that can use an Oracle TNSNAMES.ORA configuration file. The TNSNAMES.ORA file should list all the current Oracle DB server host names, IP addresses, and the associated listening ports that are set up for all Oracle DB instances. With DSN connections, you use a dialog box similar to the one shown in Figure 7-2. You configure the DSN connection by completing the following steps:

1. With user or system DSNs, select the User/System DSN option button and then use the drop-down list box to select any of the available DSNs. User and system DSNs must be on the local system.

2. With file DSNs, select the File DSN option button and then enter the full path to the DSN. File DSNs can be located anywhere on the network.

3. If you need to create a new user, system, or file DSN, click New and then use the Create New Data Source Wizard to create a new DSN. Afterward you may need to enter additional setup options.

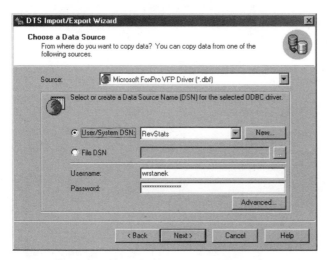

Figure 7-2. *With DSNs, you need to specify the type and name of the DSN to use and you need to supply authentication information.*

4. Type a username and password that can be used to access the data source.

5. Click Advanced to set advanced options for the driver/provider you're working with.

Server-Based Connections to Databases Other than SQL Server

You use server-based data connections to connect to databases other than SQL Server. You'll use this type of connection with Oracle, Microsoft OLE DB Provider for Internet Publishing, and Microsoft OLE DB Provider for OLAP Services. You configure server-based connections by setting Data Link properties that connect to a data source. Data Link Properties have four components:

- An OLE DB provider, which you can select using the Source or Destination selection list in the DTS Import/Export Wizard or through the Provider tab in the Data Link Properties dialog box.

- Connection options, which you set using the Connection tab in the Data Link Properties dialog box. Connection options typically include a data source name or connection string accompanied by the user name and password information needed to log on to the database.

- Advanced options, which you set using the Advanced tab in the Data Link Properties dialog box. Advanced options let you configure network settings, timeouts, and access permissions (as long as these options are configurable).

- Initialization properties, which you view using the All tab in the Data Link Properties dialog box. The initialization properties display all the options you've configured for the provider and provide a central location for editing values. Simply double-click a value to edit the associated settings.

With Oracle, the Oracle client and networking components must be installed on the system running SQL Server. If these components aren't installed, you won't be able to use the OLE DB provider. Assuming the Oracle client is installed on your system, you could set the Data Link properties for Oracle by completing the following steps:

1. In the DTS Import/Export Wizard, select Microsoft OLE DB Provider for Oracle on the Source or Destination selection list. Click Properties. This displays the Data Link Properties dialog box with the Connection tab selected.

2. As shown in Figure 7-3, type the name of the Oracle server to which you want to connect. Afterward, type the username and password needed to log on to the database.

3. To test the connection to the server, click Test Connection. If the connection fails, you may have improperly configured the Oracle client.

4. You can use the Advanced and All tabs to view additional options. Change these options as necessary.

5. Click OK.

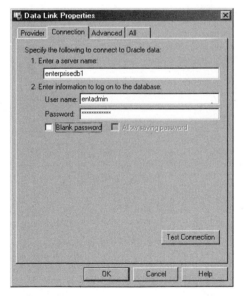

Figure 7-3. *To configure data transformation with an Oracle server you'll need to install the Oracle client software and establish a connection to the server using Data Link.*

Server-Based Connections to SQL Server

You can connect to SQL Server using an ODBC driver or an OLE DB provider. Either way, the options you have are the same as those shown in Figure 7-4, and you can configure the connection by completing the following steps:

1. Use the Server drop-down list box to select the SQL Server for the connection. The (local) option lets you choose the local system as the source or destination. Because remote procedure calls (RPCs) are used to determine available servers, the server you want to use may not be listed. In that case, click Refresh or just type in the server name.

2. Next, select an authentication method. Type a username and password, if necessary.

3. Use the Database drop-down list box to select a database to work with.

4. Click Advanced to set advanced options for the driver/provider you're working with.

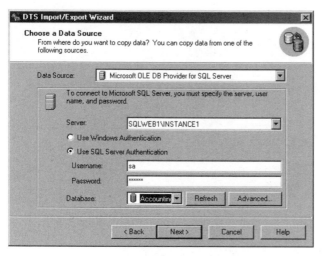

Figure 7-4. *Connecting to SQL Server is different from other types of connections.*

Importing and Exporting Text Files

You can use text files as a data source or destination. When you do, you must provide additional information about the input or output formatting. In either case, the steps are similar. To use text files as a data source, use the process below as an example and complete the following steps:

1. From the DTS Import/Export Wizard, choose the Text File option. Then enter the full filename or UNC path to the file you want to work with.

Tip If the file is in use, you'll get an error message. Click OK and then select the file again. (This forces the DTS Import/Export Wizard to try to read the file again. Otherwise, you won't see the results of the formatting.)

2. After you enter the text file information, click Next. You'll see the dialog box shown in Figure 7-5.

3. Specify how the file is delimited. If the file has fixed-width columns, select the Fixed Field option button. If the columns are delimited with commas, tabs, semicolons, or other unique characters, select the Delimited option button.

4. Select the file type using the File Type drop-down list box. The file must be formatted as ANSI (ASCII text), OEM (original equipment manufacturer), or Unicode. For importing, OEM normally refers to the native SQL Server format.

5. Specify the end-of-row delimiter using the Row Delimiter drop-down list box. The available options are

   - {CR} {LF} for carriage return and line feed
   - {CR} for carriage return only
   - {LF} for line feed only
   - Semicolon
   - Comma
   - Tab
   - Vertical bar for the | character

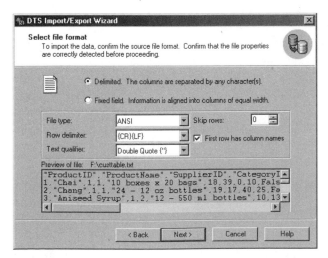

Figure 7-5. *After you enter the file information, you need to specify the file format.*

6. Use the Text Qualifier drop-down list box to specify the qualifier for text as Double Quote ("), Single Quote ('), or None.

7. If the first row contains column headers, select First Row Has Column Names.

 Tip Column headers make it easier to import data. If the file doesn't contain column names, you may want to click Cancel, add the column names to the first line, and then restart the import/export procedure.

8. To skip rows at the beginning of a file, use the Skip Rows field to set the number of rows to skip.

 Note If you indicated that the first row contains column names, the first row is read and then the specified number of rows is skipped.

9. Click Next.

10. If the file is delimited, the next screen allows you to select the delimiter as a comma, a tab, a semicolon, or another character. Use the option buttons provided to make your selection. If you choose Other, enter the characters that form the delimiter as well. As shown in Figure 7-6, the Preview area shows the data format for the options you've chosen in this dialog box and the previous dialog box.

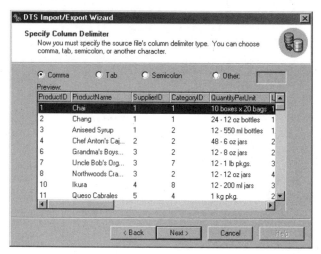

Figure 7-6. *Select a delimiter and then double-check the formatting of the file. If something is wrong, make changes before you proceed to the next stage.*

Tip If you notice data elements out of place, you can click Back to reconfigure the previous dialog box. You may also need to modify the source file. In this case, click Cancel, modify the file, and then restart the DTS Import/Export Wizard.

11. If you selected fixed-width, you'll need to tell the DTS Import/Export Wizard where columns start and end. Vertical lines indicate the start and end of columns. Add column markers by clicking in the Preview area to create a column marker. Remove column markers by double-clicking them. Move column markers by clicking them and dragging them to a new position.

12. Click Next when you're ready to select the destination for the import/export operation. After selecting the destination, you'll go on to Stage 2.

Stage 2: Copy, Query, or Transfer

With most import or export procedures, the next stage involves specifying tables and views to copy, building a query, or selecting objects to transfer. You'll select the operation using the dialog box shown in Figure 7-7, and then you'll proceed as described in the sections that follow.

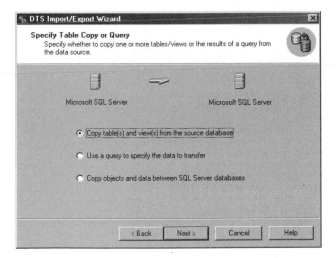

Figure 7-7. *Determine whether to copy tables and views, build a query, or transfer objects.*

Specifying Tables and Views to Copy

If you want to copy tables and views to the destination, you'll need to select which tables and views you want to copy. When a text file is the data source, making the selection is easy—there's only one table available and you can't select any views. With other data sources, you'll need to select the tables and views you want to work with. In either case the dialog box you use is the one shown in Figure 7-8.

When selecting tables, complete the following steps:

1. In the Specify Table Copy Or Query dialog box, select the Copy Table(s) And View(s) From The Source Database option button and then click Next.

2. Select a table by clicking its entry and then preview the data the table contains by clicking Preview.

3. When you find a table you want to copy, place a check in the related Source Table column.

4. By default, the destination name of the table is set to be the same as the source table name. If you want to change the table name, edit the corresponding value in the Destination Table column.

5. If you want to manipulate the row values in a table, select it and then click the corresponding button in the Transform column. Transforming row values is covered in Stage 3.

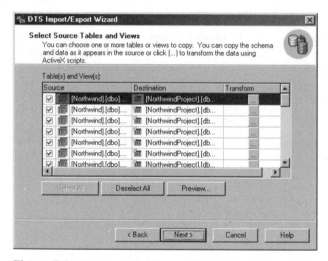

Figure 7-8. *Use the Select Source Tables And Views dialog box to specify which tables you want to copy.*

Building a Query

Another way to select data for exporting is to build a query and execute it against the source file, spreadsheet, or database. Regardless of the type of data source, you build the query in the same way by completing the following steps:

1. In the Specify Table Copy Or Query dialog box, select the Use A Query To Specify The Data To Transfer option button and then click Next.

2. In the Type SQL Statement query dialog box you can
   - Type a query directly in the text box provided and then parse it to check for accuracy using the Parse button
   - Click Query Builder to build a query using the Query Builder utility

Tip You could also create a query in your favorite query builder and then paste the results into the Type SQL Query dialog box.

3. Query Builder provides the easiest alternative, so click Query Builder. This displays the Select Columns dialog box shown in Figure 7-9.

4. Select columns for the query using the following techniques:
   - **Select all the columns in a table** Click the table name in the Source Tables list box and then choose the add button (>).
   - **Add individual columns** Click the plus sign (+) next to a table name in the Source Tables list box. This displays the columns in the table. Now select a column by clicking it and then choose the add button (>).
   - **Remove a column from the Selected Columns list box** Click it and then choose the remove button (<).
   - **Remove all selected columns from the Selected Columns list box** Click the remove all button (<<).

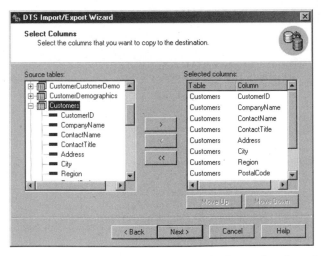

Figure 7-9. *In the Select Columns dialog box, select the columns you want to query.*

- **Change the order of selected columns** Click the column you want to reorder and then use the Move Up or Move Down button to change the column order.

5. Click Next when you're ready to continue. You can now select the sort order for columns using the dialog box shown in Figure 7-10. The buttons provided are used as follows:

- > Add the selected column
- >> Add all remaining columns using their current order
- < Remove a column from the Sorting Order list box
- << Remove all columns from the Sorting Order list box
- **Move Up** Change the order of a selected column by moving it up the list
- **Move Down** Change the order of a selected column by moving it down the list

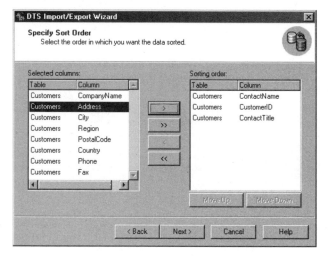

Figure 7-10. *Use the Specify Sort Order dialog box to set the sort order for the data.*

6. Set the query criteria. To choose all rows in the selection, select the All Rows option button. To set specific query criteria, select the Only Rows Meeting Criteria option button and then use the fields provided to set the query criteria. Figure 7-11 shows an example.

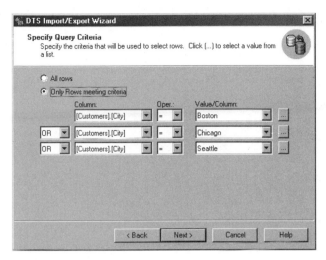

Figure 7-11. *Select the columns you want to work with and the values to search for. Use the And/Or operation to determine how to apply multiple query parameters. Use the build button (...) to the right of the query criteria to see the available values for the selected column.*

7. The result of the Query Builder procedure is a complete SQL statement that you can use to select data for exporting.

8. Click Parse to ensure that the query runs. If necessary, rebuild the *query* or *remove* statements that are causing errors.

9. Click Next to continue. The next dialog box you'll see is the Select Source Table(s) And View(s) dialog box discussed in the section of this chapter entitled "Specifying Tables and Views to Copy."

10. The default table name is Results. Click in the Destination Table column to set a new name for the destination table.

11. Click the button in the Transform column to manipulate the data before writing it to the destination. Transforming the data is covered in Stage 3.

Selecting Objects to Transfer

The only time you can select objects to transfer is when you copy between SQL Server databases. You select objects to transfer by completing the following steps:

1. In the Specify Table Copy Or Query dialog box, select the Copy Objects And Data Between SQL Server Databases option button and then click Next. This displays the Select Objects To Copy dialog box shown in Figure 7-12.

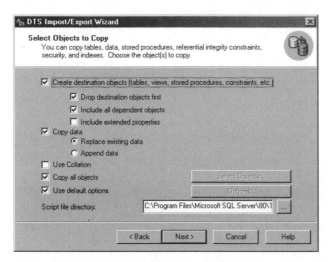

Figure 7-12. *In the Select Objects To Copy dialog box, select the objects you want to transfer.*

2. You use the options of the Select Objects To Copy dialog box as follows:

- **Create Destination Objects**   When selected, creates objects at the destination (if necessary) and allows you to determine what happens to existing objects as well as whether dependent objects are transferred.

- **Drop Destination Objects First**   Drops existing objects from the destination database.

- **Include All Dependent Objects**   Ensures that dependent objects are transferred even if they aren't explicitly selected.

- **Include Extended Properties**   Ensures extended properties are transferred even if they aren't explicitly selected.

- **Copy Data**   When selected, copies data along with the source objects. When cleared, only the objects are created at the destination.

- **Replace Existing Data**   If you choose to copy data, you can replace all existing data for the selected objects by selecting this option button.

- **Append Data**   If you choose to copy data, you can add data from the source objects to the current data in the destination database by selecting this option.

- **Use Collation**   When selected, the current collation is preserved in the destination database. Otherwise, no collation is used and the objects aren't set to a specific collation. As a result, the destination database's default collation takes effect.

- **Copy All Objects** When selected, transfers all objects from the source to the destination. Cancel this option and then click Select Objects to select individual objects.

- **Use Default Options** Select this option to use the default transfer options. To configure the options manually, clear this check box and then click Options.

- **Script File Directory** Sets the directory for scripts created when you select the Generate Scripts In Unicode option in the Advanced Options dialog box.

3. Click Next to continue to Stage 4, skipping Stage 3.

Stage 3: Formatting and Transformation

Transformation is the process of manipulating the source data and formatting it for the chosen destination. The way you transform and format data depends on the destination you've chosen. With most types of files, databases, and spreadsheets, you go through a column mapping and transformation process. But if you've chosen a text file as the destination, you must also specify the format of the output file. Because the formatting options are essentially the same as those used for importing, I won't cover them here and will instead refer you to the "Importing and Exporting Text Files" section of this chapter.

Unless you specify otherwise, the DTS Import/Export Wizard sets default mapping for all selected tables. This default mapping

- Specifies that every column in the source table is copied

- Maps the original column name, data type, nullability, size, precision, and scale to the destination table

- Appends the source data to the destination table and creates the destination table if it doesn't exist

You can override the default mappings by completing the following steps:

1. The Select Source Tables dialog box lists the results of your query or all of the available tables in the source database, spreadsheet, or file that you've selected. If you've selected a particular table, you'll find a button in the Transform column. Click this button to open the Column Mappings And Transformations dialog box shown in Figure 7-13.

2. Click the Column Mappings tab and then set the general transfer options as follows:

   - **Create Destination Table** Creates the destination table before copying source data. If the destination table exists, you must select Drop And Recreate Destination Table. Otherwise an error will occur.

   - **Delete Rows In Destination Table** Deletes all rows in the destination table before copying the source data. Indexes and constraints on the destination table remain.

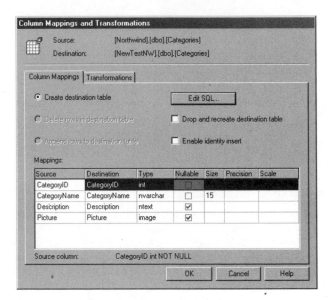

Figure 7-13. *Use the Column Mappings tab to map individual values in the selected table's columns.*

- **Append Rows To Destination Table** Inserts the source data into the destination table instead of overwriting existing data. This option doesn't affect existing data, indexes, or constraints in the destination table.

 Note Rows may not necessarily be appended to the end of the destination table. To determine where rows are inserted, use a clustered index on the destination table.

- **Drop And Recreate Destination Table** Drops and recreates the destination table before attempting to copy data into it, which permanently deletes all existing data and indexes.

 Tip If the table exists at the destination, you must drop and recreate it to map new column values to the destination table. Otherwise, you can only map source columns to different destination columns.

- **Enable Identity Insert** Allows you to insert explicit values into the identity column of a table. This option is available only on SQL Server and only if an identity column is detected.
- **Edit SQL** Displays the Create Table SQL Statement dialog box, which allows you to customize the default CREATE TABLE statement.

3. After you set the general transfer options, use the fields in the Mappings list box to determine how values are mapped from the source to the destination. The fields of this list box are all set to default values based on the source column. If you want to override these values for a new table or if you're dropping and recreating an existing table, you can modify these values. The Mapping fields are used as follows:

- **Source**   Sets the source column to map to a destination column. If you choose <ignore>, the source data isn't copied. Entering <ignore> can result in an error if there is no DEFAULT value and the destination is defined as NOT NULL.

- **Destination**   Click in this column and then select an existing column name or type a new column name for the destination table. Use the <ignore> option if the destination column shouldn't be created.

Note   If the destination column already exists and you choose <ignore>, the source data isn't copied into this column.

- **Type**   Select a data type for the Destination column. If you select a different data type than the source column, the data is converted to the new data type during the transfer.

Note   Make sure you select a valid conversion option. The DTS Import/ Export Wizard won't let you truncate data, and if you try to, an error occurs.

- **Nullable**   Select this check box if the destination allows NULL values.

- **Size**   Sets the length of the destination column. This value is applicable only for the *char, varchar, nchar, nvarchar, binary,* and *varbinary* data types.

Note   Setting the size smaller than the length of the source data can result in data truncation. If this happens, the DTS Import/Export Wizard will generate an error and won't complete the transfer.

- **Precision**   Sets the maximum number of decimal digits, including decimal places. For decimal and numeric data types only.

- **Scale**   Sets the maximum number of digits to the right of the decimal point. This value must be less than or equal to Precision and applies to decimal and numeric data types only.

4. Once you complete the mappings, you can fine tune the transformation. Click the Transformation tab. As shown in Figure 7-14, the DTS Import/Export Wizard now lets you perform the actions on the following page.

- Copy source columns directly to destination columns and set advanced flags for the transformation.
- Transform information as it's copied to the destination using a script.

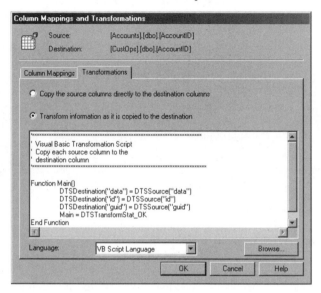

Figure 7-14. *With the Transformations tab you can set transformation options or use a script for the transformation.*

5. To copy source columns directly, select the Copy The Source Columns Directly To The Destination Columns option button. By default, all possible conversions are allowed.

6. To use a script for the transformation, select Transform Information As It Is Copied To The Destination. Next, use the Language drop-down list box to select your preferred scripting language. When you make a selection, the default script is converted to your chosen scripting language. You can then add to the default script as necessary or click Browse to find and import a script you've created in another application.

7. Click OK and then repeat this process for other tables you want to transform.

8. When you're ready to continue, click Next.

Stage 4: Save, Schedule, and Replicate

The end of the road is in sight, really! At this stage you specify when to use the package you've created and whether the package should be saved for future use. Now you should be on the Save, Schedule, And Replicate Package dialog box shown in Figure 7-15. To use this dialog box, complete the following steps:

1. Use the options under the When heading to specify when the DTS package is executed. You can use any combination of the available options, including

   - **Run Immediately**   Run the package now

   - **Use Replication To Publish Destination Data**   Set up replication between the source and destination using the package you just created

   - **Schedule DTS Package For Later Execution**   Set up a schedule for when this package should run

Tip   You don't have to select any of these options to save the package. Simply clear all the check boxes under the When heading and then select a Save DTS Package option.

2. Use the options under the Save heading to save the package for future use. If you want to save the package for use later, you should select the Save DTS Package check box and then specify where the package should be saved. The available locations are

   - **SQL Server**   Saves as a local package where the package is accessible for use on the designated server.

   - **SQL Server Meta Data Services**   Saves to the designated server's repository database, where the package can be shared with other servers through Meta Data Services.

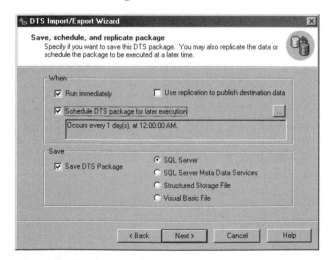

Figure 7-15. *Now that you've configured the package, you can use the Save, Schedule, And Replicate Package dialog box to run it and save it for future use.*

- **Structure Storage File** Saves as a COM-structured file. You can add additional packages to the file as long as they have a different package name. You can then copy, move, or e-mail the file to a different location.

- **Visual Basic File** Saves as a Visual Basic file, where the package can be used in Visual Basic programs.

3. When you're finished configuring run and save options, click Next.

4. If you've opted to save the package, the next dialog box lets you set the save location (see Figure 7-16). The options are slightly different depending on the save location you previously selected.

5. Type a name and description of the package using the Name and Description fields, respectively. The name should be unique for the target location.

6. If you're saving the package to SQL Server you can password-protect the package and prevent unauthorized users from working with it. Type an owner password and a user password in the fields provided. Anyone with the owner password can design, schedule, and execute the package. Anyone with the user password can only schedule or execute the package. Use the Server Name drop-down menu to select which SQL Server the package is saved to. Select the type of authentication to use by selecting one of the option buttons for either Windows Authentication or SQL Server Authentication. Provide an authorized username and password if you select SQL Server Authentication.

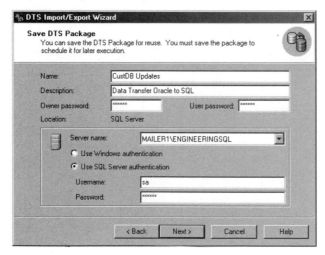

Figure 7-16. *In the Save DTS Package dialog box, provide additional information needed to save the package to a local or remote system.*

7. If you want to save the package to either a Structured Storage or Visual Basic file, set the file location using the File Name field. If you choose the SQL Server Meta Data Services option, select a destination server to save the package to by using the Server Name drop-down list box or type the server name directly. Select an authentication mode and type a username and password as needed.

8. Click Next and then Finish. If you've elected to run the package immediately, SQL Server runs the package. As each step is completed (or fails), the status is updated. If an error occurs, you can double-click its entry to view a detailed description of the error. Errors may halt execution of the package, and if they do, you'll need to redesign the package using DTS Designer or recreate the package using the DTS Import/Export Wizard.

Working with DTS Packages

SQL Server stores DTS packages as local packages, Meta Data Services packages, and file-based packages. You manage packages through Enterprise Manager, the DTS Run utility for Windows, or through the Dtsrun command-line utility.

Examining, Running, and Scheduling Packages

In Enterprise Manager you can examine, run, or schedule packages you've created by completing the following steps:

1. Start Enterprise Manager and then access the server you want to work with.

2. Click the plus sign (+) next to the server's Data Transformation Services folder.

3. You can now perform the following tasks:

   - **View local packages**   To view local packages on the selected server, click the Local Packages entry in the left pane. As shown in Figure 7-17, local packages are then listed in the right pane.

   - **View Meta Data Services packages**   To view packages in the server's repository database, click the Meta Data Services Packages entry in the left pane.

   - **View meta data**   To access the repository database's meta data, click the Meta Data entry in the left pane.

   - **Run a package**   To run a local or repository package, right-click its entry in the right pane and choose Execute Package from the shortcut menu.

   - **Schedule a package to run**   To schedule a local or repository package, right-click it and from the shortcut menu, choose Schedule Package. Then configure the package as a recurring job using the Edit Recurring Job dialog box. Scheduling is covered in Chapter 12, "Database Automation and Maintenance."

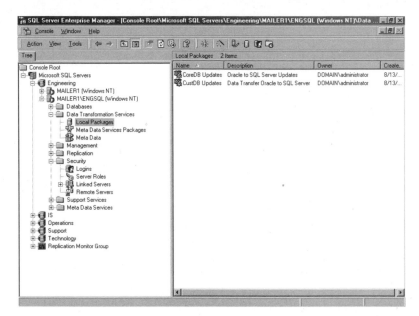

Figure 7-17. *You access packages through the Data Transformation Services folder.*

- **Modify a package's design** To modify a package's design, right-click it and from the shortcut menu, choose Design Package. This starts the DTS Designer.

- **View or modify file packages** To view or modify packages stored in files, right-click the Data Transformation Services folder, choose All Tasks from the shortcut menu, and then click Open Package. Use the Select File dialog box to select the package.

Managing Packages Using the DTS Run Utility for Windows

You can use the DTS Run utility for Windows to execute and manage DTS packages as an alternative to the Dtsrun command-line utility. The DTS Run utility for Windows provides a graphical interface to most of the execution options that are available with the Dtsrun command-line utility. You start the DTS Run utility for Windows by completing the following steps:

1. From the command line, type dtsrunui. This starts the DTS Run utility and displays the DTS Run dialog box as shown in Figure 7-18.

2. Use the Location drop-down list box to specify the type of package you'll be working with. Select either SQL Server, SQL Server Meta Data Services, or Structured Storage File.

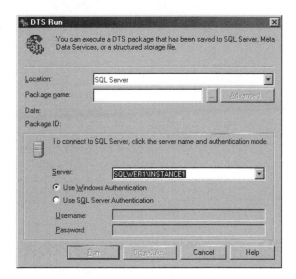

Figure 7-18. *The DTS Run utility for Windows provides a subset of the available execution options in the Dtsrun command-line utility in the form of dialog boxes.*

3. Use the Server combo box to choose an existing source server location or to specify the source server location. Afterward, choose the authentication type. With SQL Server authentication you must also provide a username and password.

4. Click the build button (...) next to the Package Name field. You'll see the Select Package dialog box as shown in Figure 7-19.

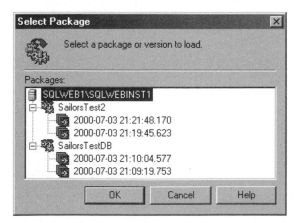

Figure 7-19. *The Select Package dialog box provides a list of available packages and specific versions associated with each package.*

5. Click the + sign next to the package that you want to execute. This will display specific versions associated with the package as shown in Figure 7-19. Select the version of the package that you want to execute and then click OK.

6. In the DTS Run dialog box, click Advanced to set additional options for global variables and logging. You can also use the Generate button to create a command-line script that executes the package.

7. To schedule the package to run at a later time, click Schedule. Specify the run schedule for the package and then click OK.

8. After you complete all modifications, click Run to run the package. The Executing DTS Package dialog box indicates the status of the package execution process. A message is displayed when the package has completed executing. Click OK to close the message dialog box. Click Done to close the Executing DTS Package dialog box.

Managing Packages from the Command Line

To manage packages from the command line, you can use Dtsrun. This utility works with all package types. By default, Dtsrun executes the specified package, but you can also use the utility to delete or overwrite packages. You delete local or repository packages to drop them from SQL Server. You overwrite file-based packages to empty their associated file. The syntax and usage for Dtsrun is shown as Sample 7-2.

Sample 7-2. Dtsrun Syntax and Usage

Syntax

```
dtsrun /~S ServerName [{[/~U UserName /~P Password] or [/E]}]

  /~N PackageName [/~M PackagePassword] [/~G PackageGuidString]

  [/~V PackageVersionGuidString] [/~A GlobalVariableName]

  [/~L LogFileName] [/~W WriteStatusToEventLogTrueOrFalse ]

  [/~F StructuredStorageUNCfilename] <overwritten if /S also
  used>

  [/~R RepositoryDatabaseName] <load package from repository if
  blank>
```

By default, Dtsrun executes the package. You can change this behavior with these options:

```
/!X <Do not execute; retrieve Package to /F filename>

/!D <Do not execute; drop package from SQL Server>

/!Y <Do not execute; output encrypted command line>

/!C <Copies command line to Windows clipboard (may be used with /
!Y and /!X)>
```

(continued)

Sample 7-2. *(continued)*
Usage

```
dtsrun /~S"zeta" /~U"sa" /~P"gorilla" /~N"DTS Customer"
```

Note The tilde (~) is optional. If you use the tilde, the parameter is specified as hexadecimal text with an encrypted value.

Understanding BCP

BCP offers a command-line alternative to DTS. The Transact-SQL counterpart to BCP import is BULK INSERT. You'll find that BULK INSERT has a similar syntax when used for importing data. To learn more about BCP, let's examine

- Basics
- Syntax
- Permissions
- Modes
- Importing data
- Exporting data

BCP Basics

Although BCP has been around for some time, it may remain a favorite of database administrators for a while longer because of its great performance and minimal overhead. You'll find that import and export processes tend to be very fast and that BCP uses very little memory to operate. BCP doesn't have a graphical user interface (GUI) and is best used in two situations:

- To import data from a text file to a single SQL Server table or view
- To export data to a text file from a single SQL Server table or view

When transferring data to or from SQL Server, BCP uses ODBC. This is a change from previous versions that communicated with SQL Server through the DB-Library.

Tip With ODBC datetime, *smalldatetime* and *money* data types are treated differently than with DB-Library. You'll find that the *datetime* format is now yyyymmdd hh:mm:ss rather than mmm dd yyy hh:mm (A.M./ P.M.) and the *money* format now has no commas with four digits after the decimal instead of commas and two digits after the decimal.

Note When importing with BCP, columns with computed values and timestamps are ignored. SQL Server can automatically assign values. To do this, use a format file to specify that the computed values or timestamp columns in the table should be skipped; SQL Server then automatically assigns values for the column. During export, computed values and timestamps are handled like other values.

BCP Syntax

Before exploring how to use BCP, let's look at the command syntax, which, as you can see from Sample 7-3, is fairly extensive. BCP switches are case and order sensitive. You must use them in the exact manner expected. If you don't, you'll have problems.

Table 7-2 provides a summary of key BCP parameters.

Sample 7-3. BCP Syntax and Usage

Syntax

```
bcp {[[dbname.][owner].]{tablename | viewname } | "query"}
  {in | out | queryout | format} datafile
  [switch1 [parameter1]] [switch2 [parameter2]]
  [switchN [parameterN]]
```

Usage

```
bcp pubs..customer out customers.txt -c -U sa -P"guerilla"
bcp pubs..customer in customers.txt -f customers.fmt -U sa
  -P"guerilla"
```

Table 7-2. Key Parameters Used with BCP

Parameter	Description
dbname	The name of the database. This parameter is optional and if it's not supplied, the user's default database is used.
owner	The owner of the table or view being used. Use the .. syntax for a general owner, such as pubs..authors instead of pubs.dbo.authors.
tablename	The name of the table to access. Use the # or ## syntax to copy a temporary table.
viewname	The name of the destination view when copying data into SQL Server; the source view when copying data from SQL Server.

(continued)

Table 7-2. *(continued)*

Parameter	Description
query	T-SQL statement that generates a result set. Using double quotation marks and specifying the queryout parameter are mandatory with this option.
in	Specifies an import process.
out	Specifies an export process.
format	Sets the creation of a format file. You must set the name of the format file with the –f switch and also specify the format for this file with n, -c, -w, or –V.
queryout	Must be used when exporting output from a SQL query or stored procedure.
datafile	The name of the file for importing or the name of the file to create when exporting. This can include the full file path.

BCP also supports a wide variety of switches. These switches and their associated parameters are summarized in Table 7-3.

Table 7-3. Switches Used with BCP

Switch	Description
-a packetsize	Sets the number of bytes in a network packet. Default is 4096 on Windows NT and 512 for MS-DOS. The valid range is 512 to 65,535 bytes.
-b batchsize	The number of rows to transfer in the batch. Each batch is copied to the server as one transaction. By default all rows are copied in a single batch. Don't use with the -h ROWS_PER_BATCH option.
-c	Character data mode (ASCII text) for transfers to and from non-SQL Server products.
-C codepage	Code page being used by the import file. Only relevant when the data contains *char*, *varchar*, or *text* columns with character values greater than 127 or less than 32. Use the code page value ACP with ANSI ISO 1252 data, RAW when no conversion should occur, OEM to use the client's default code page, or type a specific code page value, such as 850.
-e errfile	Stores error messages in the specified error file.
-E	Uses identity values. Otherwise identity values are ignored and automatically assigned new ones.
-F firstrow	Sets the number of the first row to use.
-f formatfile	Sets the name and path to a BCP format file. The default filename is BCP.FMT.

(continued)

Table 7-3. *(continued)*

Switch	Description
-h "load hints"	Used to set load hints: ROWS_PER_BATCH, KILOBYTES_PER_BATCH, TABLOCK, CHECK_CONSTRAINTS, and ORDER.
-i inputfile	Sets the name of a response file, containing responses to the command prompt questions for each field when performing a bulk copy using interactive mode.
-k	Preserves null values.
-L lastrow	Sets the last row to use.
-m maxerrors	Sets the maximum number of errors that can occur before terminating BCP. The default is 10.
-N	Sets native export for noncharacter data and Unicode character export for character data.
-n	Sets native data mode, which is SQL Server-specific.
-o outfile	File to redirect output of BCP during unattended operation.
-P password	Password to use to log on.
-q	Uses quoted identifiers.
-R	Enables regional format copy for currency, date, and time data.
-r rowterminator	Sets the row terminator.
-S servername	Sets the SQL Server name.
-t fieldterminator	Sets the field terminator.
-T	Uses a trusted connection.
-U username	Sets the username for logon.
-V	Sets the data type version for native and character formats. For SQL Server 6.0 format use 60, for SQL Server 6.5 use 65, and for SQL Server 7.0 use 70.
-v	Displays the BCP version.
-w	Sets wide character (Unicode) mode.

BCP Permissions and Modes

Although any user can run BCP, only users with appropriate permissions can access SQL Server and the specified database objects. When you run BCP, you can set logon information using the U and P switches. For unattended operations, using these switches is essential to ensure that permissions are granted appropriately. To import data into a table, the user needs Insert permission on the target table. To export data from a table, the user needs Select permission for the source table.

BCP can use three different modes:

- **Character mode** Used when you want to import or export data as ASCII text. The switch to set this mode is c.
- **Native mode** Used when you want to import or export data in native format. The switch to set this mode is n or N.
- **Wide mode** Used when you want to import or export data as Unicode text. The switch to set this mode is w.

The character and wide modes are best when copying to a non-SQL Server product. Use native mode when you're copying data between SQL Server tables. These modes all have their strengths and weaknesses. With character or wide mode files, you can view the contents and make sure that you have the right data set, but for imports you must also tell SQL Server how this data is formatted. You can do this through interactive prompts or by using a format file containing the responses to these prompts. With native mode, on the other hand, there's a tradeoff. You can't view the contents of native data files, but you don't have to specify data formatting information when importing files either.

Importing Data with BCP

With BCP you can import data in two ways. You can start an interactive session or you can set the necessary responses in a format file. The following example shows how you could start an interactive session.

```
bcp pubs..customer in customers.txt
```

To specify a format file, you use the f flag, such as

```
bcp pubs..customer in customers.txt -w -f customers.fmt
```

In an interactive session, BCP prompts you for information needed to complete the import or export process. BCP starts an interactive session when either of the following situations occur:

- You import without specifying the –c, -n, -w, or –N parameters.
- You export without specifying the –c, -n, -w, or –N parameters.

The interactive session allows you to customize the BCP process much as you do with a format file. In fact, before you try to create a format file, you should run BCP in interactive mode and then choose to have BCP create the necessary format file for you. This operation will give you a good idea of how to configure the format file.

For each column in a table you're importing, you'll see the following prompts during an interactive session:

```
Enter the file storage type of field [char]:
Enter prefix length of field [0]:
```

```
Enter length of field [5]:

Enter field terminator [none]:
```

 Tip Pressing Enter accepts the default values. To skip a column in an import file, type **0** for the prefix length, **0** for the field length, and **none** for the terminator type. You can't skip a column when exporting data.

These prompts ask you to type various kinds of information, and in every case the default value for the current column is shown in brackets. At the end of the interactive session, you'll be asked if you want to save your responses in a format file. If you answer Y, you can type the name of the format file when prompted, such as

```
Do you want to save this format information in a file? [Y/N]

Host filename [bcp.fmt]: customers.fmt
```

You can then use the format file for other BCP sessions by setting the f switch as specified earlier. Figure 7-20 shows a sample format file. Because the format file has a rigid syntax that you must follow, I recommend creating a sample file to get started. Each line in the file contains information fields that determine how data should be imported. These lines tell you the following information:

- The first line sets the version of BCP used. Here the version is 8.0.
- The second line sets the number of columns in the table you're importing. In the example the table contains 11 columns.
- Subsequent lines set the formatting of each column in the table from the first column to the last column.

```
bcp.fmt - Notepad
File  Edit  Format  Help
8.0
11
1       SQLNCHAR    2    10      " "    1     CustomerID     SQL_Lat
2       SQLNCHAR    2    80      " "    2     CompanyName    SQL_Lat
3       SQLNCHAR    2    60      " "    3     ContactName    SQL_Lat
4       SQLNCHAR    2    60      " "    4     ContactTitle   SQL_Lat
5       SQLNCHAR    2    120     " "    5     Address        SQL_Lat
6       SQLNCHAR    2    30      " "    6     City           SQL_Lat
7       SQLNCHAR    2    30      " "    7     Region         SQL_Lat
8       SQLNCHAR    2    20      " "    8     PostalCode     SQL_Lat
9       SQLNCHAR    2    30      " "    9     Country        SQL_Lat
10      SQLNCHAR    2    48      " "    10    Phone          SQL_Lat
11      SQLNCHAR    2    48      " "    11    Fax            SQL_Lat
```

Figure 7-20. *Format files are written in ASCII text and you can view them in Microsoft Notepad or any other text editor.*

The lines defining table columns are broken down into fields with each field setting a different input parameter. Normally, these fields are separated by spaces. The number of spaces doesn't really matter—provided there is at least one space. BCP treats one or more spaces as a field separator. File format fields operate in the following manner:

- Field 1 sets the column number you're describing from the data file.

- Field 2 sets the file storage type, which is simply the data type of the column.

- Field 3 sets the prefix length for compacted data. A value of zero specifies that no prefix is used.

- Field 4 sets the field length, which is the number of bytes required to store the data type. Use the default value provided whenever possible.

- Field 5 sets the field terminator. By default, BCP separates all fields but the last one with tabs (\t) and separates the last field with a carriage return and line field (\r\n).

- Field 6 sets the table column number in the database. For example, a value of 1 says the column corresponds to the first column in the database.

- Field 7 sets the table column name.

Exporting Data with BCP

When you export data, BCP creates a data file using the name you specify. With nonnative files (ASCII and Unicode text), the columns in this file are separated with tabs by default, with the last column having a carriage return and line feed. You specify a tab as a terminator with \t and carriage return and line feed with \r\n. In a format file, a tab can be an actual tab character or a series of five or more spaces.

As with importing data, you can handle data export interactively. For example, if you start an export session without specifying format information, you're prompted for this information. In the following example you export a table to a file called customers.txt and use semicolons as the delimiter:

```
bcp pubs..customer out customers.txt -c -t;
```

BCP Scripts

A BCP script is simply a batch file or a Windows Script Host file containing BCP commands. Sample 7-4 shows examples of how you could run BCP using various scripting options. If you don't know how to use batch files or Windows Script Host, two great resources are *Windows NT Scripting Administrator's Guide* (IDG Books, 1999) and *Windows 2000 Scripting Bible* (IDG Books, 2000).

Sample 7-4. Using BCP in a Script

sched-export.bat

```
@echo off
@if not "%OS%"=="Windows_NT" goto :EXIT
bcp pubs..customer out customers.txt -c -t, -Usa -P"guerilla"
:EXIT
```

sched-export.vbs

```
'Nightly Bulk Copy export for the customers table
'Writes output to cust.txt and errors to err.txt
Set ws = WScript.CreateObject("WScript.Shell")
ret = ws.Run("bcp pubs..customers out cust.txt -c -t, -Usa
  -Pguerilla -eerr.txt",0,"TRUE")
```

sched-export.js

```
\\Nightly Bulk Copy export for the customers table
\\Writes output to cust.txt and errors to err.txt
var ws = WScript.CreateObject("WScript.Shell");
ret = ws.Run("bcp pubs..customers out cust.txt -c -t, -Usa
  -Pguerilla -eerr.txt",0,"TRUE")
```

After you create a script file for the bulk copy command, you can schedule it as a task to run on your system. To schedule these scripts to run every night at midnight, you could use the following commands.

```
AT 00:00 /every:M,T,W,Th,F,S,Su "sched-export.bat"

AT 00:00 /every:M,T,W,Th,F,S,Su "cscript //B sched-export.js"

AT 00:00 /every:M,T,W,Th,F,S,Su "cscript //B sched-export.vbs"
```

> **More Info** For more information on scheduling tasks, see *Microsoft Windows NT Server 4.0 Administrator's Pocket Consultant* (Microsoft Press, 1999) or *Microsoft Windows 2000 Administrator's Pocket Consultant* (Microsoft Press, 2000).

BULK INSERT

A Transact-SQL command for importing data into a database is BULK INSERT. You can use BULK INSERT in much the same way as you use BCP. In fact, most of the parameters for BULK INSERT are the same as those used with BCP—they just have a different syntax. This syntax is shown as Sample 7-5.

Sample 7-5. BULK INSERT Syntax and Usage

Syntax

```
BULK INSERT [['dbname'.]['owner'].]{'tablename' FROM datafile}
 [WITH
 (
 [ BATCHSIZE [= batch_size]]
 [[,] CHECK_CONSTRAINTS]
 [[,] CODEPAGE [= 'ACP' | 'OEM' | 'RAW' | 'code_page']]
 [[,] DATAFILETYPE [=
 {'char' | 'native'| 'widechar' | 'widenative'}]]
 [[,] FIELDTERMINATOR [= 'field_terminator']]
 [[,] FIRSTROW [= first_row]]
 [[,] FIRETRIGGERS [= fire_triggers]]
 [[,] FORMATFILE [= 'format_file_path']]
 [[,] KEEPIDENTITY]
 [[,] KEEPNULLS]
 [[,] KILOBYTES_PER_BATCH [= kilobytes_per_batch]]
 [[,] LASTROW [= last_row]]
 [[,] MAXERRORS [= max_errors]]
 [[,] ORDER ({column [ASC | DESC]} [,...n])]
 [[,] ROWS_PER_BATCH [= rows_per_batch]]
 [[,] ROWTERMINATOR [= 'row_terminator']]
 [[,] TABLOCK]
 )
 ]
```

(continued)

Sample 7-5. *(continued)*
Usage

```
BULK INSERT pubs..customers FROM 'c:\data\customer.txt'


BULK INSERT pubs..customers FROM 'c:\cust.txt' with
 (DATAFILETYPE = 'char',
 FORMATFILE='c:\cust.fmt')
```

In order to use BULK INSERT, you must set the database properties option Select Into/Bulk Copy. To set this option, open the Properties dialog box for the database you want to work with, choose the Options tab, and then select the Select Into/Bulk Copy check box.

Chapter 8

Linked Servers and Distributed Transactions

Networking environments are becoming more and more complex. Organizations that once may have had a single Microsoft SQL Server are now finding that they need additional servers or that they need to integrate their existing server with other heterogeneous data sources. SQL Server 2000 provides several features for integrating SQL Server databases with other SQL Server databases and with other data sources, including distributed data, linked servers, and replication. This chapter focuses on linked servers and distributed data. Distributed data includes support for distributed queries, distributed transactions, and remote stored procedure execution. These distributed data features are handled through linked servers, which can be SQL Servers or non-SQL Servers. Replication is covered in the next chapter.

Working with Linked Servers and Distributed Data

Before you use distributed data, you must configure the linked servers you want to use. Linked servers depend on OLE DB providers to communicate with one another. Through OLE DB, you can link instances of SQL Server to other instances of SQL Server as well as to other data sources.

You use linked servers to handle distributed queries, distributed transactions, remote stored procedure calls, and replication. Basically, queries and transactions are distributed when they make use of two or more database server instances. For example, if a client is connected to one server instance and starts a query that accesses a different server instance, the query is distributed. On the other hand, if the same client queries two different databases on the same server instance, the query is considered a local query and is handled internally.

Using Distributed Queries

When you execute a distributed query, SQL Server interprets the command and then breaks it down for the destination OLE DB provider using rowset requests. A rowset is a type of database object that enables OLE DB data providers to support data with a tabular format. As their name implies, rowset objects represent a set of rows and columns of data. After creating the rowset objects, the OLE DB provider calls the data source, opens the necessary files, and returns the requested information as rowsets. SQL Server then formats the rowsets as result sets and adds any applicable output parameters.

 Note With SQL-92, user connections must have the ANSI_NULLS and ANSI_WARNINGS options before they can execute distributed queries. Be sure to configure these options, if necessary. For more information, see the section of Chapter 2 entitled "Configuring User and Remote Connections."

You can create ad hoc distributed queries by creating your own rowsets. To do this, you use the *Openrowset* function. When you do this, you don't need to use linked servers and you can use the *Openrowset* function in place of a table in a query as long as you pass parameters that identify the OLE DB data source and provider.

You use the *Openrowset* function in the same way that you use virtual tables. Simply replace the virtual table reference with an *Openrowset* reference. Sample 8-1 shows the syntax and usage of *Openrowset*.

Sample 8-1. *Openrowset* **Syntax and Usage**

Syntax

```
OPENROWSET('provider_name',
  {'datasource';'user_id';'password' | 'provider_string'},
  {[catalog.][schema.]object | 'query'})
```

Usage

```
USE pubs
GO
SELECT a.*
  FROM OPENROWSET('SQLOLEDB','Pluto';'netUser';'totem12',
  'SELECT * FROM pubs.dbo.authors ORDER BY au_lname, au_fname')
AS a
GO


SELECT o.*
  FROM OPENROWSET('Microsoft.Jet.OLEDB.4.0','C:\
  northwind.mdb';'Admin';"", 'Orders')
AS o
```

Using Distributed Transactions

Distributed transactions are transactions that use distributed queries or remote procedure calls (RPCs). As you might expect, distributed transactions are a bit more involved than distributed queries. This is primarily because you need a mechanism that ensures that transactions are uniformly committed or rolled back on all the linked servers. For example, if you start a transaction that updates databases on three different server instances, you want to ensure that the transaction is committed when it's successfully completed or that the transaction is rolled back if an error occurs. In this way you ensure the integrity of the databases involved in the distributed transaction.

On SQL Server, three components are required for distributed transactions to be handled properly:

- **Resource managers** You must configure resource managers, which are the linked servers used in the distributed transactions. For details, see the section of this chapter entitled "Managing Linked Servers."
- **Distributed Transaction Coordinator service** The Distributed Transaction Coordinator service must be running on all servers handling distributed transactions. If it's not, distributed transactions won't work properly.
- **Transaction manager** The transaction manager coordinates and manages distributed transactions. The transaction manager on SQL Server is the Distributed Transaction Coordinator.

Note Applications other than SQL Server can use the Distributed Transaction Coordinator. If you try to analyze Distributed Transaction Coordinator performance, you should note which applications besides SQL Server are using Distributed Transaction Coordinator.

Each server instance involved in a distributed transaction is known as a *resource manager*. Resource managers coordinate transactions through a transaction manager, such as the Microsoft Distributed Transaction Coordinator. You can use other transaction managers just as long as they support the X/Open XA specification for distributed transaction processing.

You handle distributed transactions in much the same manner as local transactions. Applications start distributed transactions in several ways:

- Explicitly, by using BEGIN DISTRIBUTED TRANSACTION
- Explicitly, by using OLE DB methods or ODBC functions to join a distributed transaction started by the application
- Implicitly, by executing a distributed query within a local transaction
- Implicitly, by calling a remote stored procedure within a local transaction (provided the REMOTE_PROC_TRANSACTIONS option is set ON)

At the end of the transaction the application requests that the transaction be either committed or rolled back. To ensure that the transaction is handled properly on all servers, even if problems occur during the transaction, the transaction manager uses a commit process with two phases:

- **Phase 1: The prepare phase** The transaction manager sends a prepare to commit request to all the resource managers involved in the transaction. Each resource manager performs any necessary preparatory tasks and then reports their success or failure to the transaction manager. If all the resource managers are ready to commit, the transaction manager broadcasts a commit message and the transaction enters phase 2, the commit phase.

- **Phase 2: The commit phase** The resource managers attempt to commit the transaction. Each resource manager then sends back a success or failure message. If all the resource managers report success, the transaction manager marks the transaction as completed and reports this to the application. If a resource manager fails in either phase, the transaction enters a pending state that must be resolved before the transaction can continue. Otherwise, the transaction is rolled back.

SQL Server applications manage distributed transactions either through Transact-SQL or through the SQL Server database application programming interface (API). SQL Server itself supports distributed transactions using the ITransactionLocal (local transaction) and ITransactionJoin (distributed transactions) OLE DB interfaces as well as the rowset objects discussed previously. If an OLE DB provider doesn't support ITransactionJoin, then only read-only procedures are allowed for that provider. Similarly, the types of queries you can execute on a linked server depend on the OLE DB provider you're using.

With distributed queries and transactions, you can use most data manipulation language (DML) commands, such as SELECT, INSERT, UPDATE, and DELETE. You can't, however, use data definition language (DDL) commands, such as CREATE, DROP, or ALTER. If you need to use DDL commands on linked servers, you may want to create stored procedures and then execute these stored procedures remotely, as necessary.

Running the Distributed Transaction Coordinator Service

The Distributed Transaction Coordinator service must run on each server that handles distributed transactions, and you'll usually want the service to start automatically when the system starts. This ensures that the distributed transactions are executed as expected. Using SQL Server Service Manager, you can control the Distributed Transaction Coordinator service just as you do other SQL Server-related services. For details, see the section of Chapter 3 entitled "Managing SQL Server Service with Service Manager."

You can also start and stop the Distributed Transaction Coordinator service in Enterprise Manager. To do this, complete the following steps:

1. Start Enterprise Manager and then access the server that you want to configure.

2. Click the plus sign (+) next to the server's Support Services folder and then right-click Distributed Transaction Coordinator.

3. To start the Distributed Transaction Coordinator service, from the shortcut menu, choose Start.

4. To stop the Distributed Transaction Coordinator service, from the shortcut menu, choose Stop.

Managing Linked Servers

To work properly, distributed queries and transactions depend on linked servers. You configure the linked servers you want to work with by registering their connection and data source information in SQL Server. Afterward, you can reference the linked server using a single logical name. If you no longer need to link to a server, you can remove the linked server connection.

Adding Linked Servers

If you want a server to be able to use distributed queries, distributed transactions, or RPCs (or all three), you must configure linked server connections to other servers. For example, if clients that access a server named Zeta make distributed queries to Pluto and Omega, you'll want to configure Pluto and Omega as linked servers on Zeta. If clients that connect to Pluto make distributed queries to Zeta and Omega, you'll want to configure Zeta and Omega as linked servers on Pluto. To add a linked server, complete the following steps:

1. Start Enterprise Manager and then access the server you want to configure.

2. Click the plus sign (+) next to the server's Security folder.

3. Right-click the Linked Servers entry and from the shortcut menu, choose New Linked Server. This opens the dialog box shown in Figure 8-1.

4. In the Linked Server field, type the name of the linked server to create.

5. If you're linking to a SQL Server, select the SQL Server option button.

6. If you're linking to a different data source, select the Other Data Source option button and then configure the data source using the input fields provided. You can't configure unavailable fields for the selected provider. The available fields are summarized in Table 8-1, and you can use them as follows:

- **Provider Name** Use the drop-down list box to select the name of the OLE DB provider to use when communicating with the specified linked server

- **Product Name** Sets the server product name for the OLE DB data source

- **Data Source** Sets the OLE DB data source, which is used to initialize the OLE DB provider

- **Provider String** Sets a provider-specific connection string that identifies a unique data source

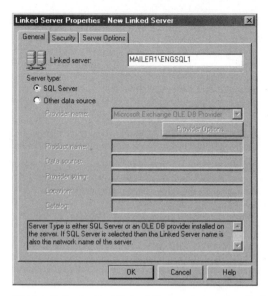

Figure 8-1. *In the Linked Server Properties dialog box, choose SQL Server or Other Data Source, and then set Linked Server options and security.*

- **Location** Sets the location of the database for the OLE DB provider
- **Catalog** Sets the catalog to use when connecting to the OLE DB provider

Real World The most commonly used option combinations are provider name and data source. For example, if you were configuring a linked server for a Microsoft Access database or a Microsoft Excel spreadsheet, you would select Microsoft Jet 4.0 OLE DB Provider and then set the data source name. With Oracle, you would select Microsoft OLE DB Provider For Oracle and then set the data source name.

7. If you're using a data source other than SQL Server, you can configure options for the OLE DB provider. Click Provider Options and then use the dialog box shown in Figure 8-2 to configure provider options.

8. Configure server-specific settings using these fields from the Server Options tab:

- **Collation Compatible** Set this option to enable SQL Server to send comparisons on character columns to the provider. Otherwise, SQL Server evaluates comparisons on character columns locally. Set this option only when the linked server has the same collation as the local server.

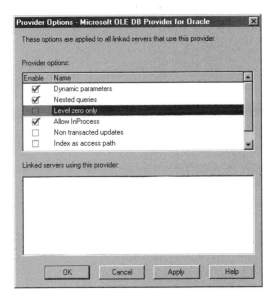

Figure 8-2. *Use the Provider Options dialog box to set options for OLE DB providers to configure or disable features, such as nested queries.*

Note Collation compatible controls sort order settings. If you don't
select this option, SQL Server uses the local sort order. This affects the
order of result sets, and you should note it when you develop SQL Server
applications or configure clients.

- **Data Access** Set this option to enable the linked server for distributed query access.

- **RPC** Set this option to enable remote procedure calls from the linked server.

- **RPC Out** Set this option to enable RPC to the linked server.

- **Use Remote Collation** Set this option to have SQL Server use the collation from the linked server's character columns. If you don't set this option, SQL Server interprets data from the linked server using the default collation of the local server instance. Note that only SQL Server databases take advantage of this option.

- **Collation Name** Set this option to assign a specific collation for queries and transactions. Note that you must clear the Collation Compatible check box before you can set this option.

- **Connection Timeout** Sets the timeout value for connections made to the remote server.

- **Query Timeout** Sets the timeout for queries made to the remote server.

9. Click OK to create the linked server. Next, you'll need to configure security settings for the linked server. You may also need to configure Distributed Transaction Coordinator. For details, see the section of this chapter entitled "Running the Distributed Transaction Coordinator Service."

The corresponding Transact-SQL command for adding linked servers is *sp_addlinkedserver*. You use this stored procedure as shown in Sample 8-2.

Sample 8-2. *sp_addlinkedserver* Syntax and Usage

Syntax

```
sp_addlinkedserver [@server =] 'server'
 [, [@srvproduct =] 'product_name']
 [, [@provider =] 'provider_name']
 [, [@datasrc =] 'data_source']
 [, [@location =] 'location']
 [, [@provstr =] 'provider_string']
 [, [@catalog =] 'catalog']
```

Usage

```
EXEC sp_addlinkedserver @server='linkedservername',
 @svrproduct=", @provider='SQLOLEDB',
  @datasrc='linkedservername'
GO
```

Table 8-1 provides a summary of parameter values you can use when configuring various OLE DB providers. The table also shows the *sp_addlinkedserver* parameter values to use for each OLE DB provider. Because some providers have different configurations, there may be more than one row for a particular data source type.

Table 8-1. Parameter Values for Configuring OLE DB Providers

OLE DB Provider	Product Name	Provider Name	Data Source	Other
Microsoft OLE DB Provider for SQL Server	SQL Server			
Microsoft OLE DB Provider for SQL Server	SQL Server	SQLOLEDB	Network name of SQL Server	Set Catalog to Database name (optional)
Microsoft OLE DB Provider for Oracle	Any	MSDAORA	SQL*Net alias for Oracle database	

(continued)

Table 8-1. *(continued)*

OLE DB Provider	Product Name	Provider Name	Data Source	Other
Microsoft OLE DB Provider for Jet	Any	Microsoft.Jet. OLEDB.4.0	Full path name of Jet database file	
Microsoft OLE DB for Jet	Any	Microsoft.Jet. OLEDB.4.0	Full path name of Excel file	Set provider string to Excel 5.0, 97-2000
Microsoft OLE DB Provider for ODBC	Any	MSDASQL	System DSN of ODBC data source	
Microsoft OLE DB for ODBC	Any	MSDASQL		Set provider string to the ODBC connection string
Microsoft OLE DB for Indexing Service	Any	MSIDXS	Indexing Service catalog name	

Configuring Security for Linked Servers

You use linked server security to control access and to determine how local logins are used. By default, new linked servers are set to have no security context when a user login isn't defined. This blocks access to all logins not explicitly mapped to the linked server.

To change the security settings for a linked server, complete the following steps:

1. Start Enterprise Manager and then access the local server that contains the linked server definitions you want to work with.

2. Click the plus sign (+) next to the server's Security folder, and then click the plus sign (+) next to the Linked Servers entry. You should now see an entry for each linked server you created on the currently selected server.

3. Right-click the icon for the linked server you want to configure and then choose Properties.

4. In the Linked Servers Properties dialog box, click the Security tab, as shown in Figure 8-3.

5. Map local logins to remote logins, as necessary, using the following fields:

   - **Local Login**   Sets the ID of a local login that can connect to the linked server.

   - **Impersonate**   Select this check box to use the local login ID to connect to the linked server. The local login ID must exactly match a login ID on the linked server.

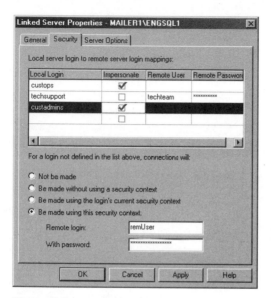

Figure 8-3. *Use the Security tab to control access to linked servers by mapping logins and by setting default security information for all other users.*

Note If you select the Impersonate check box, you can't map the local login to a remote login.

- **Remote User**   Sets the remote user to which the local login ID maps on the linked server.
- **Remote Password**   Sets the password for the remote user. If it's not provided, the user may be prompted for a password.

6. Use the option buttons and fields in the lower portion of the Security tab to set a default security context for all users who don't have a specific login setting for the linked server. These options are used as follows:

- **Not Be Made**   Users without logins aren't allowed access to the linked server.
- **Be Made Without Using A Security Context**   Blocks access to all logins not explicitly mapped to the linked server.
- **Be Made Using The Login's Current Security Context**   Logins not explicitly mapped to the linked server use their current login and password to connect to the linked server. Access is denied if the login and password don't exist on the linked server.
- **Be Made Using This Security Context**   Logins not explicitly mapped to the linked server will use the login and password provided in the Remote Login and With Password fields.

7. When you're finished configuring logins, click OK.

The related Transact-SQL command for configuring logins is *sp_addlinkedsrvlogin*. You can use this stored procedure as shown in Sample 8-3.

Sample 8-3. *sp_addlinkedsrvlogin* **Syntax and Usage**

Syntax

```
sp_addlinkedsrvlogin [@rmtsrvname =] 'rmtsrvname'
[,[@useself =] 'useself']
[,[@locallogin =] 'locallogin']
[,[@rmtuser =] 'rmtuser']
[,[@rmtpassword =] 'rmtpassword']
```

Usage

```
EXEC sp_addlinkedsrvlogin 'Pluto', 'true'

EXEC sp_addlinkedsrvlogin 'Pluto', 'false', NULL, 'remUser',
  'tangent23'

EXEC sp_addlinkedsrvlogin 'Pluto', 'false', 'Domain\GIJOE',
  'GEORGEJ', 'tango98'
```

Deleting Linked Servers

If you don't need a linked server anymore, you can delete it by completing the following steps:

1. Start Enterprise Manager and then access the local server that contains the linked server definition you want to delete.

2. Click the plus sign (+) next to the server's Security folder and then click the plus sign (+) next to the Linked Servers entry. You should now see an entry for each linked server you created on the local server.

3. Right-click the icon for the linked server you want to remove and then choose Delete. When prompted to confirm the action, choose Yes.

The Transact-SQL command to drop linked servers is *sp_dropserver*. The Transact-SQL command to drop linked server logins is *sp_droplinkedsrvlogin*. You can use these stored procedures as shown in Samples 8-4 and 8-5.

Sample 8-4. *sp_dropserver* **Syntax and Usage**

Syntax

```
sp_dropserver [@server =] 'server'
  [, [@droplogins =]{'droplogins' | NULL}]
```

(continued)

Sample 8-4. *(continued)*
Usage

```
sp_dropserver 'Pluto', 'droplogins'
```

Sample 8-5. *sp_droplinkedsrvlogin* **Syntax and Usage**

Syntax

```
sp_droplinkedsrvlogin [@rmtsrvname =] 'rmtsrvname',
  [@locallogin =]'locallogin'
```

Usage

```
sp_droplinkedsrvlogin 'Pluto', 'username'
```

Working with Remote Servers

Through a remote server, a client connected to one server can run a stored procedure on another server without having to establish another connection. The originating server handles the client's request and passes it to the remote server. The remote server then executes the referenced stored procedure and returns any results to the originating server, which in turn passes those results to the client.

You can establish remote server connections only with other SQL Servers. You can't connect to other database servers, such as Oracle. If you have existing applications that use remote server connections, you can configure remote servers and use these remote servers as you have with previous versions of SQL Server. However, if you're creating new applications, you should use the new distributed data features of SQL Server 2000. You'll find that these new features are much more versatile.

 Note SQL Server 2000 supports remote servers for backward compatibility only. On SQL Server 2000, you should use distributed queries and EXECUTE statements that execute stored procedures on linked servers. Note also that previous versions of SQL Server used remote servers for replication as well. SQL Server 2000 doesn't handle replication in this way. Instead, it uses linked servers to set up replication.

Setting Up Remote Servers in Enterprise Manager

You configure remote servers in pairs. You must make each server recognize the other as a remote server, and you must explicitly permit remote connections to each server in the pair. After you've configured the necessary connections, users logging on to either server in the pair can execute stored procedures remotely.

Tip If you have an existing application that uses remote servers, you may need to check the data services gateway setup. The only Open Data Services gateways supported by SQL Server 2000 are those that ship with SQL Server 2000. If you aren't using this version, you'll need to recompile the Open Data Services with the gateway files that ship with SQL Server 2000. Trying to call SQL Server 2000 with an older version of the gateway usually results in one of the following errors:

- Error 7399, Level 16, State 1

- OLE DB provider 'SQLOLEDB' reported an error. A provider-specific error occurred.

- Error 7304, Level 16, State 1

- Could not create a new session on OLE DB provider 'SQLOLEDB.' Reported an error.

- Error 7303, Level 16, State 1

- Unable to initialize data source object of OLE DB provider 'SQLOLEDB.'

You must configure each server in the pair to accept remote connections. You configure this SQL Server property setting as explained in the section of Chapter 2 entitled "Configuring Remote Server Connections." Don't forget to stop and start the SQL Server service on each server instance.

Next, you must configure each server in the pair to accept the other as a remote server. To do this, complete the following steps:

1. Start Enterprise Manager and then access the first server in the pair.
2. Click the plus sign (+) next to the server's Security folder.
3. Right-click the Remote Servers entry and from the shortcut menu, choose New Remote Server. This opens the dialog box shown in Figure 8-4.
4. In the Name field, type the name of the second server in the pair.
5. To enable the remote server to execute stored procedures on the current server using RPCs, select the RPC check box.
6. Determine how logins are used on the current server. You can configure logins in one of these ways:
   - To map remote logins to a local login with the same name, select Map All Remote Logins To and then select <Same Name> on the related drop-down list box.

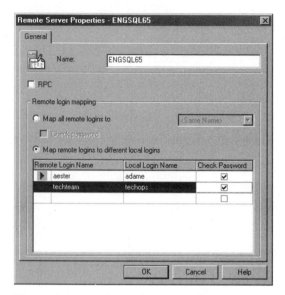

Figure 8-4. *Configure each remote server in the pair through the Remote Server Properties dialog box.*

- To map all remote logins to a single SQL Server login ID, select Map All Remote Logins To and then use the related drop-down list box to select the login ID you want to use for remote connections.

- To map each remote login to a separate SQL Server login ID, select Map Remote Logins To Different Local Logins. Then specify how the remote logins should be mapped. For example, to map the remote login genuser to the local login curruser, you would type **webuser** in the Remote Login Name field and **curruser** in the Local Login Name field. Repeat this process for each individual login you want to configure.

7. By default, all logins are trusted, which means that users aren't prompted for a password to access the remote server. If you want to prompt users for a password, select the Check Password check box for each type of login or login ID you want to verify.

8. Click OK and then repeat the process on the second server in the pair.

Setting Up Remote Servers Using Stored Procedures

You can also configure remote server pairs with *sp_addserver* and *sp_configure*. You use *sp_addserver* to add remote server connections and *sp_configure* to allow remote server connections. The syntax and usage for *sp_addserver* is shown in Sample 8-6.

Sample 8-6. *sp_addserver* **Syntax and Usage**

Syntax

```
sp_addserver [@server =] 'server'
  [,[@local =] 'local']
  [,[@duplicate_ok =] 'duplicate_OK']
```

Usage

```
EXEC sp_addserver Pluto, local
EXEC sp_addserver Zeta
```

The following example shows how you could configure the SQL Servers Zeta and Pluto as remote servers. Use this example as a starting point to configure your own server pair.

On Zeta, you would run the following SQL commands:

```
EXEC sp_addserver Zeta, local
EXEC sp_addserver Pluto
EXEC sp_configure 'remote access', 1
RECONFIGURE
GO
```

Then you would stop and restart the MSSQL Server service on Zeta. Afterward, you would configure Pluto for remote server connections to Zeta as follows:

```
EXEC sp_addserver Pluto, local
EXEC sp_addserver Zeta
EXEC sp_configure 'remote access', 1
RECONFIGURE
GO
```

Note You drop remote servers using the *sp_dropserver* stored procedure. The syntax and usage for this procedure was shown previously in
this chapter as Sample 8-4.

Then you would stop and restart the MSSQL Server service on Pluto. Now you can configure logins on the servers. You map remote logins to local logins using *sp_addremotelogin*. The syntax and usage for *sp_addremotelogin* is shown in Sample 8-7.

Sample 8-7. *sp_addremotelogin* **Syntax and Usage**

Syntax

```
sp_addremotelogin [@remoteserver =] 'remoteserver'
 [,[@loginame =] 'login']
 [,[@remotename =] 'remote_name']
```

Usage

```
EXEC sp_addremotelogin 'Pluto'

EXEC sp_addremotelogin 'Omega', 'BILLS', 'WRSTANEK'
```

You map remote logins to local logins with the same name by completing the following steps:

1. Execute this command on Zeta:

   ```
   EXEC sp_addremotelogin 'Pluto'
   ```

2. Execute this command on Pluto:

   ```
   EXEC sp_addremotelogin 'Zeta'
   ```

You map all users to a single user ID by completing the following steps:

1. Execute this command on Zeta:

   ```
   EXEC sp_addremotelogin 'Pluto', 'remUser'
   ```

2. Execute this command on Pluto:

   ```
   EXEC sp_addremotelogin 'Zeta', 'remUser'
   ```

You've just mapped all remote logins to the remUser login ID.

You can also map each remote login to a separate SQL Server login ID. For example, if you wanted to map the goteam login on Pluto to georgej on Zeta, you would use the following command:

```
EXEC sp_addremotelogin 'Pluto', 'GEORGEJ', 'GOTEAM'
```

By default, remote logins are configured to check passwords, and users may be prompted for a password. To set up a trusted login and to disable password checking, use the *sp_remoteoption* stored procedure after configuring the login. Sample 8-8 shows the syntax and usage of *sp_remoteoption*.

Sample 8-8. *sp_remoteoption* **Syntax and Usage**

Syntax

```
sp_remoteoption [[@remoteserver =] 'remoteserver']
 [,[@loginame =] 'loginame']
 [,[@remotename =] 'remotename']
```

(continued)

Sample 8-8. *(continued)*

Syntax

```
[,[@optname =] 'optname']
[,[@optvalue =] 'optvalue']
```

Usage

```
EXEC sp_remoteoption 'Pluto', 'GEORGEJ', 'GIJOE', trusted, true
```

Executing Remote Stored Procedures

You execute remote stored procedures in much the same way as any other stored procedure. The key difference is that you use a prefix to specify where the stored procedure is to be executed. For example, if you wanted to execute the *totalRevenues* stored procedure on a remote server's Customer database, you could use the following Transact-SQL command:

```
EXECUTE Pluto.Customer.dbo.totalRevenues 'December'
```

Or you could use

```
EXECUTE Pluto.Customer.totalRevenues 'December'
```

Here, Pluto is the name of the remote server, Customer is the database name, and *totalRevenues* is a user-defined stored procedure.

Chapter 9

Configuring Snapshot, Merge, and Transactional Replication

Data replication allows you to distribute data from a source database to one or more destination databases. The source and destination databases can be on other Microsoft SQL Servers or on other databases as long as an OLE DB provider is available for each destination database. You have precise control over when replication occurs, what data is replicated, and how other aspects of replication are handled. For example, you can configure replication to happen continuously or periodically. Before we examine how to implement replication, let's look at why you'd want to use replication and review its key concepts.

Note Replication is a complex subject. The discussion in this chapter is not meant to be exhaustive. Instead, as in other chapters, I focus on core administration—the replication concepts and tasks you'll use most often. In the field, I've used the tasks discussed in this chapter to configure replication on hundreds of servers. The tasks work well in most environments but they don't cover every nitty-gritty detail. See the *Microsoft SQL Server 2000 Administrator's Companion* (Microsoft Press, 2000) for more detailed information and alternative scenarios on replication.

An Overview of Replication

You use replication to copy data on one server and distribute it to other servers. You can also use replication to copy data, transform it, and then distribute the customized data to multiple servers. You generally use replication when you need to manage data on multiple servers on a recurring basis. If you need to create a copy of a database just once, you don't need replication and instead you should copy the database as discussed in the section of Chapter 4 entitled "Manipulating Databases" or in the section of Chapter 11 entitled "Restoring a Database to a Different Location." If you need to copy and transform data from one server to another server, you don't need replication either, and instead you should use the

Data Transformation Services (DTS) discussed in Chapter 7. Some reasons to use replication include:

- To synchronize changes to remote databases with a central database. For example, if the sales team uses remote laptops, you may need to create a copy of data for their sales region on the laptop. Later, a salesperson in the field may add information or make changes while disconnected from the network. Through replication these modifications would then need to be synchronized with the central database.

- To create multiple instances of a database so that you can distribute the workload. For example, if you have a central database that's updated regularly, you may want to push changes out to departmental databases as they occur. Employees can then access data through these departmental databases instead of trying to connect to the central database.

- To move specific data sets from a central server and distribute them to several other servers. For example, you'd use replication if you had a central database and needed to distribute sales data to all the databases in your company's department stores.

- To customize data and distribute it to multiple subscribers. For example, if your company sold subscriptions to your consumer credit database, you could replicate the data with subscribers, performing customization on the data as necessary for each subscriber.

Replication is designed to meet the needs of a wide variety of environments. Replication architecture is broken down into several different processes, procedures, and components, each of which is used to tailor replication for a given situation. The replication architecture includes

- **Replication components**   The server and data components used in replication
- **Replication agents**   Applications that assist in the replication process
- **Replication variants**   The types of replication you can configure

Replication Components

Before working with replication, you'll need to know the key terms and how you use them. Servers in the replication model can have one or more of the following roles:

- **Publisher**   Publishers are servers that make data available for replication to other servers. Publishers also track changes to data and maintain other information about source databases. Each data grouping has only one publisher.

- **Distributor**   Distributors are servers that distribute replicated data. Distributors store the distribution database, metadata, historical data, and (for transactional replication) transactions.

- **Subscriber**   Subscribers are the destination servers for replication. These servers store the replicated data and receive updates. Subscribers can also make changes to data. You can publish data to multiple subscribers.

The data being published for replication are referred to as *articles* and *publications*. Articles are the basic unit for replication and can consist of a table, a subset of a table, or other database objects. Publications are collections of articles that subscribers can receive. You should associate articles with a publication and then publish the publication. Articles can contain

- An entire table
- Only certain columns from a table, obtained by using a vertical filter
- Only certain rows from a table, obtained by using a horizontal filter
- A table subset containing certain rows and columns
- A view, indexed view, or user-defined function
- A stored procedure

You can also specify whether schema objects are replicated. Schema objects include constraints, indexes, triggers, collation, and extended properties. You can't publish any of the following for replication:

- The model, tempdb, and msdb databases
- System tables in the master database

In the publication and subscription model, replication involves the following steps:

1. Selecting a replication type and model
2. Performing any necessary preliminary tasks
3. Configuring a distributor and enabling publishers, publication databases, and subscribers
4. Creating a publication
5. Creating subscriptions to the publication

Replication Agents

SQL Server uses various helper applications to assist in the replication process. These applications are called *replication agents* and they include

- **Snapshot agent**   Creates snapshots of data. It includes schema and data, which are stored for distribution. The snapshot agent is also responsible for updating status information in the distribution database. The snapshot agent runs on the distributor. Each published database has its own snapshot agent that runs on the distributor and connects to the publisher. Snapshot agents are used with all types of replication.
- **Distribution agent**   Responsible for applying data from snapshot replication or transactions from transaction replication to subscribers. The distribution agent can run on the distributor or on subscribers. This agent isn't used with merge replication.
- **Merge agent**   Used to synchronize changes that occur after the initial snapshot is created. If any conflicts occur when the changes are being synchronized, the conflicts are resolved using the rules set with the conflict resolver.

Depending on the configuration, merge agents run on the publisher or on subscribers. Merge agents are used only with merge replication.

- **Log reader agent** Moves transactions marked for replication from the transaction log on the publisher to the distributor. Each database that's published using transactional replication has its own log reader agent that runs on the distributor and connects to the publisher. Log reader agents are used only with transactional replication.

- **Queue reader agent** Stores database changes in a queue where the updates can be asynchronously propagated to the publisher. This allows subscribers to modify published data and synchronize those changes without having an active network connection to the publisher. Queue reader agents are used only with snapshot and transactional replication.

- **Clean up agent** Performs replication maintenance tasks. There are several different types of clean up agents. Each clean up agent has a very specific purpose, such as removing replication agent history from distribution databases or detecting and removing expired subscriptions from distribution databases.

Replication Variants

SQL Server supports several different types of replication. These replication variants are

- **Snapshot replication** Takes a snapshot of current data and replaces the entire copy of the data on one or more subscribers. With subsequent snapshots, the entire copy of the data is again distributed to subscribers. While exact copies are a strong point of snapshot replication, this technique increases the amount of overhead and traffic on the network. Another weak point of snapshot replication is that it only runs periodically, which usually means that subscribers don't have the most current information.

- **Transactional replication** Uses transactions to distribute changes. When replication is first started, a snapshot of the data is sent to subscribers. After that, selected transactions in the publisher's transaction log are marked for replication and then distributed to each subscriber separately. Snapshots are then taken on a periodic basis to ensure that the databases are synchronized. Distributed transactions are used to ensure that incremental changes are applied consistently. A benefit of transactional replication is that you replicate individual transactions rather than an entire data set. Transactional replication can also occur on a continuous or periodic basis, which makes the procedure more versatile than snapshot replication by itself.

- **Merge replication** Allows subscribers to make changes to replicated data independently. Later, you can merge these changes into all of the related source and destination databases. Merge replication doesn't use distributed transactions and can't guarantee transactional consistency. Instead, merge replication uses a conflict resolver to determine which changes are applied.

In snapshot and transactional replication, subscribers normally don't change data. However, you have several options for allowing subscribers to change data:

- **Immediate updating** Allows subscribers to make changes and then immediately update the publisher. The publisher then replicates these changes to other subscribers.

- **Queued updating** Allows subscribers to make changes and then store those changes in a queue until they can be applied to the publisher. The publisher then replicates the changes to other subscribers. Immediate and Queued updating is only supported in Snapshot and Transactional publications.

Queued updating provides fault tolerance that may be needed when databases are geographically separated. While immediate updating requires an active connection to the publisher, queued updating doesn't. With queued updating subscribers can asynchronously apply changes, which means that they can store changes when a link is inactive and then, when the link is active, they can submit the changes to the publisher.

You can also use immediate updating with queued updating as a failover when you expect publishers and subscribers to be connected but don't want to lose the ability to make updates if a link fails. Here, you configure both updating options, using immediate updating as the primary update mechanism and then switching to queued updating when needed. You can invoke failover at any time. However, you can't fail back afterward until the subscriber and publisher are connected and the Queue Reader agent has applied all pending updates in the queue.

Both immediate updating and queued updating use transactions and the standard two-phase commit process to apply updates to the publisher. Transactions ensure that the update can be committed if it's successfully applied or rolled back if there's a problem. The transactions are applied from a specific subscriber to the publisher. After changes are made to the publisher, the publisher replicates the changes to other subscribers.

Transactions are completed automatically through the update process and managed by the Distributed Transaction Coordinator. Custom applications that modify subscriber data can be written as though they're updating a single database. To prevent changes that can't be replicated, updates to the subscriber are applied only when they can be replicated through a transaction. If the update can't be replicated through a transaction, the subscriber won't be able to modify the subscription data.

SQL Server detects subscriber changes that would conflict with changes on the publisher. If it detects a conflict, it rejects the transaction and doesn't allow the data changes. Usually, a rejection means that the subscriber needs to synchronize with the publisher before attempting to update the data locally.

When you include stored procedures as articles in a snapshot publication, SQL Server replicates the entire stored procedure from the publisher to the subscribers. Changes caused by the execution of those stored procedures are replicated with new snapshots. With transactional replication, on the other hand, you can replicate execution of the stored procedure instead of replicating the changes that the execution causes. By sending an execute command rather than data changes, you reduce the amount of data that needs to flow across the network and improve the performance of SQL applications.

If you replicate the execution of stored procedures, you have two configuration settings. You can use *standard* procedure execution, or you can use *serialized* procedure execution. With standard procedure execution, procedure execution is replicated to all subscribers, even if those procedures are executed in different transactions. Because multiple transactions may be executing at a particular time, subscribers' data can't be guaranteed to be consistent with the publisher's. With serialized stored procedures, procedures are executed in sequence as long as they are referenced within serialized transactions. If the procedures are executed outside of serialized transactions, changes to the data are replicated instead. This behavior guarantees that the subscribers' data is consistent with the publisher's.

Planning for Replication

As you've seen, the replication architecture is fairly extensive. The reason for that is to ensure that the architecture is versatile enough to meet the needs of just about any replication situation. Unfortunately, this versatility also makes replication tricky to configure. To make the replication go smoothly, you should do a bit of planning, which involves selecting a specific replication model and performing any necessary preliminary tasks before you start configuring replication.

Replication Models

The key decision you make when you select a replication model involves the physical layout of the publisher, distributor, and subscriber databases. Replication models you may want to use are

- **Central publisher model** A central publisher maintains the publisher and distributor databases on the same server, with one or more subscribers configured on other servers. The advantages of this model are manageability and ease of maintenance. The disadvantages are the extra workload and resource usage on the publication server.

 Tip The central publisher model is the most commonly used replication model. Unfortunately, you'll often find that the extra load on the publication server hampers server performance. To reduce the server load, you'll want to put the distributor on its own server. Keep in mind, though, that doing so won't entirely eliminate the workload on the publication server. The publisher and distributor still need to communicate, and they still need to pass data back and forth.

- **Central publisher with remote distributor model**   A remote distributor maintains the publisher and distributor databases on different servers, with one or more subscribers configured on other servers. The advantage of this model is that you distribute the workload. The disadvantage is that you have to maintain an additional server.

- **Central subscriber model**   A central subscriber is a single subscriber database that collects data from several publishers. For example, if you have ServerA, ServerB, and ServerC, ServerA and ServerB would act as central publishers and ServerC would act as the central subscriber. Now, when updates are distributed from ServerA and ServerB, they are collected on ServerC. A central subscriber could then republish the combined data to other servers. To use this model, all tables used in replication must have a unique primary key. Otherwise the replication model won't work properly.

- **Publishing subscriber model**   A publishing subscriber relays the distribution of data to other subscribers, and you can use it with any of the other models. For example, if you have two geographically separated sites, a publisher could replicate data to servers at site A and then have a publishing subscriber at site B that distributes the data to servers at site B.

Preliminary Replication Tasks

After selecting the replication type and model you want to use, you prepare for the replication by performing preliminary tasks. The following sections describe key tasks you should consider, according to replication type.

Preparing for Snapshot Replication

With snapshot replication, the data being replicated is copied in full to data files on the distributor. Normally these snapshot files are the same size as the data you're replicating and are stored in the SQL Server Repldata folder by default. You should make sure that the drive on which the replication data is stored has enough free space. For example, if you're using snapshot replication to distribute publication A with 5 MB of data, publication B with 42 MB, and publication C with 9 MB, you'll need at least 56 MB of free space.

You can also store snapshot data in an alternate location where subscribers can retrieve it at a later time. If you use an alternate location you have the option of compressing the snapshot file. Compressing a snapshot file reduces the disk space requirements only for the files you're compressing. It doesn't change the overall space requirements, and it doesn't always reduce the initial and final space requirements. With compression, the snapshot agent generates the necessary data files and then uses the Microsoft CAB utility to compress the files. When the subscriber receives compressed snapshot files, the files are written to a temporary location, which is either the default client working directory or an alternate location specified in the subscription properties. The subscriber uses the CAB utility to decompress the files before reading them.

Real World When you create snapshot files in the default location and in an alternate location on different drives, the files are created separately. This means that the total disk space requirements are typically what you would expect. However, when you create snapshot files in the default location and in an alternate location on the same drive, both files are initially created in the default location and then the alternate location file is copied to its final destination. This means that the total disk space requirements in the default location are twice what you would expect. Compression doesn't help. The snapshot agent generates the necessary data files and then compresses them.

Replication timing is another important consideration in snapshot replication. When the snapshot agent creates a snapshot of a published table, the agent locks the entire table while it bulk copies the data from the publisher to the distributor and, as a result, users can't update any data in the table until the lock is released. To reduce the impact on operations, you should carefully schedule when replication occurs. Some actions that may help include

- Identifying times when operations are at their lowest levels or users don't need write access to the tables you're replicating

- Identifying times when snapshots must be made and scheduling users to do work that doesn't require write access to the tables you're replicating

Preparing for Transactional Replication

Because transactional replication builds on the snapshot replication model, you'll want to prepare for both snapshot and transactional replication. With transactional replication, an initial snapshot is sent to the distributor and this snapshot is then updated on a periodic basis, such as once a week. In between snapshots, transactions are used to update subscribers. These transactions are logged in the distributor's database and are cleared out only after a new snapshot is created.

Transaction logs for published databases are extremely important to successful replication. As long as replication is enabled, pending transactions can't be cleared out of a published database until they've been passed to the distributor. Because of this, you may need to increase the size of a published database's transaction log. Furthermore, if the publisher can't contact the distributor or if the log reader agent isn't running, transactions will continue to build up in the publisher's transaction logs.

With transactional replication, all published tables must have a declared primary key. You can add a primary key to an existing table using the ALTER TABLE statement (see Chapter 6). Additionally, if a publication uses *text* or *image* data types, you must make sure that you keep the following limitations in mind:

- With WRITETEXT and UPDATETEXT statements, you must use the WITH LOG option on tables that are published for replication. You can't use the WITH NO_LOG option. While WRITETEXT is supported with any compliant database, UPDATETEXT is supported only on subscribers that are running SQL

Server version 6.0 or later. Furthermore, you must retrieve text pointers immediately prior to executing the UPDATETEXT or WRITETEXT statement in a transaction.

- The MAX TEXT REPL SIZE SQL Server configuration option controls the maximum byte size of the text and image data that can be replicated. Operations that exceed this limit will fail. Set the maximum text replication size with the *sp_configure* system stored procedure.

Preparing for Merge Replication

With merge replication, all published tables must have primary keys. If a table contains foreign keys or is used in validation, you must include the reference table in the publication. Otherwise update operations that add new rows will fail because SQL Server can't find the required primary key. Additionally, merge replication affects timestamp column usage. Timestamps are generated automatically and are guaranteed to be unique only in a specific database. Because of this, SQL Server replicates timestamp columns but doesn't replicate the literal timestamp values contained in the columns. These values are regenerated when the initial snapshot rows are applied at the subscriber.

Like transactional replication, merge replication has a few limitations when it comes to text and image columns. You must explicitly update text and image columns with an UPDATE statement. If you use WRITETEXT or UPDATETEXT to update text columns, you must follow the WRITETEXT or UPDATETEXT statement with a dummy UPDATE statement within the same transaction. Otherwise the changes may not be distributed.

With merge replication, subscribers can make changes to replicated data independently and these changes can be merged into all of the related source and destination databases. The merge agent watches for changes that conflict with other changes. If it detects a conflict, a conflict resolver is used to determine which change is applied and which change is rolled back. The merge agent can track changes at a column level or at a row level. With column-level tracking, a conflict exists when changes are made to the same column in a table in more than one copy. With row-level tracking, a conflict exists when changes are made to the same row in a table in more than one copy.

Normally, subscribers to merge publications only synchronize updates with the publisher. Subscribers can also synchronize with other servers, and they do this by designating alternate synchronization partners. Having an alternate synchronization partner is useful when you need to ensure that updates can be made even if the primary publisher is offline or otherwise unavailable.

Distributor Administration

As the name indicates, you use distributors to distribute replicated data. When you work with distributors, the core set of administration tasks you'll perform includes setting up a new distributor, updating an existing distributor, and deleting distributors.

Setting Up a New Distributor

Setting up a new distributor is the first major step in configuring replication. Before you get started, you should

- Select a replication type—either snapshot, transactional, or merge.
- Select a replication model, such as the central publisher model.
- Perform any necessary preliminary tasks. To meet certain limitations, you may need to update clients and applications that modify published databases directly.

When you're ready to proceed, configure the distributor by completing the following steps:

1. Start Enterprise Manager and then double-click the database server instance that you want to use as the distributor.

2. Right-click the Replication folder and then select Configure Publishing, Subscribers, and Distribution. This starts the Configure Publishing And Distribution Wizard.

3. Click Next to move past the Welcome screen. As shown in Figure 9-1, you can now select a distributor.

4. Because you want to set up a new distributor, choose Make <ServerName> Its Own Distributor and then click Next.

5. If SQL Server Agent is currently configured to use the System account, you'll see a dialog box prompting you to configure the agent to use a domain account. Click OK to display the SQL Server Agent Properties dialog

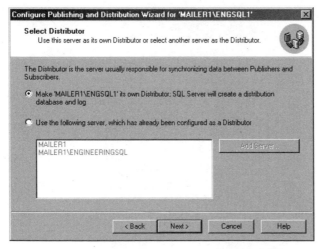

Figure 9-1. *Use the Configure Publishing And Distribution Wizard to config-ure replication. As shown here, the first step is to select a distributor.*

box. Select This Account, type a domain account name and password in the fields provided, and then click OK again.

6. Distributors use SQL Server Agent to handle replication tasks. If SQL Server Agent isn't configured to start automatically, you'll need to specify whether to automatically start the SQL Server Agent service for the currently selected database server instance. Choose the Yes option to allow automatic startup. Otherwise choose the No option and then manually start the SQL Server Agent service each time you start the server.

7. Next, specify where the snapshot folder will be stored. This folder is used to store snapshots from publishers that use the distributor. You must use a network path anytime distributor and merge agents run at subscribers. Otherwise, the agents won't be able to access snapshots.

8. As shown in Figure 9-2, you can let the wizard configure the remaining setup options for you by selecting the No, Use The Following Default Settings option button. Afterward, click Next and then click Finish. Skip the remaining steps.

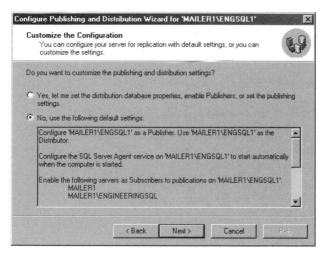

Figure 9-2. *Choose Yes to configure the distribution options yourself or No to use the default options shown.*

9. To configure the options yourself, choose the Yes option and then continue with the configuration.

10. Provide information for the distribution database using the dialog box shown in Figure 9-3. Enter a name for the distribution database and then set folder locations for the corresponding data and log files. You can't use mapped network drives.

Note   Be sure to use a descriptive name for the database, such as EmployeeDistribution or EmpDistr.

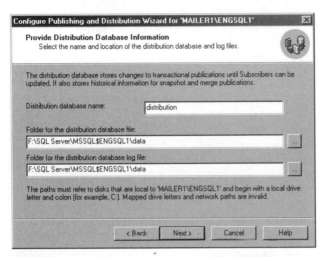

Figure 9-3. *Configure the distribution database name and the location of data and log files.*

11. As shown in Figure 9-4, you need to configure publishers for this distribution database. Only registered servers are shown. If you want to register a new server, click New.

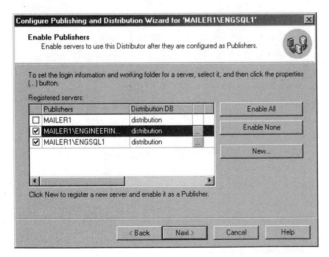

Figure 9-4. *Enable publishers and set server properties, if necessary.*

12. To the right of registered server entries, you'll see a button with three dots (...). Click this button to set publisher options for the related server. As Figure 9-5 shows, you have the following options available:

   • **Data Storage At The Distributor**   Sets the location of the folder used to store snapshots. The Snapshot folder is stored on the distribution database and can be in a different location for each publisher that uses the distribution database.

   • **Replication Agent Connection To The Publisher**   Determines how replication agents on the distributor log in to the publisher. Select Impersonate The SQL Server Agent Account to use a trusted connection. Otherwise select the Use SQL Server Authentication and then type the necessary username and password.

   • **Administrative Link To The Distributor**   Determine whether the selected publisher is trusted. If you want to require a password, choose This Publisher Requires A Password To Establish A Link To The Distributor. Otherwise clear this option. (This option is available only if the selected publisher and distributor are located on different servers.)

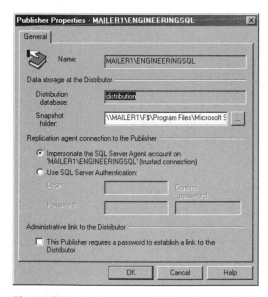

Figure 9-5. *You can set additional properties for each publisher using the distribution database. Use this dialog box to configure the available options.*

13. When you've finished enabling publishers, click Next (see Figure 9-4). As shown in Figure 9-6, you can now enable publication databases for replication. Select entries under the Trans column to enable a database for snapshot or transactional replication or both. Select entries under the Merge column to enable a database for merge replication. Click Next when you're ready to continue.

 Tip To enable a publication database for any type of replication, select both of the corresponding Trans and Merge check boxes.

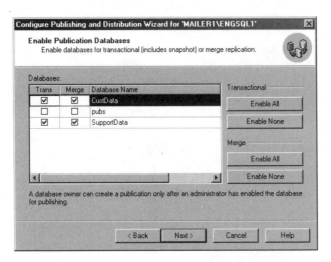

Figure 9-6. *Enable publication databases. Database owners can create publications only after you enable the database for publishing.*

14. Enable subscribers to the distribution database as shown in Figure 9-7. Again, only registered servers are shown. If you want to register a new server, click New.

15. To the right of registered server entries, you'll see a button with three dots (...). Click this button to set subscriber options for the related server. The Properties dialog box has two tabs:

- **General** Use these options to add a description for the subscriber and to determine how replication agents link to the subscriber. Select the option named Impersonate The SQL Server Agent Account to use a trusted connection. Otherwise select Use SQL Server Authentication and then type the necessary username and password.

- **Schedules** Use these options to configure when distribution and merge agents run. You can configure these agents to run continuously, which ensures that updates are made continuously, or at

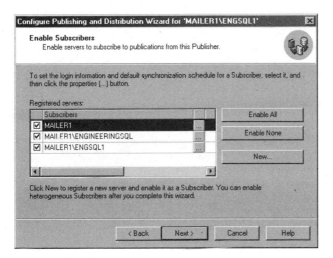

Figure 9-7. *Enable subscribers and set their properties, if desired.*

specific times, which limits updates to specific time intervals. For detailed information on scheduling jobs, see Chapter 12, "Database Automation and Maintenance."

Note While agents can run updates continuously, the updates aren't immediate. There is always some latency with replication.

16. When you're ready to continue, click Next, and then click Finish to complete the configuration. The progress of each step of the configuration process is shown in a dialog box. If the process completes successfully, click OK. If errors occur, you'll need to resolve them before you can complete the configuration.

Note The distributor must run the SQL Server Agent service. This service should be configured to run automatically. If it isn't, you'll see an error prompt. Click Yes to configure the service to start automatically. Otherwise click No (but you'll need to remember to start the service each time you restart the distributor).

17. On the distributor, a Replication Monitor is added to the folder list in Enterprise Manager. To learn how to work with this SQL Server feature, see Chapter 10, "Profiling and Monitoring Microsoft SQL Server 2000."

18. Configure publications and subscriptions as explained in the sections of this chapter entitled "Enabling Publishers," "Enabling Publication Databases," and "Enabling Subscribers."

Updating Distributors

When you configure a new distributor, you can set up a new distribution database, as discussed in the section of this chapter entitled "Setting Up a New Distributor." If you've already configured a distributor, you can update the distributor and create additional distribution databases by completing the following steps:

1. Start Enterprise Manager and then double-click the server entry for the distributor.

2. Right-click the Replication folder and then select Configure Publishing, Subscribers, and Distribution. This opens the Publisher And Distributor Properties dialog box shown in Figure 9-8.

3. You can use the options in the dialog box to change publisher, subscriber, and distributor data properties for the currently selected distributor. You use the dialog box tabs as follows:

   - **Distributor**   Configure distribution databases, agent profiles, and passwords for administrative links

   - **Publishers**   Enable and disable publishers for the distributor

   - **Publication Databases**   Enable and disable publication databases and specify which types of replication are allowed

   - **Subscribers**   Enable and disable subscribers

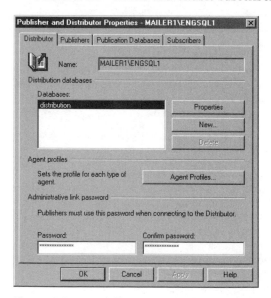

Figure 9-8. *The Publisher And Distributor Properties dialog box controls all the distributor options. You can use it to create new distribution databases and to perform many other administration tasks.*

Creating Distribution Databases

Distribution databases are used to store the information being distributed to subscribers. Each publisher that uses a distributor is assigned a distribution database to which it can connect. Publishers can share distribution databases, and you can create additional databases as necessary. If you've already configured a distributor, you can create additional distribution databases by completing the following steps:

1. Start Enterprise Manager and then double-click the server entry for the distributor.

2. Right-click the Replication folder and then select Configure Publishing, Subscribers, and Distribution. This opens the Publisher And Distributor Properties dialog box shown previously in Figure 9-8.

3. In the Distributor tab, click New. You can now configure the distribution database.

4. Enter a name for the distribution database and then set folder locations for the corresponding data and log files. You can't use mapped network drives.

5. Use the options in the Transaction Retention and History Retention areas to determine how long transactions and performance history are retained for the distribution database.

6. Click OK to create the distribution database.

Enabling Publishers

Distributors can work only with servers and databases that are enabled for their use. You can enable publishers when you create a new distributor or by completing the following steps:

1. Start Enterprise Manager and then double-click the server entry for the distributor.

2. Right-click the Replication folder and then select Configure Publishing, Subscribers, and Distribution. This opens the Publisher And Distributor Properties dialog box shown previously in Figure 9-8.

3. To enable publishers, click the Publishers tab. Use the check boxes provided to enable or disable publishers. Only registered publishers are shown. Click New to register a new publisher.

4. To the right of registered server entries, you'll see a button with three dots (...). Click this button to set publisher options for the related server. You have the following options:

   • **Data Storage At The Distributor** Sets the location of the folder used to store snapshots. The Snapshot folder is stored on the distribution database and can be in a different location for each publisher that uses the distribution database.

   • **Replication Agent Connection To The Publisher** Determines how replication agents on the distributor log in to the publisher. Select Impersonate The SQL Server Agent Account to use a trusted connection. Otherwise select the Use SQL Server Authentication and then type the necessary username and password.

- **Administrative Link To The Distributor** Determines whether the selected publisher is trusted. If you want to require a password, choose This Publisher Requires A Password To Establish A Link To The Distributor. Otherwise clear this option. (This option is available only if the selected publisher and distributor are located on different servers.)

Enabling Publication Databases

You can enable publication databases when you create a new distributor or by completing the following steps:

1. Start Enterprise Manager and then double-click the server entry for the distributor.

2. Right-click the Replication folder and then select Configure Publishing, Subscribers, and Distribution. This opens the Publisher And Distributor Properties dialog box shown previously in Figure 9-8.

3. To enable publication databases, click the Publication Databases tab. Then select entries under the Trans column to enable a database for snapshot or transactional replication (or both) or select entries under the Merge column to enable a database for merge replication.

4. To enable a publication database for any type of replication, select both the corresponding Trans and Merge check boxes.

Enabling Subscribers

You can enable subscribers when you create a new distributor or by completing the following steps:

1. Start Enterprise Manager and then double-click the server entry for the distributor.

2. Right-click the Replication folder and then select Configure Publishing, Subscribers, and Distribution. This opens the Publisher And Distributor Properties dialog box shown previously in Figure 9-8.

3. To enable subscribers, click the Subscribers tab. Use the check boxes provided to enable or disable subscribers.

4. To the right of registered server entries, you'll see a button with three dots (...). Click this button to set subscriber options for the related server. The Properties dialog box has two tabs:

- **General** Use these options to add a description for the subscriber and to determine how replication agents link to the subscriber. Select the option named Impersonate The SQL Server Agent Account to use a trusted connection. Otherwise select Use SQL Server Authentication and then type the necessary username and password.

- **Schedules**   Use these options to configure when distribution and merge agents run. You can configure these agents to run continuously, which ensures that updates are made continuously, or at specific times, which limits updates to specific time intervals. For detailed information on scheduling jobs, see Chapter 12, "Database Automation and Maintenance."

5. If you want to use a subscriber that isn't listed, click New. You can then choose the type of subscriber you want to work with and configure the subscriber, as necessary. The types of subscribers you can choose from are

   - **SQL server database**   Select SQL Server Database and then click OK. You can now register a new SQL Server to use as a subscriber.
   - **Microsoft Jet 4.0 database (Microsoft Access)**   Select Microsoft Jet 4.0 database (Microsoft Access) and then click OK. Jet 4.0 databases must be registered as linked servers on the distributor. If they aren't, click Add in the Enable Subscriber dialog box to create a new linked server as described in Chapter 8.
   - **OLE DB data source**   Select OLE DB Data Source and then click OK. OLE DB data sources must be registered as linked servers on the distributor. If they aren't, click Add in the Enable Subscriber dialog box to create a new linked server.
   - **ODBC data source**   Select ODBC Data Source and then click OK. ODBC data sources must be configured as data source names (DSNs) on the distributor. If the data source you want to use isn't available, use the ODBC Data Sources Control Panel utility to create a DSN.

Deleting Distribution Databases

Before you can delete a distribution database, you must remove all publications and disable all the publishers using the distribution database. Once you've done this, you can delete distribution databases by completing the following steps:

1. Start Enterprise Manager and then double-click the server entry for the distributor.

2. Right-click the Replication folder and then select Configure Publishing, Subscribers, And Distribution. This opens the Publisher And Distributor Properties dialog box.

3. In the Distributor tab, select the distribution database you want to delete and then click Delete.

Disabling Publishing and Distribution

Through Enterprise Manager's Disable Publishing And Distribution Wizard, you can disable publishing and distribution. When you disable publishing,

- All publications on the selected server are dropped

- All subscriptions to the affected publications are dropped
- The server is disabled as a distributor

You can disable publishing and distribution by completing the following steps:

1. Start Enterprise Manager and then double-click the server entry for the distributor.
2. Right-click the Replication folder and then select Disable Publishing And Distribution. This starts the Disable Publishing And Distribution Wizard.
3. Click Next and then choose Yes, Disable Publishing (And Publishing).
4. Click Next twice and then click Finish.

Creating and Managing Publications

Once you've configured a distributor and enabled publishers, publication databases, and subscribers, you can create publications. Afterward, you'll need to manage the publications as you would any other SQL Server resource.

Creating Publications

The easiest way to create publications is to use Enterprise Manager. To do this, complete the following steps:

1. Start Enterprise Manager and then double-click the server entry for the publisher.
2. Right-click the Replication folder, point to New, and then select Publication. This starts the Create Publication Wizard.
3. Select Show Advanced Options and then click Next.
4. Choose the database on the selected server that contains the data or objects you want to publish. You can select user databases only.
5. The first time you create a publication in a particular database, you'll have to do everything from scratch. Choose the type of replication you want to use for the publication. The options are

    - **Snapshot publication**   Creates a publication setup for snapshot replication
    - **Transactional publication**   Creates a publication setup for transactional replication
    - **Merge publication**   Creates a publication setup for merge replication

6. The next time you create a publication in a particular database, you'll have the option of using an existing publication as a publication template. To use a template, choose Yes, Use The Following Publication As A Template in the Use Publication Template window, and then select the existing publication to use as a template. Now all the default options are based on the existing

publication you've selected (but you can't change the publication type). If you would rather define the publication articles and properties separately, choose No, I Will Define The Articles And Properties.

7. If you're creating a snapshot or transactional publication, continue using the steps listed in the following section, "Snapshot and Transactional Publications."

8. If you're creating a merge publication, continue using the steps listed in the section of this chapter entitled "Merge Publications."

Snapshot and Transactional Publications

Snapshot and transactional publications are the most commonly used types of publications. With snapshot publications, the publisher periodically replaces subscriber data with an updated snapshot. With transactional publications, the publisher updates data and changes are sent to subscribers through transactions.

Once you've started a new publication, you can create a snapshot or transactional publication by completing the following steps:

1. Determine whether immediate updating subscribers or queued updating subscribers are used. These options use the Distributed Transaction Coordinator service to update the publisher. With immediate updating, SQL Server applies updates immediately. With queued updating, SQL Server writes updates to a queue before attempting to update the publisher.

Note If you want to configure immediate updating with queued updating as a failover, you can select both options. Note also that queued updating uses SQL Server queues by default. After you create the publication, you can choose Microsoft Message Queuing Server as the queue.

2. Click Next to continue. If you haven't configured updating, you can now elect to use Data Transformation Services. DTS allows you to change the data before it's distributed to subscribers. If you want to allow data transformation, choose Yes, Transform The Data. Otherwise select No, All Subscribers Receive Data Directly.

3. Select the types of subscribers that will subscribe to the publication. You can choose any or all of the following:
   - Servers Running SQL Server 2000
   - Servers Running SQL Server Version 7.0
   - Heterogeneous Data Sources

Note If all subscribers are SQL Servers and no transformations are used, snapshots are formatted using Native SQL Server format. Otherwise snapshots are formatted using Character Mode format. Additionally, if you choose SQL Server 7.0 as a data source, you can't choose properties that are new to SQL Server 2000.

4. Use the dialog box shown in Figure 9-9 to select the objects for replication. You use key elements of this dialog box as follows:

- **Object Type** Shows the types of objects that are available for replication.

Note Which objects are available depends on the types of objects in the database and can be tables, stored procedures, and views. Tables without primary keys can't be published for snapshot or transactional replication, and you'll see a key with an X through it in the Specify Articles dialog box.

- **Show** When selected, displays the related objects in the right-hand pane. For example, select Show for views, and views are displayed for selection in the right-hand pane.
- **Publish All** When selected, all of the related objects are selected for replication.
- **Owner** Shows the object owner.
- **Object** Displays the object name.
- **Show Unpublished Objects** Determines whether unpublished objects are displayed.
- **Article Defaults** Allows you to set default article options for each type of database object.

5. When you select a table, stored procedure, or view, you'll see a Properties button. Click this button to configure property settings for the related article. See the section of this chapter entitled "Setting Article Properties" for details.

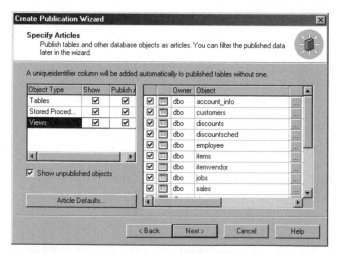

Figure 9-9. *Select tables to replicate as articles in the publication. With snapshot and transactional replication, you can also select stored procedures.*

6. After you select objects to use in the publication, click Next. If there are any issues that require changes to the publication, you'll see a prompt similar to the one shown in Figure 9-10. Read the description carefully to determine how to resolve the issue and make changes as necessary. Key issues are:

   - Tables referenced by views are required and so are objects referenced by stored procedures. If you don't select referenced tables or objects, you must create them manually at the subscriber.

   - SQL Server adds Uniqueidentifier columns to any tables you've selected for replication. Adding the Uniqueidentifier column will cause INSERT statements without column lists to fail and increase the time needed to generate the first snapshot.

   - IDENTITY columns require the NOT FOR REPLICATION option. If a published IDENTITY column doesn't use this option, INSERT commands may not replicate properly.

7. Type a name and description for the publication. If you want to list the publication in the Active Directory, select List This Publication In The Active Directory.

8. You can now determine whether default or custom properties are used. You'll usually want to use custom properties, so select the Yes option and then click Next. If you click No, the wizard uses the default options shown and clicking Next takes you to the final step of the process.

9. Specify whether and how you want to filter the data. You can filter the data vertically by column, horizontally by row, or both.

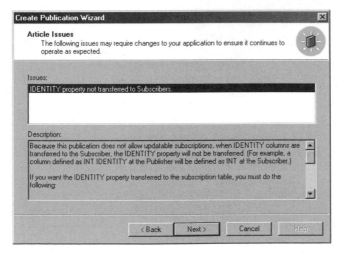

Figure 9-10. *Whenever there are issues that need your attention, you'll see this dialog box. Read the description carefully to determine how to resolve the outstanding issue.*

10. If you've elected to vertically filter table data, you'll see the Filter Table Columns window shown in Figure 9-11. To filter table data, choose a table in the left pane and then select or clear check boxes for columns in the right pane. By clearing a check box, you're excluding the related column from replication. Repeat this step for each table that you want to filter and then click Next.

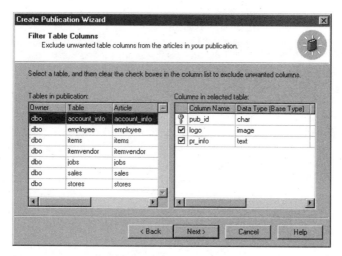

Figure 9-11. *Select columns to exclude from the publication.*

11. If you elected to horizontally filter data, you'll see the Filter Table Rows window shown in Figure 9-12. By default, all rows are published. To change this behavior, click the build (...) button for the row you want to exclude from the publication and then enter a *where* clause for the corresponding *SELECT published_columns From TableName* statement. To extend filtering on a table to a related table by defining a join, select the filtered table and the related table to filter and then define an *inner join* clause.

12. Determine whether anonymous subscriptions are allowed. Choose the Yes option to allow them. Otherwise choose the No option. Anonymous subscribers reduce the amount of administration you have to do. They allow any server to receive replicated data without your having to store information about the server in the distribution database.

 Note With anonymous subscribers, only pull subscriptions are allowed. To learn more about pull subscriptions, see the "Subscribing to a Publication" section of this chapter.

13. The next step lets you set the snapshot schedule. By default, snapshots are made once a day. To change this schedule, click Change and then set a new schedule. You can create a snapshot immediately by selecting Create First Snapshot Immediately.

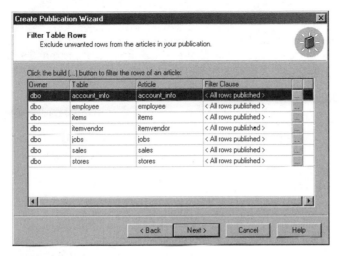

Figure 9-12. *You can also filter table rows using* where *clauses. To see a list of available column values, click Cancel and then click Back to go back to the previous wizard dialog box.*

14. Click Next and then click Finish. You'll see a dialog box that shows the progress of the creation process. If errors occur, you'll need to resolve any problems before you can continue or restart the publication definition process.

Merge Publications

Once you've started a new publication, you can create a merge publication by completing the following steps:

1. Select the types of subscribers that will subscribe to the publication. You can choose any or all of the following:

   - Servers Running SQL Server 2000
   - Servers Running SQL Server Version 7.0
   - Heterogeneous Data Sources

Note   If all subscribers are SQL Servers and no transformations are used, snapshots are formatted using Native SQL Server format. Otherwise snapshots are formatted using Character Mode format. Additionally, if you choose SQL Server 7.0 as a data source, you can't choose properties that are new to SQL Server 2000.

2. Use the dialog box shown previously in Figure 9-9 to select the objects for replication. You use key elements of this dialog box as follows:

   - **Object Type**   Shows the types of objects that are available for replication.

Note Which objects are available depends on the types of objects in the database and can be tables, stored procedures, and views. Tables without primary keys can't be published for snapshot or transactional replication, and you'll see a key with an X through it in the Specify Articles dialog box.

- **Show** When selected, displays the related objects in the right-hand pane. For example, select Show for views and views are displayed for selection in the right-hand pane.
- **Publish All** When selected, all of the related objects are selected for replication.
- **Owner** Shows the object owner.
- **Object** Displays the object name.
- **Show Unpublished Objects** Determines whether unpublished objects are displayed.
- **Article Defaults** Allows you to set default article options for each type of database object.

3. When you select a table, stored procedure, or view, you'll see a Properties button. Click this button to configure property settings for the related article. See the section of this chapter entitled "Setting Article Properties" for details.

4. After you select objects to use in the publication, click Next. If there are any issues that require changes to the publication, you'll see a prompt. Read the description carefully to determine how to resolve the issue and make changes as necessary. Key issues are:

   - Tables referenced by views are required and so are objects referenced by stored procedures. If you don't select referenced tables or objects, you must create them manually at the subscriber.
   - SQL Server adds Uniqueidentifier columns to any tables you've selected for replication. Adding the Uniqueidentifier column will cause INSERT statements without column lists to fail and increase the time needed to generate the first snapshot.
   - IDENTITY columns require the NOT FOR REPLICATION option. If a published IDENTITY column doesn't use this option, INSERT commands may not replicate properly.

5. Type a name and description for the publication. If you want to list the publication in Active Directory Services, select List This Publication In The Active Directory.

6. You can now determine whether default or custom properties are used. You'll usually want to use custom properties, so select the Yes option and then click Next. If you click No, the wizard uses the default options shown and clicking Next takes you to the final step of the process.

7. Specify whether and how you want to filter the data. You can filter the data vertically by column, horizontally by row, or both. If you don't want to use filtering, click Next without making any selections and then skip steps 8-15. Steps 8-15 are only used with filtering.

8. If you've elected to vertically filter table data, you'll see the Filter Table Columns window. To filter table data, choose a table in the left pane and then select or clear check boxes for columns in the right pane. By clearing a check box, you're excluding the related column from replication. Repeat this step for each table that you want to filter and then click Next.

9. Steps 10-15 are only used for horizontal filtering. If you aren't using horizontal filtering, skip steps 8-15.

10. Horizontal data filtering is handled in one of two ways. You can use a dynamic filter that allows individual subscribers to receive different sections of the published data, or you can use a static filter and all subscribers will receive the same data. For dynamic filters, choose Yes, Enable Dynamic Filters. Otherwise choose No, Use Static Filters.

11. In the Generate Filters Automatically window, you can specify a filter on a table and have SQL Server automatically extend the filter to other tables based on relationships you define using *where* clauses. The default setting is None – Do Not Extend Filtering. Use the Table To Filter drop-down list box to select the table you want to filter. Then enter a *where* clause for the corresponding *SELECT * From TableName* statement. Repeat this process for any additional tables you want to filter. Click Next when you're finished.

12. You'll see the Filter Table Rows window, as shown in Figure 9-13. By default, all rows are published. To change this behavior, click the build (…) button for the row you want to exclude from the publication and then enter a *where* clause for the corresponding *SELECT published_columns From TableName* statement. To extend filtering on a table to a related table by defining a join, select the filtered table and the related table to filter and then define an *inner join* clause.

13. As shown in Figure 9-13, you can extend the row filters to other tables by using *join* filters. From the list in the Filtered Table column, select a table with an existing filter. Then from the list in the Table To Filter column, select a second table to be filtered. Afterward, click the related properties button (…) to enter a *join* clause to use as the filter. Repeat this step to create additional filters. To delete a join, click <Delete Join> in the list shown in the Filtered Table column. When you click Next, SQL Server attempts to extend the filter to other tables based on their relationships.

14. With dynamic filters you can validate information at the Subscriber before each merge and the next window allows you to set related options. To enforce the validation process, select Yes, Validate Subscriber Information and then type a function to use for validation, such as **HOST_NAME() + suser_sname()**.If you do not want Subscriber information to be validated before each merge, select No, Do Not Validate Subscriber Information.

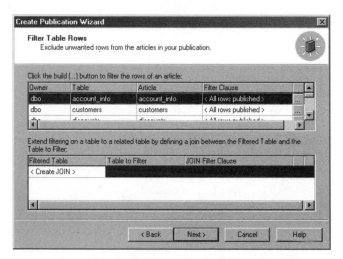

Figure 9-13. *Extend filters to other tables using a* join *clause.*

15. With horizontal filtering you can optimize synchronization by electing to maintain additional information at the publisher and thereby reduce the amount of data sent over the network. If you want to do this, select Yes, Minimize The Amount Of Data. Otherwise select No, Do Not Minimize The Amount Of Data.

16. Determine whether anonymous subscriptions are allowed. Choose the Yes option to allow them. Otherwise choose the No option. Anonymous subscribers reduce the amount of administration you have to do. They allow any server to receive replicated data without your having to store information about the server in the distribution database.

Note With anonymous subscribers, only pull subscriptions are allowed. To learn more about pull subscriptions, see the "Subscribing to a Publication" section of this chapter.

17. The next step lets you set the snapshot schedule. By default, snapshots are made once a day. To change this schedule, click Change and then set a new schedule. You can create a snapshot immediately by selecting Create First Snapshot Immediately.

18. Click Next and then click Finish. You'll see a dialog box that shows the progress of the creation process.

Updating a Publication

You can change the properties of publications any time you like. To change them, complete the following steps:

1. Start Enterprise Manager, double-click the server entry for the publisher, and then double-click the Replication folder.

2. Click the Publications folder to see a list of publications for this database.

3. Right-click the publication you want to work with and then select Properties.

4. You can now use the Properties dialog box to configure all the publication options discussed previously in the "Creating Publications" section of this chapter.

Setting Article Properties

Article properties control the behavior of replication. When you create a publication, you can set default article properties based on object type. You can override the default properties at any time. To edit article properties for an existing publication, follow these steps:

1. Start Enterprise Manager, double-click the server entry for the publisher, and then double-click the Replication folder.

2. Click the Publications folder to see a list of publications for this database.

3. Right-click the publication you want to work with and then select Properties.

4. In the Articles tab, click the build (...) button for an article you want to update. This displays the Article Properties dialog box. The available article properties depend on the replication type, and you may see one or more of the following tabs:

   - **General**   Allows you to configure basic options and is available for all replication types. You can view the article name, source table owner, and source table name. You can set the article description, destination table owner, and destination table name. With merge replication you can also specify whether row-level or column-level conflict resolution is used. With DTS and snapshot or transactional replication you can also specify whether the article should support horizontal partitions created by Data Transformation Services.

   - **Snapshot**   Sets options for snapshots, which are used with all replication types. You can set options that control what happens when a table exists at the subscriber already, what types of objects are copied, and whether user-defined data types are converted to base data types.

   - **Resolver**   Allows you to choose which resolver is used to resolve conflicts that occur in merge replication and to allow subscribers to resolve conflicts interactively during on-demand synchronizations. Merge replication only.

   - **Merging Changes**   Controls whether the subscriber verifies that the Merge Agent has permission to use INSERT, UPDATE, and DELETE commands. By default, the agent doesn't verify permissions. Indicates whether Multicolumn updates are applied during merge replication for this article. Merge replication only.

- **Commands** Controls whether INSERT, UPDATE, and DELETE commands are replaced by customized stored procedures. By default, these commands are replaced and the necessary stored procedures are created automatically when synchronizing with subscribers. Transactional replication only.

Controlling Subscription Access to a Publication

All publications have access control lists (ACLs). For publications, access control lists determine which logins can be used by pull and immediate updating subscribers to access the publication. By default, only the database owner (DBO) and administrators have subscription access to the publication. To add or remove users, complete the following steps:

1. Start Enterprise Manager, double-click the server entry for the publisher, and then double-click the Replication folder.
2. Click the Publications folder to see a list of publications for this database.
3. Right-click the publication you want to work with and then select Properties.
4. Click the Publication Access List tab. Use the buttons provided to add or remove logins.

Creating a Script for a Publication

To create a script for a publication, complete the following steps:

1. Start Enterprise Manager, double-click the server entry for the publisher, and then double-click the Replication folder.
2. Click the Publications folder to see a list of publications for this database.
3. Right-click the publication you want to work with and then select Generate SQL Script.
4. Click OK. Click Save and then save the script to a .sql file, which can be executed in Query Analyzer.

 Tip In Query Analyzer, you can access scripts by clicking the Load SQL Script button on the toolbar and then entering the location of the script.

Deleting a Publication

When you're finished using a publication, you can delete it to free up resources that it's using. But before you do this, you may want to create a script that allows you to recreate the publication automatically if you have to. After creating the script, you can delete the publication by completing the following steps:

1. Start Enterprise Manager, double-click the server entry for the publisher, and then double-click the Replication folder.
2. Click the Publications folder to see a list of publications for this server instance.

3. Right-click the publication you want to work with and then select Delete.
4. When prompted to confirm the action, click Yes.

Subscribing to a Publication

The final step in the replication process is having servers subscribe to the publication. You can do this using *push* or *pull* subscriptions.

Subscription Essentials

With push subscriptions, the publisher is responsible for replicating all changes to subscribers without subscribers asking for the changes. You'll usually use push subscriptions when you need to send changes to subscribers immediately or when you want to schedule updates periodically. Because the publisher initiates the replication, push subscriptions also offer more security than pull subscriptions. Making the publisher responsible for replicating changes, however, increases overhead on the publisher and may not be the ideal subscription model for a server that's experiencing heavy workloads.

With pull subscriptions, subscribers request periodic updates of all changes from the publisher. You'll usually use pull subscriptions when you have a large number of subscribers or when you need to reduce overhead on the publisher. You'll usually want to use pull subscriptions for independent mobile users as well. A single publication can support a mixture of push and pull subscriptions.

You can also use a special type of pull subscription called an *anonymous* subscription. With an anonymous subscription, the publisher and distributor don't maintain subscription information. Instead, the subscriber is responsible for maintaining and synchronizing the subscription, which increases the load on the subscriber but reduces the load on the publisher and distributor. Accordingly, anonymous subscriptions are most useful when you have a large number of subscribers or when you allow subscriptions using the Internet.

Note   You create anonymous subscriptions to publications just like pull subscriptions. If the publication is enabled for anonymous subscriptions and the server isn't registered as a subscriber, the Pull Subscription Wizard creates an anonymous subscription automatically.

The Distribution Agent and Merge Agent are responsible for synchronizing subscriptions and resetting their retention period. If these agents aren't running, subscriptions become out of sync with their publications and are marked as deactivated. A deactivated subscription is a subscription that has exceeded the publication retention period. Deactivated subscriptions no longer receive updates during synchronization and you must mark these subscriptions for reinitialization in order to reenable them. If you don't reenable deactivated subscriptions before they expire, the Expired Subscription Clean Up Agent will delete them.

Creating Pull Subscriptions

The subscriber initiates pull subscriptions. You configure pull subscriptions by completing the following steps:

1. In Enterprise Manager, access the database server instance that will act as the subscriber. Right-click the Replication folder, point to New, and then select Pull Subscription. This starts the Pull Subscription Wizard.

2. Select Show Advanced Options In This Wizard and then click Next.

3. You use the next dialog box (see Figure 9-14) to specify where you want to look for a publication. You can look at publications from registered servers, search in Active Directory services for publications, or specify the publication information manually. You can only search the Active Directory for publications or enter the information manually when you are running SQL Server 2000 in a Windows 2000 Active Directory domain. Click Next after you've made your selection.

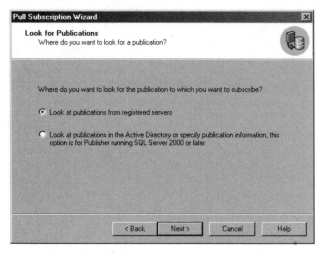

Figure 9-14. *Look For Publications allows you to look for publications from registered servers, search Active Directory for publications, or specify publication information manually.*

4. If you elected to look at publications from registered servers, you can browse available publications from the list of registered publishers in the Choose Publication dialog box (see Figure 9-15). Display a list of available publications by clicking the plus sign (+) next to a registered publisher. Then select the publication to which you want to subscribe. Afterward, click Next. You can also register a new server by clicking the Register Server button.

5. If you elected to search the Active Directory for publications or to enter information manually, you will see the Specify Publication dialog box as shown in Figure 9-16. To browse an Active Directory for publications, click the Browse button and then use the Find SQL Server Publications dialog box

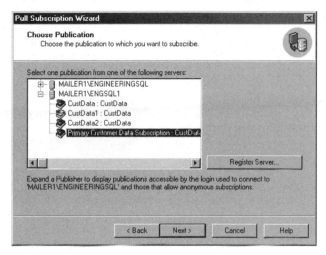

Figure 9-15. *Choose Publication allows you to access a list of currently available publications from registered servers.*

to find the publication you want to use. To specify the publication information, manually type the name of the publisher, the publication database, and the publication. Whether you specify the information manually or select a publication from Active Directory, you must also specify the authentication technique to use for the connection. If you choose SQL Server Authentication, type the SQL login name and password as well.

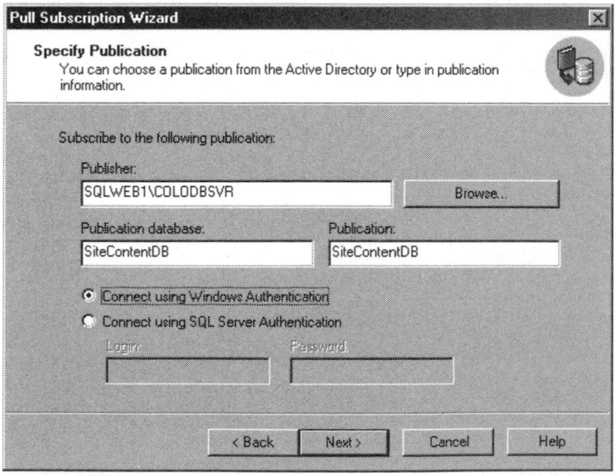

Figure 9-16. *You can use Specify Publication to enter specific publication information manually, or you can browse the Active Directory for registered publications by clicking Browse.*

Note In some situations you may need to specify the login used by the synchronization agent to connect to the publisher and distributor. Typically this occurs when you're accessing publishers that are members of a domain from a SQL Server that isn't a member of the domain, or you logged in locally to the server and are not an authenticated user of the domain. You specify the login information using the Specify Synchronization Agent Login dialog box. The agent can either impersonate the SQL Server Agent account (recommended) or use a specific SQL Server login name and password. Either way, the account you choose must be listed on the publication access list.

6. Use the Choose Destination Database window to select an existing database in which to create the subscription or click New to create a new database for the subscription. Click Next when you're ready to continue.

7. If you selected a publication that does not use immediate updating or queued updating, skip steps 8 and 9. Steps 8 and 9 are only used when immediate updating or queued updating are selected.

8. If immediate updating, queued updating, or both was specified when the snapshot or transactional publication was created, the next dialog box will be Updatable Subscriptions (see Figure 9-17). This dialog box allows you to enable these options for the subscription. Select None – Changes Are Not Replicated if you don't want to create an updatable subscription at this time. Keep in mind that when you use immediate updating with queued updating as a failover, you must manually switch into queued updating mode and then switch back to immediate updating once the connection is restored and the queue is empty.

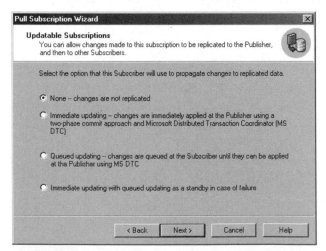

Figure 9-17. *Updatable subscriptions allow changes made to a subscription to be replicated to the publisher and then to other subscribers.*

9. If you choose to create an updatable subscription using immediate updating, the next dialog box allows you to configure the technique used by the subscriber to access the publisher (see Figure 9-18). You can use an existing linked server or remote server to establish the connection, provided you've already configured these options as described in Chapter 8. Or you can use a SQL Server login id, provided the login is listed on the publication access list.

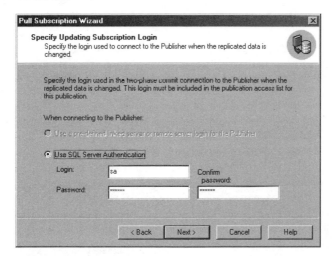

Figure 9-18. *Specify the login method used to access the publisher when making updates. You can use linked servers, remote logins, or SQL Server Authentication.*

10. Use the Initialize Subscription window to determine whether the subscription database should be initialized. The options available are different depending on the type of publication that is being subscribed to. Some options are dimmed and are unavailable. Choose the Yes option to initialize the schema and data. Choose the No option if you're updating an existing database with the same schema.

Note   Keep in mind that initialization is handled by the Snapshot and Distribution Agents. The Snapshot Agent creates the initial view of the schema and data, and then when it next runs, the Distribution Agent applies the snapshot.

11. If you elect to initialize the schema and data, the next dialog box lets you specify where to access the snapshot files. You can access the snapshot files in the default snapshot folder for the publication or in an alternate location. For an alternate location, type the full folder path, such as C:\data\snapshots.

12. Set the Distribution Agent or Merge Agent schedule using one of the following options:

- **Continuously** Select this option to continuously check for updates on the publisher.

- **Using The Following Schedule** Select this option and then click the Change button to set a periodic schedule, such as once an hour.

- **On Demand Only** Select this option if you want to update the subscription database manually.

13. If you chose a snapshot or transactional publication and want to transform the publication data before sending it to subscribers, you must now specify the DTS package that defines the transformations for the subscription. As shown in Figure 9-19, specify the package location on the distributor or on the subscriber and then enter a package name. If required, enter the owner password for the package as well.

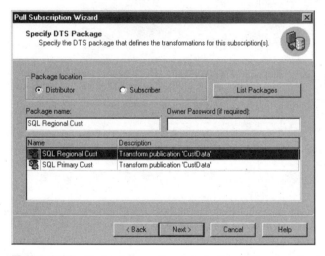

Figure 9-19. *To transform the data before delivering it, specify the package location, name, and optional owner password.*

14. If you are subscribing to a merge publication, you can choose the priority setting of the publisher to resolve subscriber conflicts or you can set the priority level manually (see Figure 9-20).

15. If necessary, determine whether required services should be started. To start a service, select the check box to the left of the service name. Services that aren't started automatically will need to be started manually for the subscription to work.

16. If the SQL Server Agent service isn't configured to start automatically, you'll next need to specify whether the SQL Server Agent should start automatically. Choose Yes for automatic startup or choose No if you plan to manually start the agent.

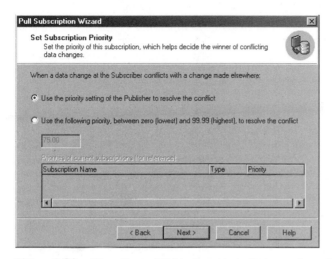

Figure 9-20. *Allow the publisher to set priority to resolve subscriber conflicts or set a priority level manually.*

17. Check the setup and click Finish when you're ready to create the pull subscription.

Updating, Maintaining, and Deleting Pull Subscriptions

To update, maintain, or delete a pull subscription, complete the following steps:

1. Start Enterprise Manager. Double-click the server entry for the subscriber and then double-click the Replication folder.

2. Click the Subscriptions folder to see a list of subscriptions for this server instance.

3. Right-click the pull subscription you want to work with and then choose one of the following options:

- **Copy Subscription Database** Writes a copy of the subscription database to a subscription file that can be replicated through FTP to remote locations. Subscription files end with the .msf extension and are saved to the REPLDATA folder for the SQL Server instance by default.

- **Delete** Deletes the subscription. Confirm the action by clicking Yes when prompted.

- **Generate SQL Script** Creates a SQL script that you can use to recreate or delete the subscription. Generally, it's a good idea to create a script for a subscription before you delete it. This way, you can easily recreate the subscription if necessary.

- **Job History** Shows a history of all SQL Server Agent jobs that are run to create, maintain, and manage the subscription. If a job fails because SQL Server is unable to determine if the job owner has access to a server, it means the login id for the distributor or publisher isn't listed in the publication's access control list.

- **Properties** Displays the Subscription Properties dialog box. The dialog box has four tabs: General, Synchronization, Security, and Snapshot File Location. Use the General tab to view subscription information. Use the Synchronization tab to view or change replication agent properties, configure synchronization, and specify where to start the merge agent. Use the Security tab to set distributor and publisher logins. Use the Snapshot File Locations tab to specify alternative snapshot locations and to specify a temporary working folder to use when creating snapshots.

- **Reinitialize** Reinitialize the snapshot in the subscription database. Use this option to create a new snapshot of the data and restart synchronization for a deactivated subscription.

- **Start Synchronization** Starts the synchronization process for an active subscription. Use this option to manually update the subscription.

- **Stop Synchronization** Stops the synchronization process if it's in progress. Use this option if you need to stop the update before it's written to the subscription.

- **View Conflicts** Starts the Replication Conflict Viewer, which shows current conflicts that are unresolved. If you've configured the subscription so that conflicts are resolved interactively, you use the Replication Conflict Viewer to manually resolve conflicts.

Creating Push Subscriptions

You can initiate push subscriptions from the publisher by completing the following steps:

1. In Enterprise Manager, access the publisher. Double-click the Replication folder and then double-click the Publications folder.

2. Right-click the publication you want to configure and then select Push New Subscription. This starts the Push Subscription Wizard.

3. Select Show Advanced Options In This Wizard. Click Next to access the dialog box shown in Figure 9-21. Select one or more subscribers for the publication. Servers that are currently enabled are listed in the Enabled Subscribers group. If a server you want to use as a subscriber isn't listed, click Cancel, enable the server as a subscriber, and then restart the wizard.

4. Type the name of the destination database on the subscriber. Click the Browse Or Create button to select an existing database or to create a new database on the subscriber. Click Next when you're ready to continue.

Figure 9-21. *Select the subscribers for the publication.*

5. Choose whether the Distribution Agent should run at the distributor or at the subscriber. If you choose to run the agent at the subscriber, you must also enter the computer name of the subscriber.

Note The Distribution Agent is responsible for applying data from snapshot replication or transactions from transactional replication to subscribers. In most cases, the agent should run on the distributor. However, if you want to move some of the workload off a distributor that is also acting as a publisher, this is one way to do it.

6. Set the distribution agent schedule using one of the following options:

   • **Continuously** Select this option to have the publisher send updates continuously.

   • **Using The Following Schedule** Select this option and then click Change to set a periodic schedule, such as once an hour.

7. Determine whether the subscription database should be initialized. Choose the Yes option to initialize the schema and data. Choose the No option if you're updating an existing database with the same schema. If you choose Yes, you can also choose to start the snapshot agent so that it can begin the initialization process.

8. If you configured merge replication, you can now configure the subscription priority for data changes as shown in Figure 9-22. When a data change at the subscriber conflicts with a change elsewhere, you can use the priority setting of the publisher to resolve the conflict or to set a specific priority between 0.00 (lowest) and 99.99 (highest).

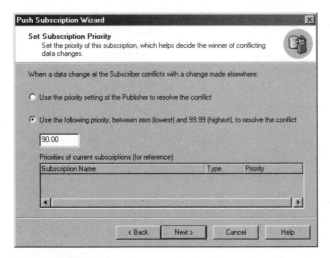

Figure 9-22. *Subscription priority determines the winner of conflicting changes.*

 Tip The priorities of existing subscriptions to the publication are listed for reference. If you want to ensure that changes to a particular subscription have precedence, set the priority of this subscription to be higher than that of other subscriptions and the default priority of the publisher. If you want to ensure that changes to a particular subscription are discarded when there's a conflict, set the priority of this subscription to be lower than that of other subscriptions and the default priority of the publisher.

9. If you specified immediate updating, queued updating, or both when creating the publication, the next dialog box allows you to enable these options for the subscription. Select None – Changes Are Not Replicated if you don't want to create an updatable subscription at this time. Keep in mind that when you use immediate updating with queued updating as a failover, you must manually switch into queued updating mode and then switch back to immediate updating once the connection is restored and the queue is empty.

10. If you chose to transform the publication data before sending it to subscribers, you must now specify the DTS package that defines the transformations for the subscription. Specify the package location on the distributor or on the subscriber and then enter a package name. If required, enter the owner password for the package as well.

11. Determine whether required services should be started. To start a service, if necessary, select the check box to the left of the service name. Services that aren't started automatically will need to be started manually for the subscription to work.

12. Check the setup and click Finish when you're ready to create the push subscription.

Updating, Maintaining, and Deleting Push Subscriptions

To update, maintain, or delete a push subscription, complete the following steps:

1. Start Enterprise Manager. Double-click the server entry for the publisher and then double-click the Replication folder.

2. Double-click the Publications folder. Click the publication whose subscriptions you wish to manage.

3. Right-click the push subscription you want to work with and then choose one of the following options:

- **Delete** Deletes the subscription. Confirm the action by clicking Yes when prompted.

- **Properties** View and change subscription properties. The only property you can change is the run location of the merge agent, which is either at the distributor or at the subscriber.

- **Reinitialize** Reinitializes the snapshot in the subscription database. Use this option to create a new snapshot of the data and restart synchronization for a deactivated subscription.

- **Start Synchronization** Starts the synchronization process for an active subscription. Use this option to manually update the subscription.

- **Stop Synchronization** Stops the synchronization process if it's in progress. Use this option if you need to stop the update before it's written to the subscription.

Transforming Published Data

You can use Data Transformation Services (DTS) to manipulate publication data before sending it to subscribers. This technique is useful if individual subscribers need different views of the data or if you need to map information from one table or data format to another table or data format. You can configure both snapshot and transactional publications for data transformation, provided the publications aren't configured to allow updatable subscriptions.

Configuring data transformation for publications and subscriptions requires several steps. You must create a publication that allows data transformation and then you must create a DTS package that's enabled for replication. After you create a publication that allows data transformation, you use the Transform Published Data Wizard to create the replication-enabled package. You access and use this wizard by completing the steps on the following page.

1. Start Enterprise Manager. Double-click the server entry for the publisher and then double-click the Replication folder.

2. Click the Publications folder to see a list of publications for this server instance.

3. Right-click the publication you want to work with and then select Define Transformation Of Published Data. This starts the Transform Published Data Wizard. Click Next.

4. As shown in Figure 9-23, use the Destination drop-down list box to select the provider type for the destination database. You use the provider to generate the subscriber data. If the subscriber is a SQL Server database, you'll want to use the Microsoft OLE DB Provider for SQL Server. Other providers are available as well.

5. Fill in any additional information required to establish a connection to the destination. The destination you select determines what information you need to supply. With SQL Server, be sure to choose the destination database. This database must be the one that was designated as the distribution database when you created the publication.

6. Now you need to define transformations for the objects in the publication as explained next.

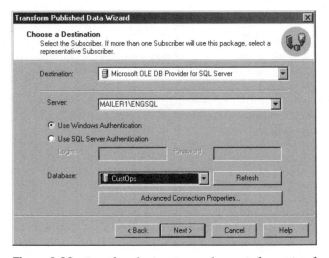

Figure 9-23. *Specify a destination and enter information for the provider and database.*

Transformation is the process of manipulating the source data and formatting it for the chosen destination. Select a table or view that you want to manipulate and then click the corresponding button in the Transform column. Unless you specify otherwise, the wizard sets default mapping for all objects in the publication. This default mapping

• Specifies that every object in the source publication is copied

- Maps the original object name and properties to the destination object
- Drops any existing object with the same name and creates it

You can override the default mappings using a procedure similar to the one outlined in the section of Chapter 7 entitled "Stage 3: Formatting and Transformation." When you're finished configuring all the necessary transformations, click Next in the Transform Published Data Wizard. The final steps allow you to specify the package location, name, and an optional owner password.

Managing Replication Monitors

SQL Server 2000 provides two ways to monitor replication:

- Use replication monitors at the server level.
- Use replication monitor groups at the enterprise level.

Once monitors are enabled, you can use the monitor to view the status of replication agents and troubleshoot potential problems with distributors. All replication agents have options that you can set to customize their behavior.

You can set agent profiles that control the exact behavior of the agent as well as agent properties that control other configuration settings.

Configuring Server-Level Monitoring

Server-level monitoring lets you check replication on a specific distributor. To check replication at the server level, follow these steps:

1. In Enterprise Manager, access the database server instance that is acting as the distributor and then select the Replication Monitor node.

2. Use the Publishers folder to control replication publishers, publications, and subscriptions.

3. Use the Agents folder to configure and manage replication agents for the currently selected distributor as described in "Setting Agent Profiles" and "Setting Agent Properties" below.

Configuring Enterprise-Level Monitoring

Enterprise-level monitoring lets you check replication on multiple distributors throughout the enterprise. Before you can view enterprise-level monitors, you must enable the Replication Monitor Group and add distributors to monitor as specified in the following steps:

1. In Enterprise Manager, right-click Microsoft SQL Servers and then choose Display Replication Monitor Group. The Replication Monitor Group is added to the console root.

2. Right-click Replication Monitor Group and then choose Add Distributor To Monitor.

3. In the Add Distributor To Monitor dialog box, select one or more distributors and then click OK. If the distributor you want to use isn't registered, click Register Server and then complete the Registered SQL Server Properties dialog box.

Setting Agent Profiles

Profile settings are useful for updating agents to work with slow connections, to configure verbose logging, and more. You set a profile for any of the available agents by completing the following steps:

1. In Enterprise Manager, access the distributor whose agent you want to configure in the Replication Monitor Group. If this group isn't displayed, you can display it as described under "Configuring Enterprise-Level Monitoring."

2. Double-click the distributor's entry and then double-click the related Agents folder. You can now configure profiles for the agents that use this distributor.

3. Click the folder for the type of agent you want to work with, such as Snapshot Agents. A list of the related agents should be displayed in the right pane.

4. Right-click the agent you want to work with and then select Agent Profiles. The Agent Profiles dialog box is displayed.

5. Select an existing profile using the option buttons in the Default column.

6. Create a new profile by selecting Copy and configuring the Replication Agent Profile Details dialog box.

7. To force all existing distribution agents to use the new profile, select Change All Existing Agents To Use The Selected Profile.

8. Click OK.

Setting Agent Properties

The snapshot agent and the distribution agent are the key agents you'll want to set properties for. You configure the snapshot agent properties for publications and the distribution agent properties for pull subscriptions.

To change property settings for the snapshot agent, complete the following steps:

1. In Enterprise Manager, access the distributor whose agent you want to configure in the Replication Monitor Group. If this group isn't displayed, you can display it as described under "Configuring Enterprise-Level Monitoring."

2. Double-click the distributor's entry and then double-click the related Agents folder. You can now configure profiles for the agents that use this distributor.

3. Click the folder for the type of agent you want to work with, such as Snapshot Agents. A list of the related agents should be displayed in the right pane.

4. Right-click the agent you want to work with and then select Agent Properties. The Agent Properties dialog box is displayed.

5. Use the related Properties dialog box to configure the agent.

Part IV

Performance, Optimization, and Maintenance

This part of the book covers administration tools that you'll use to enhance and maintain Microsoft SQL Server 2000. Chapter 10 provides the essentials for working with server logs, monitoring SQL Server performance, and solving performance problems. Chapter 11 starts by explaining how to create a backup and recovery plan and then discusses common tasks for creating and restoring backups. Chapter 12 explores database automation. You'll learn how to configure alerts, schedule jobs, and manage database operators. You'll also learn how to create maintenance plans and resolve database consistency problems.

Chapter 10

Profiling and Monitoring Microsoft SQL Server 2000

Monitoring server performance, tracking user activity, and troubleshooting errors are essential parts of database administration, and Microsoft SQL Server has several tools that you can use to perform these tasks. Performance Monitor, the standard Microsoft Windows 2000/NT tool for monitoring servers, has updated counters for SQL Server. These counters allow you to track many different server resources and activities. SQL Server Profiler, an analysis and profiling tool, allows you to trace server events. Other tools and resources are available, such as stored procedures and the SQL Server logs.

Monitoring Server Performance and Activity

Monitoring SQL Server isn't something you should do haphazardly. You need to have a plan—a set of goals that you hope to achieve. Let's look at some reasons you may want to monitor SQL Server and the tools you can use to do this.

Why Monitor SQL Server?

Troubleshooting SQL Server performance problems is a key reason for monitoring. For example, users may be having problems connecting to the server, and you may want to monitor the server to troubleshoot these problems. Here, your goal would be to track down the problem using the available monitoring resources and then solve it.

Another common reason for wanting to monitor SQL Server is to improve server performance. To achieve optimal performance, you need to minimize the time it takes for users to see the results of queries and maximize the total number of queries that the server can handle simultaneously. You do this by

- Resolving hardware issues that may be causing problems. For example, if slow disk drives are delaying queries, work on improving disk input/output (I/O).
- Monitoring memory and CPU usage and taking appropriate steps to reduce the load on the server, as necessary. For example, other processes running on the server may be using memory and CPU resources needed by SQL Server.

- Cutting down the network traffic load on the server. With replication, for example, configure remote stored procedure execution rather than transmit large data changes individually.

Unfortunately, when it comes to resource usage you often have to make tradeoffs. For example, as the number of users accessing SQL Server grows, you may not be able to reduce the network traffic load, but you may be able to improve server performance by optimizing queries or indexing.

Getting Ready to Monitor

Before you start monitoring SQL Server, you may want to establish baseline performance metrics for your server. To do this, you measure server performance at various times and under different load conditions. You can then compare the baseline performance with subsequent performance to determine how SQL Server is performing. Performance metrics that are well above the baseline measurements may indicate areas where the server needs to be optimized or reconfigured.

After you establish the baseline metrics, you should formulate a monitoring plan. A comprehensive monitoring plan involves the following steps:

1. Determine which server events should be monitored to help you accomplish your goal.
2. Set filters to reduce the amount of information collected.
3. Configure monitors and alerts to watch the events.
4. Log the event data so that it can be analyzed.
5. Analyze the event data and replay the data as necessary to find a solution.

These procedures are examined later in this chapter in the section entitled "Monitoring SQL Server Performance." While you should develop a monitoring plan in most cases, sometimes you may not want to go through all these steps to monitor SQL Server. For example, if you want to check current user activity levels, you may not want to use Performance Monitor and may want to run the stored procedure *sp_who* instead. Or you may simply want to examine this information in the Current Activity window in Enterprise Manager.

Monitoring Tools and Resources

The primary monitoring tools you'll use are Windows Performance Monitor and SQL Server Profiler. Other resources for monitoring SQL Server include

- **SQL Server error logs** Use information in these error logs to troubleshoot SQL Server problems.
- **SQL Server Agent error logs** Use information in these error logs to troubleshoot SQL Server Agent problems.
- **Event logs** Use information in the event logs to troubleshoot system-wide problems, including SQL Server and SQL Server Agent problems.

- **Enterprise Manager Current Activity window** This provides information on current users, processes, and locks.
- *sp_helpdb* This stored procedure displays information about databases.
- *sp_helpindex* This stored procedure reports information about indexes on a table.
- *sp_helpserver* This stored procedure provides information in SQL Server instances configured for remote access or replication.
- *sp_lock* This stored procedure shows information concerning object locks.
- *sp_monitor* This stored procedure shows key SQL Server usage statistics, such as CPU idle time and CPU usage.
- *sp_spaceused* This stored procedure shows an estimate of disk space used by a table or database.
- *sp_who* This stored procedure shows a snapshot of current SQL Server users and processes.
- **DBCC statements** Use this set of commands to check SQL Server statistics, to trace activity, and to check database integrity.

Beyond log files and Transact-SQL statements, you'll find a set of built-in functions that return system information. Table 10-1 provides a summary of key functions and their usages. The values returned by these functions are cumulative from the time SQL Server was last started.

**Table 10-1. Built-In Functions for Monitoring
SQL Server Performance and Activity**

Function	Description	Example
@@connections	Returns the number of connections or attempted connections	select @@connections as 'Total Login Attempts'
@@cpu_busy	Returns CPU processing time in milliseconds for SQL Server activity	select @@cpu_busy as 'CPU Busy,' getdate() as 'Since'
@@idle	Returns SQL Server idle time in milliseconds	select @@idle as 'Idle Time,' getdate() as 'Since'
@@io_busy	Returns I/O processing time in milliseconds for SQL Server	select @@io_busy as 'IO Time,' getdate() as 'Since'
@@pack_received	Returns the number of input packets read from the network by SQL Server	select @@pack_received
@@pack_sent	Returns the number of output packets written to the network by SQL Server	select @@pack_sent

(continued)

Table 10-1. *(continued)*

Function	Description	Example
@@*packet_errors*	Returns the number of network packet errors for SQL Server connections	select @@*packet_errors*
@@*total_errors*	Returns the number of disk read/write errors encountered by SQL Server	select @@*total_errors* as 'Total Errors,' getdate( ) as 'Since'
@@*total_read*	Returns the number of disk reads by SQL Server	select @@*total_read* as 'Reads,' getdate( ) as 'Since'
@@*total_write*	Returns the number of disk writes by SQL Server	select @@*total_write* as 'Writes,' getdate( ) as 'Since'

Working with the Error Logs

Error logs are your primary resource for tracking SQL Server errors. SQL Server writes events to the SQL Server error logs, the SQL Server agent error logs, and the Windows application log. You can use all three logs to track messages related to SQL Server. However, there are some things you should know:

- Some events aren't logged in the application log and you can control the logging of most noncritical events through the Manage SQL Server Messages dialog box in Enterprise Manager. To display this dialog box, choose the Manage SQL Server Messages option from the Tools menu.

- Only the application log provides additional information on all applications running on the server, and only the application log provides features for filtering events based on type. For example, you can filter events so that only error and warning messages are displayed.

- If you start the MSSQLServer or MSSQL$*instancename* service from the command prompt, events are logged to the SQL Server error log and to standard output. No events are recorded in the Windows application log.

SQL Server error messages are cryptic and difficult to read if you don't understand the formatting. Messages logged by SQL Server can have

- **An error number that uniquely identifies the error message** System error numbers have one to five digits. System errors are numbered from 1 to 50,000. User-defined errors start at 50,001.

- **A severity level that indicates how critical the message is** Severity levels go from 1 to 25. Messages with a severity level of 10 are informational messages. Severity levels from 11 to 16 are generated by users and users can correct them. Severity levels from 17 to 25 indicate software or hardware errors that you should examine.

- **An error state number that indicates the source of the error** Error state numbers have one to three digits and a maximum value of 127. Normally, error state numbers indicate the line number in the SQL Server code that generated the message.

- **A message that provides a brief description of the error**

ODBC (open database connectivity) and OLE (object linking and embedding) return errors from SQL Server that contain similar information as well.

Examining the Application Log

The application log contains entries for all database server instances running on the computer as well as entries for other business applications. You access the application log by completing the following steps:

1. Access the Start menu, choose Programs, choose Administrative Tools (Common), and then choose Event Viewer. This starts Event Viewer.

2. Event Viewer displays logs for the local computer by default. If you want to view logs on a remote computer, right-click the Event Viewer entry in the console tree (left pane) and then select Connect To Another Computer. Afterward, in the Select Computer dialog box, enter the name of the computer you want to access and then click OK.

3. In the console tree (left pane), click Application Log. You should see the application log shown in Figure 10-1. Use the information in the Source column to determine which service or database server instance logged a particular event.

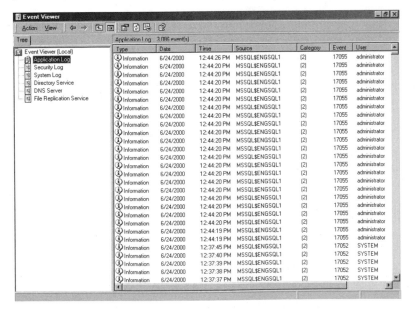

Figure 10-1. *The Windows application log.*

The entries in Event Viewer's main window provide a quick overview of when, where, and how an event occurred. To obtain detailed information on an event, double-click its entry. A summary icon that tells you the event type precedes the date and time of the event. Event types include

- **Informational** An informational event that's generally related to a success-ful action
- **Success audit** An event related to the successful execution of an action
- **Failure audit** An event related to the failed execution of an action
- **Warning** A noncritical error that provides a warning. Details for warnings are often useful in preventing future system problems.
- **Critical error** A critical error, such as the failure of a service to start

In addition to the date, time, and the event type indicator, the summary and detailed event entries provide the following information:

- **Source** The application, service, or component that logged the event
- **Category** The category of the event, which is sometimes used to further describe the related action
- **Event** An identifier for the specific event
- **User** The user account that was logged on when the event occurred
- **Computer** The computer name where the event occurred
- **Description** In the detailed entries, this provides a text description of the event
- **Data** In the detailed entries, this provides any data or error code output by the event

Warnings and critical errors are the two key types of events that you'll want to examine closely. Whenever these types of events occur and you're unsure of the cause, double-click the entry to view the detailed event description. If you want to see only warnings and errors, you can filter the log by completing the follow-ing steps:

1. From the View menu, choose the Filter option. This opens the dialog box shown in Figure 10-2.
2. Clear the following check boxes: Information, Success Audit, and Failure Audit.
3. Select the Warning and Error check boxes.
4. Click OK. You should now see a list of warning and error messages only. Keep in mind that these messages are for all applications running on the server and not just SQL Server.

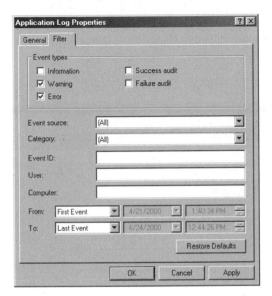

Figure 10-2. *In the Application Log Properties dialog box, you can filter events so that only warnings and errors are displayed.*

Examining the SQL Server Error Logs

The SQL Server logs record information, warnings, errors, and auditing messages pertaining to SQL Server activity. New logs are created when you start the SQL Server service or when you run the *sp_cycle_errorlog* stored procedure. When a new log is created, the current log is cycled to the archive. SQL Server maintains up to six archived logs.

You can view the SQL Server error logs in Enterprise Manager or through a text editor. In Enterprise Manager, you access the error logs by completing the following steps:

1. Start Enterprise Manager and then access the database server instance whose logs you want to examine.

2. Click the plus sign (+) next to the server's Management folder, and then double-click the SQL Server Logs entry.

3. The current log is shown with the label Current.

4. Archived logs are shown with the label Archive # N, such as Archive # 1.

5. To view the properties of an error log entry, double-click it.

To access the error logs in a text editor, complete the steps on the following page.

1. Start the text editor and then use its Open dialog box to access the SQL Server Log folder that's normally located in mssql\Log or mssql$*instancename*\Log.

2. Open the log you want to examine. The current log file is named ERRORLOG with no file extension. The most recent log backup has the extension .1, the second most recent has the extension .2, and so on.

Examining the SQL Server Agent Error Logs

The SQL Server Agent logs record information, warnings, and errors pertaining to SQL Server Agent activity. The only time new logs are created is when you start the SQL Server Agent service. When a new log is created, the current log is cycled to the archive. SQL Server maintains up to six archived logs.

In Enterprise Manager, you access the current SQL Server Agent log by completing the following steps:

1. Start Enterprise Manager and then access the database server instance whose logs you want to examine.

2. Click the plus sign (+) next to the server's Management folder. Right-click SQL Server Agent and then select Display Error Log. This displays the SQL Server Agent Error Log dialog box.

3. Use the Type selection list to choose the type or event to view. The available options are All Types, Error, Warning, and Information.

4. To view the properties of a log entry, double-click it.

To access archived SQL Server Agent error logs in a text editor, complete the following steps:

1. Start the text editor and then use its Open dialog box to access the SQL Server Log folder, which is normally located in mssql\Log or mssql$*instancename*\Log.

2. Open the log you want to examine. The current log file is named SQLAGENT.OUT. The most recent log backup has the extension .1, the second most recent has the extension .2, and so on.

Monitoring SQL Server Performance

Windows Performance Monitor is the tool of choice for monitoring SQL Server performance. Performance Monitor graphically displays statistics for the set of performance parameters you've selected for display. These performance parameters are referred to as *counters*.

When you install SQL Server on a system, Performance Monitor is updated with a set of counters for tracking SQL Server performance parameters. These counters can also be updated when you install services and add-ons for SQL Server. For example, when you configure replication on a server, the Replication Monitor window is added to Enterprise Manager, and Performance Monitor is again updated with a set of objects and counters for tracking replication performance.

Performance Monitor creates a graph depicting the various counters you're tracking. You can configure the update interval for this graph, but it's set to 3 seconds by default. As you'll see when you work with Performance Monitor, the tracking information is most valuable when you record the information in a log file and when you configure alerts to send messages when certain events occur or when certain thresholds are reached, such as when a database log file gets close to running out of free space.

The following sections examine key techniques you'll use to work with Performance Monitor.

Note Performance Monitor isn't available with Windows 95 or Windows 98 desktop installations.

Starting Performance Monitor

You can start Performance Monitor in two ways. You can

* Choose the Performance Monitor option from the Administrative Tools menu
* In Enterprise Manager, right-click the Replication Monitor entry and then, from the shortcut menu, choose Performance Monitor

The technique you use to start Performance Monitor depends on the tasks you want to accomplish. If you start Performance Monitor from the Administrative Tools menu, no default counters are configured. On the other hand, if you start Performance Monitor from Enterprise Manager, default counters are configured automatically for tracking. These counters show the replication defaults.

Choosing Counters to Monitor

Performance Monitor displays information only for counters you're tracking. Over a hundred SQL Server counters are available—and if you've configured replication, there are even more. These counters are organized into object groupings. For example, all lock-related counters are associated with the MSSQL:Locks object.

To select which counters you want to monitor, complete the following steps:

1. Start Performance Monitor. As Figure 10-3 shows, any default counters are shown in the lower portion of the Performance Monitor window.

2. Performance Monitor has several views. Make sure you're in Chart view. Click the View Chart button on the toolbar.

3. To delete a default counter, click its entry in the lower portion of the Performance Monitor window and then press the Delete key.

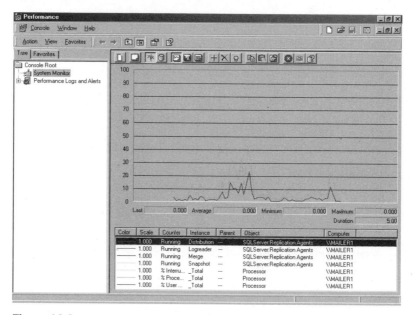

Figure 10-3. *Counters are listed in the lower portion of the Performance Monitor window.*

4. To add counters, click the Add button on the toolbar. This displays the Add Counters dialog box shown in Figure 10-4. The key fields are

- **Use Local Computer Counters**   Configures performance options for the local computer.

- **Select Counters From Computer**   Enters the UNC (Uniform Naming Convention) name of the SQL Server you want to work with, such as \\ZETA.

- **Performance Object**   Selects the type of object you want to work with, such as MSSQL:Locks.

Note   The easiest way to learn what you can track is to explore the objects and counters available in the Add Counters dialog box. Select an object in the Performance Object field, click Explain, and scroll through the list of counters for this object.

- **All Counters**   Selects all counters for the current object.

- **Select Counters From List**   Selects one or more counters for the current object. For example, you could select Lock Requests/sec, Lock Timeouts/sec, and Number of Deadlocks/sec.

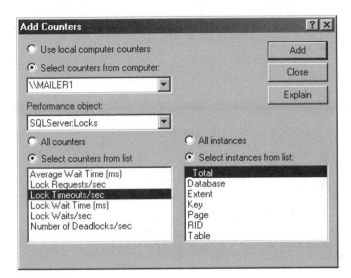

Figure 10-4. *In the Add Counters dialog box, select the counters you want to monitor.*

- **All Instances**   Selects all counter instances for monitoring.
- **Select Instances From List**   Selects one or more counter instances to monitor. For example, you could select instances of the Lock Requests/sec counter for Database, Extent, and Page.

Tip   Don't try to chart too many counters or counter instances at once. You'll make the display too difficult to read and you'll use system resources—namely CPU time and memory—that may affect server responsiveness.

5. When you've selected all the necessary options, click Add to add the counters to the chart. Repeat this process as necessary to add other performance parameters.

6. Click Close when you're finished.

Creating and Managing Performance Monitor Logs

You can use performance logs to track the performance of SQL Server, and you can replay them at a later date. As you set out to work with logs, keep in mind that the parameters you track in log files are recorded separately from the parameters you're charting in the Performance Monitor window. You can configure log files to update counter data automatically or manually. With automatic logging, a snapshot of key parameters is recorded at specific time intervals, such as every 10 seconds. With manual logging, you determine when snapshots are made. Two types of performance logs are available:

- **Counter Logs** Record performance data on the selected counters when a predetermined update interval has elapsed
- **Trace Logs** Record performance data whenever their related events occur

Creating and Managing Performance Logging

To create and manage performance logging, complete the following steps:

1. Access the Performance console by choosing the Performance option from the Administrative Tools menu.

2. Expand the Performance Logs and Alerts node by clicking the plus sign (+) next to it. If you want to configure a counter log, select Counter Logs. Otherwise select Trace Logs.

3. As shown in Figure 10-5, you should see a list of current logs (if any) in the right pane. A green log symbol next to the log name indicates logging is active. A red log symbol indicates logging is stopped.

4. You can create a new log by right-clicking in the right pane and choosing New Log Settings from the shortcut menu. A New Log Settings box appears asking you to give a name to the new log settings. Type a descriptive name here before continuing.

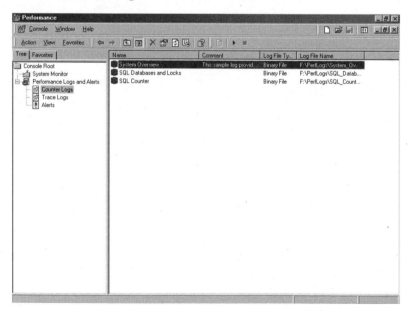

Figure 10-5. *Current performance logs are listed with summary information.*

5. To manage an existing log, right-click its entry in the right pane and then select one of the following options:
   - **Start**   To activate logging
   - **Stop**   To halt logging
   - **Delete**   To delete the log
   - **Properties**   To display the log properties dialog box

Creating Counter Logs

Counter logs record performance data on the selected counters at a specific sample interval. For example, you could sample performance data for the CPU every 15 minutes. To create a counter log, complete the following steps:

1. Select Counter Logs in the left pane of the Performance console and then right-click in the right pane to display the shortcut menu. Choose New Log Settings.

2. In the New Log Settings dialog box, type a name for the log, such as System Performance Monitor or Processor Status Monitor. Click OK.

3. In the General tab, click Add to display the Select Counters dialog box. This dialog box is identical to the Add Counters dialog box shown previously in Figure 10-4.

4. Use the Select Counters dialog box to add counters for logging. Click Close when you're finished.

5. In the Sample Data Every ... field, type in a sample interval and select a time unit in seconds, minutes, hours, or days. The sample interval specifies when new data is collected. For example, if you sample every 15 minutes, the log is updated every 15 minutes.

6. As shown in Figure 10-6, click the Log Files tab and then, using the following fields, specify how the log file should be created:
   - **Location**   Sets the folder location for the log file.
   - **File Name**   Sets the name of the log file.
   - **End File Names With**   Sets an automatic suffix for each new file that's created when you run the counter log. Logs can have a numeric suffix or a suffix in a specific date format.
   - **Start Numbering At**   Sets the first serial number for a log that uses an automatic numeric suffix.
   - **Log File Type**   Sets the type of log file to create. Use Text File – CSV for a log file with comma separated entries. Use Text File – TSV for a log file with tab separated entries. Use Binary File to create a binary file that can be read by Performance Monitor. Use Binary Circular File to create a binary file that overwrites old data with new data when the file reaches a specified size limit.

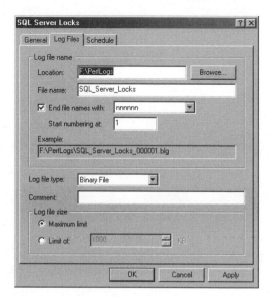

Figure 10-6. *Configure the log file format and usage in the Log Files tab.*

 Tip If you plan to use Performance Monitor to analyze or view the log, use one of the binary file formats.

- **Comment** Sets an optional description of the log, which is displayed in the Comment column.
- **Maximum Limit** Sets no predefined limit on the size of the log file.
- **Limit Of** Sets a specific limit in KB on the size of the log file.

7. As shown in Figure 10-7, click the Schedule tab and then specify when logging should start and stop.

8. You can configure the logging to start manually or automatically at a specific date. Select the appropriate option and then specify a start date if necessary.

 Tip Log files can grow in size very quickly. If you plan to log data for an extended period, be sure to place the log file on a drive with lots of free space. Remember, the more frequently you update the log file, the higher the drive space and CPU resource usage on the system.

9. You can configure the log file to stop
- Manually
- After a specified period of time, such as seven days

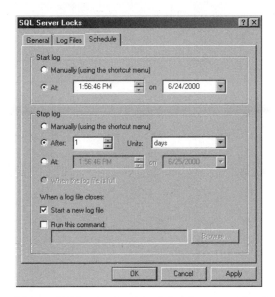

Figure 10-7. *Use the Schedule tab to specify when logging starts and stops.*

- At a specific date and time
- When the log file is full (if you've set a specific file size limit)

10. Click OK when you've finished setting the logging schedule. The log is then created and you can manage it as explained in the "Creating and Managing Performance Logging" section of this chapter.

Creating Trace Logs

Trace logs record performance data whenever events for their source providers occur. A source provider is an application or operating system service that has traceable events. On domain controllers you'll find two source providers: the operating system itself and Active Directory:NetLogon. On other servers the operating system will probably be the only provider available.

To create a trace log, complete the following steps:

1. Select Trace Logs in the left pane of the Performance console and then right-click in the right pane to display the shortcut menu. Choose New and then select New Log Settings.

2. In the New Log Settings dialog box, type a name for the log, such as Database Locks Trace or SQL Server Trace. Then click OK. This opens the dialog box shown in Figure 10-8.

3. If you want to trace operating system events, select the Events Logged By System Provider option button. As shown in Figure 10-8, you can now select system events to trace.

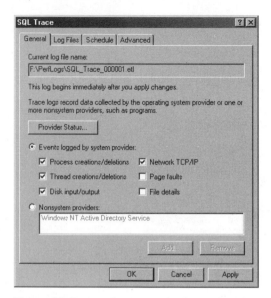

Figure 10-8. *Use the General tab to select the provider to use in the trace.*

 Caution Collecting page faults and file detail events puts a heavy load on the server and causes the log file to grow rapidly. Because of this, you should collect page faults and file detail events only for a limited time.

4. If you want to trace another provider, select the Nonsystem Providers option button and then click Add. This displays the Add Nonsystem Providers dialog box, which you'll use to select the provider to trace.

5. When you're finished selecting providers and events to trace, click the Log Files tab. You can now configure the trace file as detailed in step 6 of the section of this chapter entitled "Creating Counter Logs." The only change is that the log file types are different. With trace logs, you have two log types:

   - **Sequential Trace File** Writes events to the trace log sequentially up to the maximum file size (if any)

   - **Circular Trace File** Overwrites old data with new data when the file reaches a specified size limit

6. Choose the Schedule tab and then specify when tracing starts and stops.

7. You can configure the logging to start manually or automatically at a specific date. Select the appropriate option and then specify a start date if necessary.

8. You can configure the log file to stop manually, after a specified period of time, (such as seven days), at a specific date and time, or when the log file is full (if you've set a file size limit).

9. When you've finished setting the logging schedule, click OK. The log is then created, and you can manage it as explained in the section of this chapter entitled "Creating and Managing Performance Logging."

Replaying Performance Logs

When you're troubleshooting problems, you'll often want to log performance data over an extended period of time and analyze the data later. To do this, complete the following steps:

1. Configure automatic logging as described in the "Creating and Managing Performance Monitor Logs" section of this chapter.

2. When you're ready to analyze the data, load the log file in Performance Monitor. To do this, select the View Log File Data button on the Performance Monitor toolbar. This displays the Select Log File dialog box.

3. Use the Look In selection list to access the log directory, and then select the log you want to view. Click Open.

4. Counters you've logged are available for charting. Click Add on the toolbar and then select the counters you want to display.

Configuring Alerts for Performance Counters

You can configure alerts to notify you when certain events occur or when certain performance thresholds are reached. You can send these alerts as network messages and as events that are logged in the application event log. You can also configure alerts to start applications and performance logs.

To add alerts in Performance Monitor, complete the following steps:

1. Select Alerts in the left pane of the Performance console, and then right-click in the right pane to display the shortcut menu. Choose New Alert Settings.

2. In the New Alert Settings dialog box, type a name for the alert, such as Database Alert or SQL Server Locks Alert. Then click OK. This opens the dialog box shown in Figure 10-9.

3. In the General tab, type an optional description of the alert in the Comments field. Then click Add to display the Select Counters To Log dialog box. This dialog box is identical to the Add Counters dialog box shown previously in Figure 10-4.

4. Use the Select Counters To Log dialog box to add counters that trigger the alert. Click Close when you're finished.

5. In the Counters panel, select the first counter and then use the Alert When Value Is ... field to set the occasion when an alert for this counter is triggered. Alerts can be triggered when the counter is over or under a specific value. Select Over or Under, and then set the trigger value. The unit of measurement is whatever makes sense for the currently selected counter(s). For example, to alert if processor time is over 95 percent, you would select Over and then type **95**. Repeat this process to configure all counters you've selected.

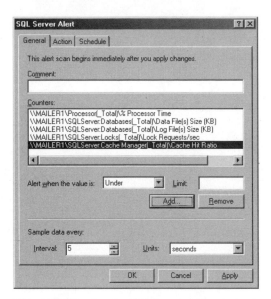

Figure 10-9. *Use the SQL Server Alert dialog box to configure counters that trigger alerts.*

6. In the Sample Data Every … field, type in a sample interval and select a time unit in seconds, minutes, hours, or days. The sample interval specifies when new data is collected. For example, if you sample every 10 minutes, the log is updated every 10 minutes.

 Caution Don't sample too frequently. You'll use system resources, and you may cause the server to become slow in responding to user requests.

7. Click the Action tab as shown in Figure 10-10. You can now specify any of the following actions to be taken when an alert is triggered:

- **Log An Entry In The Application Event Log** Creates log entries for alerts

- **Send A Network Message To** Sends a network message to the computer specified

- **Start Performance Data Log** Sets a counter log to start when an alert occurs

- **Run This Program** Sets the complete file path of a program or script to run when the alert occurs

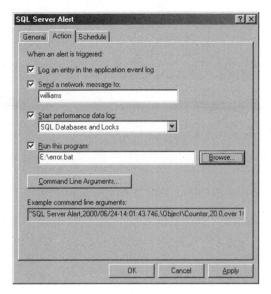

Figure 10-10. *Use the Action tab to set actions that are executed when the alert occurs.*

Tip   You can run any type of executable file, including batch scripts with
the .bat or .cmd extension and Windows scripts with the .vb, .js, .pl, or
.wsc extension. To pass arguments to a script or application, use the
options of the Command Line Arguments panel. Normally, arguments are
passed as individual strings. However, if you select Single Argument
String, the arguments are passed in a comma-separated list within a
single string. The Sample Arguments List at the bottom of the panel
shows how the arguments would be passed.

8. Click the Schedule tab and then specify when you want alerting to start and
   stop. For example, you could configure the alerts to start on Friday evening
   and stop on Monday morning. Then each time an alert occurs during this
   period, the specified action(s) are executed.

9. You can configure alerts to start manually or automatically at a specific date.
   Select the appropriate option and then specify a start date if necessary.

10. You can configure alerts to stop manually, after a specified period of time
    (such as seven days), or at a specific date and time.

11. When you've finished setting the alert schedule, click OK. The alert is then
    created and you can manage it in much the same way that you manage
    counter and trace logs.

Solving Performance Problems with Profiler

Whether you're trying to track user activity, troubleshoot connection problems, or optimize SQL Server, SQL Server Profiler is one of the best utilities available. Profiler enables you to trace events that occur in SQL Server. Events you can track in Profiler are similar to counters you can monitor in Performance Monitor. They're organized into groups called *event classes*, and you can track one or more events for any of the available event classes. Profiler's strength is in its advanced features and extensive customization capabilities.

You can record and replay Profiler traces when you want to analyze the data—and this is one area where Profiler excels. You can

- Use the information to find slow-running queries and then determine what's causing the queries to run slowly
- Go through statements a step at a time to find the cause of a problem
- Track a series of statements that cause a particular problem and then replay the trace on a test server to determine the cause
- Use trace information to determine the cause of deadlocks
- Monitor user and application activity to determine actions that are using CPU time or queries that are taking a long time to process

Let's look at how you can work with Profiler. Afterward I'll cover creating and managing traces.

Using Profiler

You can start Profiler in two ways. You can

- Choose the Profiler option from the Microsoft SQL Server menu
- In Enterprise Manager, from the Tools menu, choose SQL Server Profiler

Figure 10-11 shows Profiler in the process of running a trace. The columns shown for the trace, such as Event Class and Event SubClass, are completely configurable when you're setting up the trace, allowing you to select or clear columns as necessary. Two columns you'll want to pay particular attention to are Duration and CPU. The Duration column shows how long a particular event has been running in milliseconds. The CPU column shows the event's processing time by the CPU in milliseconds.

Stored procedures provide an alternative to Profiler. Using these stored procedures gives you some options that you don't have with SQL Server Profiler. You can

- Store traces in the Windows application log
- Autostart a trace when SQL Server starts
- Forward event data to another computer running SQL Server (Windows NT or Windows 2000 only)

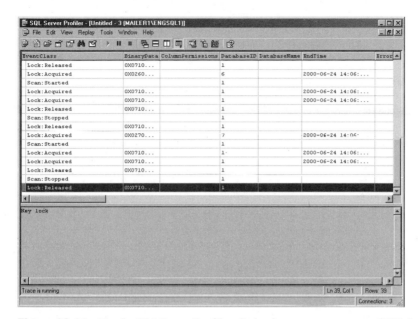

Figure 10-11. *Use the SQL Server Profiler dialog box to create traces of SQL Server events.*

To create traces with stored procedures, complete the following steps:

1. Create a trace definition using *sp_trace_create*.

2. Set events to capture using *sp_trace_setevent*.

3. Set event filters using *sp_trace_setfilter*.

Creating New Traces

You use traces to record events generated by local and remote SQL servers. You run traces in the Profiler window and store them for later analysis.

To start a new trace, complete the following steps:

1. Start SQL Server Profiler and then click the New Trace button. Or select File, then New, and then Trace. You'll see the Connect To SQL Server dialog box.

2. Select the SQL Server instance that you want to trace and then configure the authentication technique to use for the connection. Afterward, click OK.

3. You'll see the Trace Properties dialog box, as shown in Figure 10-12.

4. In the Trace Name field, type a name for the trace, such as Data Trace or Deadlock Trace For CustomerDB.

5. The Profiler window displays traces automatically. You can store traces as they are being created by setting the Save To File or the Save To Table option, or

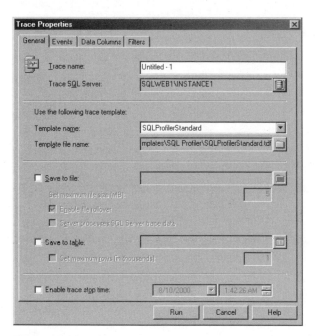

Figure 10-12. *Configure the trace using the tabs and fields in the Trace Properties dialog box.*

both. Or you can store a running trace later by selecting File, then selecting Save As, and then choosing either the Trace File option or the Trace Table option.

Tip As you might imagine, there are advantages and disadvantages to using trace files and trace tables. With trace files, you can store traces quickly and efficiently while using minimal system resources. With trace tables, you get ease of use by being able to store a trace directly in a table on another server, but you use much more system resources and usually have slower response times. Note also that storing a trace only saves the trace data. It doesn't save the trace definition. To reuse the trace definition, you'll have to export the trace definition.

6. SQL Profiler templates are used to save trace definitions that contain the events, data columns, and filters used in a trace. Use the Template Name selection list to choose a template to use as the basis of the trace. If you don't see the template you want to use, click the folder button to the right of the Template File Name field and then use the Open File dialog box to find a different template file. SQL Profiler templates end with the .tdf file extension.

7. Click the Events tab, as shown in Figure 10-13. Over 75 individual events are available. Available Event Classes lists all events available to be traced.

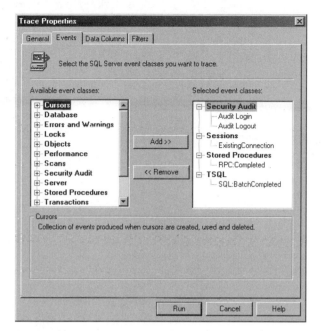

Figure 10-13. *Use the Events tab to select event classes or individual events to add to the trace.*

Selected Event Classes lists all events selected to be traced. The best way to learn the types of events you can trace is to select each event or event class and read its description in the lower portion of the Events tab.

8. Select events to add to the trace. Use the Add button to add event classes or individual events to a trace definition. Use the Remove button to remove event classes or individual events from a trace definition. Remember, the more events you trace, the more events will be generated on the source server, which can use up system resources and bog down the trace queue.

9. Click the Data Columns tab, as shown in Figure 10-14. Then select data columns to collect in the trace. The data columns you select determine the columns of information displayed with the trace. For example, if you select the ApplicationName column, you'll see the corresponding column in the trace data.

Tip   If you're tracking distributed queries, be sure to add the HostName column that corresponds to the ServerName in the display window. For transactions, be sure to add the TransactionID column. Also, if you plan to replay the trace for troubleshooting, look in the section of this chapter entitled "Replaying Traces" for specific event classes and data columns that you need to select.

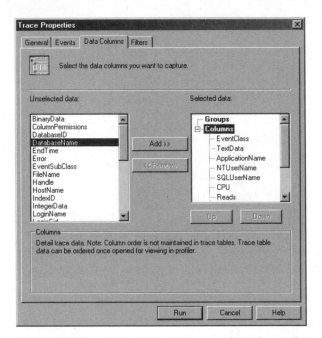

Figure 10-14. *Use the Data Columns tab to choose data columns to display for traced events. The default settings are usually fine.*

10. To focus the trace on specific types of data, you may want to set criteria that exclude certain types of events. If so, click the Filters tab and then set filter criteria. For each event category, you can use different filtering criteria. You use these criteria as follows:

- **Equals, Not Equal To, Greater Than Or Equal, or Less Than Or Equal** Set the values that trigger the event. Events with values outside the specified range are excluded. For example, with the CPU event category you can specify that only events that use greater than or equal to 1000 milliseconds of CPU time are captured. If events use less CPU time than this, they're excluded.

- **Like or Not Like** Enter strings to include or exclude for this event category. Use the wildcard character (%) to match a series of characters. Use the semicolon (;) to separate multiple strings. For example, with the Application Name category, you could exclude all application names that start with MS and SQL Server by typing **MS%;SQL Server%**.

11. When you're finished configuring the trace, click OK to create the trace.

Working with Traces

Profiler displays information for multiple traces in separate windows that can be cascaded or tiled. Use the buttons on the Profiler toolbar to control the active trace. Using the buttons on the Profiler toolbar, you can

- Create a new trace by clicking the New Trace button and then configuring the trace using the New Trace dialog box.
- Create a trace template by clicking New Template, setting trace properties, and then clicking Save.
- Start the current trace by clicking the Start Selected Trace button.
- Pause the current trace by clicking the Pause Selected Trace button. You can then use the Start Selected Trace button to resume the trace where it left off.
- Stop the current trace by clicking the Stop Selected Trace button. If you start the trace again with the Start Selected Trace button, the Profiler display starts over from the beginning of the trace process; new data is appended to the files or tables to which you're capturing data.
- Edit trace properties by clicking the Properties button.

Saving a Trace

When you create traces in Profiler, you create trace data and trace definitions. The Profiler window displays trace data, and you can also store it in a file or a table, or both. The trace data records a history of events that you're tracking, and you can use this history to replay the events for later analysis. The Trace Properties dialog box displays the trace definition. You can use the trace definition to create a new trace based on the existing trace.

To save trace data, complete the following steps:

1. Access the Profiler window that displays the trace you want to save.
2. Select File, point to Save As, and then select Trace File or Trace Table.
3. Use the Save As dialog box to select a folder location. Type the filename and then click Save. Trace files end with the .trc extension.

To save a trace definition, complete the following steps:

1. Access the Profiler window that displays the trace whose definition you want to save.
2. Select File, point to Save As, and then select Trace Template.
3. Use the Save As dialog box to select a folder location. Type the filename and then click Save. Trace templates end with the .tdf extension.

Replaying Traces

One of the main reasons for creating traces is that it gives you the ability to save traces and replay them later. When replaying traces, Profiler can simulate user connections and authentication, which allows you to reproduce the activity recorded in the trace. To aid in troubleshooting, you can

- Execute traces step by step to closely monitor each step in the trace
- Execute traces using the original timeline to simulate user loads
- Execute traces with a high replay rate to stress test servers

As you monitor the trace execution, you can look for problem areas. Then, when you identify the cause of problems you're trying to solve, you can correct them and then rerun the original trace definition. If you're still having problems, you'll need to reanalyze the trace data or look at other areas that may be causing problems. Keep in mind that you may need to specify different events to capture in the subsequent trace.

Requirements for Replaying Traces

Traces that you want to replay must contain a minimum set of events and data columns. If the trace doesn't contain the necessary elements, you won't be able to replay the trace. The required elements are in addition to any other elements that you want to monitor or display with traces. Events that you must capture in order to allow a trace to be replayed and analyzed correctly are

- Connect
- CursorExecute (required only when replaying server-side cursors)
- CursorOpen (required only when replaying server-side cursors)
- CursorPrepare (required only when replaying server-side cursors)
- Disconnect
- Exec Prepared SQL (required only when replaying server-side prepared SQL statements)
- ExistingConnection
- Prepare SQL (required only when replaying server-side prepared SQL statements)
- RPC:OutputParameter
- RPC:Starting
- SQL:BatchStarting

Data columns that you must capture to allow a trace to be replayed and analyzed correctly are

- Application Name
- Binary Data
- Connection ID or SPID
- Database ID

- Event Class
- Event SubClass
- Host Name
- Integer Data
- Server Name
- SQL User Name
- Start Time
- Text

Replaying Traces on a Different Server

You can replay a trace on a server other than the server originally traced. This server is called the *target system*. When replaying traces on the target, you should ensure that all logins contained in the trace

- Are created on the target system and are in the same database as the source system
- Have the same permissions they had originally
- Have the same passwords they had originally
- Are set to use a default database that matches the database on the source system

If these settings aren't the same, you'll see errors, but the replay operation will continue. Also, database IDs on the target system must be the same as those on the source system. The easiest way to set up databases on the target is to complete the following steps:

1. Back up the master database on the source and any user databases used in the trace.

2. Restore the databases on the target as explained in the section of Chapter 11 entitled "Restoring a Database to a Different Location."

Replaying and Analyzing a Trace

Replaying a trace allows you to analyze problems. To get started, start Profiler and then select the Open Trace File or Open Trace Table button, as appropriate for the type of trace you want to replay. After you select the trace to replay, the trace is then loaded into the Profiler window. As Figure 10-15 shows, events and commands recorded in the trace are summarized in the Profiler window. You can select an entry to see an expanded list of commands executed.

As Figure 10-15 also shows, the window toolbar for replay is different from the standard toolbar. The buttons provide just about everything that you need to debug traces, including

- **Start Replay** Starts executing the trace
- **Pause Replay** Pauses execution of the trace
- **Stop Replay** Stops execution of the trace

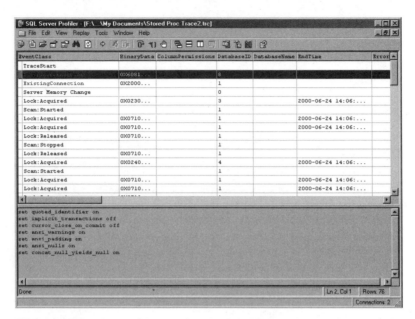

Figure 10-15. *The Profiler window displays all the commands executed and the events collected in the trace.*

- **Execute One Step**   Allows you to move through the trace one step at a time
- **Run To Cursor**   Allows you to move through the trace using cursor sets
- **Toggle Breakpoint**   Allows you to set breakpoints for the trace execution

When you start the replay, you'll get an initial dialog box that asks you to configure replay options (see Figure 10-16). You configure the options in the Replay SQL Server dialog box to control where and how the playback takes place. Start by setting the destination server for the replay operation. Then set replay options.

The replay options determine how closely the replay mirrors the original event execution. You can choose

- **Replay Events In The Order They Were Traced**   Events are started in the order in which they originally started. This enables debugging but doesn't guarantee timing of event execution. Events may be executed sooner than their original start time or after their original start time, depending on current activity levels, the current speed of connections, and other factors.
- **Replay Events Using Multiple Threads**   Events are replayed as quickly as they can be processed. No timing is maintained between events. When one event completes, the next event is started. This optimizes performance and disables debugging.

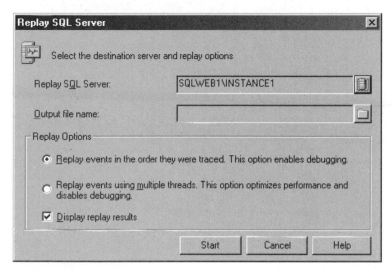

Figure 10-16. *Replay options in the Replay SQL Server dialog box allow you to control where and how the playback takes place.*

The Display Replay Results check box controls whether the replay results are displayed in the Profiler window. To display results, select this option. Otherwise, clear this option.

You can also select an output file to save the result of the replay for later viewing. The output file allows you to review the replay just as you would any other trace file.

Chapter 11

Database Backup and Recovery

Information is the fuel that drives the enterprise, and the most critical information is often stored in databases. Databases are where you'll find an organization's customer account information, partner directories, product knowledge base, and other important data. To protect an organization's data and to ensure the availability of its databases, you need a solid database backup and recovery plan.

Backing up databases can protect against accidental loss of data, database corruption, hardware failures, and even natural disasters. It's your job as a database administrator to perform backups and store them in a safe and secure location.

Creating a Backup and Recovery Plan

Creating and implementing a backup and recovery plan is one of your most important duties as a database administrator. Think of database backup as an insurance plan for the future—and for your job. Important data is accidentally deleted all the time. Mission-critical data can become corrupt. Natural disasters can leave your office in ruins. With a solid backup and recovery plan you can recover from any of these situations. Without one, you're left with nothing to fall back on.

Initial Backup and Recovery Planning

Creating and implementing a backup and recovery plan takes time. You'll need to figure out which databases need to be backed up, how often the databases should be backed up, and more. To help you create a plan, consider the following:

- **What type of database are you backing up?** System and user databases often have different backup and recovery needs. For example, the master database is essential for all Microsoft SQL Server operations. If the master database fails or becomes corrupt, it takes the whole server down with it. But you don't need to back up master every hour or every half hour—as you might have to do with a critical user database that handles real-time customer transactions. You need to back up master only after you create a database, change configuration values, configure SQL logons, or perform similar activities that make changes to the database.

- **How important is the data in the database?** How you judge the data's importance can go a long way toward determining *when* and *how* you should back it up. While you may back up a development database weekly, you would probably back up a production database at least daily. The data's importance also drives your decision about the *type* of backup. With that development database, you'd probably do a full backup once a week. With an in-house customer order database that's updated throughout the week-day, you'd probably perform full backups twice a week and supplement this with daily differential backups and hourly backups for the transaction logs. You may even want to set named log marks that allow recovery up to a specific point of work.

- **How often are changes made to the database?** The frequency of change can drive your decision about how often the database should be backed up. Because a read-only database doesn't ordinarily change, it doesn't need to be backed up regularly. On the other hand, a database that's updated nightly should be backed up after the nightly changes are posted. A database that's updated around the clock should be backed up continually.

- **How quickly do you need to recover the data?** It's important to consider time when you create a backup plan. For mission-critical databases, you may need to get the database back online swiftly; to do this, you may need to alter your backup plan. Instead of backing up to tape, you may want to back up to disk drives or use multiple backup devices. Both options are much faster than restoring from a single tape device.

- **Do you have the equipment to perform backup?** You need backup hardware to perform backups. If you don't have the hardware, you can't per-form backups. To perform timely backups, you may need several backup devices and several sets of backup media. Backup hardware includes a tape drive, optical drives, removable disk drives, and plain old disk drives. Gen-erally, tape drives are less expensive but slower than other types of drives.

- **What's the best time to schedule backups?** You'll want to schedule back-ups when database usage is as low as possible. This will speed the backup process. However, in the real world you can't always schedule backups for off-peak hours. So you'll need to carefully plan when key databases are backed up.

- **Do you need to store backups off-site?** Storing copies of backup tapes off-site is essential to the recovery of your systems in the case of a natural disaster. In your off-site storage location, you should also include copies of the software you may need to install in order to restore operations on a new system.

Backing up a database is a bit different than backing up a server or a workstation. This is primarily because you'll often need to combine all (or nearly all) of the available techniques to ensure that you can recover a database completely. The basic types of backups you can perform include

- **Complete database backups** Perform a full backup of the database, including all objects, system tables, and data. When the backup starts, SQL Server copies everything in the database and also includes any needed portions of the transaction log as the backup is in progress. Because of this, you can use a complete backup to recover the complete state of the data in the database at the time the backup operation finishes.

- **Differential backups** Designed to back up data that has changed since the last complete backup. Because you store only the changes, the backup is faster and you can perform it more often. As with complete backups, differential backups include needed portions of the transaction logs, which allow you to restore the database to the time when the backup operation finishes.

Tip You can use differential backups only in conjunction with complete backups, and you can't perform differential backups on the master database. Don't confuse differential backups with incremental backups. Differential backups record all changes since the last full backup (which means the size of the incremental backup grows over time). Incremental backups record changes since the most recent full or incremental backup (which means the size of the incremental backup is usually much smaller than a full backup).

- **Transaction log backups** Transaction logs are serial records of all database modifications and are used during recovery operations to commit completed transactions and to roll back uncompleted transactions. When you back up a transaction log, the backup stores the changes that have occurred since the last transaction log backup and then truncates the log, which clears out transactions that have been committed or aborted. Unlike complete and differential backups, transaction log backups record the state of the transaction log at the time the backup operation starts (not when it ends).

- **File and filegroup backups** Allow you to back up database files and filegroups rather than the entire database. This is useful with large databases where, to save time, you want to back up individual files rather than the entire database. Many factors affect file and filegroup backups. When you use file and filegroup backups, you must back up the transaction log as well. Because of this dependency, you can't use this backup technique if Truncate Log On Checkpoint is enabled. Furthermore, if objects in the database span multiple files or filegroups, you must back up all the related files and filegroups at the same time.

SQL Server 2000 uses recovery models to help you plan backups. The types of databases you are backing up and the types of backups you perform drive the choices for recovery models. The three recovery models shown on the following page are available:

- **Simple** The simple recovery model is designed for databases that need to be recovered to the point of the last backup. The backup strategy with this model should consist of full and differential backups. You cannot perform transaction log backups when the simple recovery model is enabled. SQL Server 2000 turns on the Truncate Log On Checkpoint option, which clears out inactive entries in the transaction log on checkpoint. Because this model clears out transaction logs, it is ideal for most system databases.

- **Full** The full recovery model is designed for databases that need to be recovered to the point of failure or to a specific point in time. With this model all operations are logged, including bulk operations and bulk loading of data. The backup strategy with this model should include full, differential, and transaction log backups, or full and transaction log backups only.

- **Bulk-logged** The bulk-logged recovery model reduces the log space usage yet retains most of the flexibility of the full recovery model. With this model, bulk operations and bulk loads are minimally logged and cannot be controlled on a per operation basis. You'll need to manually redo bulk operations and bulk loads if the database fails before you perform a full or differential backup. The backup strategy with this model should include full, differential, and transaction log backups, or full and transaction log backups only.

Each database can have a different recovery model. By default, master, msdb, and tempdb use the simple recovery model, and the model database uses the full recovery model. Model is the template database for all new databases, so if you change the default setting all new databases for the database server instance use the new default model. You set the recovery model by completing the following steps:

1. Start Enterprise Manager and then in the left pane (Console Root) click the plus sign (+) next to the server group you want to work with.

2. If plan to switch from bulk-logged recovery to simple recovery, perform a transaction log backup prior to making the change and then change your backup strategy so that you no longer perform transaction log backups.

3. Click the plus sign (+) next to the server you want to work with again and then click the plus sign (+) next to the Databases folder.

4. Right-click the database you want to work with and then, from the shortcut menu, choose Properties. This displays the database's Properties dialog box.

5. Use the Model selection list in the Options tab to change the recovery model and then click OK.

6. If you switched from simple recovery to full or bulk-logged recovery, add transaction log backups to your backup strategy for the database.

Planning for Backups of Replicated Databases

Databases that are replicated present a special problem for backup and restore. This is primarily because the traditional database architecture is extended to include three server roles:

- **Publisher** Servers that make data available for replication, track changes to data, and maintain other information about source databases.
- **Distributor** Servers that distribute replicated data and store the distribution database.
- **Subscriber** The destination servers for replication. They store the replicated data, receive updates, and in some cases can also make changes to data.

Because of these roles, you'll need to use additional strategies for backing up and restoring replicated databases. For complete details see the section of the SQL Server Books Online entitled "Backing Up and Restoring Replication Databases." (Click Start, then Programs, then Microsoft SQL Server 2000, and then choose Books Online.)

Planning for Backups of Very Large Databases

When backing up and restoring very large databases, you may want to take advantage of parallel backup and restore. Parallel backup and restore allow SQL Server 2000 to use multiple threads to read and write data. This means SQL Server can read data from, and write data to, multiple data sources. Backup and restore use parallel input/output (I/O) in different ways:

- Backup uses one thread per disk device to read data from the database when a database has files on several disk devices.
- Restore uses one thread per disk device while it initializes a database that it's creating for the restore process, provided the database is defined with files on several disks.
- Both backup and restore use one thread per backup device when a backup set is stored on multiple backup devices.

As you can see from the previous list, to take advantage of parallel I/O you must implement your backup strategy so that databases use

- Multiple disk drives for storing data
- Multiple backup devices for backing up and restoring data

Once you determine the backup operations you'll use on each database and how often you'll back up each database, you can select backup devices and media that meet these requirements. The next section covers backup devices and media.

Selecting Backup Devices and Media

Many different solutions are available for backing up data. Some are fast and expensive. Others are slow but very reliable. The backup solution that's right for your organization depends on many factors, including

- **Capacity** The amount of data that you need to back up on a routine basis. Can the backup hardware support the required load given your time and resource constraints?

- **Reliability** The reliability of the backup hardware and media. Can you afford to sacrifice reliability to meet budget or time needs?

- **Extensibility** The extensibility of the backup solution. Will this solution meet your needs as your organization grows?

- **Speed** The speed with which data can be backed up and recovered. Can you afford to sacrifice speed to reduce costs?

- **Cost** The cost of the backup solution. Does the solution fit within your budget?

Capacity, reliability, extensibility, speed, and cost are the issues that will influence your choice of a backup plan. If you determine the relative value of these issues to your organization, you'll be on the right track to selecting an appropriate backup solution. Some of the most commonly used backup solutions include

- **Tape drives** Tape drives are the most common backup devices. They use magnetic tape cartridges to store data. Magnetic tapes are relatively inexpensive but aren't highly reliable. Tapes can break or stretch. They can also lose information over time. The average capacity of tape cartridges ranges from 100 MB to 2 GB. Compared with other backup solutions, tape drives are fairly slow. Still, the key selling point is the low cost of tape drives and magnetic tapes.

- **DAT drives** DAT (digital audio tape) drives are quickly replacing standard tape drives as the preferred backup devices. DAT drives use 4-mm tapes and 8-mm tapes to store data. DAT drives and tapes are more expensive than standard tape drives and tapes, but they offer higher speed and more capacity. DAT drives that use 4-mm tapes typically can record over 30 MB per minute and have capacities of up to 16 GB. DAT drives that use 8-mm tapes typically can record more than 10 MB per minute and have capacities of up to 10 GB (with compression).

 Tip To perform faster backup and recovery operations, you can use multiple backup devices with SQL Server. For example, if it normally takes four hours to perform a full backup or restoration of the database, you can cut the backup and restoration time in half using two backup devices; with four backup devices you could fully back up or restore the database in an hour.

- **Autoloader tape systems** Autoloader tape systems use a magazine of tapes that create extended backup volumes capable of meeting the high capacity needs of the enterprise. With an autoloader system, tapes within the magazine are automatically changed as needed during the backup or recovery process. Most autoloader tape systems use DAT tapes. The typical system uses magazines with between 4 and 12 tapes. The key drawback to these systems is the high cost.

- **Magnetic optical drives** Magnetic optical drives combine magnetic tape technology with optical lasers to create a more reliable backup solution than

DAT. Magnetic optical drives use 3.5-inch disks and 5.25-inch disks that look similar to floppies but are much thicker. Typically, magnetic optical disks have capacities of between 1 GB and 4 GB.

- **Tape jukeboxes** Tape jukeboxes are similar to autoloader tape systems. Jukeboxes use magnetic optical disks rather than DAT tapes to offer high-capacity solutions for the enterprise. These systems load and unload disks stored internally for backup and recovery operations. The key drawback to tape jukeboxes is the high cost.

- **Removable disks** Removable disks, such as Iomega Jaz, are increasingly being used as backup devices. Removable disks offer good speed and ease of use for a single drive or single system backup. However, the disk drives and the removable disks tend to be more expensive than standard tape or DAT drive solutions.

- **Disk drives** Disk drives provide the fastest way to back up and restore databases. With disk drives, you can often accomplish in minutes what a tape drive takes hours to do. When your needs mandate a speedy recovery, nothing beats a disk drive. The drawbacks to disk drives, however, are high cost and low extensibility.

Although backup device selection is an important step in implementing a backup and recovery plan, it isn't the only step. You also need to purchase the tapes or the disks, or both, that will allow you to implement your backup and recovery plan. The number of tapes, disks, or drives you need depends on

- How much data you'll be backing up
- How often you'll be backing up the data
- How long you'll need to keep additional data sets

The typical way to implement backups is to use a rotation schedule whereby you rotate through two or more sets of tapes, disks, or files. The idea is that you can increase media longevity by reducing media usage and at the same time reduce the number of actual tapes, disks, or files you need to ensure that you have data on hand when necessary.

Best Practice For important databases, I recommend using four media sets. Use two sets for regular rotations. Use the third set for the first rotation cycle at the beginning of each month. Use the fourth set for the first rotation cycle of each quarter. This technique allows you to recover the database in a wide variety of situations.

Using Backup Strategies

Table 11-1 lists backup strategies you may want to use. As you can see, these backup strategies are based on the type of database as well as the type of data. Two key things to keep in mind when planning a backup strategy are shown on the following page.

- The master database stores important information about the structure of other databases, including the database size. Any time database information or structure changes, master can get updated without your knowing about it. For example, the size of most databases changes automatically, and when this happens master is updated. Because of this, often the best backup strategy for master is to schedule backups every other day and to rotate through several backup sets so that you can go back to several different versions of master if necessary.

- You can use transaction logs to recover databases up to the point of failure and up to a point of work. To recover to a point of work you must insert named log marks into the transaction log using BEGIN TRANSACTION WITH MARK. You can then recover to a mark in the log using RESTORE LOG WITH STOPATMARK or RESTORE LOG WITH STOPBEFOREMARK.

Table 11-1. Backup Strategies for System and User Databases

Database Type	Details	Strategy
User	Recovery up to the minute	Run complete backups twice a week, if possible. Use nightly differential backups and back up the recovery transaction log every 10 minutes during business hours. Don't use Truncate Log On Checkpoint, as this will make it impossible to recover some transactions. To improve backup restore speed, use multiple backup devices whenever possible.
	Recovery up to a point of work	Run complete backups twice a week, if possible. Use nightly differential backups and back up the recovery transaction log every 10 minutes during business hours. Don't use Truncate Log On Checkpoint. Use named transactions to insert named marks into the transaction logs. To improve backup/restore speed, use multiple backup devices whenever possible.
	Recovery up to the hour	Run complete backups twice a week, if possible. Use nightly differential backups and back up the recovery transaction log every 30 minutes during business hours. Don't use Truncate Log On Checkpoint. To improve backup/restore speed, use multiple backup devices whenever possible.

(continued)

Table 11-1. *(continued)*

Database Type	Details	Strategy
	Recovery of daily changes	Run complete backups at least once a week. Use daily nightly differential backups and back up the changes transaction log every four hours during business hours. Don't use Truncate Log On Checkpoint.
	Read-only	Schedule a complete backup of the database every 30 days and supplement this with an additional complete backup whenever the database is modified.
System	distribution	Available when you configure replication and the server is acting as a distributor. Schedule complete backups after snapshots. With transactional replication, schedule regular log backups.
	master	Run complete backups immediately after creating or removing databases, changing the size of a database, adding or removing logons, or modifying server configuration settings. Don't forget to maintain several backup sets for master.
	msdb	If you schedule jobs through the SQL Server Agent, back up this database regularly because this is where the job schedule and history is maintained and backup history is stored.
	model	Treat like a read-only database.
	tempdb	Normally doesn't need to be backed up. This database is recreated each time you start SQL Server.

Creating a Backup Device

Previous versions of SQL Server required you to configure backup devices before you could back up databases. With SQL Server 2000, this is no longer the case, and you don't need to explicitly define backup devices. Nevertheless, backup devices do provide an easy way to ensure that you create backups that have the same filename and location time after time. With consistent names and locations, you can more easily manage the backup and recovery process.

To create a backup device using Enterprise Manager, complete the following steps:

1. Start Enterprise Manager and then access the database server instance you want to work with.

2. Click the plus sign (+) next to the server's Management folder.

3. Right-click Backup and then, from the shortcut menu, choose New Backup Device. This opens the dialog box shown in Figure 11-1.

4. In the Name field, type the name of the logical backup device. Use a short but descriptive name, such as Customer Device or Master Device, to make the device easier to work with.

5. If you've installed a tape drive and want to back up to the tape drive, select the Tape Drive Name field and then use the related drop-down list box to select the target drive.

6. If you're backing up to a file, select the File Name option button and then enter the full path to the backup file you want to associate with this device, such as E:\MSSQL\BACKUP\CUSTOMER.BAK.

7. Click OK.

With Transact-SQL, you create backup devices using *sp_addumpdevice*. The syntax and usage for this command is shown in Sample 11-1. This command uses many different arguments, including *device_type, logical_name, physical_name, controller_type,* and *device_status*. The *device_type* is the type of device you're using—disk, tape, or pipe. The *logical_name* is the name of the backup device. The *physical_name* is the full path to the backup file. The *controller_type* is 2 for a disk, 5 for a tape, and 6 for a named pipe. The *device_status* is either *noskip,* to read ANSI tape headers, or *skip,* to skip ANSI tape headers.

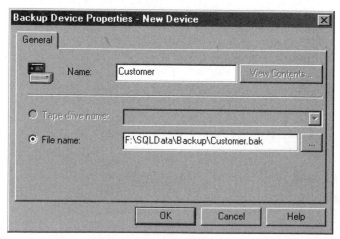

Figure 11-1. *Create a backup device to make it easier to manage backups.*

Sample 11-1. *sp_addumpdevice* **Syntax and Usage**

Syntax

```
sp_addumpdevice [@devtype =] 'device_type',
  [@logicalname =] 'logical_name',
  [@physicalname =] 'physical_name'
  [, {
    [@cntrltype =] controller_type |
    [@devstatus =] 'device_status'
  }
  ]
```

Usage

```
EXEC sp_addumpdevice 'disk', 'Customer',
  'c:\mssql\backup\cust.bak'


EXEC sp_addumpdevice 'disk', 'Customer on Backup Server',
  '\\omega\backups\cust.bak'


EXEC sp_addumpdevice 'tape', 'Customer on Tape', '\\.\tape0'
```

Performing Backups

Backups are an essential part of database administration. They're so important that SQL Server provides multiple backup procedures and several backup-related wizards—all designed to help you better manage database backup and recovery. In this section I'll look at standard backup procedures, the Backup Wizard, and the Transact-SQL backup process. The final ingredient for backups involves database maintenance plans, which you'll learn about in Chapter 12, "Database Automation and Maintenance."

Creating Backups in Enterprise Manager

In Enterprise Manager you can start the backup process using any of these techniques:

- Select the server you want to work with and then, from the Tools menu, choose Backup Database. This opens the SQL Server Backup dialog box.
- Select the server you want to work with and then, from the Tools menu, choose Wizards. This opens the Wizards dialog box. Click the plus sign (+) next to Management and then double-click Backup Wizard.

- Right-click the database you want to back up, point to All Tasks, and then select Backup Database.

Regardless of which technique you use, the steps you follow are similar. Rather than covering the same information twice, I'll focus on the SQL Server Backup dialog box and how you can use it to perform backups in these situations:

- Creating a new backup set
- Adding to an existing backup set

You can use these techniques with the Backup Wizard as well. The key difference is that you'll need to go through a series of dialog boxes.

Creating a New Backup Set

Whenever you back up a database for the first time or start a new rotation on an existing backup set, follow these steps to create the backup:

1. Select the server you want to work with and then, from the Tools menu, choose Backup Database. This opens the SQL Server Backup dialog box shown in Figure 11-2.

2. Use the Database drop-down list box to select the database you want to back up.

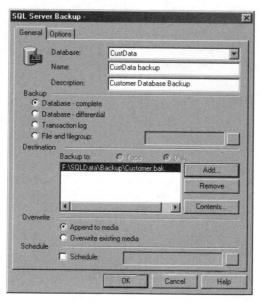

Figure 11-2. *Use the SQL Server Backup dialog box to start or schedule a backup. If this is the first time you're running Backup, some of the backup types may be unavailable.*

3. In the Name field, type a name for the backup set you're creating. This is an ordinary nontechnical name that'll help you tell at a glance what the backup contains. For example, name the first backup set for the customer database Customer Backup Set 1. Then you can add the complete, differential, and transaction log backups for this rotation to the set.

4. In the Description field type a description of the backup, such as "Set 1 contains the weekly complete, daily differential, and hourly transaction log backups."

5. In the Backup area, use the option buttons to select the type of backup. Because this is your first time running a backup on the database, some of the options may be unavailable. Don't worry—once you run a complete or differential backup, the other options should become available.

Note The only available backup option for the master database is Database – Complete. That's because you can run only complete backups on master.

6. If a backup set exists and is listed in the Destination area, select it and click Remove.

7. Click Add to display the Select Backup Destination dialog box shown in Figure 11-3. To use a file as the backup destination, select the File Name option button and enter the full path to the backup file, such as E:\DATA\ BACKUPS\CUST.BAK or \\OMEGA\BACKUPS\CUST.BAK. To use a backup device, select the Backup Device option button and then choose the backup destination using the drop-down list box. Click OK when you're ready to continue.

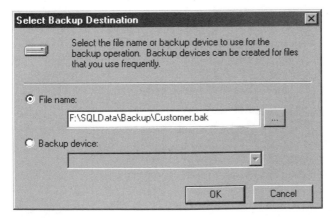

Figure 11-3. *Use the Select Backup Destination dialog box to select a file or backup device to use as the backup destination.*

8. To schedule the backup, click Schedule and then configure the backup schedule as discussed in Chapter 12, "Database Automation and Maintenance."

9. To set additional options for the backup, click the Options tab (see Figure 11-2). You use the available options as follows:

- **Verify Backup Upon Completion**   Reads the entire backup and checks for errors.

- **Eject Tape After Backup**   Set to eject the tape after the backup (only valid with tape devices).

- **Remove Inactive Entries From The Transaction Log**   Cleans out entries that are no longer needed after the backup. These entries are for transactions that have been committed or rolled back. (Set by default for transaction log backups.)

Tip   You'll usually want to perform one last log backup before you try to restore a corrupt database. When you do, you'll want to clear the option and perform the log backup without truncation. This option is the same as running BACKUP LOG NO_TRUNCATE.

- **Check Media Set Name And Backup Set Expiration**   Ensures that you're writing to the correct tape set and that the tape expiration date has not been reached.

- **Backup Set Will Expire On**   When backing up to a tape device, you can check this option and then set an expiration date. This option allows the backup to overwrite the media after a specified date or period.

- **Initialize And Label Media**   When backing up to tape devices, you can use this option to erase the previous contents of the media and then add a new label and description.

10. Click OK to start the backup or confirm that you want to schedule the backup. For an immediate backup, you'll see the Backup Progress dialog box, which displays a progress bar as the backup proceeds. If you opted to verify the data, the verification process starts immediately after the backup ends.

Adding to an Existing Backup Set

When you want to add to an existing backup set, complete the following steps:

1. Select the server you want to work with and then, from the Tools menu, choose Backup Database. This opens the SQL Server Backup dialog box shown previously in Figure 11-2.

2. Use the Database drop-down list box to select the database to be backed up.

3. In the Backup area, use the option buttons to select the type of backup you want to perform:

- Database – Complete

- Database – Differential

- Transaction Log
- File And Filegroup

4. A backup set should be listed in the Destination area. If one isn't, click Add to display the Choose Backup Destination and then enter the location of the existing backup. Click OK when you're ready to continue.

5. If you want to add data to the existing backup set, select the Append To Media option button.

Real World   Whether you back up to a tape or disk drive, you should use the tape rotation philosophy. Create multiple tape sets and then write to these sets on a rotating basis. With a disk drive, for example, you could create these backup files on different network drives and use them as follows:

- //omega/data1drive/backups/cust_set1.bak Used on week 1, 3, 5, and so on for complete and differential backups of the customer database.

- //omega/data2drive/backups/cust_set2.bak Used on week 2, 4, 6, and so on for complete and differential backups of the customer database.

- //omega/data3drive/backups/cust_set3.bak Used on the first week of the month for complete backups of the customer database.

- //omega/data4drive/backups/cust_set4.bak Used on the first week of the quarter for complete backups of the customer database.

Don't forget that each time you start a new rotation on a tape set, you should overwrite the existing media. For example, you would append all backups on week 1. Then, when starting the next rotation on week 3, you would overwrite the existing media for the first backup and then append the remaining backups for the week.

6. Click the Options tab to double-check the backup options. For transaction log backups, you'll usually want to select the Remove Inactive Entries From Transaction Log check box. This ensures that inactive entries are cleared out of the transaction log after a backup.

7. To schedule the backup, click Schedule and then configure the backup schedule as discussed in Chapter 12, "Database Automation and Maintenance."

8. Click OK to start the backup or to confirm that you want to schedule the backup. For an immediate backup, you'll see the Backup Progress dialog box, which displays a progress bar as the backup proceeds. If you opted to verify the data, the verify process starts immediately after the backup ends.

Using Striped Backups with Multiple Devices

Through a process called *parallel striped backups*, SQL Server can perform backups to multiple backup devices simultaneously. As you can imagine, writing multiple backup files at the same time can dramatically speed backup operations. The key to this speed, however, lies in having physically separate devices, such as three different tape devices or three different drives that you're using for the backup. You can't write parallel backups to a single tape device and you can't write parallel backups to the same drive.

Multiple devices used in a backup operation are referred to as a *media set*. SQL Server allows you to use from 2 to 32 devices to form the media set. These devices must be of the same type. For example, you can't create a striped backup with one backup tape device and one backup drive device.

The two main operations you'll perform are

- Creating a new media set
- Adding to an existing media set

Creating a New Media Set

To create a new media set using multiple devices, complete the following steps:

1. Select the server you want to work with and then create each of the backup devices you need in the media set as described in the section of this chapter entitled "Creating a Backup Device."

2. Open the SQL Server Backup dialog box by going to the Tools menu and choosing Backup Database. (You can't create a multiple device backup with the Backup Wizard.)

3. Follow the steps outlined in the section of this chapter entitled "Creating a New Backup Set." Repeat step 7 for each backup device you want to use in the media set.

Adding to an Existing Media Set

To add to an existing media set, complete the following steps:

1. Open the SQL Server Backup dialog box by going to the Tools menu and choosing Backup Database. (You can't create a multiple backup with the Backup Wizard.)

2. Follow the steps outlined in the "Adding to an Existing Backup Set" section of this chapter. The only change is that in step 4 you should see a list of all backup devices used in the media set. If you don't, you'll need to add them one by one using the Add button and the related Choose Backup Destination dialog box.

Using Transact-SQL Backup

An alternative to the backup procedures in Enterprise Manager is to use the T-SQL BACKUP statement. You'll use BACKUP DATABASE to back up databases and BACKUP LOG to back up transaction logs.

Tip If you back up databases using Transact-SQL, you lose one of the biggest benefits of SQL Server—the automated recovery process. With automated recovery, you don't have to worry about which backup to apply when, which command flags to use when, and more. Furthermore, because you can schedule automated and unattended backups, you don't really need to run backups manually through SQL as often as you used to. So I recommend using the Enterprise Manager backup and restore process whenever possible.

BACKUP DATABASE has dual syntax. Sample 11-2 shows the syntax and usage for complete and differential backups. A complete backup is the default operation.

Sample 11-2. BACKUP DATABASE Syntax and Usage for Complete and Differential Backups

Syntax

```
BACKUP DATABASE {database_name | @database_name_var}

TO <backup_device> [,...n]

[WITH

  [BLOCKSIZE = {blocksize | @blocksize_variable}]

  [[,] DESCRIPTION = {text | @text_variable}]

  [[,] DIFFERENTIAL]

  [[,] EXPIREDATE = {date | @date_var}

   | RETAINDAYS = {days | @days_var}]

  [[,] PASSWORD = {password | @password_variable}]

  [[,] FORMAT | NOFORMAT]

  [[,] {INIT | NOINIT}]

  [[,] MEDIADESCRIPTION = {text | @text_variable}]

  [[,] MEDIANAME = {media_name | @media_name_variable}]

  [[,] MEDIAPASSWORD = {mediapassword | @mediapassword_variable}]

  [[,] [NAME = {backup_set_name | @backup_set_name_var}]

  [[,] {NOSKIP | SKIP}]

  [[,] {NOREWIND | REWIND}]

  [[,] {NOUNLOAD | UNLOAD}]

  [[,] [RESTART]
```

(continued)

Sample 11-2. *(continued)*
Syntax

```
 [[,] STATS [= percentage]]
]
```

Usage

```
USE master

EXEC sp_addumpdevice 'disk', 'Customer Backup Set 1',
 'f:\data\backup\Cust2.dat'

BACKUP DATABASE 'Customer' TO 'Customer Backup Set 1'
```

Sample 11-3 shows the BACKUP DATABASE syntax for file and filegroup backups.

Sample 11-3. BACKUP DATABASE Syntax and Usage for File or Filegroup Backups

Syntax

```
BACKUP DATABASE {database_name | @database_name_var}

 <file_or_filegroup> [,...n]

TO <backup_device> [,...n]

[WITH

 [BLOCKSIZE = {blocksize | @blocksize_variable}]

 [[,] DESCRIPTION = {text | @text_variable}]

 [[,] EXPIREDATE = {date | @date_var}

  | RETAINDAYS = {days | @days_var}]

 [[,] PASSWORD = {password | @password_variable}]

 [[,] FORMAT | NOFORMAT]

 [[,] {INIT | NOINIT}]

 [[,] MEDIADESCRIPTION = {text | @text_variable}]

 [[,] MEDIANAME = {media_name | @media_name_variable}]

 [[,] MEDIAPASSWORD = {mediapassword | @mediapassword_variable}]

 [[,] [NAME = {backup_set_name | @backup_set_name_var}]

 [[,] {NOSKIP | SKIP}]

 [[,] {NOREWIND | REWIND}]

 [[,] {NOUNLOAD | UNLOAD}]
```

(continued)

Sample 11-3. *(continued)*
Syntax

```
[[,] [RESTART]

[[,] STATS [= percentage]]

]
```

Usage

```
USE master

EXEC sp_addumpdevice 'disk', 'Customer Backup Set 1',
  'f:\data\backup\Cust2.dat'

BACKUP DATABASE Customer

  FILE = 'Customer_data',

  FILEGROUP = 'Primary',

  FILE = 'Customer_data2',

  FILEGROUP = 'Secondary'

  TO 'Customer Backup Set 1'
```

Sample 11-4 shows the syntax for BACKUP LOG. By default, this command truncates the log after the backup.

Sample 11-4. BACKUP LOG Syntax and Usage

Syntax

```
BACKUP LOG {database_name | @database_name_var}

{

  [WITH

    { NO_LOG | TRUNCATE_ONLY }]

}

TO <backup_device> [,...n]

  [WITH

    [BLOCKSIZE = {blocksize | @blocksize_variable}]

    [[,] DESCRIPTION = {text | @text_variable}]

    [[,] EXPIREDATE = {date | @date_var}

      | RETAINDAYS = {days | @days_var}].

    [[,] PASSWORD = {password | @password_variable}]
```

(continued)

Sample 11-4. *(continued)*
Syntax

```
[[,] FORMAT | NOFORMAT]

[[,] {INIT | NOINIT}]

[[,] MEDIADESCRIPTION = {text | @text_variable}]

[[,] MEDIANAME = {media_name | @media_name_variable}]

[[,] MEDIAPASSWORD = {mediapassword | @mediapassword_variable}]

[[,] [NAME = {backup_set_name | @backup_set_name_var}]

[[,] NO_TRUNCATE]

[[,] {NOSKIP | SKIP}]

[[,] {NOREWIND | REWIND}]

[[,] {NOUNLOAD | UNLOAD}]

[[,] [RESTART]

[[,] STATS [= percentage]]
]
```

Usage

```
USE master

EXEC sp_addumpdevice 'disk', 'Customer_log1',
  'f:\data\backup\Cust_log.dat'

BACKUP LOG Customer

  TO Customer_log1
```

Performing Transaction Log Backups

Transaction logs are essential to the timely recovery of SQL Server databases. Unlike database backups, which can be complete or differential, transaction log backups are usually incremental. This means that each transaction log backup has a record of transactions only within a certain time frame. Transaction logs are always applied in sequence—with the completion time of the last complete or differential backup marking the beginning of a transaction log sequence.

Consequently, in order to restore the database you must apply each transaction logon sequence up to the point of failure. For example, if you run a complete backup at 1 P.M. and the database fails at 1:46 P.M., you would restore the last complete backup and then apply each transaction log created after that time, such as the backups at 1:15 P.M., 1:30 P.M., and 1:45 P.M. As you can see, without the incremental transaction log backups you'd lose all the transactions that took place after the 1 P.M. complete backup.

You can perform transaction log backups like any other backup. Still, there are a few details that you should know beforehand, and the following sections cover these details.

Options and Commands that Invalidate Log Sequences

Although the normal backup process for transaction logs is fairly straightforward, SQL Server throws a few curveballs by providing option flags that you can set for the backup or the database, or both. The following database options prevent you from using a transaction log sequence to recover a database:

- **Truncate Log On Checkpoint**   A database option that clears out inactive entries in the transaction log on checkpoint
- **Using Non-Logged Operations**   Commands that bypass the log invalidate a log backup sequence
- **ALTER DATABASE**   Adding or deleting files with ALTER DATABASE invalidates a backup sequence

Tip   As I stated earlier, the completion time of the last complete or differential backup marks the beginning of a transaction log sequence. If you use any of the previous commands and invalidate a log sequence, perform a complete or differential backup to start a new sequence.

Log Truncation Options

When you back up transaction logs, you have several options that determine how the backups are made. With SQL Server Backup in Enterprise Manager, you can use the Remove Inactive Entries From The Log option. Setting this option clears committed transactions out of the log after a log backup. The BACKUP LOG command normally clears out committed or aborted transactions after a log backup as well. However, you can override this behavior with these options:

- **TRUNCATE_ONLY**   Removes inactive entries from the log without creating a backup. This invalidates the log sequence.
- **NO_LOG**   Same as TRUNCATE_ONLY but doesn't log the BACKUP LOG command in the transaction log. This option is designed for a situation where the transaction log or its home drive is full and you must truncate the log without writing to the log device.
- **NO_TRUNCATE**   Writes all the transaction log entries from the last backup to the point of failure. Use this option when the database is corrupt and you're about to restore it.

Tip   After you use TRUNCATE_ONLY or NO_LOG, always perform a complete or differential backup. This revalidates the log sequence. Additionally, because you can grow logs automatically, you should rarely encounter a situation where you need to truncate the log without logging. The log can run out of space only if you set a maximum size or the drive(s) that the log uses runs out of space.

Restoring a Database

Occasional database corruption, hardware failure, and natural disasters are facts of life, and as a database administrator you need to be able to restore the database if any of these mishaps occur. Even if you're an old pro at backup and restore, keep in mind that restoring a database is a bit different from restoring an operating system or recovering other types of applications. The mix of complete, differential, and transaction log backups ensures that you can get up-to-the-minute recovery of a database, but it complicates the recovery process.

In the section that follows you'll find tips and advice on troubleshooting database corruption. In the sections after that you'll find step-by-step procedures for restoring a database in various situations, including

- Restoring a database using backups created in Enterprise Manager
- Restoring a file or filegroup
- Restoring a database from a device
- Restoring a database to a different location
- Restoring a database using Transact-SQL

Database Corruption and Problem Resolution

All your database administration know-how comes into play in one defining moment. That's the moment when you attempt to restore a database. The techniques you use to restore a database depend on the backup options you've used and the state of the database. As you know, the backup techniques available are complete, differential, transaction log, and file/filegroups. What you may not know is how to restore a database when these techniques are combined.

Table 11-2 lists some suggested recovery strategies. These strategies show how to recover a database with various combinations of the available backup operations. If you use Enterprise Manager for backup and restore, these procedures are done for you automatically in most cases. The actual step-by-step process is covered later in this chapter.

Table 11-2. Recovery Strategies for Databases

Backup Type	Restore Process
Complete backups only	Restore the database using the last complete backup.
Complete and differential backups	Restore the last complete backup with NORECOVERY. Then restore the last differential backup with RECOVERY.
Complete and transaction log backups	Back up the current transaction log with NO_TRUNCATE. Restore the last complete backup with NORECOVERY. Apply log backups from that time forward in sequence and using NORECOVERY.

(continued)

Table 11-2. (*continued*)

Backup Type	Restore Process
	Apply the last differential backup with RECOVERY option.
Complete, differential, and transaction log backups	Back up the current transaction log with NO_TRUNCATE. Restore the last complete backup with NORECOVERY and transaction log and then the last differential backup with NORECOVERY. Apply log backups from that time forward in sequence and using NORECOVERY. Apply the last backup using the RECOVERY option.

All right, now you know in theory how to restore a database. But before you pull out all the stops, you should make sure the database is really corrupt and can't be recovered by other means. To troubleshoot database problems and potential corruption, complete the following steps:

1. Start with the error logs. See what types of error messages are in the logs, paying particular attention to errors that occur during database startup. Also take a look at user-related errors. If you find errors, you can look up the error numbers in the SQL Server Books Online or the Microsoft Online Support Web site (*http://search.support.microsoft.com*). You access the server logs through the Management folder in Enterprise Manager.

2. Check the state of the database. Every time you start SQL Server, it goes through a recovery process on each database. If the recovery process has problems, the mode or state of the database may be abnormal. To check mode or state, use these properties of the *databaseproperty* function:

   - **IsShutDown**   If set to 1, the database is shut down because of problems during startup.

   - **IsEmergencyMode**   If set to 1, the database is in emergency mode, which allows a suspect database to be used.

   - **IsSuspect**   If set to 1, the database is suspect, which means there is possible corruption.

   - **IsInLoad**   If set to 1, the database is going through the loading process.

   - **IsInRecovery**   If set to 1, the database is going through the recovery process.

3. If possible, try to use the DBCC command to further troubleshoot or repair the database. DBCC is covered in Chapter 12, "Database Automation and Maintenance."

4. If these procedures indicate a corrupt database that can't be repaired, restore the database from backup.

You can use the *databaseproperty* function as shown in Sample 11-5.

Sample 11-5. The *databaseproperty* Function Syntax and Usage

Syntax

databaseproperty('database','property')

Usage

select databaseproperty('Customer','IsEmergencyMode')

Restoring a Database from a Normal Backup

Enterprise Manager tracks all the backups you create for each database; when you need to restore a database, Enterprise Manager automatically configures the restore. You can restore a database using these default settings or fine-tune the restore operation as necessary.

To restore a database, complete the following steps:

1. If you're using transaction logs and the database is still running, you should back up the current transaction log with NO_TRUNCATE. When you're using the SQL Server Backup dialog box, this means you should cancel the option labeled Remove Inactive Entries From Transaction Log before running the backup.

2. You must have exclusive access to the database. Close all active connections to the database or have users log off, or both.

3. In Enterprise Manager, select the server you want to work with and then, from the Tools menu, choose the Restore Database option. This opens the Restore Database dialog box.

4. Use the Restore As Database drop-down list box to specify which database to restore and then select the Database option button.

5. Select the database again using the Show Backups Of Database option. This option is provided to allow you to restore a database to a different location, as described in the section of this chapter entitled "Restoring a Database to a Different Location."

6. Use the First Backup To Restore option to select which backup you want to apply first. Only complete backups are available in this drop-down list box. By default, the last complete backup should be selected.

 Real World Normally, you'll want to start with the last complete backup. However, if you know that the last backup is bad or contains transactions that you don't want to apply, such as a massive table deletion, go back to a previous complete backup by selecting a different backup as the starting point.

7. If multiple backups are available, you may be able to select a point in time for the restore. For example, if you know that GOTEAM accidentally deleted

the Accounts table at 12:16 P.M., you could restore the database to a point just prior to this transaction, such as 12:15 P.M. To use the point in time option, select the Point In Time Restore check box. This opens the Point In Time Restore dialog box shown in Figure 11-4. Select a date and time using the fields provided and then click OK.

8. The lower portion of the Restore Database dialog box provides a backup history for the selected database. You can use the information in the history as follows:

* **Restore**   Allows you to select which backup sets to restore. Default selections are based on the first backup to restore and go forward in time through differential and transaction log backups. You should rarely change the default selections.

* **Type**   Icons in this field are just about the only indicators of the type of backup. A backup device with a yellow database symbol behind it indicates a complete backup. A backup device with a bluish-green database symbol behind it indicates a differential backup. A backup device with a notebook symbol behind it indicates a transaction log.

* **Backup Set Date**   Shows a date and time stamp for the backup entry.

* **Size**   Shows the size of the backup.

* **Restore From**   Shows the location of the related backup file.

* **Backup Set Name**   Shows the name of the backup set.

Tip   Select an entry and then click Properties to see a more detailed summary of the backup.

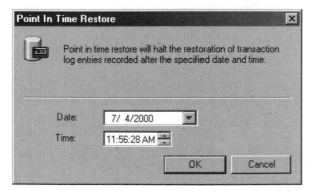

Figure 11-4. *Optionally, use the Point In Time Restore dialog box to select a point in time for the database restore operation.*

9. Click the Options tab to configure options for the restore operation. The Options tab is shown in Figure 11-5. You use the available options as follows:

- **Eject Tapes (If Any) After Restoring Each Backup** Automatically ejects tapes from the tape drive when a restore completes. This is a time-saver if you have to deal with lots of tapes.

- **Prompt Before Restoring Each Backup** Automatically prompts after completing a successful restore and before starting the next restore. The prompt includes a Cancel button, which is useful to cancel the restore operation after a particular backup is restored.

- **Force Restore Over Existing Database** Automatically overwrites existing database files.

- **Restore Database Files As** Allows you to change the restore location for database files.

- **Leave Database Operational** Completes the entire restore process and applies all the selected backups, which can include a complete backup, a differential backup, and multiple transaction log backups. All completed transactions are applied, and any uncompleted transactions are rolled back. When the restore process is completed, the database is returned to ready status and you can use it for normal operations.

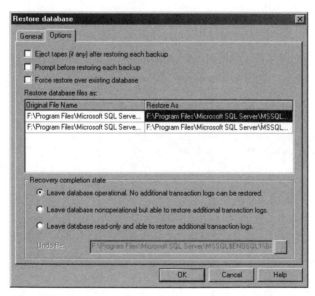

Figure 11-5. *Use the Options tab to configure options for the restore operation, as necessary.*

- **Leave Database Nonoperational**   Essentially a manual restore that allows you to go step-by-step through the backups. SQL Server completes the entire restore process and applies all the selected backups, which can include a complete backup, a differential backup, and multiple transaction log backups. When the restore is completed, the database isn't returned to ready status and you can't use it for normal operations. All transactions haven't been processed, and the database is waiting for you to apply additional transaction logs. Apply these transaction logs using this mode, and then for the last transaction log set the mode to Leave Database Operational. All completed transactions are then applied, and any uncompleted transactions are rolled back.

- **Leave Database Read-Only**   Essentially the same as Leave Database Nonoperational, with some exceptions. When the restore process ends, the database is in Read-Only mode and ready for additional transaction logs to be applied. In Read-Only mode, you can check the data and test the database. If necessary, apply additional transaction logs. For the last transaction log, set the mode to Leave Database Operational. All completed transactions are then applied, and any uncompleted transactions are rolled back.

Tip   With Leave Database Read-Only, SQL Server also creates an Undo file, which you can use to undo the restore operation. To commit the restore operations and the final transactions, if possible, without restoring another transaction log, you could use

- RESTORE DATABASE Customer

- WITH RECOVERY

This commits final transactions (if possible), deletes the Undo file, and puts the database back in operations mode. Although you may want to use WITH RECOVERY at this stage, you probably don't want to use WITH NORECOVERY because you'll undo all the changes from the restore and may end up with an empty database.

10. When you're ready to start the restore operation, click OK. Restore Database shows the progress of each backup. Stop the restore at any time by clicking Stop. If an error occurs, you'll see a prompt with an error message. The most common error is Database In Use. This error occurs when you don't have exclusive access to the database, which means that someone is still connected to the database, and you can't proceed until the connection is closed.

Restoring Files and Filegroups

You can restore files and filegroups from database backups or file backups either individually, in combination with each other, or all together. If any changes were made to the files or filegroups, you must also restore all transaction log backups that were created after the files or filegroups were backed up.

Although you can usually recover individual files or filegroups, there are exceptions. If tables and indexes are created that span multiple filegroups, all the related filegroups must be restored together. Don't worry, SQL Server generates an error prior to starting the restore if a needed filegroup is missing. Further, if the entire database is corrupted, you must restore all files and filegroups in the database. In both cases you must also apply transaction log backups created after the file or filegroup backups you're restoring.

To restore files or filegroups, complete the following steps:

1. You must have exclusive access to the database. Close all active connections to the database or have users log off, or both.

2. In Enterprise Manager, select the server you want to work with and then, from the Tools menu, choose the Restore Database option.

3. Use the Restore As Database drop-down list box to specify which database to restore and then select the Filegroups Or Files option button. This changes the Restore Database dialog box, as shown in Figure 11-6.

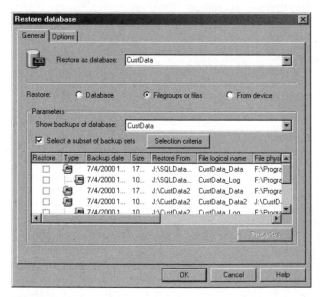

Figure 11-6. *When you restore from files or filegroups, you have different options than with a normal backup.*

4. Select the database you're restoring again using the Show Backups Of Database drop-down list box. This option is provided to allow you to restore a database to a different location, as described in the section of this chapter entitled "Restoring a Database to a Different Location."

5. If you want to specify criteria for determining which files to use in the backup, choose Select A Subset Of Backup Sets and then click Selection Criteria. This opens the Filter Backup Sets dialog box, shown in Figure 11-7. The options of this dialog box determine which of the available backups are selected, and you use them as follows:

   - **Only The Backup Sets Of The Data Files On Drive** Choose this option to restore only data files that are on a specific drive, such as F.

   - **Only The Backup Sets Completed After** Choose this option to filter backup sets by creation date and time.

   - **Only Backup Sets Of The Following Filegroups And Files** Choose this option to filter restore by filegroup and file.

6. The lower portion of the Restore Database dialog box provides a backup history for the files and filegroups in the selected database. By setting selection criteria, you remove options from the history and narrow the choices based on your filters. You can use the information in the history as follows:

   - **Restore** Allows you to select which backup files to restore. No default selections are made and you must choose the files manually.

Figure 11-7. *Use the Filter Backup Sets dialog box to filter the available backup sets by drive, creation date, or filename.*

- **Type** Icons in this field indicate the type of backup. A backup device with a folder symbol behind it indicates a file backup. A backup device with a notebook symbol behind it indicates a transaction log.
- **Backup Date** Shows a date and time stamp for the backup entry.
- **Size** Shows the size of the backup.
- **File Logical Name** Shows the logical name of the file.
- **File Physical Name** Shows the complete file path for the backup entry.

Tip Select an entry and then click Properties to see a more detailed summary of the backup.

7. Select the backup files you want to restore. When you do this, Restore Database automatically selects related transaction logs that must be restored with this file.

8. Click the Options tab to configure options for the restore operation. The available options are the same as those discussed in the section of this chapter entitled "Restoring a Database from a Normal Backup."

9. When you're ready to start the restore operation, click OK. Restore Database shows the progress of each backup. You can stop the restore at any time by clicking Stop.

Restoring a Database from a Device

Restoring a database from a tape device or other backup device is different from a normal backup. This is primarily because you have to work with backup media (tapes) that may contain multiple backups, as well as multiple backup media sets (tape sets). Although you can use this procedure to restore a disk backup device, the normal backup procedure is especially designed for this purpose and is much easier to use.

To restore a database from a device, complete the following steps:

1. You must have exclusive access to the database. Close all active connections to the database or have users log off, or both.

2. In Enterprise Manager, select the server you want to work with and then, from the Tools menu, choose the Restore Database option.

3. Use the Restore As Database drop-down list box to specify which database to restore and then select the From Device option button. This changes the Restore Database dialog box, as shown in Figure 11-8.

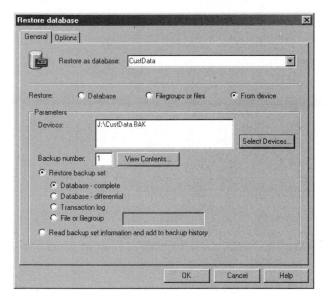

Figure 11-8. *When you restore a database from a device, you have additional options for selecting devices and accessing media.*

4. Click Select Devices to display the Choose Restore Devices dialog box, which is shown in Figure 11-9.

5. To restore from disk, select the Disk option button. Otherwise select the Tape option button.

6. Click Add to choose the file or backup device for the restore operation. With multiple backup devices, repeat this step to select additional files or backup devices.

7. When restoring from tape, you can ensure that you're backing up from the right tapes by selecting Only Restore From Media With The Following Name and then typing the name of the backup set in the Media Name field.

8. In the Backup Set field, type the number of the backup set you're restoring. If you're restoring the first backup set on the tape, type **1**. For the second backup set type **2**, and so on. To make sure that you've set the right backup, click View Contents and double-check the information provided.

9. To restore the backup set, select the Restore Backup Set option button, and then specify the type of backup you're restoring using these option buttons:
   - Database – Complete
   - Database – Differential
   - Transaction Log
   - File Or Filegroup

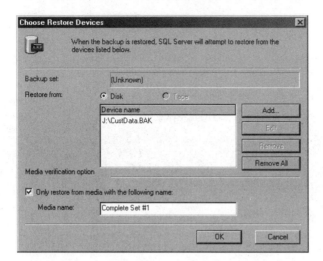

Figure 11-9. *In the Choose Restore Devices dialog box, choose the restore devices and specify media criteria.*

10. To read the backup information and add to backup history rather than perform a restore, select Read Backup Set Information And Add To Backup History.

11. Click the Options tab to configure options for the restore operation. The available options are almost the same as those discussed in the "Restoring a Database from a Normal Backup" section of this chapter. You also have the option of reading from the tape to ensure that you have the right backup set. To do this, click Read From Media.

12. When you're ready to start the restore operation, click OK. Restore Database shows the progress of each backup. You can stop the restore at any time by clicking Stop.

Restoring a Database to a Different Location

When you restore a database to a different location, you're essentially copying the database from the backups. If you use this procedure to copy a database to a new location on the same computer, you create a copy of the database that can have separate files and a different database name. Restoring a database to a different location is similar to the discussion in the previous section. The key differences are as follows:

1. In the Restore As field, type a new name for the database. For example, if you're restoring the Customer database to a new location, name the copy Customer 2 or CustomerCopy.

2. When you access the Options tab, you override the default destination paths and enter new destination paths for all of the files you're restoring. Simply

click in the Restore As or Move To Physical File Name field associated with a backup and then enter a new file path.

If you use this procedure to copy a database to a different computer, you can create a working copy of the database on another server. You don't need to create a new database or perform any preliminary work. The exception is that if you want to use backup devices on the destination server, you should set these up beforehand. Also, before you begin the restore, you should ensure that the destination computer is using the same code page, sort order, Unicode collation, and Unicode locale as the source server. If these configuration settings aren't identical, you won't be able to run the database on the destination server.

Recovering Missing Data

If you suspect part of the database is missing or corrupted, you can perform a partial restore to a new location so that you can recover the missing or corrupted data. To do this, you use the PARTIAL option with the RESTORE DATABASE statement. You can restore partial databases only at the filegroup level. The primary file and filegroup are always restored along with the files that you specify and their corresponding filegroups. Files and filegroups that aren't restored are marked as offline and you can't access them.

To carry out the restore and recovery process, complete the following steps:

1. Perform a partial database restore. Give the database a new name and location in the RESTORE DATABASE statement and use MOVE/TO to move the original database source files to new locations, such as:

   ```
   RESTORE DATABASE new_custdb_partial

   FILEGROUP = 'Customers2'

   FROM DISK='g:\cust.dmp'

   WITH FILE=1,NORECOVERY,PARTIAL,

   MOVE 'cust' TO 'g:\cu2.pri',

   MOVE 'cust_log' TO 'g:\cu2.log',

   MOVE 'cust_data_2' TO 'g:\cu2.dat2'

   GO
   ```

2. Extract any needed data from the partial restore and insert it into the database from which it was deleted.

Creating Standby Servers

The notion of restoring a backup to a different computer can be extended to create a standby backup server that you can bring online if the primary server fails. When you create a standby you have two options. You can

- Create a cold standby that you synchronize manually

- Create a warm standby that SQL Server synchronizes automatically

Creating a Cold Standby

To create a standby that you synchronize manually, complete the following steps:

1. Install SQL Server on a new server system using an identical configuration. This means that the destination server should use the same code page, sort order, Unicode collation, and Unicode locale as the source server.

2. Copy all of the databases on the primary server to this new system by specifying a different restore location in the Restore Database dialog box.

3. Maintain the copies of the databases by periodically applying the transaction log backups from the primary to the standby.

4. You may want to leave the standby server in Standby mode so that the database is read-only. This allows users to access the database but not make changes.

If one or more databases on the primary server fails for any reason, you can make the corresponding databases on the standby available to users. However, before you do this you should synchronize the primary and the standby by completing the following steps:

1. On the standby server, apply any transaction log backups created on the primary server that haven't been applied yet. You must apply these backups in the proper time sequence.

2. Create a backup of the active transaction log on the primary server and apply this backup to the database on the standby server. This ensures up-to-the-minute synchronization. Be sure to recover the database or specify that the database should be put in operational mode after this backup is applied.

 Tip If you need to make the standby appear to be the primary, you may need to take the primary off the network and rename it. Then rename the standby so that it appears to be the primary.

3. After you restore the primary server to working condition, any changes to the standby's databases need to be restored to the primary server. Otherwise those changes are lost when you start using the primary server again.

 Note Standby servers aren't the same as a SQL Server failover cluster, which is created using the SQL Server Failover Cluster Wizard and Windows 2000 Microsoft Cluster Service. Standby servers store a second copy of databases on their hard disk drives. Virtual servers use a single copy of databases that is accessed from a shared storage device.

Creating a Warm Standby

SQL Server 2000 Enterprise Edition includes a feature called *log shipping*. You can use log shipping to create a standby server that's automatically synchronized with the primary server. To do this, follow these steps:

1. Install SQL Server on a new server system using an identical configuration. This means that the destination server should use the same code page, sort order, Unicode collation, and Unicode locale as the source server.

2. Copy all of the databases on the primary server to this new system by specifying a different restore location in the Restore Database dialog box.

3. On the primary server, create a database maintenance plan for log shipping as described in the section of Chapter 12 entitled "Creating Maintenance Plans for Log Shipping."

The primary server is referred to as the *source server*. The servers receiving the logs are referred to as *destination servers*. After configuring log shipping, you should check the status of log shipping on the source and destination servers periodically.

If one or more databases on the primary server fail for any reason, you can make the corresponding databases on the standby available to users. To do that, follow these steps:

1. Make sure that the most recent logs have been applied by checking the status of log shipping on the destination server.

2. Take the primary off the network and rename it.

3. Rename the standby so that it appears to be the primary.

4. Check connections to the new primary server.

After you restore the primary server to working condition, any changes to the standby's databases need to be restored to the primary server. Otherwise those changes are lost when you start using the primary server again.

Using Transact-SQL Restore

You can also restore databases using Transact-SQL. The commands you'll use are RESTORE DATABASE and RESTORE LOG. You can use RESTORE DATABASE to restore an entire database, specific files and filegroups, or part of a corrupted database. Sample 11-6 shows the syntax and usage for a complete restore. The option WITH RECOVERY is the default mode.

Sample 11-6. RESTORE DATABASE Syntax and Usage for a Complete Restore

Syntax

```
RESTORE DATABASE {database_name | @database_name_var}
[FROM <backup_device> [,...n]]
[WITH
 [RESTRICTED_USER]
 [[,] FILE = file_number]
```

(continued)

Sample 11-6. *(continued)*

Syntax

```
  [[,] PASSWORD = {password | @password_variable}]

  [[,] MEDIANAME = {media_name | @media_name_variable}]

  [[,] MEDIAPASSWORD = {mediapassword | @mediapassword_variable}]

  [[,] MOVE 'logical_file_name' TO 'operating_system_file_name']

   [,...n]

  [[,] KEEP_REPLICATION]

  [[,] {NORECOVERY | RECOVERY | STANDBY = undo_file_name}]

  [[,] {NOREWIND | REWIND}]

  [[,] {NOUNLOAD | UNLOAD}]

  [[,] REPLACE]

  [[,] RESTART]

  [[,] STATS [= percentage]]
]
```

Usage

```
RESTORE DATABASE Customer
 FROM Customer_1
 WITH NORECOVERY
```

```
RESTORE DATABASE Customer
 FROM Customer_1
 WITH FILE = 2
```

Usage

```
RESTORE DATABASE Customer
 FROM TAPE = '\\.\tape0'
```

Usage

```
RESTORE DATABASE Customer
 FROM Customer_1
 WITH NORECOVERY,
  MOVE 'CustomerData1' TO 'F:\mssql7\data\NewCust.mdf',
  MOVE 'CustomerLog1' TO 'F:\mssql7\data\NewCust.ldf'
```

(continued)

Sample 11-6. *(continued)*

Usage

```
RESTORE LOG Customer
  FROM CustomerLog1
  WITH RECOVERY
```

With RESTORE DATABASE you can also restore files and filegroups. The related syntax and usage is shown in Sample 11-7.

Sample 11-7. RESTORE DATABASE Syntax and Usage for File and Filegroup Restore

Syntax

```
RESTORE DATABASE {database_name | @database_name_var}
  <file_or_filegroup> [,...n]
[FROM <backup_device> [,...n]]
[WITH
  [RESTRICTED_USER]
  [[,] FILE = file_number]
  [[,] PASSWORD = {password | @password_variable}]
  [[,] MEDIANAME = {media_name | @media_name_variable}]
  [[,] MEDIAPASSWORD = {mediapassword | @mediapassword_variable}]
  [[,] NORECOVERY]
  [[,] {NOREWIND | REWIND}]
  [[,] {NOUNLOAD | UNLOAD}]
  [[,] REPLACE]
  [[,] RESTART]
  [[,] STATS [= percentage]]
]
```

Usage

```
RESTORE DATABASE Customer
  FILE = 'Customerdata_1',
  FILE = 'Customerdata_2',
  FILEGROUP = 'Primary
  FROM Customer_1
```

(continued)

Sample 11-7. *(continued)*
Usage

```
WITH NORECOVERY

RESTORE LOG Customer

FROM CustomerLog1
```

Sample 11-8 shows the syntax for performing a partial restore. This command creates a new database that's based on a partial copy of the backup data. With this procedure, the database_name represents the new name for the database and MOVE/TO is used to move the original database source files to new locations.

Sample 11-8. RESTORE DATABASE Syntax and Usage for Partial Restore

Syntax

```
RESTORE DATABASE { database_name | @database_name_var }

 < file_or_filegroup > [ ,...n ]

[ FROM < backup_device > [ ,...n ] ]

[ WITH

 [ RESTRICTED_USER ]

 { [ , ] PARTIAL }

 [ [ , ] FILE = file_number ]

 [ [ , ] PASSWORD = { password | @password_variable } ]

 [ [ , ] MEDIANAME = { media_name | @media_name_variable } ]

 [ [ , ] MEDIAPASSWORD =
   { mediapassword | @mediapassword_variable } ]

 [ [ , ] MOVE 'logical_file_name' TO operating_system_file_name'
]

  [ ,...n ]

 [ [ , ] NORECOVERY ]

 [ [ , ] { NOREWIND | REWIND } ]

 [ [ , ] { NOUNLOAD | UNLOAD } ]

 [ [ , ] REPLACE ]

 [ [ , ] RESTART ]

 [ [ , ] STATS [= percentage ] ]

]
```

(continued)

Sample 11-8. *(continued)*

Usage

```
RESTORE DATABASE cust_part
 FILEGROUP = 'Customers2'
 FROM DISK='g:\cust.dmp'
 WITH FILE=1,NORECOVERY,PARTIAL,
 MOVE 'cust' TO 'g:\cu2.pri',
 MOVE 'cust_log' TO 'g:\cu2.log',
 MOVE 'cust_data_2' TO 'g:\cu2.dat2'
GO

RESTORE LOG cust_part
 FROM DISK = 'g:\cust.dmp'
 WITH FILE = 2,RECOVERY
GO
```

Sample 11-9 shows how you can use RESTORE LOG.

Sample 11-9. RESTORE LOG Syntax and Usage

Syntax

```
RESTORE LOG {database_name | @database_name_var}
[FROM <backup_device> [,...n]]
[WITH
 [RESTRICTED_USER]
 [[,] FILE = file_number]
 [[,] PASSWORD = {password | @password_variable}]
 [[,] MEDIANAME = {media_name | @media_name_variable}]
 [[,] MEDIAPASSWORD = {mediapassword | @mediapassword_variable}]
 [[,] {NORECOVERY | RECOVERY | STANDBY = undo_file_name}]
 [[,] {NOREWIND | REWIND}]
 [[,] {NOUNLOAD | UNLOAD}]
 [[,] RESTART]
 [[,] STATS [= percentage]]
```

(continued)

Sample 11-9. *(continued)*
Syntax

```
[[,] STOPAT = {date_time | @date_time_var}
 | [[,] STOPATMARK = 'mark_name' AFTER date_time]
 | [[,] STOPBEFOREMARK = 'mark_name' AFTER date_time]
]
```

Usage

```
RESTORE DATABASE Customer
 FROM Customer_1, Customer_2
 WITH NORECOVERY

RESTORE LOG Customer
 FROM CustomerLog1
 WITH NORECOVERY

RESTORE LOG Customer
 FROM CustomerLog2
 WITH RECOVERY, STOPAT = 'Dec 11, 1999 3:30 PM'
```

Restoring the Master Database

The master database is the most important database on SQL Server. This database stores information about all the databases on the server, server configuration, server logons, and other important information. If master gets corrupted, operations on the server may grind to a halt, and you'll have to recover master using one of two techniques.

If you can start SQL Server, you can restore master from backup much like you would any other database. To do this, complete the following steps:

1. You can only back up master using a complete backup. As a result, no differential or transaction log backups will be available. This means you may not be able to restore master exactly as it was before the failure, and that you should normally use the Recovery Complete state of Leave Database Operation.

2. When you finish restoring the master database, you may need to manually apply any changes made since the last complete backup.

3. After you check the server and verify that everything is okay, make a complete backup of master.

If you can't start SQL Server and you know master is the cause of the problem, you can restore master by completing the following steps:

1. Run the Rebuild Master utility discussed in Chapter 2.

2. Once you rebuild master and get SQL Server back online, you can restore the last backup of master in order to return the server to its most current state.

3. Because Rebuild Master rebuilds the msdb and model databases, you may need to restore these databases from backup as well.

4. Recreate any backup devices, if necessary.

5. Reenter logons and other security settings, if necessary.

6. Restore distribution, if necessary.

7. Restore or attach user databases, if necessary.

8. Restore other server configuration settings, if necessary.

As you can see from the step-by-step procedure, restoring master can take a lot of time and work, which is why regularly backing up master is so important. When you finish recovering the server, be sure to make a complete backup of the master database.

Chapter 12

Database Automation and Maintenance

Automation and maintenance go hand in hand. You can automate many routine database administration tasks, most of which have to do with maintenance issues, such as backing up databases or running consistency checks. Automation allows you to increase productivity, complete tasks while away from your computer, and more. You can configure the server to monitor processes and user activities, to check for errors, and to alert you when related events occur. If you configure alerts properly, Microsoft SQL Server 2000 can monitor itself and you can focus on other areas of administration. You can also schedule jobs to automate routine administration tasks. You can configure these jobs to run on a onetime basis or on a recurring basis, such as once a week or, say, the third Tuesday of every month.

Using SQL Server Agent

SQL Server Agent is the driving force behind database automation. It's responsible for processing alerts and running scheduled jobs. When alerts are triggered and when scheduled jobs fail, succeed, or complete, you can notify SQL Server operators. Operator notifications are also processed through SQL Server Agent.

Accessing Alerts, Operators, and Jobs

You can use Enterprise Manager to access resources related to SQL Server Agent by completing the following steps:

1. In Enterprise Manager, access the Management folder on the database server instance you want to work with.

2. Select the SQL Server Agent entry in the left pane.

3. You should see entries for Alerts, Operators, and Jobs. Select one of these entries in the left pane to display its properties in the right pane, as shown in Figure 12-1.

4. Double-click an alert, operator, or job entry to access its associated properties dialog box.

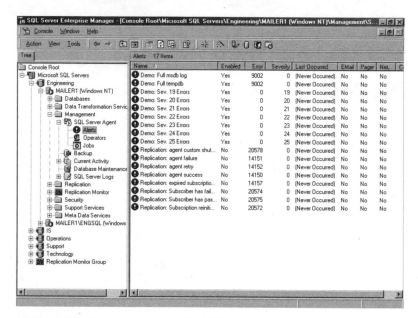

Figure 12-1. *Summary entries for alerts provide an overview of each individual alert. You can also access summaries for operators and jobs.*

 Note If you've configured replication on the server, you'll see many alerts and jobs that you configure to make it easier to monitor replication. To start these alerts or jobs, you need to enable them and set the appropriate property settings.

Configuring the SQL Server Agent Service

For SQL Server Agent to work properly, you should configure the SQL Server Agent service to run automatically. Start SQL Server Service Manager by double-clicking the SQL Server shortcut on the taskbar or by selecting Start, then Programs, then Microsoft SQL Server, and finally Service Manager. You can then configure the SQL Server Agent service with Service Manager by completing the following steps:

1. Use the Server selection list to choose an available server or enter the server name.

2. From the Services selection list, choose SQL Server Agent.

3. Choose Start to start the service, if necessary.

4. Choose Auto-Start Service When OS Starts. This will cause SQL Server Agent service to start automatically when the system boots.

Configuring SQL Server Agent

SQL Server Agent has different properties that you can configure to control how the service works. You configure Agent properties through the SQL Server Agent Properties dialog box shown in Figure 12-2. To access this dialog box, right-click the SQL Server Agent entry in Enterprise Manager's Management folder and then select Properties. The following sections of this chapter use a task-oriented approach to explore the most frequently used configuration options.

Configuring SQL Server Agent Startup Account

The startup account used by the SQL Server Agent service determines SQL Server Agent's access permissions. If the startup account doesn't have appropriate permissions, SQL Server Agent won't run properly. In most cases you'll want to use a Microsoft Windows domain account that's a member of the sysadmin role. This ensures that SQL Server Agent can generate alerts, run jobs, and restart services, as necessary.

You set the startup account by completing the following steps:

1. Click the General tab of the SQL Server Agent Properties dialog box.

2. Choose System Account to use the built-in system account as the startup account. Otherwise select the This Account option button and then type the username and password of a Windows domain account.

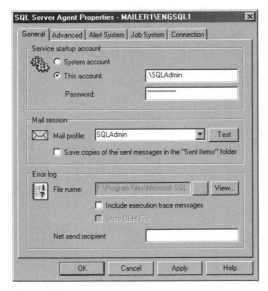

Figure 12-2. *Configure SQL Server Agent properties using the available tabs and fields in the SQL Server Agent Properties dialog box.*

3. If the startup account doesn't have appropriate permissions for making connections to SQL Server, access the Connection tab and then select an authentication method. With SQL Server authentication, you'll also need to specify a login account and password.

4. Click OK.

Setting the SQL Server Agent Mail Profile

SQL Server Agent sends e-mail and pager notifications through the SQL Server Agent service. In order for mail to work properly, you must set the name of the mail profile you want to use for sending these notifications. Type this profile name in the Mail Profile field of the SQL Server Agent Properties dialog box's General tab. For more information on configuring mail, see the section of Chapter 3 entitled "Managing SQL Mail and SQL Server Agent Mail."

Using SQL Server Agent to Restart Services Automatically

You can configure SQL Server Agent to automatically restart the SQL Server and SQL Server Agent services if they stop unexpectedly. Configuring automatic restart of these services is a good idea that'll keep you from getting paged at 3:00 A.M. on a Tuesday morning.

To configure automatic service restart, complete the following steps:

1. Access the Advanced tab of the SQL Server Agent Properties dialog box.

2. Select Auto Restart SQL Server If It Stops Unexpectedly. Select Auto Restart SQL Server Agent If It Stops Unexpectedly.

3. Click OK.

Viewing SQL Server Agent Logs

SQL Server Agent writes output to a separate log file. You can access this log file by completing the following steps:

1. In Enterprise Manager, access the Management folder on the server running SQL Server Agent.

2. Right-click SQL Server Agent and then, from the shortcut menu, choose Display Error Log.

Managing Alerts

Using alerts, you can send e-mail, pager, or Net Send alerts when errors occur or when performance conditions are reached. For example, you can configure an alert to send a message when a Log File Is Full error occurs, or when the number of deadlocks per second is more than five. You can also execute a job on an alert event.

Default Alerts

Default alerts are configured when you install SQL Server and when you configure key features, such as replication. The names of alerts configured for a new installation of SQL Server begin with Demo: and include

- **Demo: Full tempdb** An example alert triggered for a full log file in the tempdb database.

- **Demo: Full msdb log** An example alert triggered for a full log file in the msdb database.

- **Demo: Sev. 19 errors** An example alert triggered for an error with a severity of 19, which is the first level of fatal errors. Other alerts handle severity levels 20–25.

The demo alerts are enabled for use but don't have operators configured to receive the alerts. Because the alerts for fatal errors are the most useful, you'll probably want to edit their properties and configure them for use on the server.

The names of alerts configured when you set up replication begin with Replication:. The replication alerts include

- **Replication: Agent Success** Tells you that the replication agent was successful

- **Replication: Agent Failure** Tells you that the replication agent failed

- **Replication: Agent Retry** Tells you that the replication agent failed and is retrying

- **Replication: Expired Subscription Dropped** Tells you that an expired subscription was dropped, which means the subscriber won't be updated anymore

- **Replication: Subscriber Has Failed Data Validation** Tells you that data in the subscriber's subscription couldn't be validated

- **Replication: Subscriber Has Passed Data Validation** Tells you that data in the subscriber's subscription was validated

- **Replication: Subscriber Reinitialized After Validation Failure** Tells you that data in the subscriber's subscription was reinitialized with a new snapshot

The replication alerts are disabled and don't have operators assigned either. So if you want to use these alerts, you'll need to enable them and assign operators.

Creating Error Message Alerts

Error message alerts are triggered when SQL Server generates an error message. You can create an error message alert by completing the steps on the following page.

1. In Enterprise Manager, access the Management folder on the server running SQL Server Agent.

2. Select the SQL Server Agent entry in the left pane.

3. Right-click Alerts and then, from the shortcut menu, choose New Alert. This opens the New Alert Properties dialog box.

4. Type a short but descriptive name for the alert in the Name field, as shown in Figure 12-3.

5. In the Type selection list, choose SQL Server Event Alert. You can now set alerts according to the number or severity level of error messages.

6. To set alerts by error number, choose Error Number and then type an error number in the related field. To search for an error number, click the build button (...) and then use the Manage SQL Server Messages dialog box to find an appropriate message.

7. To set alerts by severity level, choose Severity and then use the related selection list to choose a severity level that triggers the alert. You'll usually want to configure alerts for severity levels 19–25.

8. Use the Database Name selection list to choose the database in which the error must occur in order to trigger the alert. To specify all databases on the server, select the (All Databases) option.

9. To restrict alerts to messages containing specific text strings, type the filter text in the Error Message Contains This Text field.

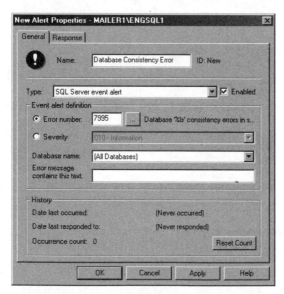

Figure 12-3. *Use the New Alert Properties dialog box to configure new alerts for error messages.*

10. Click Apply and then configure the alert response as explained in the next section of this chapter, "Handling Alert Responses."

Handling Alert Responses

In response to an alert, you can execute SQL Server jobs or notify operators of the alert, or both. To configure the alert response, complete the following steps:

1. In Enterprise Manager, access the Management folder on the server running SQL Server Agent.

2. Select the SQL Server Agent entry in the left pane.

3. Select the Alerts entry in the left pane and then double-click the alert you want to configure. Then click the Response tab, as shown in Figure 12-4.

4. To execute a job in response to the alert, select Execute Job and then use the related selection list to select a job to execute. If you want to create a new job, choose the (New Job) entry and then configure the job as discussed in the section of this chapter entitled "Scheduling Jobs."

5. Operators configured to handle alerts and schedule jobs are shown in the Operators To Notify area. The available notification methods depend on how the operator account is configured. You can select E-Mail, Pager, or Net Send notification, or all three.

Figure 12-4. *You can respond to alerts by executing jobs or notifying operators of the alert, or both.*

6. Use the Include Alert Error Text In check boxes to specify whether error text is sent with the notification message. By default, error text is sent only with E-Mail and Net Send notifications.

7. Set an additional message to operators using the Additional Notification Message To Send text box.

8. Set the delay between responses for subsequent alert notifications using the Delay Between Responses fields labeled Minutes and Seconds.

 Tip To limit the number of alert responses triggered, you'll probably want to set a delay response value of five minutes or more.

9. Click OK to complete the configuration.

Deleting, Enabling, and Disabling Alerts

Deleting an alert removes its entry from the alerts list. Because old alerts may be useful to you (or another DBA) in the future, you may want to disable them instead of deleting them. When an alert is disabled, no alerts are triggered if the related event occurs.

To delete, enable, or disable an alert, complete the following steps:

1. In Enterprise Manager, access the Management folder on the server running SQL Server Agent.

2. Select the SQL Server Agent entry in the left pane and then select Alerts.

3. To enable or disable an alert, double-click its entry in the Alerts list to open the related properties dialog box. Then, in the General tab, select or clear the Enabled check box to enable or disable the alert.

4. To delete an alert, click it and then press Delete. When prompted to confirm the deletion, choose Yes.

Managing Operators

Operators are special accounts that can be notified when alerts are triggered and when scheduled jobs fail, succeed, or complete. Before operators become available, you need to register them. After you register operators, you can enable or disable them for notifications.

Registering Operators

You register operators by completing the following steps:

1. In Enterprise Manager, access the Management folder on the server running SQL Server Agent.

2. Select the SQL Server Agent entry in the left pane.

3. Right-click the Operators entry in the left pane and then, from the shortcut menu, choose New Operator. This opens the New Operator Properties dialog box shown in Figure 12-5.

4. Type a name for the operator in the Name field.

5. Specify E-Mail, Pager, or Net Send accounts (or all three) to notify. If you can't remember the account you want to use, click the build button (...) to display the Contacts list from your address book, and then select the account to use.

6. Click the Notifications tab to specify existing alerts that the operator should receive (if any). Existing alerts are listed in the Alert Name column. If you find an alert that the operator should receive, select the corresponding check boxes in the E-Mail, Pager, and Net Send columns as appropriate.

7. Once you've configured the Notifications tab, you can click Send E-Mail to send the operator an e-mail that lists that operator's alert responsibilities.

Tip If you specify a pager account for the operator, you can set a duty schedule for the pager using the Pager On Duty Schedule area's fields and check boxes. This option is helpful if you have operators who should be notified only during working hours. To set default configuration settings for pagers, access the Alert System tab of the SQL Server Agent Properties dialog box.

8. Click OK to register the operator.

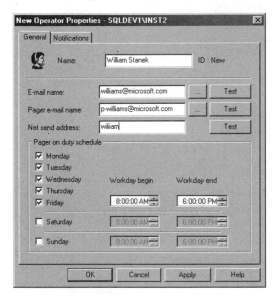

Figure 12-5. *Operators can receive alert and job notifications. To associate the operator with multiple users, reference a group e-mail account.*

Deleting and Disabling Notification for Operators

When DBAs leave the organization or go on vacation, you may want to delete or disable their associated operator accounts. To do this, complete the following steps:

1. In Enterprise Manager, access the Management folder on the server running SQL Server Agent.

2. Select the SQL Server Agent entry in the left pane and then select Operators.

3. To disable an operator, double-click the operator entry in the right pane. This opens the Operator Properties dialog box. Now click the Notifications tab and then clear Operator Is Available To Receive Notifications.

4. To delete an operator, click its entry in the right pane and then press Delete. If the operator has been selected to receive alert or job notifications, you'll see the Delete Operator dialog box shown in Figure 12-6. To reassign notification duty, select a different operator using the Re-Assign To selection list and then click Reassign.

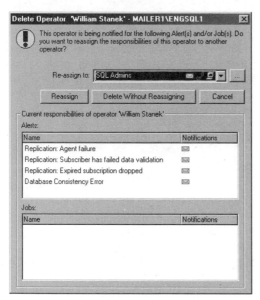

Figure 12-6. *In the Delete Operator dialog box you can reassign notification duties when deleting an operator registration.*

Configuring a Fail-Safe Operator

When things go wrong with notification, operators don't get notified and problems may not be corrected in a timely manner. To prevent this, you may want to designate a fail-safe operator. The fail-safe operator is notified when

- SQL Server Agent can't access system tables in the msdb database, which is where operator definitions and notification lists are stored.
- All pager notifications to designated operators have failed or the designated operators are off duty (as defined in the pager schedule).

Note Using the fail-safe operator on pager notification failure may seem strange, but it's the way to go. E-mail and Net Send messages almost always reach their destination—whether someone is watching their mail or sitting at their computer to receive Net Send messages is another matter altogether.

To configure a fail-safe operator, complete the following steps:

1. Right-click the SQL Server Agent entry in Enterprise Manager's Management folder and then select Properties.
2. In the SQL Server Agent Properties dialog box, click the Alert System tab and then use the Operator selection list to choose an operator to designate as the fail-safe operator. You can reassign the fail-safe duty by selecting a different operator or disable the feature by selecting (No Fail-Safe Operator).
3. Use the Notify Using check boxes to determine how the fail-safe operator is notified.
4. Click Apply.

Scheduling Jobs

Job scheduling is a key part of database automation. You can configure SQL Server jobs to handle just about any database task.

Creating Jobs

You create jobs as a series of steps that contain actions in the sequence in which you want to execute them. When you schedule jobs in conjunction with other SQL Server facilities, such as database backups or data transformation services (DTS), the necessary commands are configured for you. Normally these commands are set as step 1, and all you need to do is set a run schedule for the job. You can add extra steps to these jobs and thus perform other tasks. For example, after importing data through DTS, you may want to back up the related database. In the DTS Wizard, you would schedule the import and then you would edit the associated job in Enterprise Manager to add an additional step for backing up the database. By coordinating the two processes, you ensure that the import operation is completed before starting the backup.

Another reason for editing a job created by another SQL Server facility is to add notifications based on success, failure, and completion of the job. In this way you can notify operators of certain conditions, and you don't have to search through logs to determine whether the job executed properly.

When you schedule jobs to execute for alerts, you configure the entire job process from start to finish. You

- Create a job definition
- Set steps to execute
- Configure a job schedule
- Handle completion, success, and failure notification messages

Assigning or Changing Job Definitions

Whether you're creating a new job or editing an existing job, the steps for working with job definitions are the same. Complete the following steps:

1. In Enterprise Manager, access the Management folder on the server running SQL Server Agent.

2. Select the SQL Server Agent entry in the left pane and then double-click Jobs.

3. Existing jobs are shown in the right pane. Double-click a job to access its related properties dialog box, which is essentially the same as the New Job Properties dialog box shown in Figure 12-7.

4. To create a new job, right-click the Jobs entry and, from the shortcut menu, choose New Job. This displays the New Job Properties dialog box shown in Figure 12-7.

5. In the Name field, type a descriptive name for the job. The name can be up to 128 characters long. If you change the name of an existing job, the job is displayed with the new name. Any references to the old job name in logs or history files remain the same and aren't modified.

6. If job scheduling across multiple servers is configured, select the target server. The target server is the server on which the job runs. To run on the currently

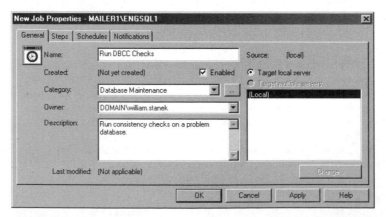

Figure 12-7. *Use the General tab of the New Job Properties dialog box to name, describe, and categorize the job.*

selected server, select Target Local Server. To run on multiple servers, select Target Multiple Servers and then choose the target servers.

7. Job categories help to organize jobs so they can be easily searched and differentiated. The default category is Uncategorized (Local). Use the Category selection list to choose a different category for the job.

Note Job categories are created and managed through a separate process. To create a new job category or update an existing category, use the techniques described in the section of this chapter entitled "Managing Job Categories."

8. By default, the current user owns the job. Administrators can reassign jobs to other users. To do this, use the Owner selection list. You can use only predefined logons. If the logon you want to use isn't available, you'll need to create a logon for the account.

9. Type a description of the job in the Description text box. You can use up to 512 characters.

10. Click Apply to create the job definition. Then set Steps, Schedules, and Notifications as explained in the following sections.

Setting Steps to Execute

Jobs can have one or more steps. While SQL Server Agent always attempts to execute the Start step, additional steps can be executed conditionally, such as only when the Start step succeeds or fails. You work with steps using the Steps tab in the New Job Properties dialog box, as shown in Figure 12-8. The dialog box displays any existing steps for the job. You can use the fields and buttons in this dialog box as listed on the following page.

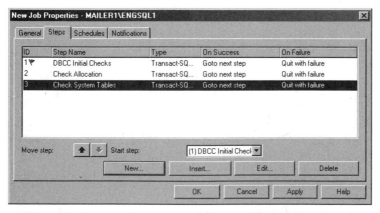

Figure 12-8. *Using the Steps tab in the New Job Properties dialog box, you can execute steps conditionally and in any sequence you specify.*

- **New**   Creates a new step.
- **Insert**   Inserts a step before the currently selected step.
- **Edit**   Allows edits to the selected step.
- **Delete**   Deletes the selected step.
- **Move Step Up/Down**   Changes the order of the selected step.
- **Start Step**   Sets which step is executed first. The green flag icon highlights the start step in the step list.

When you create or edit a step, you see a dialog box similar to the one shown in Figure 12-9. To configure this dialog box, complete the following steps:

1. Type a short but descriptive name for the step in the Step Name field.
2. Use the Type selection list to choose a step type. Each step can

- **Execute Transact-SQL commands**   Type Transact-SQL commands in the Command area or load the statements from a Transact SQL script. To load commands from a script, click Open and then select the Transact-SQL script you want to use. The entire contents of the script are then stored with this step.

- **Run ActiveX scripts**   You can write ActiveX scripts in VBScript, JScript, or another active scripting language configured for use on the system. Enter script statements directly into the Command area or load the statements from a script file. Again, the entire contents of the script are then stored with this step, and later changes to the script file aren't updated automatically.

- **Execute operating system commands**   Enter the operating system commands on a separate line, making sure that you specify

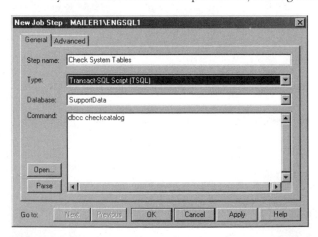

Figure 12-9. *Set summary information and commands to execute for the step you're configuring using the fields in the General tab of the New Job Step dialog box.*

the full path to commands and in command parameters. Commands can run batch scripts, Windows scripts, command-line utilities, or applications.

- **Pass Transact-SQL commands to replication agents**   You can script the Distributor, Snapshot, Merge, and Transaction LogReader agents with Transact-SQL commands. To see examples, refer to the existing jobs that are configured to handle replication, distribution, and subscription processes on the server (if available).

Tip   Subsequent changes to scripts aren't updated automatically. You'll need to edit the step properties and reload the script file. Additionally, you shouldn't edit existing replication jobs. Instead, modify the replication process as described in Chapter 9, "Configuring Snapshot, Merge, and Transactional Replication."

3. When executing Transact-SQL commands, use the Database selection list to set the database on which the commands are executed.

4. Click the Advanced tab as shown in Figure 12-10.

5. In the On Success Action selection list, set the action to take when the step succeeds. You can

   - Go to the next step to continue sequential execution of the job

   - Go to a different step to continue execution of the job on a different step

   - Quit the job and report success or failure

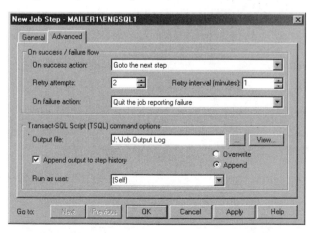

Figure 12-10. *Control the behavior and logging of the step using the fields in the Advanced tab.*

6. By default, Retry Attempts is set to zero and SQL Server Agent doesn't try to execute steps again. You can change this behavior by setting the number of retry attempts and a retry interval. You do this by using the Retry Attempts and Retry Interval (Minutes) fields, respectively. The retry interval is the delay in minutes between retries.

7. If the job fails on all retry attempts (if any), the action set in the On Failure Action selection list is executed. The available options are the same as those for success.

8. If desired, configure a file for logging output from Transact-SQL and CmdExec commands. Type the filename and path in the Output File field or use the find file button (...) to search for an existing file. An alternative is to append output to the step history.

 Tip You may want to create a central log file for the output of all jobs or only all jobs in a particular category. If you do this, be sure to select the Append option button rather than the Overwrite option button. This ensures that the output file doesn't get overwritten.

9. Set the login to use when executing commands using the Run As User selection list. By default, commands are run using the current login ID.

10. Choose Apply to complete the step configuration.

Configuring Job Schedules

You track schedules in the Schedules tab of the New Job Properties dialog box, as shown in Figure 12-11. Jobs can have one or more schedules associated with them, and just as you can enable or disable jobs and their individual steps, you can enable or disable individual schedules. This makes the job scheduling

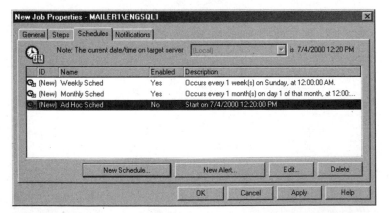

Figure 12-11. *Track schedules in the Schedules tab of the New Job Properties dialog box. Jobs can have multiple schedules associated with them.*

process very flexible. For example, you could set one schedule to execute the job on weekdays at 2 A.M., another to execute the job on Saturday and Sunday at 8 A.M., and another for ad hoc execution at 10 P.M.

Whether you're creating a new job or editing an existing job, you work with schedules in the Schedules tab as follows:

- **Create a new schedule**   Click New Schedule to configure a new schedule.

- **Edit a schedule**   Select an existing schedule and then click Edit to view or modify its properties.

- **Delete a schedule**   Select an existing schedule and then click Delete to remove the schedule.

You create or edit schedules by completing the following steps:

1. Click New Schedule to open the New Job Schedule dialog box, or click Edit to open the Edit Job Schedule dialog box. These dialog boxes are essentially the same except for the title. Figure 12-12 shows the New Job Schedule dialog box.

2. Type a name for the schedule and then select one of the following schedule types:

   - **Start Automatically When SQL Server Agent Starts**   Runs the job automatically whenever SQL Server Agent starts.

   - **Start Whenever The CPU(s) Become Idle**   Runs the job whenever the CPU is idle. CPU idle time is specified in the Advanced tab of the SQL Server Agent Properties dialog box.

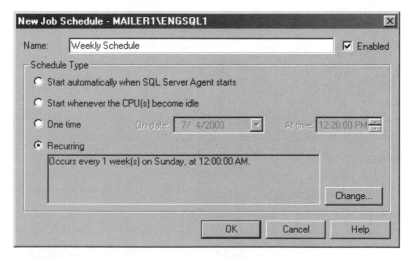

Figure 12-12. *Use the New Job Schedule dialog box to set the schedule name and type.*

- **One Time** Runs the job once at the date and time specified in the On Date and At Time fields.

- **Recurring** Runs the job according to the recurring schedule displayed.

3. Recurring jobs are the ones that need the most explanation. When you click Change, you'll see the Edit Recurring Job Schedule dialog box shown in Figure 12-13. You can schedule recurring jobs to run on a daily, weekly, or monthly basis.

4. To run the job on a daily basis, select the Daily option button. Then use the Every Day field to set when the job runs. Daily recurring jobs can run every day, every other day, or every Nth day.

5. To run the job on a weekly basis, select the Weekly option button. Then configure the job using these fields:

- **Every Nth Week(s)** Allows you to run the task every week, every other week, or every Nth week

- **Day Of Week** Sets the day(s) of the week when the task runs, such as on Monday or on Monday, Wednesday, and Friday

6. To run the job on a monthly basis, select the Monthly option button. Then configure the job using these fields:

- **Day N Of Every Nth Month** Sets the day of the month and on which months the job runs. For example, if you select Day 15 of every second month, the job runs on the 15th day of alternating months.

- **The Nth Day Of Every Nth Month** Sets the job to run on the Nth occurrence of a day in a given month, such as the second Monday of every month or the third Sunday of every other month.

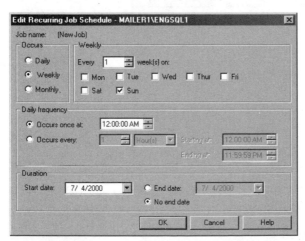

Figure 12-13. *Configure a recurring schedule in the Edit Recurring Job Schedule dialog box.*

7. Set the Daily Frequency for the daily, weekly, or monthly job. You can configure jobs to run one or more times on their scheduled run date. To run the
job once on a given date, select Occurs Once At and then set a time. To run
the job several times on a given date, select Occurs Every and then set a time
interval in hours or minutes. Afterward, set a start and end time, such as from
7:30 A.M. to 5:30 P.M.

8. By default, schedules begin on the current date and don't have a designated
end date. To change this behavior, select the End Date option button and
then use the Start Date and End Date fields to set a new duration for the
schedule.

9. Click OK to close the Edit Recurring Job Schedule dialog box and then click
OK again to close the New Job Schedule dialog box, which completes the
schedule process.

Handling Notification Messages

Notification messages are generated when a job succeeds, fails, or completes. You
can handle these messages in several ways. You can notify operators, log
the related event, automatically delete the job, or do all three. To configure
notification, complete the following steps:

1. Access the Notifications tab of the job you want to configure. This tab is shown
in Figure 12-14.

2. You can notify operators by e-mail, pager, or Net Send message. Select the
check box for the technique you want to use. Choose an operator to handle
the notification. Then choose a notification type. Repeat this process to
configure other notification methods.

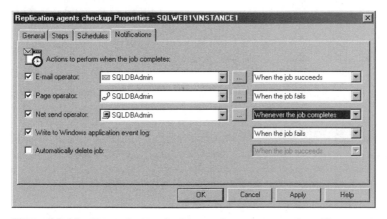

Figure 12-14. *Using the Notifications tab, you can send notification messages
to operators, log them in the event log, or use them to automatically delete a
job.*

3. To log a particular type of notification message in the event log, select Write To Windows Application Event Log and then select the notification type to log. Usually, you'll want to log failure, so select When The Job Fails.

4. To delete a job upon notification, select Automatically Delete Job and then choose the notification type that triggers the deletion.

5. Choose Apply.

Managing Existing Jobs

In Enterprise Manager, you manage jobs with the SQL Server Agent. To do that, complete the following steps:

1. Access the SQL Server Agent window in the console root. You'll see an entry labeled Jobs.

2. Select Jobs in the left pane and you'll see existing jobs in the right pane.

3. You can now double-click a job entry to access its related properties dialog box or right-click a job entry to display a shortcut menu. Key options on the shortcut menu are

- **Delete**   Deletes the job definition. Before deleting a complex job, you may want to create a script that can be used to recreate the job.

- **Disable Job**   Disables the job so it won't run.

- **Download**   If you've configured multiserver administration, use this option to post scheduled job instructions to a target server. Downloading jobs to a target allows you to immediately start execution of a job or to use the job on the target at a later date.

- **Script Job**   Select All Tasks and then choose Script Job to access the Generate SQL Script dialog box. This dialog box enables you to generate a Transact-SQL script that you can use to recreate the job.

- **Start Job**   Starts the selected job if it's not already running.

- **Stop Job**   Stops the selected job if it's running.

- **View Job History**   Displays the Job History dialog box. This dialog box enables you to view summary or detail information on the job execution.

Managing Job Categories

You use job categories to organize jobs into topical folders. When you install SQL Server, default job categories are created automatically. You can add new job categories and change the existing categories at any time.

Working with Job Categories

To create a new job category or update an existing category, complete the following steps:

1. In Enterprise Manager, access the SQL Server Agent window in the console root.

2. Right-click the Jobs node. Select All Tasks, and then choose Manage Job Categories. This displays the Job Categories dialog box.

3. You can delete a category by selecting it and then pressing Delete.

4. You can view the properties of a category by selecting it and then clicking Properties.

5. To add categories or to change the properties of a category, follow the steps outlined in the following sections, "Creating Job Categories" or "Updating Job Categories," respectively.

Creating Job Categories

You can create a new job category by completing the following steps:

1. Access the Job Categories dialog box as explained previously. Click Add to display the New Job Categories dialog box.

2. Type a name for the category in the Name field, and then select Show All Jobs.

3. All jobs defined on the current server should now be listed. Add a job to the new category by selecting the corresponding check box in the Member column. Remove a job from the new category by clearing the corresponding check box in the Member column.

4. Click OK when you're finished.

Updating Job Categories

You can update an existing job category by completing the following steps:

1. Access the Job Categories dialog box as explained previously. Click Properties to display a properties dialog box.

2. Select Show All Jobs. All jobs defined on the current server should now be listed.

3. Add a job to a new category by selecting the corresponding check box in the Member column. Remove a job from the category by clearing the corresponding check box in the Member column.

4. Click OK when you're finished.

Automating Routine Server-to-Server Administration Tasks

Anytime you deploy multiple SQL Servers or multiple instances of SQL Server within an organization, you'll need a way to handle routine server-to-server administration tasks. For example, if you have a database on one server, you may need to copy or move the database to a different server. SQL Server 2000 allows you to automate routine server-to-server administration tasks using DTS packages. You can run the packages immediately, schedule them to run periodically, or save them for later use.

The server-to-server administration tasks you can automate include

- Copying logins from one server to another
- Copying scheduled jobs from one server to another
- Copying shared stored procedures from one server to another
- Copying user-defined error messages from one server to another
- Copying or moving user-defined databases from one server to another

The sections that follow explain how you can create DTS packages to automate these administration tasks.

Copying Logins to Another Server

SQL Server uses two types of logins: standard SQL logins and Windows logins. Logins can be assigned default settings, server roles, and database access permissions. Rather than manually recreating login settings each time you want to use the same login on another server, you can copy logins and their settings to a target server. You copy logins with the Transfer Logins Task in DTS Designer as shown in the following steps:

1. Start Enterprise Manager and then access the server you want to work with.
2. Right-click the server's Data Transformation Services folder and then select New Package. This displays the DTS Designer window in Enterprise Manager.
3. In DTS Designer, choose Task and then click Transfer Logins Task. This adds the Transfer Logins Task icon to the DTS Designer window.
4. Double-click the Transfer Logins Task icon. This displays the Transfer Logins Properties dialog box shown in Figure 12-15.

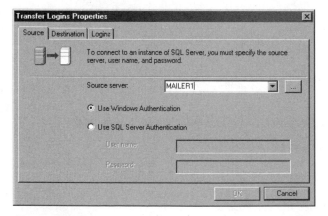

Figure 12-15. *Use the Transfer Logins Properties dialog box to configure the task options. You can select all logins for transfer or logins for selected databases.*

5. In the Source tab, use the Source Server selection list to specify the SQL Server instance that contains the logins you want to transfer. Afterward, specify the authentication technique to use when connecting to the server. If you're logged on using a Windows domain account that's a member of the sysadmin role on the source server, select Use Windows Authentication. Otherwise select Use SQL Server Authentication and then enter the user name and password of a login that's a member of the sysadmin role.

6. In the Destination tab, use the Destination Server selection list to specify the SQL Server instance to which you want to transfer logins. Afterward, specify the authentication technique to use when connecting to the server. Again, make sure you use a login that's a member of the sysadmin role.

Note You can't set the source and destination server to the same value. You must configure the transfer from one server to another.

7. Click the Logins tab as shown in Figure 12-16. You can
   - Copy all logins to the destination server by choosing All Server Logins Detected At Package Runtime.
   - Copy only the logins for the databases you select by choosing Logins For Selected Databases and then selecting the databases to use.

8. Click OK to close the Transfer Logins Properties dialog box.

9. To run the package immediately, click the Execute button (the green arrow button located on the menu bar) or choose Package from the menu and then click Execute. If you want to save the package for later use or for scheduling, continue with the remaining steps. Otherwise skip the remaining steps.

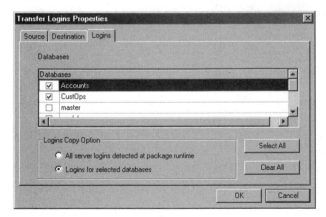

Figure 12-16. *Use the Logins tab to specify the logins to transfer.*

10. To save the package for later use, choose Package and then click Save. You'll see the Save DTS Package dialog box as shown in Figure 12-17.

11. Type a name for the package in the Package Name field. The package name should be unique for the target location.

12. If you're saving the package to SQL Server, you can password-protect the package and prevent unauthorized users from working with it. Type an owner password and a user password in the fields provided. Anyone with the owner password can design, schedule, and execute the package. Anyone with the user password can only schedule or execute the package.

13. Use the Location field to specify where the package should be saved. The available locations are

    - **SQL Server**   Saves as a local package where the package is accessible for use on the designated server.

    - **SQL Server Meta Data Services**   Saves to the designated server's repository database, where the package can be shared with other servers through Meta Data Services.

    - **Structure Storage File**   Saves as a COM-structured file. You can add packages to the file as long as they have a different package name. You can then copy, move, or e-mail the file to a different location.

    - **Visual Basic File**   Saves as a Visual Basic file where the package can be used in Visual Basic programs.

14. The lower portion of the Save DTS Package dialog box changes according to the location selection. When you save to SQL Server or to SQL Server Meta Data Services, you must specify the target server and authentication

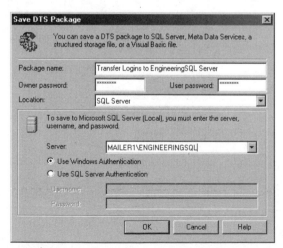

Figure 12-17. *Use the Save DTS Package dialog box to configure the save options for the package.*

information. When you save to a Structure Storage file or a Visual Basic file, you must specify the file name and path.

15. Click OK to save the package to the specified location. Once you've saved the package, you can run or schedule the package for execution as described in the section of Chapter 7 entitled "Examining, Running, and Scheduling Packages."

Copying Scheduled Jobs to Another Server

You use scheduled jobs to automate routine administration tasks. If you've already created jobs on one server, there's no reason you can't reuse the jobs on another server. To do this, you would copy the jobs to the target server and then edit the job properties to ensure that they make sense for the target server. For example, if you created a set of jobs to periodically check the Support database and then added custom steps to handle various database states, you could copy these jobs to another server and then edit the job properties to apply the tasks to the Customer database on the target server.

You copy jobs from one server to another server with the Transfer Jobs Task in DTS Designer. To do that, complete the following steps:

1. Start Enterprise Manager and then access the server you want to work with.

2. Right-click the server's Data Transformation Services folder and then select New Package. This displays the DTS Designer window in Enterprise Manager.

3. In DTS Designer, choose Task and then click Transfer Jobs Task. This adds the Transfer Jobs Task icon to the DTS Designer window.

4. Double-click the Transfer Jobs Task icon. This displays the Transfer Msdb Jobs dialog box shown in Figure 12-18.

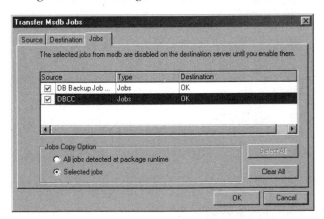

Figure 12-18. *Use the Transfer Msdb Jobs dialog box to configure the task options. You can select all jobs for transfer or specify jobs to transfer individually.*

5. In the Source tab, use the Source Server selection list to specify the SQL Server instance that contains the jobs you want to transfer. Afterward, specify the authentication technique to use when connecting to the server. If you're logged on using a Windows domain account that's a member of the sysadmin role on the source server, select Use Windows Authentication. Otherwise select Use SQL Server Authentication and then enter the username and password of a login that's a member of the sysadmin role.

6. In the Destination tab, use the Destination Server selection list to specify the SQL Server instance to which you want to transfer jobs. Afterward, specify the authentication technique to use when connecting to the server. Again, make sure you use a login that's a member of the sysadmin role.

Note You can't set the source and destination server to the same value. You must configure the transfer from one server to another.

7. Click the Jobs tab as shown previously in Figure 12-18. You can

   • Copy all jobs to the destination server by choosing All Jobs Detected At Package Runtime.

   • Copy only the jobs you select by choosing Selected Jobs and then choosing the jobs to transfer.

8. Click OK to close the Transfer Jobs dialog box.

9. To run the package immediately, click the Execute button (the green arrow button located on the menu bar) or choose Package and then click Execute. If you want to save the package for later use or for scheduling, continue with the remaining steps. Otherwise skip the remaining steps.

10. To save the package for later use, choose Package and then click Save. As shown previously in Figure 12-17, you'll see the Save DTS Package dialog box.

11. Type a name for the package in the Package Name field. The package name should be unique for the target location.

12. If you're saving the package to SQL Server, you can password-protect the package and prevent unauthorized users from working with it. Type an owner password and a user password in the fields provided. Anyone with the owner password can design, schedule, and execute the package. Anyone with the user password can only schedule or execute the package.

13. Use the Location field to specify where the package should be saved. The available locations are

   • **SQL Server**   Saves as a local package where the package is accessible for use on the designated server.

   • **SQL Server Meta Data Services**   Saves to the designated server's repository database where the package can be shared with other servers through Meta Data Services.

- **Structure Storage File**   Saves as a COM-structured file. You can add packages to the file as long as they have a different package name. You can then copy, move, or e-mail the file to a different location.
- **Visual Basic File**   Saves as a Visual Basic file where the package can be used in Visual Basic programs.

14. The lower portion of the Save DTS Package dialog box changes according to the location selection. When you save to SQL Server or to SQL Server Meta Data Services, you must specify the target server and authentication information. When you save to a Structure Storage file or a Visual Basic file, you must specify the file name and path.

15. Click OK to save the package to the specified location. Once you've saved the package, you can run or schedule the package for execution as described in the section of Chapter 7 entitled "Examining, Running, and Scheduling Packages."

Copying Shared Stored Procedures to Another Server

Shared stored procedures are stored in the master database. If you've created shared stored procedures on one server, you can transfer them to another server using the Transfer Master Stored Procedures Task in DTS Designer. To do that, complete the following steps:

1. Start Enterprise Manager and then access the server you want to work with.

2. Right-click the server's Data Transformation Services folder and then select New Package. This displays the DTS Designer window in Enterprise Manager.

3. In DTS Designer, choose Task and then click Transfer Master Stored Procedures Task. This adds the Transfer Master Stored Procedures Task icon to the DTS Designer window.

4. Double-click the Transfer Master Stored Procedures Task icon. This displays the Transfer Master Stored Procedures dialog box as shown in Figure 12-19.

5. In the Source tab, use the Source Server selection list to specify the SQL Server instance that contains the shared stored procedures you want to transfer. Afterward, specify the authentication technique to use when connecting to the server. If you're logged on using a Windows domain account that's a member of the sysadmin role on the source server, select Use Windows Authentication. Otherwise select Use SQL Server Authentication and then enter the username and password of a login that's a member of the sysadmin role.

6. In the Destination tab, use the Destination Server selection list to specify the SQL Server instance to which you want to transfer shared stored procedures. Afterward, specify the authentication technique to use when connecting to the server. Again, make sure you use a login that's a member of the sysadmin role.

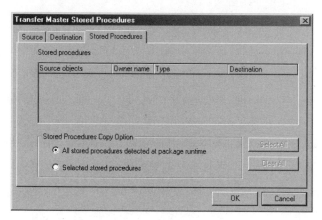

Figure 12-19. *Use the Transfer Master Stored Procedures dialog box to configure the task options. You can select all shared stored procedures for transfer or specify shared stored procedures to transfer individually.*

 Note You can't set the source and destination server to the same value. You must configure the transfer from one server to another.

7. Click the Stored Procedures tab as shown previously in Figure 12-19. You can

   • Copy all shared stored procedures to the destination server by choosing All Stored Procedures Detected At Package Runtime.

   • Copy only the shared stored procedures you select by choosing Selected Stored Procedures and then choosing the stored procedures to use.

8. Click OK to close the Transfer Master Stored Procedures dialog box.

9. To run the package immediately, click the Execute button (the green arrow button located on the menu bar) or choose Package and then click Execute. If you want to save the package for later use or for scheduling, continue with the remaining steps. Otherwise skip the remaining steps.

10. To save the package for later use, choose Package and then click Save. As shown previously in Figure 12-17, you'll see the Save DTS Package dialog box.

11. Type a name for the package in the Package Name field. The package name should be unique for the target location.

12. If you're saving the package to SQL Server, you can password-protect the package and prevent unauthorized users from working with it. Type an owner password and a user password in the fields provided. Anyone with the owner password can design, schedule, and execute the package. Anyone with the user password can only schedule or execute the package.

13. Use the Location field to specify where the package should be saved. The available locations are

- **SQL Server** Saves as a local package where the package is accessible for use on the designated server.

- **SQL Server Meta Data Services** Saves to the designated server's repository database, where the package can be shared with other servers through Meta Data Services.

- **Structure Storage File** Saves as a COM-structured file. You can add packages to the file as long as they have a different package name. You can then copy, move, or e-mail the file to a different location.

- **Visual Basic File** Saves as a Visual Basic file where the package can be used in Visual Basic programs.

14. The lower portion of the Save DTS Package dialog box changes according to the location selection. When you save to SQL Server or to SQL Server Meta Data Services, you must specify the target server and authentication information. When you save to a Structure Storage file or a Visual Basic file, you must specify the file name and path.

15. Click OK to save the package to the specified location. Once you've saved the package, you can run or schedule the package for execution as described in the section of Chapter 7 entitled "Examining, Running, and Scheduling Packages."

Copying User-Defined Error Messages to Another Server

You use user-defined error messages to create custom error messages for database applications. If you've created user-defined error messages on one server, you can transfer them to another server using the Transfer Error Messages Task in DTS Designer. To do that, complete the following steps:

1. Start Enterprise Manager and then access the server you want to work with.

2. Right-click the server's Data Transformation Services folder and then select New Package. This displays the DTS Designer window in Enterprise Manager.

3. In DTS Designer, choose Task and then click Transfer Error Messages Task. This adds the Transfer Error Messages Task icon to the DTS Designer window.

4. Double-click the Transfer Error Messages Task icon. This displays the Transfer Error Messages dialog box as shown in Figure 12-20.

5. In the Source tab, use the Source Server selection list to specify the SQL Server instance that contains the user-defined error messages you want to transfer. Afterward, specify the authentication technique to use when connecting to the server. If you're logged on using a Windows domain account that's a member of the sysadmin role on the source server, select Use Windows

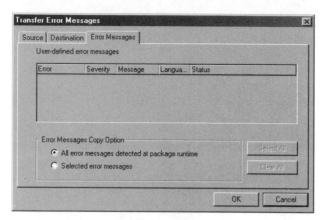

Figure 12-20. *Use the Transfer Error Messages dialog box to configure the task options. You can select all user-defined error messages for transfer or specify user-defined error messages to transfer individually.*

Authentication. Otherwise select use SQL Server Authentication and then enter the user name and password of a login that's a member of the sysadmin role.

6. In the Destination tab, use the Destination Server selection list to specify the SQL Server instance to which you want to transfer user-defined error messages. Afterward, specify the authentication technique to use when connecting to the server. Again, make sure you use a login that's a member of the sysadmin role.

 Note You can't set the source and destination server to the same value. You must configure the transfer from one server to another.

7. Click the Error Messages tab as shown previously in Figure 12-20. You can

   • Copy all user-defined error messages to the destination server by choosing All Error Messages Detected At Package Runtime.

   • Copy only the user-defined error messages you select by choosing Selected Error Messages and then choosing the error messages to transfer.

8. Click OK to close the Transfer Error Messages dialog box.

9. To run the package immediately, click the Execute button (the green arrow button located on the menu bar) or choose Package and then click Execute. If you want to save the package for later use or for scheduling, continue with the remaining steps. Otherwise skip the remaining steps.

10. To save the package for later use, choose Package and then click Save. As shown in previously Figure 12-17, you'll see the Save DTS Package dialog box.

11. Type a name for the package in the Package Name field. The package name should be unique for the target location.

12. If you're saving the package to SQL Server, you can password-protect the package and prevent unauthorized users from working with it. Type an owner password and a user password in the fields provided. Anyone with the owner password can design, schedule, and execute the package. Anyone with the user password can only schedule or execute the package.

13. Use the Location field to specify where the package should be saved. The available locations are

   - **SQL Server**   Saves as a local package where the package is accessible for use on the designated server.

   - **SQL Server Meta Data Services**   Saves to the designated server's repository database where the package can be shared with other servers through Meta Data Services.

   - **Structure Storage File**   Saves as a COM-structured file. You can add packages to the file as long as they have a different package name. You can then copy, move, or e-mail the file to a different location.

   - **Visual Basic File**   Saves as a Visual Basic file where the package can be used in Visual Basic programs.

14. The lower portion of the Save DTS Package dialog box changes according to the location selection. When you save to SQL Server or to SQL Server Meta Data Services, you must specify the target server and authentication information. When you save to a Structure Storage file or a Visual Basic file, you must specify the file name and path.

15. Click OK to save the package to the specified location. Once you've saved the package, you can run or schedule the package for execution as described in the section of Chapter 7 entitled "Examining, Running, and Scheduling Packages."

Copying or Moving User-Defined Databases to Another Server

You can copy or move user-defined databases from one SQL Server to another using the Copy Database Wizard or through the DTS Designer. I recommend using the Copy Database Wizard. Both processes create a DTS package that you can run or save for later use, but only the wizard makes it easy to manage this complex process. Either way, you can only copy or move user-defined databases. You can't copy or move system databases. Further, you can't copy or move user-defined databases that already exist on the destination server or that are configured for replication with the destination server.

How Are Databases Copied or Moved?

The Copy Database Wizard creates a package that automates all the tasks that you'd have to perform manually to copy or move a database. The copy process follows the steps listed on the following page.

1. At the beginning of a copy, the wizard attempts to put the database in single-user mode. The wizard can only do this when there are no active sessions in the database.

2. Once the database is in single-user mode, the wizard detaches the source database, and then, if successful in detaching the database, the wizard copies the database files associated with the database to the destination server.

3. Once the files are copied to the destination server, the wizard attaches the database on the source and then attaches the database on the destination server.

4. The wizard then tests the destination database by logging in as the database administrator.

The move process is slightly different:

1. At the beginning of a move, the wizard attempts to put the database in single-user mode. The wizard can do this only when there are no active sessions in the database.

2. Once the database is in single-user mode, the wizard detaches the source database, and then, if successful in detaching the database, the wizard copies the database files associated with the database to the destination server.

3. Once the files are copied to the destination server, the wizard attaches the database on the destination server but doesn't reattach the database on the source server. The database files on the source still exist and could be used to reattach the database. Or you could manually delete the files.

4. The wizard then tests the destination database by logging in as the database administrator.

Copying or Moving Databases

You use the Copy Database Wizard to copy or move a user-defined database by completing the following steps:

1. Start Enterprise Manager and then access the server you want to work with. If the database you want to use has active user sessions, you'll need to terminate these sessions before continuing. The wizard won't complete the operation when there are active sessions.

2. Right-click the source server entry, point to All Tasks, and then choose Copy Database Wizard.

3. You'll see the Copy Database Wizard dialog box. Read the welcome page and then click Next.

4. Use the Source Server selection list to specify the SQL Server instance that contains the database(s) you want to copy or move. Afterward, specify the authentication technique to use when connecting to the server. If you're logged on using a Windows domain account that's a member of the sysadmin role on the source server, select Use Windows Authentication. Otherwise select

Use SQL Server Authentication and then enter the username and password of a login that's a member of the sysadmin role.

5. Click Next and then use the Destination Server selection list to specify the SQL Server instance to which you want to copy or move the selected database(s). Afterward, specify the authentication technique to use when connecting to the server. Again, make sure you use a login that's a member of the sysadmin role.

Note   You can't set the source and destination server to the same value. You must configure the transfer from one server to another.

6. Select the user-defined databases to move or copy as shown in Figure 12-21. You can't select system databases, and you can't select databases that already exist on the destination server.

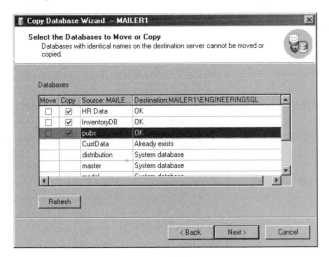

Figure 12-21. *Select the user-defined databases to move or copy.*

7. As Figure 12-22 shows, the next dialog box summarizes the database file information for the copy and move operations you're performing. You use the key fields in the dialog box as follows:

- **Files**   Specifies the type of database file.
- **Destination Drives**   Specifies the destination drive on the target server.
- **Size**   Specifies the total disk space the files will use on the destination drives.
- **Status**   Specifies the file status. A green checkmark indicates the files are ready to move or copy. A red X indicates a problem.

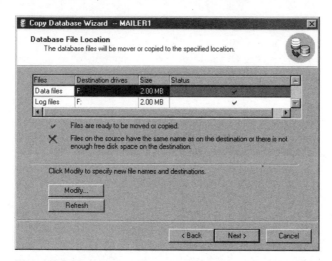

Figure 12-22. *The Database File Location dialog box provides a summary for the database files you're working with.*

- **Modify** Displays the Database Files dialog box, which you can use to get more detailed file information and to set new source file names and destinations for database files.

- **Refresh** Refreshes the file and drive usage information.

8. As shown in Figure 12-23, select the related objects that you want to copy or move with the selected database(s). The objects you can select are: Logins,

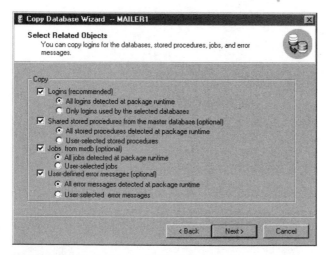

Figure 12-23. *Select the related objects that you want to copy or move with the selected database(s).*

Shared Stored Procedures, Jobs, and User-Defined Error Messages. All related objects are selected by default. To cancel an object, clear the related check box.

9. The option buttons in the Select Related Objects dialog box control which objects of a particular type are copied or moved. Changing the options changes which of the related objects are used and may also cause additional dialog boxes to be displayed in later steps. The options are

- **All Logins Detected At Package Runtime** Copies all logins to the destination server

- **Only Logins Used By The Selected Databases** Copies only the logins for the databases you select in a subsequent dialog box

- **All Stored Procedures Detected At Package Runtime** Copies all shared stored procedures to the destination server

- **User-Selected Stored Procedures** Copies only the shared stored procedures you select in a subsequent dialog box

- **All Jobs Detected At Package Runtime** Copies all jobs to the destination server

- **User-Selected Jobs** Copies only the jobs you select in a subsequent dialog box

- **All Error Messages Detected At Package Runtime** Copies all user-defined error messages to the destination server

- **User-Selected Error Messages** Copies only the user-defined error messages you select in a subsequent dialog box

10. After you configure any special dialog boxes displayed as a result of object selections, you'll have the option of scheduling the DTS package to run. You can

- **Run Immediately** Run the package now

- **Run Once** Set the package to run once at a specified date and time

- **Schedule DTS Package To Run Later** Set a schedule for when the package should run

11. Click Next and then click Finish to complete the process. If you elected to run the package immediately, SQL Server runs the package. As each step is completed (or fails), the status is updated. If an error occurs, you can double-click its entry to view a detailed description of the error. Errors may halt execution of the package and if they do, you'll need to recreate the package. If you scheduled the package to run later, you can manipulate the package as described in the section of Chapter 7 entitled "Examining, Running, and Scheduling Packages."

Multiserver Administration

With multiserver administration you use one server to centrally manage alerts and job scheduling for other servers. You centrally manage alerts through event forwarding. You centrally manage job scheduling by designating master servers and target servers.

Event Forwarding

If you have multiple instances of SQL Server running on multiple systems throughout the network, event forwarding is a time and resource saver. With event forwarding, you can forward application log events to a central server and then process those events on this server. Thus, rather than having to configure alerts on 12 different server instances, you configure event forwarding on 11 servers and have one server handle all the incoming events. You could then use the application log's Computer field to determine the system on which the event occurred and take the appropriate corrective actions using scripts or remote procedure calls.

To configure event forwarding, complete the following steps:

1. Access the Advanced tab of the SQL Server Agent Properties dialog box, as shown in Figure 12-24.

2. Select Forward Events To A Different Server.

3. Use the Server selection list to choose the server that will handle the events. Choose <New Forwarding Server> to register a new server.

4. Set the type of events to forward by selecting Unhandled Events or All Events. An unhandled event is one that you haven't configured alerts for on the current server.

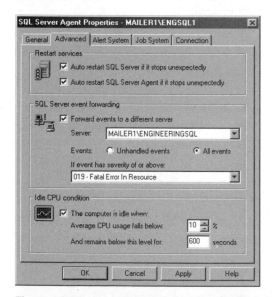

Figure 12-24. *Event forwarding can be helpful in reducing the time you spend configuring alerts on individual servers.*

5. In the If Event Has Severity Of Or Above selection list, determine the severity threshold for events that are forwarded.

Tip To reduce network traffic caused by event forwarding, set the severity threshold to a fairly high value. Fatal errors have a severity level of 19–25.

6. Click Apply.

Multiserver Job Scheduling

When you want to centrally manage job scheduling, you'll need to create a master server and one or more target servers. The SQL Server Agent running on the master server

- Centrally manages jobs for the target servers. Then you create jobs on the master that runs on the targets. For details, see the section of this chapter entitled "Assigning or Changing Job Definitions."
- Can also download jobs to a target. For details, see the "Managing Existing Jobs" section of this chapter.

Multiserver Scheduling Requirements

For the master/target relationship to work correctly, you must

- Make sure that the master server and all target servers are running SQL Server 2000.
- Use domain accounts, not local accounts, when configuring the master and target.
- Make sure that SQL Server Agent is running on the master server and all target servers.

Configuring Master Servers

To create a master server, complete the following steps:

1. In Enterprise Manager, access the SQL Server Agent window on the server you want to configure as the master.

2. Right-click SQL Server Agent, point to Multiserver Administration, and then select Make This A Master. This starts the Make MSX Wizard.

3. Read the welcome dialog box and then click Next.

4. As shown in Figure 12-25, create a special operator to handle multiserver job notifications. This operator, called MSXOperator, is created on the master and all target servers that use this master. Set an e-mail, pager, and Net Send address, as appropriate. You can change this information later by editing the MSXOperator properties on the master server.

5. Select the target servers to associate with this master server. The process of associating target servers with a master is called *enlisting*. Later, you can remove the association by right-clicking SQL Server Agent in Enterprise

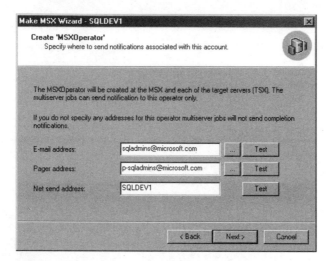

Figure 12-25. *Use the Make MSX Wizard to configure the MSXOperator to handle multiserver job notifications.*

Manager, selecting Multi Server Administration, and then selecting Manage Target Servers.

6. Click Next and then click Finish. The wizard performs the necessary tasks and reports its progress. You'll be notified of any errors.

Configuring Target Servers

You can configure one or more target servers for each master server. You create target servers by completing the following steps:

1. In Enterprise Manager, access the SQL Server Agent window on the server you want to configure as the target.

2. Right-click SQL Server Agent and then select the Multiserver Administration option. From the shortcut menu, choose Make This A Target. This starts the Make TSX Wizard.

3. Read the welcome dialog box and then click Next.

4. Set a valid Windows domain account that can be used to access network resources. Type an account name and a password.

5. In the next dialog box, type the name of the master server for this target.

6. Click Next and then click Finish. The wizard performs the necessary tasks and reports its progress. You'll be notified of any errors, and you can click Pause to stop the operation.

Database Maintenance

Database maintenance involves different tasks. Because most of these tasks have been discussed in previous chapters, this section doesn't go into detail on the tasks already covered. Instead, it provides a checklist that you can use as a starting point for your maintenance efforts. Then it explains how to set up maintenance plans and run database consistency checks.

Database Maintenance Checklist

The following is a checklist for daily, weekly, and monthly maintenance tasks:

Daily

✓   Monitor application, server, and agent logs. Configure alerts for important errors that aren't configured for alert notification.

✓   Check for performance and error alert messages.

✓   Monitor job status, particularly jobs that back up databases and perform replication.

✓   Review the output from jobs in the job history or output file, or both.

✓   Back up databases and logs (as necessary and if not configured as automatic jobs).

Weekly

✓   Monitor available disk space on drives.

✓   Monitor the status of linked, remote, master, and target servers.

✓   Check the maintenance plan reports and history to determine the status of maintenance plan operations.

✓   Generate an updated record of configuration information by executing *sp_configure.*

Monthly

✓   Monitor server performance, tweaking performance parameters as necessary to improve response time.

✓   Manage logins and server roles.

✓   Audit server, database, and object permissions to ensure that only authorized users have access.

✓   Review alert, job, and operator configurations.

As Needed

✓   Back up the SQL Server Registry data.

✓   Update the Emergency Repair Disk.

✓   Run database integrity checks and update database statistics. (SQL Server 2000 handles this automatically in most cases.)

Using Maintenance Plans

Maintenance plans provide an automated way to optimize databases, check database integrity, create backups, and ship transaction logs to a standby server. You can run a maintenance plan against a single database or multiple databases. You can also generate report histories for maintenance plan execution.

You create maintenance plans with the Database Maintenance Plan Wizard. The wizard generates jobs to handle the maintenance tasks you select. You should manage these jobs through the Database Maintenance Plan dialog box, as discussed in the section of this chapter entitled "Viewing, Editing, and Deleting Maintenance Plans."

Creating Maintenance Plans

You can create a maintenance plan by completing the following steps:

1. In Enterprise Manager, access the Management folder on the server you want to work with.

2. Right-click Database Maintenance Plans and then select New Maintenance Plan. This starts the Database Maintenance Plan Wizard.

3. Read the welcome dialog box and then click Next.

4. As shown in Figure 12-26, select the databases that'll use this maintenance plan. You can use the maintenance plan with all databases, all system databases, all user databases, or a combination of one or more individual databases.

 Tip For most installations, I recommend configuring separate maintenance plans for system and user databases. This gives you greater flexibility when it comes to how and when maintenance operations are performed. For large installations you may want to have separate maintenance plans for each database. This way you can work with different databases on different days or at different times of the day.

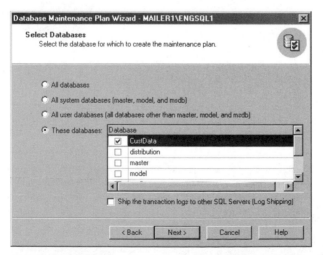

Figure 12-26. *Using the Database Maintenance Plan Wizard, select the database(s) that'll use this maintenance plan.*

5. Select database optimization operations to perform and then set a schedule for these operations, as shown in Figure 12-27.

6. If you prefer, select the Reorganize Data And Index Pages check box to drop and recreate current table indexes with a new fill factor. Then select one of the following options:

- **Reorganize Pages With The Original Amount Of Free Space** Recreates indexes with the original fill factor that was specified when the indexes were created.

- **Change Free Space Per Page Percentage To** Specifies a new fill factor. The higher the percentage, the more free space is reserved on the index pages and the larger the index grows. The default is 10 percent. Valid values are from 0 to 100.

Note Fill factors are discussed in Chapter 2 in the section entitled "Setting the Index Fill." Reorganizing pages changes table indexes and thus invalidates existing statistics. You can't reorganize data and update statistics in the same plan, and you may want to create separate maintenance plans for handling each of these important tasks.

7. If you prefer, select the Update Statistics Used By Query Optimizer check box to resample the distribution statistics of each index created on user tables. SQL Server uses distribution statistics to optimize performance when executing statements on tables. Then set a percentage of the database to sample using the Sample % Of The Database field. A higher percentage generates more accurate statistics than a lower percentage. The default value is 10 percent. Valid values are from 1 through 100.

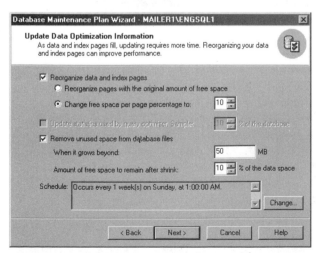

Figure 12-27. *Choose optimization options and then set a schedule for execution.*

Note If you set the sample value to low, SQL Server automatically adjusts the sample size to ensure that a sufficient sample is collected.

8. If you prefer, select the Remove Unused Space From Database Files check box to remove any unused space from the database. Then set values for these fields:

   - **When It Grows Beyond** Free space is removed only when its size exceeds this value. The default value is 50 MB, which means that if there is more than 50 MB of free space, SQL Server should shrink the database to the size specified in the next field.

   - **Amount Of Free Space To Remain After Shrink** Sets the amount of unused space to remain after the database is reduced in size. The value is based on the percentage of the actual data in the database. The default value is 10 percent. Valid values are from 0 through 100.

9. Click Change and then set a schedule for the optimization operations you've selected. This schedule can be different from other schedules in the maintenance plan.

10. As shown in Figure 12-28, determine whether you want to perform integrity checks. Integrity checks can detect inconsistencies and errors in databases by running DBCC CHECKDB.

11. To run database integrity checks, select Check Database Integrity and then configure additional options as follows:

   - **Include Indexes** Checks the data and index pages in the database during the integrity tests.

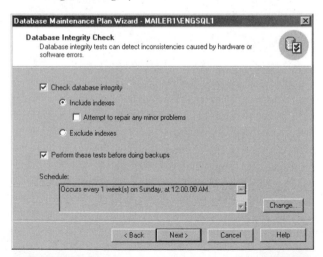

Figure 12-28. *Check and repair the database according to the integrity check schedule.*

- **Attempt To Repair Any Minor Problems** Attempts to automatically correct minor problems detected during the database integrity checks. This option is recommended and is available only when you include indexes in the checks.

- **Exclude Indexes** Checks data pages only during integrity tests and doesn't check indexes. Because fewer database pages are tested, this option executes faster than the Include Indexes option.

Note If you exclude indexes, you can't repair minor problems automatically; you'll need to handle this manually instead.

12. If you prefer, select the Perform These Tests Before Doing Backups check box to perform consistency checks before backing up databases or logs. This ensures that the databases or logs are backed up only if the integrity checks are normal. Otherwise, if the integrity tests detect inconsistencies, the affected databases or logs aren't backed up.

13. Click Change and then set a schedule for the integrity operations you've selected. This schedule can be different from other schedules in the maintenance plan.

14. Specify a database backup plan for the selected databases, as shown in Figure 12-29. If you select Backup The Database As Part Of The Maintenance Plan, complete backups are performed at the scheduled times. You can also verify the backup after completion.

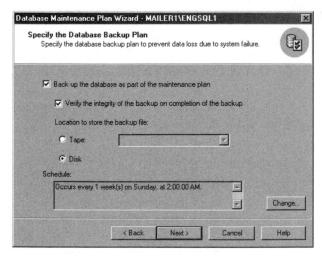

Figure 12-29. *Configure when complete backups of the database are performed.*

15. Select the location of the backup as Tape or Disk. Then click Change to set a backup schedule.

16. After you configure the backup plan, you need to set storage options for the backups, as shown in Figure 12-30. With disk-based backups, you can set a specific backup directory and create subdirectories for each database being backed up. You can also set the file extension for the backups. The default extension is .bak.

17. An interesting option for backups is the ability to automatically remove old backups. Select the Remove Files Older Than check box and then set a specific time period in minutes, hours, days, weeks, or months. For example, you could remove backups more than three weeks or two months old.

18. Set backup options for the transaction logs associated with the selected databases. These options are basically the same as those shown in Figure 12-30.

19. Set storage options for transactions logs. These options are basically the same as those shown in Figure 12-30.

20. The remaining dialog boxes let you generate maintenance reports and a maintenance history. Maintenance reports are stored in a directory you designate, and you can specify that old reports should be automatically deleted. Maintenance history information is stored in msdb and by default is limited to 1000 rows of data. If you increase this value or create several plans, make sure that msdb is sized appropriately to handle this data.

21. After you've configured reporting and history, click Finish to complete the process and generate jobs to handle the designated maintenance tasks. These jobs are labeled

    * Optimizations Job for DB Maintenance Plan <Plan Name>

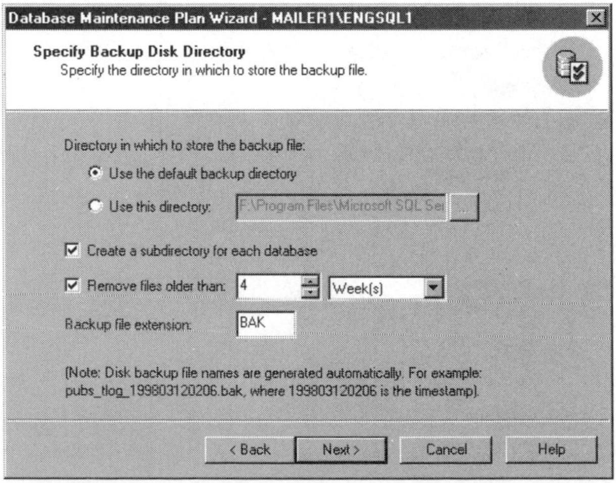

Figure 12-30. *Configure the backup location and storage options.*

- Integrity Checks Job for DB Maintenance Plan <Plan Name>
- DB Backup Job for DB Maintenance Plan <Plan Name>
- Transaction Log Backup Job for DB Maintenance Plan <Plan Name>

Creating Maintenance Plans For Log Shipping

You use log shipping to create a standby server that's automatically synchronized with a primary server. Log shipping is configured through maintenance plans and is available only with SQL Server 2000 Enterprise Edition. To get started, configure the standby server as described in the section of Chapter 11 entitled "Creating a Warm Standby" and then configure a separate log shipping plan for each database that you want to synchronize.

You create a database maintenance plan for log shipping by completing the following steps:

1. Log on to the primary server. The primary is the database server instance that you want to ship logs from.

2. Use Windows Explorer to create a folder for storing the transaction logs that you want to ship. Be sure the associated drive has ample free space.

3. Share the folder on the network and set the access permissions so that the SQL Server Agent domain account has access permissions.

Tip A good resource for creating shared folders and setting shared folder permissions is *Microsoft Windows 2000 Administrator's Pocket Consultant* (Microsoft Press, 2000). See the sections of Chapter 13 entitled "Creating Shared Folders" and "Managing Share Permissions."

4. Start Enterprise Manager. In Enterprise Manager, access the primary server's Management folder.

5. Right-click Database Maintenance Plans and then select New Maintenance Plan. This starts the Database Maintenance Plan Wizard.

6. Read the welcome dialog box and then click Next.

7. In the Select Databases dialog box of the Database Maintenance Plan Wizard, select These Databases and then check the database to log ship.

Caution If you select more than one database, log shipping won't work, and the log shipping option won't be available. Also, you aren't allowed to select a database that's already configured for log shipping.

8. Check Ship The Transaction Logs To Other SQL Servers (Log Shipping).

9. If you have an existing maintenance plan for this database, continue through the wizard, skipping all the database maintenance options, until you get to the Specify the Transaction Log Share dialog box. Be sure to clear Back Up The Database As Part Of The Maintenance Plan in the Specify The Database Backup Plan dialog box.

10. If you don't have an existing maintenance plan for this database, continue through the wizard, setting appropriate database maintenance options, until you get to the Specify the Transaction Log Share dialog box.

11. Type the UNC path for the network share where the transaction logs are created on the primary server, such as \\ENGSQL\Data\Logs. Or click the build (...) button if you want to browse for a folder location.

12. In the Specify The Log Shipping Destinations dialog box, click Add to add a destination database. This displays the Add Destination Database dialog box shown in Figure 12-31.

13. Use the Server Name selection list to choose the destination server name. The server must be registered and running SQL Server 2000 Enterprise Edition to appear in the drop-down list.

14. The destination directory for the transaction logs you're shipping is set by default. To change the default location, type a new directory path or click the build (...) button and browse for an existing directory.

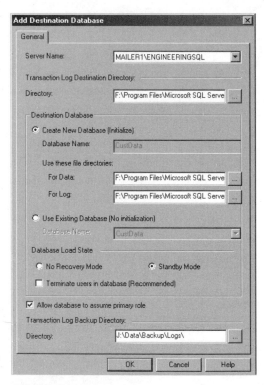

Figure 12-31. *In the Add Destination Database dialog box, specify the destination database for log shipping.*

15. If you want to enable the destination to become the primary in case of failure, select Allow Database To Assume Primary Role. If this box isn't checked, the destination database won't be able to assume the primary role in the future. Then use the Transaction Log Backup Directory field to specify the backup directory for logs on the destination server. You must set a value for this field.

16. If the source database doesn't exist on the destination server, select Create New Database (Initialize). The Database Name will default to the source database name. If you've chosen to allow the destination database to assume the primary role, you can't change the database name from the default. Otherwise you can specify a new name if you like.

17. If you've elected to create a new database, you must also specify the file directories for data and logs on the destination database. Use the For Data and For Log fields.

18. If the source database already exists on the destination server, select Use Existing Database (No Initialization) and then use the Database Name selection list to choose the database. The database must have been restored using the WITH STANDBY option to properly accept logs.

19. Set the Database Load State to either No Recovery Mode or Standby Mode and then click OK. Then click Next in the Specify The Log Shipping Destinations dialog box.

20. In the Initialize the Destination Databases dialog box, specify whether to Take Full Database Backup Now or to Use Most Recent Backup File to initialize the destination database. If the existing backup file is selected but isn't in the log shipping share, the file is copied to that location. Click Next when finished.

21. From the Log Shipping Schedules dialog box shown in Figure 12-32, view the default log shipping schedule. If you would like to alter the schedule, click Change and then set a new schedule.

22. Use the Copy/Load Frequency fields to set the frequency in minutes or hours that you want the destination servers to back up and restore the transaction logs from the source server. The default is 15 minutes.

23. Use the Load Delay fields to set the delay in minutes or hours that you want the destination database to wait before it restores the transaction log from the source server. By default there is no delay, which means the destination server should immediately restore any transaction log backups.

24. Use the File Retention Period fields to specify the length of time that must elapse before a transaction log can be deleted. The default is 24 hours. Click Next when you're finished.

25. In the Log Shipping Thresholds dialog box, set the Backup Alert Threshold. The backup alert threshold sets the maximum elapsed time since the last transaction log backup was made on the source server. If the elapsed time exceeds this threshold, the monitor server generates an alert.

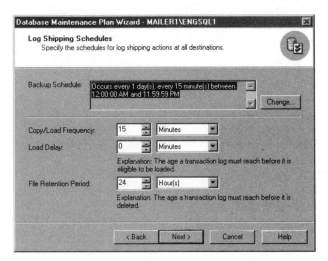

Figure 12-32. *Set log shipping schedules in the Log Shipping Schedules dialog box.*

26. Set the Out of Sync Alert by specifying the maximum elapsed time between the last transaction log backup on the source server and the last transaction log restore on the destination server. If the elapsed time exceeds this threshold, the monitor server generates an alert. Click Next when you're finished.

27. In the Specify the Log Shipping Monitor Information dialog box, select the server that will monitor log shipping and then choose either Use Windows Authentication or Use SQL Server Authentication to connect to the monitor server. If you choose to use SQL Server authentication, you must specify a password. The log_shipping_monitor_probe login name is fixed and must be used to connect to the monitor server. If this is a new account, choose a new password and the account will be created. If the account already exists on the monitor server, you must specify the existing password.

28. The remaining dialog boxes let you generate maintenance reports and a maintenance history. Maintenance reports are stored in a directory you designate, and you can specify that old reports should be automatically deleted. Maintenance history information is stored in msdb and by default is limited to 1000 rows of data. If you increase this value or create several plans, make sure that msdb is sized appropriately to handle this data.

29. After you've configured reporting and history, click Finish to complete the process and generate jobs to handle the designated maintenance tasks.

The jobs on the primary server are labeled

- Log Shipping Alert Job – Backup
- Log Shipping Alert Job – Restore
- Transaction Log Backup Job For DB Maintenance Plan <Plan Name>

The jobs on the destination server are labeled

- Log Shipping Copy For <Server.Database>
- Log Shipping Restore For <Server.Database>

Checking Maintenance Reports and History

Creating a maintenance plan is only the beginning. After you create the plan, you'll need to check the maintenance reports and history periodically. Maintenance reports are stored as text files in the designated directory. You can view these reports in a standard text editor or word processor. To access the maintenance history through Enterprise Manager, complete the following steps:

1. In Enterprise Manager, access the Management folder on the server you want to work with.

2. Right-click Database Maintenance Plans and then select Maintenance Plan History. This displays the Database Maintenance Plan History dialog box shown in Figure 12-33.

3. Use the Status selection list to view all jobs, only successful jobs, or only failed jobs.

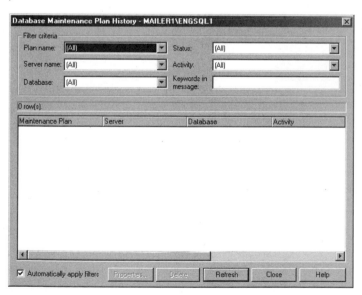

Figure 12-33. *Periodically check the Database Maintenance Plan History dialog box to ensure that maintenance jobs are successfully executing.*

Viewing, Editing, and Deleting Maintenance Plans

You can view, edit, or delete maintenance plans by completing the steps on the following page.

1. In Enterprise Manager, access the Management folder on the server you want to work with.

2. Select Database Maintenance Plans in the left pane. You'll see the existing maintenance plans in the right pane.

3. To view or edit a maintenance plan, double-click the maintenance plan entry in the right pane. This displays the Database Maintenance Plan dialog box shown in Figure 12-34. The options of this dialog box are almost identical to those provided by the Database Maintenance Plan Wizard.

4. To delete a maintenance plan, select its entry and then press Delete. When prompted to confirm the deletion, click Yes.

Figure 12-34. *Options in the Database Maintenance Plan dialog box are almost identical to those available in the Database Maintenance Plan Wizard.*

Checking and Maintaining Database Integrity

With SQL Server 6.5 you had to perform database consistency checks frequently to ensure that databases didn't get corrupted. With the improved architecture of SQL Server 7.0 and SQL Server 2000, you rarely have to perform database integrity checks, and when you do, you can use maintenance plans to handle most of the work for you. On those rare occasions when you perform consistency checks manually, you'll use the DBCC command. DBCC stands for *database consistency check*. While there are many different DBCC commands, the ones you'll use most often to maintain a database are covered in the following sections.

Using DBCC CHECKDB

The DBCC CHECKDB command checks the consistency of the entire database and is the primary technique you'll use to check for database corruption. The command ensures that

- Index and data pages are linked correctly
- Indexes are up to date and sorted properly
- Pointers are consistent
- The data on each page is up to date
- Page offsets are up to date

Sample 12-1 shows the syntax and usage for the DBCC CHECKDB command. When you run the command without a repair option, errors are reported but not corrected. To correct errors, you need to put the database in single-user mode and then set a repair option. After you repair the database, create a backup.

Sample 12-1. DBCC CHECKDB Syntax and Usage

Syntax

```
DBCC CHECKDB

 ( 'database_name'

  [ , NOINDEX

   | { REPAIR_ALLOW_DATA_LOSS

   | REPAIR_FAST

   | REPAIR_REBUILD }
  ]

 )     [ WITH { [ ALL_ERRORMSGS ]

       [ , [ NO_INFOMSGS ] ]

       [ , [ TABLOCK ] ]

       [ , [ ESTIMATEONLY ] ]

       [ , [ PHYSICAL_ONLY ] ] ] }

       ]
```

Usage

```
DBCC CHECKDB ('customer', NOINDEX)

DBCC CHECKDB ('customer', REPAIR_REBUILD)
```

The REPAIR_FAST option performs minor repairs that don't consume a lot of time and won't result in data loss. The REPAIR_REBUILD option performs comprehensive error checking and correction that requires more time to complete but doesn't result in data loss. The REPAIR_ALLOW_DATA_LOSS option performs all the actions of REPAIR_REBUILD and adds new tasks that may result in data loss. These tasks include allocating and deallocating rows to correct structural problems and page errors as well as deleting corrupt text objects.

Tip When trying to fix database problems, start with REPAIR_FAST or REPAIR_REBUILD. If these options don't resolve the problem, use REPAIR_ALLOW_DATA_LOSS. Keep in mind that running the REPAIR_ALLOW_DATA_LOSS option may result in unacceptable loss of important data. To ensure that you can recover the database in its original state, place the DBCC command in a transaction. This way you can inspect the results and roll back the transaction, if necessary.

Using DBCC CHECKTABLE

To correct problems with individual tables, you can use the DBCC CHECKTABLE command. As Sample 12-2 shows, the syntax and usage for this command is almost the same as DBCC CHECKDB.

Sample 12-2. DBCC CHECKTABLE Syntax and Usage

Syntax

```
DBCC CHECKTABLE
  ( 'table_name' | 'view_name'
   [ , NOINDEX
    | index_id
    | { REPAIR_ALLOW_DATA_LOSS
     | REPAIR_FAST
     | REPAIR_REBUILD }
   ]
  )     [ WITH { [ ALL_ERRORMSGS | NO_INFOMSGS ]
        [ , [ TABLOCK ] ]
        [ , [ ESTIMATEONLY ] ]
        [ , [ PHYSICAL_ONLY ] ] ] }
       ]
```

(continued)

Sample 12-2. *(continued)*

Usage

```
DBCC CHECKTABLE ('receipts')

DBCC CHECKTABLE ('receipts', REPAIR_REBUILD)
```

Using DBCC CHECKALLOC

To check the consistency of database pages, you can use DBCC CHECKALLOC. Again, the syntax for this command is nearly identical to the previous DBCC commands. One item worth noting is that although Sample 12-3 shows a NOINDEX option, it's maintained only for backward compatibility with previous SQL Server versions. The command always checks the consistency of page indexes.

Sample 12-3. DBCC CHECKALLOC Syntax and Usage

Syntax

```
DBCC CHECKALLOC

    (     'database_name'

    [,        NOINDEX

    |

    {       REPAIR_ALLOW_DATA_LOSS

      | REPAIR_FAST

      | REPAIR_REBUILD }
    ]

    )     [ WITH { [ ALL_ERRORMSGS | NO_INFOMSGS ]

          [ , [ TABLOCK ] ]

          [ , [ ESTIMATEONLY ] ] ] }

          ]
```

Usage

```
DBCC CHECKALLOC ('customer')

DBCC CHECKALLOC ('customer', REPAIR_REBUILD)
```

Using DBCC CHECKCATALOG

Another useful DBCC command is CHECKCATALOG. You use this command to check the consistency of a database's systems tables. Sample 12-4 shows the syntax and usage of the command.

Sample 12-4. DBCC CHECKCATALOG Syntax and Usage

Syntax

```
DBCC CHECKCATALOG

(      'database_name'

) [WITH NO_INFOMSGS]
```

Usage

```
DBCC CHECKCATALOG ('customer')
```

Using DBCC DBREINDEX

To rebuild one or more indexes on a database, you can use DBCC DBREINDEX.
Sample 12-5 shows the syntax and usage of the command.

Sample 12-5. DBCC DBREINDEX Syntax and Usage

Syntax

```
DBCC DBREINDEX

( ['database.owner.table_name'

   [, index_name

   [, fillfactor ]

   ]

   ]

) [WITH NO_INFOMSGS]
```

Usage

```
DBCC DBREINDEX ('customer.dbo.customers', PK_cust, 75)

DBCC DBREINDEX (customers, '', 85)
```

Index

About the Author

William R. Stanek has a master of science in information systems degree and 15 years of hands-on experience with advanced programming and development. He is a leading network technology expert and an award-winning author. Over the years, his practical advice has helped programmers, developers, and network engineers all over the world. He is also a regular contributor to leading publications like *PC Magazine*, where you'll often find his work in the "Solutions" section. He has written, coauthored, or contributed to over 20 computer books. His current or forthcoming books include *Microsoft Windows 2000 Administrator's Pocket Consultant, Microsoft Exchange 2000 Server Administrator's Pocket Consultant, Microsoft Web Administrator's Pocket Consultant,* and *Windows 2000 Scripting Bible.*

Mr. Stanek has been involved in the commercial Internet community since 1991 and has been working with SQL Server since 1990. Before that he worked mostly with Unix networks and Sybase. Lately, he has been doing advanced research and development for Windows 2000 Datacenter Server, SQL Server 2000, and Exchange 2000 Server. During 1998 and 1999, he worked as a senior member of the technical staff at Intel Corporation's iCat e-commerce division. William's core networking experience comes from more than 11 years of military service. He is proud to have served in the Persian Gulf War as a combat crewmember on an electronic warfare aircraft. He flew on numerous combat missions into Iraq and was awarded nine medals for his wartime service, including one of the highest U.S. flying honors, the Air Force Distinguished Flying Cross. Currently, he resides in the Pacific Northwest with his wife and children.

The author prepared and submitted the manuscript for this book in electronic form using Microsoft Word 2000 for Windows. Pages were composed by nSight, Inc., in Cambridge, MA, using Adobe PageMaker 6.5 for Windows, with text in Garamond Light and display type in ITC Franklin Gothic. Composed pages were delivered to the printer as electronic prepress files.

Cover Designer
Tim Girvin Design

Cover Illustrator
Tom Draper

Layout Artist
Mary Beth McDaniel

Project Manager
Lisa A. Wehrle

Tech Editor
John Panzarella

Copy Editor
Joseph Gustaitis

Proofreaders
Renee Cote, Rebecca Merz, and Elina Pellebon

Indexer
Jack Lewis